NUMBERS, LANGUAGE, AND THE HUMAN MIND

What constitutes our number concept? What makes it possible for us to employ numbers the way we do? Which mental faculties contribute to our grasp of numbers? What do we share with other species, and what is specific to humans? How does our language faculty come into the picture? This book addresses these questions and discusses the relationship between numerical thinking and the human language faculty, providing psychological, linguistic, and philosophical perspectives on number, its evolution, and its development in children. Heike Wiese argues that language as a human faculty plays a crucial role in the emergence of systematic numerical thinking. She characterises number sequences as powerful and highly flexible mental tools that are unique to humans and shows that it is language that enables us to go beyond the perception of numerosity and to develop such mental tools: language as a mental faculty not only lies at the heart of what makes us human, it is also the capacity that lays the ground for our concept of number.

HEIKE WIESE is Assistant Professor of Linguistics at the Institute for German Language and Linguistics, Humboldt University Berlin. She has published in the fields of linguistics, cognitive science, didactics of mathematics, and philosophy.

NUMBERS, LANGUAGE, AND THE HUMAN MIND

HEIKE WIESE

CAMBRIDGE
UNIVERSITY PRESS

PUBLISHED BY THE PRESS SYNDICATE OF THE UNIVERSITY OF CAMBRIDGE
The Pitt Building, Trumpington Street, Cambridge, United Kingdom

CAMBRIDGE UNIVERSITY PRESS
The Edinburgh Building, Cambridge, CB2 2RU, UK
40 West 20th Street, New York, NY 10011–4211, USA
477 Williamstown Road, Port Melbourne, VIC 3207, Australia
Ruiz de Alarcón 13, 28014 Madrid, Spain
Dock House, The Waterfront, Cape Town 8001, South Africa

http://www.cambridge.org

First published 2003
Reprinted 2005

Printed in the United Kingdom at the University Press, Cambridge

Typeface Adobe Garamond 11/12.5 pt.   *System* LATEX 2$_\varepsilon$ [TB]

A catalogue record for this book is available from the British Library

Library of Congress Cataloguing in Publication data
Wiese, Heike.
Numbers, Language, and the Human Mind / Heike Wiese.
p.   cm.
Includes bibliographical references and index.
ISBN 0 521 83182 2
1. Grammar, Comparative and general – Numerals.   2. Language and languages.
3. Psycholinguistics.   4. Language acquisition.   1. Title.
P275.W54   2003
401′9 – dc21

ISBN 0 521 83182 2 hardback

*To my mother, Ilse Wiese, who shared her fascination for numbers
and numerical thinking and her enthusiasm for scientific inquiry*

Contents

vii

Acknowledgments

Researching and writing this book was a particularly appealing project for me, bringing together two topics I have always found fascinating, the human language faculty and numerical cognition. I was lucky to have had the support of many people who share my fascination with numbers and language and who helped to shape this book.

One of the enjoyable things I will remember from the writing process are several afternoons spent in cafés discussing the manuscript for this book with Horst Simon. His constructive and thorough criticism is highly appreciated. Thanks are also owing to all the people who shared their own works and gave me the opportunity to discuss various aspects of my account, of whom I particularly want to mention Ray Jackendoff, Terrence Deacon, Karen Wynn, Ewald Lang, Kevin Durkin, and Anne Sinclair. Special thanks go also to five anonymous reviewers for detailed and very helpful comments on earlier drafts.

I also would like to thank the people who were early influences on my view of language and number, dating back to my years as a student at Göttingen University. Dieter Cherubim started my interest in the language/number relationship in a seminar series on 'Language and the World' in the early 1990s; Erich Fries, Günther Patzig, and Wolfgang Carl were the crucial influences for my interest in Frege and the foundations of mathematics, and Michael Heidelberger was the first to introduce me to the philosophical background of measurement theory and its applications in psychology.

The linguistic analysis of number words I present in the final chapter draws on results from a book that evolved out of my doctoral dissertation at Humboldt-University Berlin, which benefited from discussions and input from numerous people, particularly Norbert Fries, Manfred Bierwisch, and Ede Zimmerman.

Finally very special thanks to my husband, Charles Stewart, who contributed to this project at every stage and helped me shape my thoughts in countless and sometimes night-long discussions – for his time, his support, and most of all for his enthusiasm and his gift to get involved. This book would definitely not be the same without him.

I would like to thank the following organisations and individuals for their permission to use graphics and text quotes:
The Libyan Tourist Board for the desert photograph used for the jacket illustration.
Blackwell Publishing Ltd. for Figure 28 from Saxe, Geoffrey B., Body parts as numerals: a developmental analysis of numeration among the Oksapmin in Papua New Guinea, *Child Development* 52 (1981);
Artibus Asiae for Figure 40 from Karel Absolon, Dokumente und Beweise der Fähigkeiten des fossilen Menschen zu zählen im mährischen Paläolithikum, *Artibus Asiae* 20(2/3) (1957);
Jean Clottes, conservateur général du patrimoine, Ministère de la culture et la communication (French Ministry of Culture and Communication) for Figure 41;
Schroedel Verlag for Figure 55 from Hendrik Radatz, Wilhelm Schipper, Rotraut Dröge, and Astrid Ebeling, *Handbuch für den Mathematikunterricht, 2. Schuljahr* (1998) © Schroedel Verlag;
Eichborn-Verlag for Figure 65 from Manfred Hofmann, *Wo fehlt's uns denn? Dein Körper in gesunden und kranken Tagen* © Eichborn AG, Frankfurt am Main, 1994;
Knut Rickmeyer for Figure 66 from Rickmeyer, Knut, 'Die Zwölf liegt hinter der nächsten Kurve und die Sieben ist pinkrot': Zahlenraumbilder und bunte Zahlen, *Journal für Mathematik-Didaktik* 22(1) (2001);
Kluwer Academic / Plenum Publishers for Figure 67 from Anne Sinclair, F. Siegrist, and Hermine Sinclair, Young children's ideas about the written number system, in: D. R. Rogers and J. A. Sloboda (eds.), *The Acquisition of Symbolic Skills* (1983);
Psychology Press for Figure 67 from Penny Munn, Symbolic function in pre-schoolers, in: Chris Donlan (ed.) (1998), *The Development of Mathematical Skills*;
Clarendon Press, Oxford, for the excerpt from John Locke, Of number, in: *Essay Concerning Human Understanding* (1690; 1975);
Elsevier Science for the excerpts from Karen C. Fuson, and James W. Hall, The acquisition of early number word meanings: a conceptual analysis and review, in: H. P. Ginsburg (ed.), *The Development of Mathematical Thinking* (Academic Press), © 1983; Karen Wynn, Children's acquisition of

the number words and the counting system, *Cognitive Psychology* 24 © 1992;
Patrice Hartnett, and Rochel Gelman, Early understandings of numbers:
paths or barriers to the construction of new understandings? *Learning and
Instruction* 8(4) © 1998;
The Bertrand Russell Peace Foundation for the excerpt from Bertrand
Russell, Letter to Heijenoort (1962), in: J. van Heijenoort (ed.), *From Frege
to Gödel. A Source Book in Mathematical Logic* (1967);
MIT Press for the excerpts from Willard Van Orman Quine, *Word and
Object* (1960); Noam Chomsky, *Language and Problems of Knowledge. The
Managua Lectures* (1988);
The British Journal of Developmental Psychology Society for the excerpts
from Kevin Durkin, Beatrice Shire, Roland Riem, Robert D. Crowther,
and D. R. Ruttner, The social and linguistic context of early number word
use, *British Journal of Developmental Psychology* 4(3) (1986) © The British
Psychological Society;
Open Court Publishing Company, a division of Carus Publishing Company, Peru, Ill., for the excerpt from Ferdinand de Saussure, *Course in
General Linguistics*, translated by Roy Harris, edited by C. Bally and A.
Sechehaye © 1986, Open Court;
HarperCollins Publishers Inc. for the excerpt from Steven Pinker, *The
Language Instinct* © 1994 by Steven Pinker;
The Economic and Social Research Council for the excerpt from Martin
Hughes, Learning about Number. *ESRC Newsletter* 52 (1984).

Introduction

Numbers play a central role in our lives. Numbers and number expressions arise early both in human history and in the individual development of children. Numerical notations existed long before the invention of script, and archaeological evidence suggests that at least 30,000 years ago our ancestors used notches as primitive representations for collections of things. Newborns in their first week of life can already distinguish two from three objects, and children start using number words and engage in counting games as early as two years of age. In our everyday life we use numbers in a wide range of different contexts; we employ them not only for counting, but also for telling the time, on price tags, for football scores, to rank runners in a marathon, for bus lines, as telephone numbers, in lotteries, and so on. And in one way or the other, numbers play a role in the spiritual contexts of most cultures. They are employed in fortune-telling, and in many cultures certain numbers, say 13, are associated with bad luck, or certain kinds of number assignments fall under taboo restrictions, for instance, it might be considered imprudent to count people or to count your own children.

What makes numbers such a fascinating topic? I think the fascination that numbers have for us arises from their great significance as reasoning devices, as powerful and highly flexible mental tools. Here is a passage by the nineteenth- to twentieth-century mathematician Richard Dedekind that emphasises the role that this concept of numbers plays in our thinking:

Of all the devices the human mind has created to make its life – that is, the task of reasoning – easier, there is none that has such a great effect and is so indivisibly connected to its innermost nature, as the concept of *number* . . . Every thinking human, even if he does not feel it clearly, is a numerical being.[1]

What is it that makes us 'numerical beings'? What does our concept of number encompass? One aspect that initially comes to mind is cardinality, the property that we ask for in 'How many?' We assess this property in

---

[1] Richard Dedekind, in Ewald (1996: vol. 2, p. i), emphasis in the original (my translation, H. W.).

a cardinal number assignment; for example, I could count the pens that lie on my desk and, as a result, assign them the number 3. This kind of number assignment allows us, among other things, not only to distinguish two from three objects, but also to acknowledge the difference between, say, 102 and 103 objects. Employing numbers to identify cardinalities enables us to grasp relations far beyond the limits of our perception.

In the context of numbers, one tends to first think of these cardinal number assignments. However, as the examples of bus lines and marathon runners above might have suggested, an important point for our investigation will be that there is more to numbers than cardinality. Numbers, I will argue, are flexible tools that can be used to identify a whole range of properties of which cardinality is just one, and crucially not the only one. Apart from cardinality, numbers can be employed to identify, for instance, the ranks of runners (an ordinal number assignment) or the identity of bus lines (a nominal number assignment). Cardinal assignments play an important role in our number concept, though, and in fact our everyday usage of the word 'number' often does not distinguish between numbers and cardinality: we use 'number' not only when talking about, say 'the natural numbers', but also when we want to refer to the cardinality of a set, as for instance in 'the number of stars'. Since it is crucial for our discussion to distinguish these two meanings, I will use the term 'number' only in the first sense, while 'number' in the second sense will always be called 'cardinality'.

Books on numbers and numerical thinking usually concentrate on this cardinal aspect of numbers. The present investigation complements these works by integrating cardinality into a wider view of the number domain. In order to do so, I will distinguish numbers and the properties they can identify in number assignments. Among others, this allows us to take into account not only cardinal number contexts, but also the ordinal and nominal number contexts I mentioned above. What brings together these different contexts? How can we employ the same numbers for such diverse purposes? In this book, I will show that it is a certain pattern of linking up numbers and objects that makes this possible, and I will argue that it is the human language faculty that lays the foundations for this kind of linking. Hence – as I hope to convince you – language plays a crucial role in the emergence of systematic numerical thinking in humans.

Now this will strike you as a bit odd – after all, it was only some paragraphs before that I mentioned that infants can already distinguish three from two objects in their first week of life, hence at a time long before they exercise their language faculty. And, what is more, this capacity is not restricted to humans; a lot of other species – among others, monkeys, dolphins, rats, and even canaries – have been shown to discriminate between small sets of different sizes, for instance between two dots and three dots on a display. However, note that this does not mean that they have a full grasp of number. It means that they grasp the different cardinalities of different small sets of dots, that is, they grasp the property of cardinality, but this does not yet involve applying numbers to this property. As a result, a canary might be able to tell two sunflower seeds from three, but not 102 seeds from 103.

What does it mean, then, to apply numbers? When would we say that somebody has a grasp of numbers? The answer I am going to offer is twofold. On the one hand, I spell out the crucial properties that a number sequence must have, a list of criteria that help us to identify numbers (I will call this the 'criteria-based approach to numbers'). On the other hand, I show what it takes to employ numbers in the different kinds of number assignments. In particular, I show that it is not enough to simply link up a number with an object or a set of objects – say, linking up a number with a set of pens, or with a marathon runner, or with a bus line. Rather, for a systematic number assignment we have to link up relations from two different *systems* (a system of numbers and a system of objects). This kind of linking will be called '(system-)dependent linking'.

This gives us the basis to identify possible number sequences and to understand what it needs to employ them as numerical tools. And this, then, is the point where language comes in. I will argue that language as a mental capacity allows us to employ dependent links in a systematic way, namely when we correlate words and objects, and I will show how this pattern of dependent linking can be transferred to the numerical domain, where it allows us to link up *numbers* and objects. In this context, counting words – sequences like 'one, two, three, . . .' as we use them in counting – will play a crucial role as a bridge between language and number in the emergence of systematic numerical cognition. I will show that the counting sequences of natural languages make it possible to use the powerful pattern of dependent linking in the numerical domain. It is this transfer of dependent linking, I will argue, that enables us to develop a unified concept of number, a concept that encompasses cardinal, ordinal, and nominal aspects alike.

Before we start our investigation, let me give you an idea of how this book is organised. Apart from this introduction, there are eight chapters in the book. The first three chapters introduce the central notions and arguments for our account of numerical thinking. Drawing on these foundations, chapter 4 investigates the cognitive capacities on which our concept of number can build. Crucially, it is here that I make the case for a linguistic foundation of systematic numerical cognition. The last four chapters apply this approach to different areas that are relevant for our investigation: the acquisition and representation of numbers, the architecture of the cognitive number domain, the status of arabic numerals, and the linguistic behaviour of number words.

The following paragraphs give a brief overview of the questions we will ask in the different chapters, and how they will contribute to our topic of numbers, language, and the human mind.

CHAPTER 1: NUMBERS AND OBJECTS

How do we use numbers? What properties of numbers are crucial when we apply them to objects? What have three pens, the third runner, and bus #3 in common?

To find out what a number is, we will ask what we do when we employ numbers and apply them to objects. This chapter introduces a threefold distinction of number contexts that will feature prominently in our further discussion: cardinal contexts like 'three pens' and 'three litres of wine', ordinal contexts like 'the third runner', and nominal contexts like 'bus #3'. We analyse the properties of numbers that we make use of in each context, and by so doing identify the crucial features that numbers need to have. I introduce the notion of dependent linking and show that it is this kind of linking that makes the different kinds of number assignments significant.

CHAPTER 2: WHAT DOES IT MEAN TO BE A NUMBER?

How can we account for numbers? What can we learn from the philosophical tradition?

This chapter connects our investigation with the philosophical tradition, and in particular with the controversy on the foundations of mathematics that took place at the end of the nineteenth and beginning of the twentieth century. These logico-mathematical approaches to number were not so much concerned with the particular way in which numbers are represented in the human mind, but set out to define numbers as the primary objects of mathematics. However, I will show that they can contribute to our understanding of the cognitive domain of numbers as a whole, as each of them can account for different concepts related to our numerical cognition. The discussion in this chapter, together with the 'number characteristics' from the first chapter, will lead us to a criteria-based account of numbers that will serve as the foundation for our approach to numbers as mental tools.

CHAPTER 3: CAN WORDS BE NUMBERS?

What would be a good example of numerical tools? How about counting words?

Equipped with our criteria-based account, we identify counting words of natural languages as numerical tools. I argue that these words – verbal entities – can be employed as elements of a number sequence: they do not refer to numbers, they *serve as* numbers (they serve as the tools in our number assignments). I show that this approach to counting words can account for their special status within the grammatical system and in language acquisition. At the same time, it suggests an intimate relationship between the linguistic and the numerical domain that will be further explored in the following chapters.

CHAPTER 4: THE LANGUAGE LEGACY

What role does language play for the emergence of numerical thinking? Can canaries count? How could a systematic number concept evolve in the history of our species?

We are now in a position to investigate the role that language plays for the foundation of our numerical thinking. We discuss evidence from animal studies and studies with human babies, suggesting that our number concept can build on prelinguistic capacities that allow us to grasp those properties of objects that are relevant in the different kinds of number assignments (among others, cardinality). I argue that it is our language faculty that then enables us to grasp the pattern of dependent linking that we identified as the constitutive feature of systematic number assignments. I show how a development that starts from iconic cardinality representations, building on prelinguistic (and pre-numerical) capacities, can lead to the emergence of a systematic number concept once language comes in and our representations get dissociated from their iconic roots.

CHAPTER 5: CHILDREN'S ROUTE TO NUMBER: FROM ICONIC REPRESENTATIONS TO NUMERICAL THINKING

How do children master systematic number assignments? Why is finger counting so popular? Where does language come in?

In this chapter, our results on numerical thinking and the role of language give us a new perspective on the way children first learn to count. We have a look at the acquisition of counting sequences and discuss how children learn to represent them as numerical tools, taking into account our results from the first chapters on the characteristic features of numbers and the status of counting words. We then investigate how children acquire cardinal number assignments when they learn to count and to tell how many. We find that individual development starts from iconic stages (with finger counting as a prominent example), before dependent linking sets in and with it the emergence of a systematic number assignment – a striking analogy to our evolutionary scenario from chapter 4. With our previous results on the language/number relationship in mind, we discuss the role of children's linguistic development in this transition.

CHAPTER 6: THE ORGANISATION OF OUR COGNITIVE NUMBER DOMAIN

What are the different aspects of our number concept, and how do they come together?

We can now integrate the acquisition of counting sequences and cardinal number assignments into a comprehensive view of the cognitive number domain. We discuss the acquisition of different numerical concepts, using our distinction of number contexts from the first chapter as a guideline, and see how the characteristics we identified for each kind of number assignments show up in individual development. In this chapter, we talk about our concept of cardinality and its abstraction in arithmetical reasoning, we talk about measure concepts that cover, among others, properties like weight, temperature, time, distance, and trade value, and we give an account of ordinal and nominal number concepts and their prenumerical underpinnings. We bring together our results in a model for the architecture of our number domain.

CHAPTER 7: NON-VERBAL NUMBER SYSTEMS

Where do arabic numerals come in? How are non-verbal numerals and counting words linked up?

In this chapter we have a closer look at non-verbal systems like that of the arabic numerals (1, 2, 3, . . .), which are not part of a particular language (say, English) or of an alphabet (for instance the Latin one), but have a status that sets them apart from language and script. We find that, once numerical thinking has emerged, such numeral systems can develop as a non-verbal, visual alternative to counting sequences, that is, as an alternative system that meets the number criteria defined in our approach. Our analysis will reveal crucial parallels between these non-verbal and verbal sequences, indicating that our account of numerical tools is independent of a specific modality. We integrate non-verbal numerals into our model of the number domain and show how they can be correlated with counting words, not as an alternative way of spelling number words and also not as an alternative way of naming numbers, but as elements of an independent numerical system.

CHAPTER 8: NUMBERS IN LANGUAGE: THE GRAMMATICAL INTEGRATION OF NUMERICAL TOOLS

What can the grammar of number word constructions tell us about the relationship between language and number?

We distinguish counting words, which have a special status as numerical tools, and the different kinds of number word constructions that refer to numerical concepts: cardinal constructions ('three pens'; 'three litres of wine'), ordinal constructions ('the third runner'), and '#'-constructions ('bus #3'). I show that the grammatical behaviour of referential number words can be related to a particular interplay between linguistic and conceptual structures. In particular, we identify syntactic and semantic parallels between the different kinds of number words and certain non-numerical expressions, namely quantifier constructions like 'few pens' and 'many pens', superlatives like 'the youngest runner', and constructions with proper nouns like 'my sister Karen'. I motivate the grammatical properties of number words within a broader model of numerical tools, counting words, and language.

In short, then, this book is about our concept of numbers and its foundations, and it is dedicated to exploring the distinctive way in which numerical cognition is intertwined with the human language faculty. Adopting an interdisciplinary perspective, my argumentation will draw on results from different fields related to cognitive science, among them psychology, linguistics, and the philosophy of mathematics. As I hope to convince you in this book, it is this interdisciplinary perspective that has the potential to give us new insights into the rich and fruitful relationship between numbers and language.

With this in mind, I have taken care not to presuppose a particular specialised background for the discussion, but to develop the concepts we need in a largely non-technical manner, without introducing a lot of formal machinery. Since I do not want to leave you without explicit formal accounts of the analyses I develop, though, the discussion in the main body of the text is complemented by 5 appendices that provide the respective definitions that formalise our model of numerical cognition.

CHAPTER I

Numbers and objects

A striking feature of numbers is their enormous flexibility. A quality like colour, for instance, can only be conceived for visual objects, so that we have the notion of a red flower, but not the notion of a red thought. In contrast to that, there seem to be no restrictions on the objects numbers can apply to. In 1690 John Locke put it this way, in his 'Essay Concerning Human Understanding':

number applies itself to men, angels, actions, thoughts; everything that either doth exist, or can be imagined. (Locke 1690: Book II, ch. XVI, § 1)

This refers to our usage of numbers as in 'four men' or 'four angels', where we identify a cardinality. This number assignment works for any objects, imagined or existent, no matter what qualities they might have otherwise; the only criterion here is that the objects must be distinct in order to be counted. In a seminal work on numbers from the nineteenth century, the mathematician and logician Gottlob Frege took this as an indication for the intimate relationship between numbers and thought, a relationship that will be a recurring topic throughout this book:

The truths of arithmetic govern all that is numerable. This is the widest domain of all; for to it belongs not only the existent, not only the intuitable, but everything thinkable. Should not the laws of number, then, be connected very intimately with the laws of thought?[1] (Frege 1884: § 14)

And this is only one respect in which numbers are flexible. Not only can we assign them to objects of all kinds, we can also assign them to objects in ways that are so diverse that, on first sight, they seem not to be related at all. Of these number assignments, the cardinality assignment that is based on counting is probably the first that comes to mind when thinking of

---

[1] This is quoted from the translation provided by John Austin (1950). One might want to replace 'numerable' by the more specific term 'countable' here, since this translation would be closer to Frege's term 'zählbar' in the German original.

numbers and objects, but it is by no means the only way we can assign numbers to objects.[2]

The same number, say 3, can be used to give the cardinality of pens on my desk ('three pens'); to indicate, together with a unit of measurement, the amount of wine needed for a dinner with friends ('three litres of wine') or the temperature of the mineral water in my glass ('water of 3 °C'); it can tell us the rank of a runner in a Marathon race ('the third runner'); or identify the bus that goes to the opera ('bus #3' / 'the #3 bus'). The following example from a paper on the acquisition of number concepts by Karen Fuson and James Hall illustrates, in one sentence, the various ways in which we employ numbers in our daily lives:

Despite a *seventy-eight yard run* by *number thirty-four* the Bears lost by *two touchdowns* and dropped into *sixth place*. (Fuson and Hall 1983: 49)

What is it that makes numbers so flexible, allowing them to occur naturally in so many different contexts? How are their different usages related to each other? To answer these questions, let us have a closer look at the different ways numbers apply to objects. In a first approach, let us distinguish three kinds of number assignments: cardinal, ordinal, and nominal assignments. To give you an idea of what I mean by this classification, I give a brief characterisation for each of these number assignments in the following paragraphs (we will analyse them in more detail later in this chapter).

We encounter cardinal number assignments in contexts like 'three pens', 'three litres of wine' and 'three degrees Celsius', where the number indicates how many. In our examples the number indicates how many pens there are, how many litres of wine, and how many degrees Celsius. In the first case, 'three' identifies the cardinality of a set of objects: it tells us how many elements the set of pens has. In the second case, 'three' quantifies over litres, and by so doing identifies, say, the amount of wine needed for dinner. In 'three degrees Celsius', 'three' quantifies over degrees of temperature.

Ordinal number assignments are illustrated by our Marathon example above, 'the third runner'. Unlike in cardinal assignments, the number does not apply to a set, but to an individual element of a set; more precisely, to an individual element of a sequence. For instance, in 'the third runner', 3 is not the number of the entire set of Marathon participants:

---

[2] Although I speak of 'numbers *and* objects' here, you should be aware of the fact that numbers themselves might also be among the objects, that is, for instance, among the things that are counted.

it indicates the rank of one particular person within the sequence of runners.

Nominal number assignments are ones like 'bus #3'. This is probably not what you would call a typical number context (Fuson and Hall (1983) go so far as to call them '*non-numerical* number contexts', which sounds a bit like a contradiction in terms). However, nominal number assignments are actually quite common in our daily lives; we encounter them in the numbering of football players, in subway and bus systems, and also in telephone numbers and in the numbers on an ID card, to name just a few examples. What these cases have in common is the fact that the numbers identify objects within a set: in nominal assignments, numbers are used like proper names. So rather than thinking of names like 'Mike' or 'Lucy' for buses, we just assign them numbers when we want to identify them, in the same way that we assign numbers to the members of a football team, employ them as telephone numbers, or use ID numbers as a means to identify students within a university.

Figure 1 shows a photograph I took on Fehmarn, an island in the Baltic Sea. As you can see, the lamb in this picture was given the number '289'. This is an instance of a nominal number assignment that distinguishes sheep and might for instance help the farmer to keep track of which lamb belongs to which mother sheep, or which sheep are on which part of the dyke.

So when we investigate the different ways we apply numbers to objects, we must include in our analysis nominal number assignments as well as cardinal and ordinal usages of numbers. A theory that allows us to discuss the different usages under a unified notion of number assignments is the Representational Theory of Measurement, a theory that has been developed within the fields of philosophy and psychology.[3] The Representational Theory of Measurement is concerned with the features that make a number assignment significant; it aims to establish the criteria that make sure that the number we assign to an object does in fact tell us something about the property we want to assess (this property might be, for instance, cardinality, or volume, or the rank in a sequence).

I will use the machinery of this theory for a somewhat different purpose, putting it into service for our investigation of numbers and objects. In particular, I am going to employ the Representational Theory of Measurement

[3] Cf. Stevens (1946); Suppes and Zinnes (1963); Krantz et al. (1971); Roberts (1979); Narens (1985). The Representational Theory has its roots in the philosophical works of Fechner (1858); Helmholtz (1887); Mach (1896); Hölder (1901); and Russell (1903).

Figure 1 Nominal number assignment: a numbered lamb on Fehmarn

as a generalised theory of number assignments that can give us a handle on the different ways we assign numbers to objects and allows us to find out which properties of numbers we make use of in each case. As a result, we will be in a position to identify the crucial properties that numbers need to have.

In order to take into account all meaningful assignments of numbers to objects, the Representational Theory takes a very broad view of 'measurement'. Within this framework, any assignment of numbers to objects is regarded as an instance of measurement, as long as certain relations between the numbers represent relations between the objects. So, for example, we can regard the correlation between the pile of books in Figure 2 and the numbers from 1 to 6 as a kind of measurement, because the numbers express a relation that holds between the books, namely the relation 'lies further up'. In our example, books receive higher or lower numbers depending on the higher or lower position they occupy within the pile: if a book lies further to the top than another book, it receives a higher number than that book; and vice versa, if a book receives a higher number than another book, you know that it must lie further up than that book.[4] This is depicted in Figure 2: the bottom book has been assigned the number 1, the next book has been numbered '2', and so on, with the top book receiving the highest number in our set, namely 6. Hence, the property we 'measure' in Figure 2 is the position of a book in relation to other books in the pile, and this

---

[4] Hence, this number assignment is not an instance of counting, where the books could receive numbers in any order, that is, their relative position would not play a role. We will discuss counting as a subroutine in number assignments below.

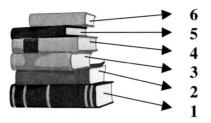

Figure 2 Numbering of books as a form of 'measurement'

property is identified by the '>' relation that holds between the numbers we assigned to the books. (Note that '>' is just the ordering relation for our number sequence here, hence '2 > 1' can be understood as '2 comes after 1 in the number sequence' and does not necessarily relate to a quantitative view of numbers, as the reading 'greater than' might suggest. For the time being we leave it open what status numbers have and how their ordering might work. We will tackle this question in the following two chapters.)

Calling this kind of book numbering an instance of 'measurement' may strike you as a bit odd, since this is not what we normally mean when we talk about measuring objects. Our use of the term 'measurement' is normally restricted to cases like the three litres of wine from our dinner-example above, that is, cases where the number assignment tells us something about properties like volume (as in the dinner-example), weight, length, temperature, and so on.

However, while being at odds with our pre-theoretical terminology, it is exactly this generalisation that makes the Representational Theory so powerful for our investigation of number contexts. By expanding the notion of 'measurement' to include all meaningful assignments of numbers to objects, the Representational Theory can capture the whole range of number contexts within one unified framework.

To avoid unnecessary terminological confusion, though, I will talk of *measurement*^{RTM} when I use 'measurement' as a technical term within the Representational Theory of Measurement, and where possible I will use the more intuitive term '(meaningful) number assignment'. Without superscript, 'measurement' will refer to those number assignments where we measure properties like weight, length, or temperature (in accordance with our pre-theoretical terminology).

Applying the Representational Theory to our analysis of the relationship between numbers and objects does not only allow us to determine what is common to all number contexts. As I am going to show in this chapter, it will also enable us to identify the characteristic features of the different kinds of number assignments, and to relate them to each other within a unified framework. Together this will give us a clear idea how numbers work and, in doing so, will give us the key to see what properties are crucial for our concept of numbers and what it is that makes them so powerful.

Let me now introduce the basic elements of the Representational Theory. As mentioned in the introduction, here I will concentrate on the essential theoretical concepts that are relevant for our investigation of numbers and the purpose they serve within the model, while the technical definitions are spelled out in the appendices. You can find the definitions relevant to the present chapter in Appendix 1.

The Representational Theory of Measurement is based on three principal notions: *measurement^{RTM}*, the *scales* underlying a number assignment, and the features that make a numerical statement *meaningful*. Let us have a look at these in turn.

'Measurement^{RTM}' is defined as a mapping between empirical objects (in the above example, the books) and numbers. As mentioned above, we want to express certain relations between our objects by this mapping. This is determined by two requirements. The first requirement is that the objects and the numbers form *relational structures*, that is, sets of elements that stand in specific relationships to each other. For instance, in the book example we regarded the books not as unrelated individual objects, but as elements of a particular pile. The relational structure is here constituted by the relation 'lies further up'. The relation between the numbers that we focused on in our number assignment was '>'. All other relations that might hold between the objects (for example, the size of the books) or between the numbers (for example, odd numbers versus even numbers) are ignored for the purposes of this measurement. The two relational structures are distinguished as *numerical relational structure* (the relational structure constituted by the numbers) and *empirical relational structure* (the one established by the objects, here: the pile of books).

The second requirement for measurement^{RTM} is that the mapping underlying our number assignment be *homomorphic*. This means that it should translate the property we want to measure in the objects into a property of our numbers. A mapping from a relational structure A (for example, the pile of books) into a relational structure B (the numbers) is homomorphic when it not only correlates the elements of A and B, but also preserves the relations between them. In our example we did not just randomly line up books and numbers, but we linked them in a way such that the relation 'lies further up' from the empirical relational structure (the pile of books) was associated with the '>' relation in our numerical relational structure (the numbers). So if I tell you that one book received the number 1 and another book got the number 3, you know that the second book lies further up than the first one, because 3 > 1.

Had I assigned numbers to books without taking into account the relation 'lies further up', it would not help you at all to know which numbers two books received if you wanted to find out which one lies further up in the pile. For instance, it might easily turn out that the lowest book had been given the 3, while a higher book had the 1. The mapping was not homomorphic with respect to the two relations. However, this does not necessarily mean that the mapping was random and did not preserve any relations at all. I might not have bothered about which book lies further up in the pile, but my numbering might have focused on another property of the books, for instance their age. In this case, the book that got the 1 might not lie further up in the pile than the one that got the 3, but it would be newer. Hence, the mapping would indeed have been homomorphic, it would have preserved a relation between the books, although a different one: I regarded the books as elements of a different relational structure, namely one that is based on the relation 'is newer than' (rather than the relation 'lies further up than').

Another possibility would be that I focused on the same empirical property as before, namely the position of books in the pile, but employed a different relation between the numbers, for instance the relation 'lesser than'. In this case, you would know that the book with the number 1 lies further up in the pile than the book with the number 3, because 1 < 3. Again, the mapping would be homomorphic, but this time with respect to a different numerical relational structure.

The interesting aspect for our investigation of numbers and objects is now that from this analysis, it follows that number assignments are essentially links between relations: for the purpose of number assignment it is not so much the correlation between individual objects and individual numbers that counts, but the association between relations that hold between the empirical objects and relations that hold between the numbers. For instance, in our initial number assignment for the book pile, the links between the books and the numbers were grounded in the association of two relations, 'lies further up' and '>', but we could also associate other relations, for instance, the relations 'is newer than' and '>', or the relations 'lies further up' and '<', and as a result we might get different links between individual

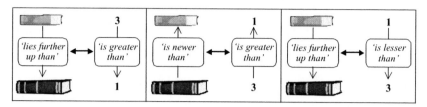

Figure 3   Measurement as an association of relations

books and individual numbers. Figure 3 gives an illustration for the different associations we discussed.

In our example from Figure 2 (illustrated by the graphic on the left), there is no reason why one should assign the number 3 to the grey book on the top if one looks at the book and the number as individuals in their own standing, and there is nothing in the number 1 itself that makes it particularly prone to be assigned to the black book on the bottom. We are associating relational structures here: it is because of their relations with other numbers and with other books, respectively, that 3 is linked up with the grey book and 1 with the black book. To put it plainly: we link up 3 with the grey book and 1 with the black book because 3 is greater than 1 and the grey book is higher in the pile than the black one – and not because 3 has anything to do with the grey book or 1 with the black book if we look at them as individuals outside their respective systems (namely, the number sequence and the pile of books). The links are dependent on the systems. Accordingly, I will call such a linking an instance of 'system-dependent linking', or in short: *dependent linking.*

So when assigning numbers to objects, we are not interested in numbers as individuals in their own right; it is the relations between them that we want. Accordingly, when analysing the different kinds of number assignments, I will focus on the *relations* between numbers that are relevant in each case, that is, I will focus on the numerical relations that reflect, in each case, the properties we want to assess in the objects.

The homomorphism that establishes the number assignment identifies its underlying *scale*: given a certain empirical property, the scale tells us which relation between the numbers is relevant in the assignment, that is, which numerical relational structure the mapping employs. Accordingly, in number assignments that are based on the same type of scale, the empirical property is reflected by the same relation between the numbers. This means that the number assignments can be transformed into each other. For instance in the measurement of weight, we can transform a number assignment like 'The pumpkin weighs 3 kg' into 'The pumpkin weighs 6.6138 lb', because both are based on the same type of scale.

In this example, the '>' relation between numbers reflects the property 'weight' (more precisely: it reflects the relation 'weighs more' between the objects), so if you tell me your measurement yielded '3 kg' for one pumpkin, and '2 kg' for another pumpkin, I know that the first one weighs more than the second one, and in just the same way I know that a 6 lb pumpkin weighs more than one of 4 lb. In both cases, the '>' relation between the numbers is associated with the relation 'weighs more than' in a particular way: in both cases, the numbers tell us that the first pumpkin weighs $1\frac{1}{2}$ times as much as the second pumpkin. We can always transform one number assignment into another one, as long as the association between the relevant numerical and empirical relations stays intact, because it is this association of relations that establishes our number assignment. The transformations that satisfy this requirement are the *admissible transformations* for a scale.

A numerical statement can now be defined as *meaningful* if and only if its truth-value is constant under admissible scale transformations (cf. Suppes and Zinnes 1963: 66). This means that if a numerical statement is true (or false), it should still be true (or false, respectively) when we translate it into another numerical statement, as long as this transformation is one that is allowed for the type of scale that underlies our number assignment. To put it plainly, if you tell me that 'The pumpkin weighs 3 kg' is true, but 'The pumpkin weighs 6.6138 lb' turns out to be false, something is wrong with your measurement. In this case, the numbers you apply to your objects seem not to reflect the property you intended to measure (namely, weight).

This is now a good point to see where we have got so far in our investigation of numbers and objects. Using the Representational Theory of Measurement, we have outlined a unified view of number assignments as mappings from empirical objects to numbers, and we have spelled out the characteristic features of this mapping: the empirical objects enter the number assignment with respect to a particular property, the property we want to assess. This property is then associated with a relation that holds between the numbers, and it is this association that determines the correlation between numbers and objects and makes the number assignment meaningful. According to this analysis, the numbers and objects are not correlated as individuals, but as elements of two systems, they are correlated in a way we described as 'dependent linking'.

Having thus spelled out the framework for our investigation, we are now in a position to examine the different ways in which we assign numbers to objects, as different instances of the same general scheme of 'measurement^RTM'. Above, I identified three different types of number assignments: cardinal, ordinal, and nominal assignments. Let us have a look at each of the three types in turn. In each case, we will ask which properties of numbers we make use of, that is, which properties numbers need to have in order to represent properties of empirical objects in a meaningful way. In our discussion I will concentrate on the natural numbers starting from 1, that is on the positive integers, ignoring, for the time being, 0, negative numbers, rational numbers, and so forth.

CARDINAL NUMBER ASSIGNMENTS:[5] '3 PENS', '3 KG', '3 °C'

In cardinal number assignments, the mapping from empirical objects to numbers takes advantage of the numerical relation '>' (or '<', respectively). As mentioned above, we can distinguish two subclasses of cardinal number assignments: those like '3 pens', on the one hand, and those like 'a 3 kg pumpkin' or 'bathwater of 3 °C' on the other hand. In the first case, the number identifies the cardinality of a set, that is, '3' tells us how many elements the set has, in this case: how many pens there are on my desk. The second class of cardinal assignments is the kind we mean when talking about 'measurement' in the familiar, pre-theoretical usage of the word. In these cases, '3' does not give us the cardinality of the measured objects (the pumpkin or the bathwater in our examples), but instead the cardinality of certain units of measurement (kg or °C). With the help of these units, we can use numbers to measure properties like weight or temperature. In 'a 3 kg pumpkin', '3' tells us how many kilograms, and '3 kg' specifies the pumpkin's weight. In 'bathwater of 3 °C', '3' tells us how many degrees Celsius, and '3 °C' specifies the temperature of the bathwater. As I am going to argue later in this section, we can regard these measurements as a special case of cardinal number assignments. (Admittedly bathwater of 3 °C is not a very pleasant image. If this causes you cold shivers, just think of a spa where you might want to dip into a 3 °C bath tub after a really hot sauna . . .)

Cardinality assignments for sets of objects: '3 pens'

In a number assignment like '3 pens', we apply a number to a set of objects; for instance the number 3 to the set of pens on my desk. This number tells us the cardinality of that set; it tells us how many pens there are

---

[5] Recall that with this terminology I refer to a classification of number assignments, that is, by 'cardinal number assignments' I do not mean the assignment of 'cardinal numbers', but number assignments that are cardinal in nature.

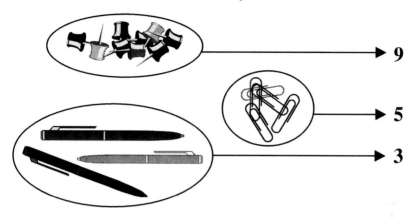

Figure 4 'Measurement^{RTM}' of cardinality

on my desk. This is what distinguishes these from other kinds of number assignments: when we use numbers to represent cardinalities, it is crucial that the empirical objects in our assignment are not individuals, but sets. The empirical relation that we focus on in our number assignment is 'has more elements than', and it is linked up with the numerical relation '>'.

Figure 4 illustrates this kind of number assignment. The sets in my example are different sets of utensils from my desk: a set of plastic pins, a set of paperclips, and the by now well-known set of pens. What makes this number assignment meaningful? How can numbers indicate cardinalities of sets? 3, 5, and 9 in Figure 4 occur as single objects. So where does the cardinality come from; what property of numbers do we make use of when we 'measure^{RTM}' cardinality in our empirical objects? To answer this question, let us have an explicit demonstration of the procedure that leads to a cardinal number assignment. The task is to tell the cardinality of the set in Figure 5, or, to put it a bit clumsily in measurement terms: to map the empirical object 'set of stars' in Figure 5 onto a number that indicates its cardinality.

The most straightforward way to determine the correct number is to assign a number to every star, starting with 1, then 2, and so on, until all the stars have a number; in short: we count the stars. Then we use the last number from the counting procedure – which will be 20 if the count is correct – in order to indicate the cardinality of the whole set of stars: 20 stars.

This gives us an insight into what lies behind our cardinal number assignment: first, we map the *elements* of the empirical object (that is, the

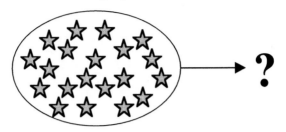

Figure 5 How many stars?

elements of our set) onto numbers, we 'count' the set; in our example: we mapped the elements of our empirical object 'set of stars' onto the numbers from 1 to 20. On the basis of this 'auxiliary number assignment', we then map the whole set onto one number, namely onto the last number we used in counting.

What makes this assignment meaningful is the fact that the counted set has as many elements as the initial sequence of numbers we used in counting: there are as many stars as there are numbers from 1 to 20. This is because when counting the stars, we match each star with exactly one number. We establish a one-to-one-mapping between stars and numbers that guarantees that the set of stars and the set of numbers we used in counting have the same cardinality.

So the number we assigned to the set of stars, 20, is something like a placeholder for a whole set of numbers, the numbers from 1 to 20. The cardinality of this *number set* represents the cardinality of our empirical object, the set of stars. In a nutshell, in cardinal number assignments we map a set onto a number n such that the set of numbers less than or equal to n – the number sequence from 1 to n – has as many elements as that set.

Accordingly, when employing counting as a verification procedure for our cardinal number assignment, we do not use numbers in random order. For instance, in Figure 5, you presumably did not count "5, 7, 1, 12, 24, 8, 3", and so on, and then suddenly came up with 20 as your last number. Much more likely, you started with 1, then 2, and so on, applying numbers to stars sequentially, with each number being followed by its successor in the number line. This is crucial to make sure the last number, 20, is the endpoint of a particular subsequence of the set N of natural numbers, namely the sequence <1, 2, 3, . . . , 20>. This sequence consists of the number 20 and all predecessors of 20 within the number line.

In Figure 6, this procedure is illustrated for our set of pens: we establish an ordered one-to-one mapping between the pens and the numbers from 1 to 3, in sequential order (column A). On this basis, we assign the number 3

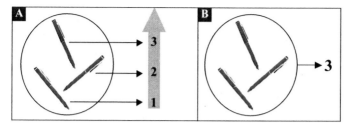

Figure 6 Procedure underlying cardinal number assignments ('3 pens')

to the entire set of pens (column B): 3 functions as a place-holder for the set consisting of the numbers 1, 2, and 3 – a set that has as many elements as the set of pens. By so doing, 3 can indicate the cardinality of the set of pens.

Let me sum up our analysis of cardinal number assignments. In cardinal number assignments, the empirical objects are sets, and the property we want to assess is their numerical quantity: their cardinality as identified by a number. When we apply a number n to a set s, we want to specify how many elements s has. The numerical statement is meaningful if and only if the number sequence from 1 to n has the same cardinality as the set s, that is, if there is a one-to-one-mapping between the numbers up to n and the elements of s. This one-to-one-mapping can be established via counting.

Cardinal number assignments like the ones described here – that is, those that are about cardinality and not about properties like weight or temperature – are based upon absolute scales. These scales do not allow any transformations but the identity transformation, hence a transformation that does not change the number assignment at all: it yields for a numerical statement like 'There are 3 pens on my desk' the very same statement ('There are 3 pens on my desk'). This is because in these cardinal number assignments, we unambiguously refer to the sequence of numbers starting with 1, and set them in a one-to-one correlation with the elements of the empirical set. Accordingly, there is always only one number that applies to a given set.

For our investigation of numbers we now want to know what it is in particular that qualifies numbers for this kind of assignment: what enables numbers to represent cardinalities the way they do? What is the system on which the dependent linking is based in this case? As we have seen, when indicating a cardinality, a number n points to the set of numbers less than or equal to n. The elements of this set form a sequence from 1 to n, they constitute an initial sequence of the natural numbers N. This is possible because of the sequential order of numbers, as established by the '<'-relation: every number has a fixed position within N, hence, for a particular number *n*, we can always specify the set of numbers up to *n*, the sequence from 1 to *n*. This sequence is unique for every number, and it has always a unique cardinality.

Take any two natural numbers, say 3 and 5, and you can always identify the respective sets of predecessors (including the numbers themselves) that are relevant in cardinal number assignments: the set with the elements '1, 2, 3' in the case of 3, and '1, 2, 3, 4, 5' in the case of 5. These sets are different for any two different numbers, and they never have the same cardinality, because two different numbers will always occupy different positions within the number line, so they will always have a different set of predecessors.

In our example, the set we identified for 5 has more elements than that for 3, and it has either more or less elements than the sequence from 1 to *n* for any other number *n*. This might sound trivial, but it is part and parcel of our use of numbers in cardinal number assignments. If 3 and 5 were not elements of a sequence – and what is more, of the same sequence – in these assignments, we would have no guarantee that they indicate different cardinalities, or any cardinalities at all. Figure 7 depicts the way 3 and 5 relate to sets of unique cardinalities – namely to distinct initial sequences of N – due to their position in the number sequence.

The sequential position within N is hence the crucial numerical feature in cardinal number assignments. It is the sequential order of N that enables us to represent cardinalities with numbers the way we do. What is more, it is the only feature N needs to have for this task. As our discussion has shown, there are no other requirements on numbers in cardinal number assignments; their sequential position within N was the only feature we referred to when using numbers to identify the cardinalities of our empirical objects. Being an element of a sequence is hence an essential property of numbers.

We can define a sequence as a particular set that is ordered by a relation R (for instance, '>') with the following properties: R is antireflexive

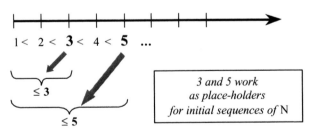

Figure 7 Sequential order as the basis for cardinal number assignments

(no number is greater than itself), asymmetric (if a number x is greater than another number y, then y cannot be greater than x), and transitive (if a number x is greater than another number y, and y is greater than a third number z, then x is also greater than z), and the order introduced by R must be total (for any two different numbers x and y, one is greater than the other). If we want to use this sequence in counting, we must make sure that there is a unique path to each of its elements. This is the case if each of its elements has only finitely many predecessors, starting with an initial element, '1'. I will call a sequence that fulfils these conditions a 'progression' (cf. also the definition given in Appendix 1).

Cardinal number assignments including measures: *'a 3 kg pumpkin', 'water of 3 °C'*

The second kind of cardinal number assignments is the measurement we meet in examples like 'a 3 kg pumpkin' or 'bathwater of 3 °C'. This is the kind of number assignment we refer to when using the term 'measurement' in the familiar sense. Unlike in number assignments such as '3 pens', the empirical objects in measurement – the pumpkin and the bathwater in our examples – are not treated as sets. Of course, they can be sets anyway, as in '3 kg of apples' (where we measure the weight of a set of apples), but this is not what the number assignment takes into account; there is no set-specific feature of the empirical objects (like cardinality) that the number assignment refers to. My three pens weigh together 20 g, and this is about as much as the floppy disc lying next to them on my desk, but to find that out, I totally ignore the fact that the pens form a set of three, whereas the floppy disc is a single object – for the purpose of measurement, it comes out just the same.

So whereas in cardinality assessments it is imperative for the number assignments that the empirical objects be sets, we ignore this feature in measurement; sets and non-sets are treated alike. In fact, cardinality assessments are the only kind of number assignments where the numbers apply to sets *as sets*, and only to sets. This is because only for sets can we identify the number of elements. Only sets have a cardinality, whereas the properties we identify in other kinds of number assignments apply to individual objects as well as sets, so 'set-ness' is not a feature we need to focus on; it is not part of our empirical relational structure in the number assignment.

In measurement, we are concerned with empirical properties like weight, length, or temperature: dimensional properties other than cardinality. As for all cardinal number assignments, we associate the empirical property with the numerical relation '>' in our mapping. Let us distinguish two kinds of measurement with respect to the property we relate to: measurement of extensive properties like weight and length, and measurement of non-extensive properties like temperature.

An extensive property is one that depends on the amount of the measured objects. This is the case because an extensive property changes with the size of our empirical sample; it increases when we add more objects with the same property. Take weight: when you have a basket with apples, and you add more apples, it becomes heavier (its weight increases), because the property 'weight' is extensive. It is the same with volume: pour more wine into a glass, and the volume of wine in that glass increases. And two of my pens, if arranged end to end in a line, are together longer than one pen, because 'length' is an extensive property, too.

In contrast to this, a non-extensive property like temperature does not increase if we add 'more of the same'. When you add more wine of the same temperature to the wine in a glass, the wine becomes more, but it does not become warmer: the volume of the wine – an extensive property – increases, but its temperature does not. The tea in my mug might become hotter when I add fresh tea from the thermos to it, but that is because when we mix fluids their temperature equals out, not because it adds up.

Direct measurement: 'a 3 kg pumpkin'

Let us first have a look at measurements as expressed in 'a 3 kg pumpkin'. I call this 'direct measurement', because – as we will see below – in this instance of measurement we have a direct link between cardinality and our units of measurement. In this kind of number assignment, we want the numbers to tell us something about an extensive property of the empirical objects. In particular, we want the relation '>' between the numbers to reflect differences in this extensive property between our empirical objects.

Figure 8 illustrates this kind of cardinal number assignment. In the example, we measure the weight of three empirical objects: a watermelon, a pumpkin, and a squash. Higher or lower numbers are applied with respect to higher or lower weight: the watermelon as the heaviest object receives the highest number, 5; the squash is the lightest vegetable with 1, and the pumpkin is in the middle and gets the number 3. This does not quite look like a weight measurement as we know it. What is missing in this example is the specification of measurement units. When asking for the weight of a pumpkin in a grocery store, you would probably not be satisfied with an answer like '3'. What you expect the sales person to tell you is rather something like '3 kg' or '3 pounds'. Expressions like 'kg' or 'pound'

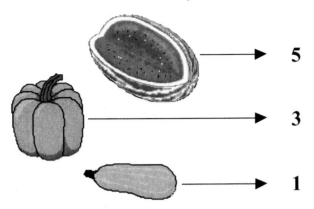

Figure 8 Direct measurement as a cardinal number assignment: measurement of weight

identify different units for the measurement of weight; they introduce supporting measure items that we employ for our number assignment. In the following discussion, I am going to argue that measure items relate extensive properties like weight to cardinality and thus enable us to draw on the cardinal aspect of numbers in the course of measurement.

Before we discuss the use of measure items in detail, let me first illustrate this with an example, to give you an idea of the procedure that underlies this kind of number assignment. Figure 9 spells out the use of measure items for the pumpkin from our example. To measure the pumpkin's weight, I employed objects of 1 kg as measure items. I then found a set of these items that weigh together as much as the pumpkin. Counting the elements of this set yielded the number I assigned to the pumpkin. Hence I identified the weight of the pumpkin via the cardinality of a set of measure items: three kilograms. Let us have a look at what lies behind the usage of measure items illustrated in Figure 9. How does it work? And why do we employ measure items in the first place? The problem we face in measurement is that we want the '>' relation between numbers to indicate 'more' ('weighs more than', 'is longer than' etc.) – measurement being a form of cardinal number assignment – but, since our empirical objects are not sets, we cannot employ the counting procedure for them that worked so well in our first kind of cardinal number assignments (i.e., assignments as in '3 pens') – it is of no use to try and count a pumpkin in order to find out its weight.

However, when measuring extensive properties like weight, there is always a way to relate the property we want to measure to some cardinality. Remember our apple example from page 23 above: when we add more apples to a basket of apples, it becomes heavier. So the total weight of the

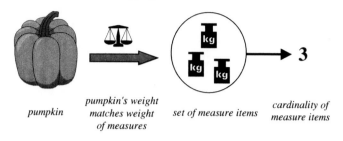

pumpkin | pumpkin's weight matches weight of measures | set of measure items | cardinality of measure items

Figure 9 Procedure underlying direct measurement: weight ('a 3 kg pumpkin')

apples increases with their cardinality – the more apples, the heavier the basket. If we find a way to employ this relation between cardinality and weight for our measurement, we can base our measurement on numerical quantification after all. This is what the seventeenth- to eighteenth-century philosopher Gottfried Wilhelm Leibniz called the 'recourse from continuous quantity to discrete quantity', when he discussed the measurement of size ('grandeur'), another example of measurement:

we cannot distinctly recognise sizes without having recourse to whole numbers . . . , and so, where distinct knowledge of size is sought, we must leave continuous quantity and have recourse to discrete quantity. (Leibniz 1703/05: § 4)

If we use standardised measure items now instead of apples, we have an elegant way to realise this recourse, that is, to measure an extensive property like weight via cardinality. Two requirements are important for the objects that are to fulfil the task of measure items:

(1) The measure items must possess the empirical property that we want to measure, and they must be identical with respect to this property.
(2) The property must be additive, that is, it must be a property that can be associated with cardinality. More precisely, there must be a physical operation of concatenation for the objects that has the effect of addition if we represent it numerically.

The first requirement means, for instance, that for the measurement of weight each measure item must have the same weight. This might sound circular at first – after all, was not weight what we set out to measure eventually? So how are we supposed to know whether our measure items have the same weight beforehand? This is possible because, in order to know whether two objects have *the same weight*, we need not know *which weight* they have. We can compare the weight of two metal blocks that we might want to use as measure items and determine whether they have the same weight or not, for instance by using a balance, without measuring their weight in terms of numbers and units of measurements. And, similarly, we can arrange two objects parallel to each other, starting at the same point, in order to determine whether they have the same length. This is a general phenomenon: we can always compare two objects with respect to an empirical property without employing a number assignment.

The second requirement, namely that the relevant property of our measure items must be additive, is met by extensive properties. As illustrated in our examples above, the values of these properties for several objects add up. For instance, the weight of our set of apples increased and decreased along with its cardinality. In this case, to 'concatenate' means 'put together': if we put together two apples, their total weight adds up. Similarly, the total length of several pens, when arranged end to end in a straight line ('concatenation' of length), increases and decreases along with their cardinality: if we lay two pens end to end, their total length adds up.

If these requirements are met, the cardinality of a set of measure items is linked up with the property we want to measure (more precisely: the two properties are monotonically covarying). For instance, when we measure weight as illustrated in Figure 9 above, our measure items could be metal blocks of 1 kg each. Since each of these blocks has the same weight, the cardinality of the set of blocks indicates their total weight – if we know how many blocks there are, we know how heavy they are together.

Using this set of measure items, we can then measure the weight of an empirical object like our pumpkin. All we have to do is make sure that the total weight of our set of measure items matches that of the pumpkin. And again, in order to do this, we do not have to employ numbers yet, but can make a simple comparison, for example with the help of a balance as sketched in Figure 9. The cardinality of the set of metal blocks then indicates the weight of the pumpkin: the cardinality tells us the total weight of the blocks, and, since the blocks together weigh as much as the pumpkin, it also tells us the pumpkin's weight. This way, measure items mediate between cardinality and an extensive property like weight, and it is this correlation that makes the number assignment meaningful.

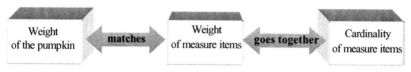

Figure 10 Measure items as agents between an extensive property (weight) and cardinality

Standardised units like 'kg' or 'metre' point to measure items of a specified weight or length, respectively; so when using these units in our number assignments, we do not have to identify the particular objects one might use in the course of measurement (particular metal blocks etc.), but can relate to standardised units. We will come back to the use of different measure items in our discussion of measure concepts in chapter 6. What is important for our present investigation is that the introduction of measure items enables us to base direct measurement *entirely* on cardinality assignments, as far as numbers are concerned. We do not make use of any properties of numbers here that we did not use in simple cardinality assignments (as in '3 pens') anyway. All we need to ask from our numbers is that they form a progression, so we can use them to identify cardinalities. The additional features of measurement come in with measure items, but they do not put any further requirements on numbers.

Let me summarise the analysis of direct measurement that I have proposed here. In direct measurement, the empirical objects are not sets; they do not have any elements that we can count for the number assignment. So what we do in this case is we find something that *is* a set and quantify it instead. This set is a set of measure items, that is, its cardinality is connected with the extensive property we want to measure items in our empirical objects. The cardinality of this set of measure items can therefore identify our extensive property. In a nutshell, direct measurement boils down to a cardinality assignment for measure items. Accordingly, nothing is required for numbers over and above the condition that they are elements of a progression[6] – the numerical feature we need for cardinality assignments.

Because there are always different kinds of measure items one can use to measure the same property (that is, measure items of a different – standardised – weight, length etc.), this kind of number assignment is not based on absolute scales (like our first kind of cardinal number assignments), but on rational scales. This means that you can always multiply the numbers you used in our measurement with a positive real number – provided you are using the same number in each measurement procedure – without changing the truth (or falsity) of your numerical statement. So for rational scales, the numbers themselves are not kept invariant (as is the case for absolute scales), only the ratios between them are: in a number assignment based on a rational scale, we determine uniquely the ratios between the values we assign to our empirical objects.

---

[6] That is, they are elements of a sequence each of whose elements has only finitely many precursors (see the definition of a progression on p. 23 above).

For instance, if we measure the weight of our objects from Figure 8 in grams instead of kilograms, we have to multiply the numbers we assigned them with 1000; if we measure in pounds, we have to multiply with 2.2046: the watermelon weighs 5000 g or 11.023 lb or 5 kg; the pumpkin weighs 3000 g, 6.6138 lb, or 3 kg, and the squash weighs 1000 g, 2.2046 lb, or 1 kg. The numbers we assigned our empirical objects changed, but the ratio between them stayed the same. In each case, the watermelon weighs 5 times and the pumpkin 3 times as much as the squash, and the pumpkin weighs 0.6 times as much as the watermelon.

Indirect measurement: 'Bathwater with a temperature of 3 °C'
The number assignment expressed in 'The bathwater has a temperature of 3 °C.' works a bit differently from the direct measurement I analysed in the previous paragraphs. Let us have a look at this indirect measurement now, in order to find out which features of numbers are crucial here. In particular, we want to know if there are any additional properties of numbers we want to relate to when assigning them to our empirical objects in a meaningful way.

Figure 11 gives a first impression of indirect measurement. In the example, I assigned numbers to an ice cone, a warm pretzel, and a hot dog, to indicate their temperature. The warmer a food item was, the higher the number I assigned to it: the '>' relation between the numbers reflects the relation 'is warmer than' between the empirical objects.

Unlike in the measurement of weight, here we do not have a set of measure items that directly relates the property we want to measure to a cardinality. For the number assignments in Figure 11, I did not use measure items that systematically link up temperature with cardinality, such that

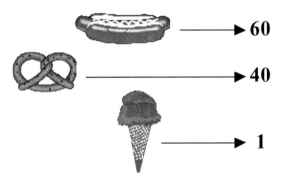

Figure 11 Measurement of temperature

each of them has the same temperature as the ice cream, 40 of them are together as warm as the pretzel, and 60 are as hot as the frankfurter. Rather, measurement units like °C or °F relate temperature to cardinality in an indirect way. In this measurement procedure, we employ a mediating object that enables us to measure a non-extensive property via an extensive property. An instance for such a mediating object is the mercury column in a thermometer. Its temperature is linked up with the extensive property 'height' (more precisely, the two properties are positively covarying): the warmer the mercury is, the higher the mercury column. The height of the column can hence be used to indicate its temperature.

Similarly to what we do in direct measurement, we have to make sure that the mercury has the same temperature as the object we want to measure, say the water in a bathtub. And again, we can do that without employing numbers – conventionally we make sure that the mercury is as warm as the water by holding the thermometer into the bathtub. The height of the mercury column can then tell us not only the temperature of the mercury, but also – by way of match – the temperature of the bathwater. So all we have to do now is to measure the height of the column. Since height is an extensive property, we can do that along the lines we figured out for the measurement of weight: find a set of measure items such that each of them has the same length (for instance, the individual units on a ruler), and such that they are together as long as the column, and count them.

So, in the end, the cardinality of this set of length units can identify the temperature of our bathwater, via their (total) height, the height of the mercury column and the mercury's temperature. It is this line of linked-up properties that makes sure that the number assignment is meaningful, that is, it guarantees that the numbers we assign to empirical objects in fact tell us something about their temperature. Figure 12 summarises this correlation between cardinality and the measured property in indirect measurement.

This is what makes indirect measurement indirect. As in direct measurement, we use the cardinality of a set of measure items as an indicator of an extensive property; however, this object (the mercury column) is not yet the empirical object we want to measure, but a mediating object that links

Figure 12 Measure items and the mediating object in indirect measurement

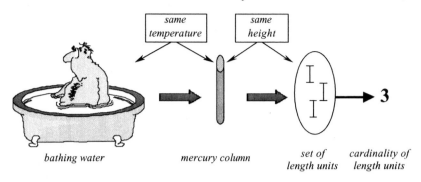

Figure 13 Procedure underlying indirect measurement of temperature ('water of 3 °C')

up this extensive property with the property we set out to measure in the first place (temperature).

What is crucial here for our discussion of numbers is that the only place where numbers come in is the cardinality assignment for the set of measure items, just as in direct measurement. That is, as far as numbers are concerned, all that is needed here is sequential order within a progression again. All the additional sophistication that enables us to quantify temperature with numbers, comes from the employment of measure items and of a mediating object for the purpose of measurement.

In Figure 13, I spell out the procedure underlying indirect measurement for the example of bathwater with a temperature of 3 °C. There is one respect in which my illustration is not quite accurate: what I identified as 'mercury column' is actually not the whole mercury column, but only that part of it that is above a particular height, which is marked '0'. When measuring in degrees Celsius, the zero point marks the height of the mercury column at the temperature of freezing water. Obviously, the mercury does not disappear at that temperature. Its height does not become '0'; it just reaches a particular point that we decided to call '0' as a convention (and accordingly, we conventionally use negative numbers to identify how far the column is below that point at colder temperatures).

This starting point '0' is determined more or less arbitrarily; we can agree upon any point we might find convenient. Accordingly, unlike in direct measurement, there are different temperatures called '0 degrees' for different units of measurement that can be used here (for instance, Celsius and Fahrenheit). This kind of measurement is based on interval scales, scales that allow all transformations that keep invariant the ratios of the *intervals* between the numbers that we assign to our empirical objects. In addition to multiplying our numbers with a positive real number (as in rational scales), we are allowed to add something to them (more precisely: we can add a positive or a negative real number). This addition has the effect of marking a different point as 'o'. If you are using the same multiplier and the same increment for all the numbers in one instance of measurement, this transformation will not affect the truth or falsity of your numerical statement.

In other words, bathwater of 3 °C or of $33\frac{2}{3}$ °F comes out just the same (the bathwater either has 'both' temperatures, or none), because $33\frac{2}{3} = 32 + \frac{5}{9} \times 3$, and the transformation rule from Celsius to Fahrenheit is: n °C $\triangleq (32 + \frac{5}{9}n)$ °F, that is, we multiply by $\frac{5}{9}$ and add 32, an admissible transformation. (Because of this rather tiresome computation procedure, for temperature unlike for weight or height, in everyday life most people do not bother to do the calculation each time they want to transform °C into °F or the other way round – for instance, when abroad in a country where people use an unfamiliar unit. Instead, one often just memorises some correlations that might be useful, say the matching figures for 'nice weather', 'cold weather', and 'really chilly', or for the oven temperatures needed to bake a cake and to cook a lasagne.)

In addition to Celsius and Fahrenheit, we have to account for measurement units like Kelvin and Rankine that relate temperature to the kinetic energy of molecules. When we measure temperature in Kelvin or Rankine, the lowest possible value is a point of 'absolute zero', the theoretical temperature where molecular motion ceases and a body would have no heat energy. Accordingly, all possible temperatures are positive. This kind of number assignment is therefore based on rational scales: if we transform the numbers we assigned to our empirical objects, we may multiply them with a positive real number, but we do not add anything, because – unlike in temperature measurements using Celsius and Fahrenheit – the starting point 'o' is fixed. Since the Kelvin degree is the same size as the Celsius degree, and the Rankine degree is the same size as the Fahrenheit degree, we have to multiply by $\frac{5}{9}$ to get from Kelvin to Rankine: n K $\triangleq$ $\frac{5}{9}n$ °R (recall that the transformation rule from Celsius to Fahrenheit was: n °C $\triangleq (32 + \frac{5}{9}n)$ °F). As the example illustrates, we can regard rational scales as a special case of interval scales, namely as ones which allow only o as an increment in number transformations.

Let me recapitulate the results for our investigation of numbers and objects at this point. In the last paragraphs, we investigated three different ways in which we assign numbers to objects in cardinal number assignments: the assignment of cardinality to sets, as in '3 pens', direct measurement as expressed in 'a 3 kg pumpkin', and indirect measurement such as 'bathwater of 3 °C'. The discussion of these cardinal number assignments has shown that the homomorphism from empirical objects to numbers draws in each case on the cardinal aspect of numbers, and that this cardinal aspect is based on a particular sequential ordering of the number line, an ordering that makes it a progression. It is this ordering that allows us to identify a unique set of predecessors from 1 to n for each natural number n; a set that has a different cardinality for each number. Hence each natural number, by pointing to this predecessor set, can identify a unique cardinality.

Following this account of cardinal number assignments, the relevant numerical property here, that is, the property we need in numbers to use them the way we do, is their sequential order within a progression, and it is the *only* numerical property we need. Let us have a look at the two remaining kinds of number assignments, ordinal and nominal assignments, and see how we employ numbers in those cases, in order to find out if there are additional numerical properties we want to relate to in our number assignments.

ORDINAL NUMBER ASSIGNMENTS: 'THE THIRD RUNNER'

In ordinal number assignments, we use a number to identify the rank of an empirical object within a sequence. For instance in 'Mick is the third runner in the race', the number 3 identifies the rank of Mick in a sequence of runners. Figure 14 illustrates this kind of number assignment. The empirical objects are participants of a race who are ordered according to their speed. In this kind of number assignment, the ' $<$ ' relation between the numbers represents the sequential ordering of the empirical objects: in our example, ' $<$ ' represents the ordering of Charles, Karen, Mick, and Paul by 'is faster than'. For instance, since Karen is faster than both Mick and Paul, she got a smaller number than both men; Charles received a smaller number than Karen, and Mick's number is smaller than Paul's.

Let us have a closer look at how this number assignment works. For this purpose, imagine yourself as the judge in this race. Your job is to announce the participants' ranks, that is, you are to announce who wins, who comes second, etc. To that end, you stand at the finishing line and assign numbers to the runners; in other words: you map the empirical objects 'runners in this race' onto numbers, by way of an ordinal number assignment. How do you do that? Very simply, you assign the number 1 to the first runner who reaches the goal (Charles), the number 2 to the one who comes directly

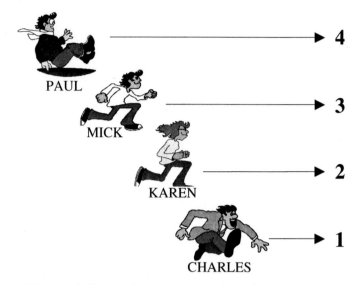

Figure 14 Ordinal number assignment (ranking of runners in a race)

after (Karen), the number 3 to the next one (Mick), and so on. Hence you establish a one-to-one-mapping from the runners, depending on the order of their arrival, to the sequence of natural numbers, starting with 1.

This procedure looks very much like the 'counting' routine we discussed for cardinal number assignments above. However, counting differs from ordinal number assignments in an interesting way. As I argued above, counting is a subroutine we employ for another number assignment, the assignment of a cardinality. By counting the elements of a set, we make sure that this set has as many elements as the sequence from 1 to a particular number *n*. It is this number *n* that we then assign to our empirical object, the set.

Accordingly, the individual correlations we establish between numbers and the elements of a set in the course of counting are of no relevance for our cardinal number assignment. In contrast to that, the correlations between the numbers and the runners in our race *are* the ordinal number assignment. Therefore, the order of the empirical objects is irrelevant in counting, but it is crucial in ordinal number assignments, since it is this order that determines which number an object gets. So, when I count the pens that lie on my desk in front of me, it does not matter whether I start with the red one or the blue one, as long as every pen gets one and only one number in the process of counting.

This would be the same if we *counted* our runners, instead of employing the ordinal number assignment I described above. If you just want to know how many participants there are in the race, you need not care about their order when counting them. For instance, in the process of counting, you could (a) start with Mick and assign him the number 1, then go on with Charles, and so on; or alternatively you could (b) start with Charles, then Karen, and assign Mick the number 3. Whichever way you choose will make no difference for the outcome of your cardinal number assignment. If the assignment of numbers is meant to be ordinal, however, the choice between (a) and (b) would make a world of a difference, and Charles – as the rightful winner of the race – would probably object quite a bit when getting the number 2, as in option (a). In ordinal number assignments, it is crucial for the mapping from objects to numbers that our empirical objects are ordered with respect to each other; for example, by the relation 'is faster than'.

Just as for numbers, this ordering relation has to be antireflexive (no runner is faster than him-/herself), asymmetric (if Karen is faster than Mick, then Mick cannot be faster than Karen), and transitive (if Charles is faster than Karen, and Karen is faster than Mick, then Charles is also faster than Mick). These requirements make sure that our empirical relational structure is a sequence. Again, like the number line, this sequence has to be a progression; it must have an initial element that will receive the 1 in our number assignment. In our runner example, this element was Charles. Obviously, it would not do to define him as the 'first' runner, because that would be kind of circular ('The first runner is the one that gets the number 1'). Instead, we can identify him with respect to our ordering relation, 'faster than': Charles is the fastest runner in our race; in other words, there is no runner who is faster than Charles.

To sum up, the empirical objects in ordinal number assignments are elements of a progression, and the numbers we assign to them tell us their respective ranks within this progression. For this task, we focus on the sequential order of numbers. The homomorphism that constitutes our number assignment correlates the sequential position of numbers with the empirical objects' position within a progression. Accordingly, in our example above we assigned Mick the number 3, because his rank within the sequence of runners is the same as the rank of 3 within the number sequence – we have an instance of dependent linking that associates sequential ranks.

So, like cardinal number assignments, ordinal number assignments rely on the sequential ordering of N, but they do so in a more direct way. In this kind of number assignment, every number stands for its sequential

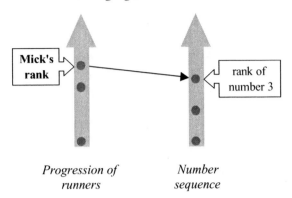

Figure 15 Procedure underlying ordinal number assignment ('Mick is the third runner.')

position, and we use this position to identify the relative position of an object within an empirical progression.

Ordinal number assignments are based on ordinal scales. This means that all those transformations are allowed that keep the order of the numbers invariant (all transformations based on a monotone increasing function). So, in principle, we could use a numerical relational structure consisting of odd numbers only, assigning 1 to Charles, 3 to Karen, and 5 to Mick; or we could restrict ourselves to prime numbers greater than 23, which would yield 29 for Charles, 31 for Karen, and 37 for Mick. As a rule, any *sequence* of numbers would do.

This is because ordinal number assignments are all about order; there is no quantification involved. Assigning Mick a higher number than Karen does not say anything about the distance between them. It just means that Mick comes after Karen, not that the distance between Mick and Karen is the same as between the respective numbers we assigned to them (in order to emphasise this, in Figure 15 I positioned the dots that indicate the runners' ranks in varying distances to each other). In other words, that Karen gets a '2' and Mick a '3' in our assignment only tells us that she is faster than Mick, it does not tell us how much faster she is, and that Paul gets a '4' does not mean that Karen is twice as fast as Paul or that the distance between Karen and Mick is the same as the distance between Mick and Paul. There is no analogy to the quantification involved in cardinality assignments and measurement when it comes to ordinal assignments.

Accordingly, any number assignment where the order of the numbers reflects the order of our empirical objects would be a meaningful ordinal assignment. However, conventionally we use the sequence of natural

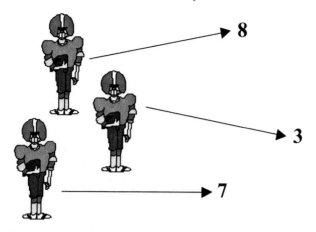

Figure 16 Nominal number assignment (labelling of football players)

numbers starting with 1 as our numerical relational structure, and this is what I will assume for the following discussion.

NOMINAL NUMBER ASSIGNMENTS: 'BUS #3', 'FOOTBALL PLAYER #3'

In nominal number assignments we use numbers as labels for empirical objects. The number we assign an object works like a proper name for it; it helps us distinguish it from other objects. In these number assignments, the empirical objects are elements of a set, for instance a set of bus lines or a team of football players. Unlike in ordinal number assignments, this set does not have to be a progression, there needs to be no ordering relation on the objects. Figure 16 gives an illustration: the empirical relational structure is a set of football players, and the numbers I have assigned to them are 3, 7, and 8. I have placed the numbers in random positions to emphasise that we do not make use of their sequential order here. Nominal number assignments are the only kind of 'measurement[RTM]' where the sequential order of numbers is irrelevant. This is the case because numbers do not tell us a rank or a cardinality here, they are employed to identify the empirical objects themselves. To this end, it suffices if the homomorphism that constitutes the mapping from objects to numbers takes into account the identity and non-identity of the objects, and associates it with identity and non-identity among the numbers: the systems in our dependent linking need not be sequences, but just unordered sets of objects.

Accordingly, the only rule for nominal number assignments is: never assign the same number to more than one object, because if you did, this number could not uniquely identify an object anymore. The meaningfulness of the numerical statement is established by the fact that the number we assign to one object is well distinguished from the numbers we assign to other objects. Hence the only property of numbers that is relevant here is the fact that they are well-distinguished entities.

The distinctness of numbers is actually a prerequisite for the other number assignments, too; we just took it for granted. After all, if we cannot tell apart one number from the other, there is no way we can distinguish their respective sequential positions either. In order to talk about sequential order in the first place, we need well-distinguished entities. As a consequence, this feature of distinctness is something one feels should go without saying. However, since we want to get to the very basics of which properties we need in numbers, let us not take anything for granted, and include this feature in our list of essential numerical properties.

Since nominal number assignments make use of very little of what numbers are, they are less central to our concept of number and mastered later by young children than cardinal and ordinal assignments of numbers (I will come back to this phenomenon when discussing the development of number concepts and the organisation of our cognitive number domain in chapter 6). The fact that we use only the distinctness of numbers in nominal number assignments means also that we can use other, non-numerical labels for the task of identification in just the same way. Numbers come in handy, because there are so many of them that we never run out of new labels. They are inexhaustible and readily available proper names. However, apart from this, elements of other sets do just as well.

An obvious example are conventional proper names, that is, names like 'Karen' or 'Mick'. In some parts of the Arab Emirates, for instance, houses are not numbered, but have names – while streets are numbered and not named. So if you lived in Dubai your address could be, say, Al-Ahmad apartment block in #12 street (this was in fact my address when I once stayed in Dubai) – a neat mirror to an address like house #12 in Al-Ahmad Street, which you might have in another country. An example from the non-linguistic domain are colours. Once we settle on a certain set of distinct colours, we can use them to identify objects, just as we identify objects with numbers in nominal number assignments. An example where we use both kinds of labels (numerical: numbers; non-numerical: colours) are subway systems. In particular in cities with only a few subway lines, one often uses colours to distinguish them, rather than numbers. In addition, letters of the alphabet are often used in a way similar to the way we assign numbers in nominal number assignments. Since the alphabet forms a sequence, too, this also occurs for ordinal contexts. In particular, letters are sometimes used to indicate subsequences within a sequence identified by numbers. An example would be the numbering of chapters and subsections in a book by numbers in combination with letters, for instance '1a', '1b', '2a', '2b' etc.

Nominal number assignments are based on nominal scales. These scales allow almost any transformation; the only restriction here is that objects that were given different numbers should still have different numbers after the transformation (that is, any injective function is allowed[7]). For instance, in the course of a complete reorganisation of the bus numbering in a city, we could rename the lines with the effect that bus #4 becomes #12, what used to be bus #3 is now bus #6, and so on, and we would still have a valid nominal number assignment, equivalent to the one we used to have, as long as all the lines that were distinguished before still have different numbers after renumbering.

Apart from prototypical nominal number assignments like the numbering of bus lines, there are also number assignments that are nominal in principle, but imply something I call a 'secondary ordinal aspect'. I am thinking of cases like house numbers, where the number that is assigned to a house does not only identify it, but can often also tell us something about its position among other houses. For instance, if you are looking for a house with the number 5, you might expect it between house 4 and house 6, or between the houses with the numbers 3 and 7, depending on the house numbering system in that area. On first sight, this might suggest an ordinal basis for the number assignment.

However, this ordinal aspect is just an addition that sometimes comes in handy when we are using numbers as labels: since these labels are ordered anyway, we might as well use their order to indicate an order that holds within our empirical objects. The actual purpose of our number assignment, though, is a nominal one, namely the identification of the houses (or premises) themselves and not the identification of their positions in a sequence. The dependent linking does not rely on the ordering relation. This becomes evident when the ranks of the houses change, while their identity remains the same: in this case, their numbers can remain the same, too, which indicates that we have a nominal, rather than an ordinal basis for our number assignment.

---

[7] An injective function is one that links every element from the source domain to a unique element of the target domain, that is, no element of the target domain is shared.

Imagine for instance that house number 4 in your street is torn down to make place for a park. This has an effect for the sequence of houses: from house 5 onwards, houses will be lower in rank – house number 5 is not the fifth house in line anymore, but the fourth one now, while house number 6 is the fifth one, and so on. If the numbers were to reflect an ordinal number assignment, we would have to change all those house numbers in the street.[8] However, since this is a nominal number assignment we can keep the old numbering. The ordinal aspect that comes in for house numbers is a practical back-up for the identification task, not a necessary implication of the number assignment. Accordingly, skipping one number might be a bit confusing for strangers, but it does not render the number assignment invalid.

To sum up, this secondary ordinal aspect does not have any impact on the number assignment; it is a feature one might want to introduce for reasons of practicality in cases where our empirical objects are ordered anyway – and where it is therefore easier to find an object with a particular number if this order is reflected in their labels. I am speaking from experience here: I have just come back from the library where I looked up some of the references for this chapter, and when I wanted to leave it took me nearly ten minutes to track down the locker in which I had left my bag. The reason for this was that in the course of a recent renovation all the lockers got mixed up, with the result that for instance locker 802 ended up next to 946 and right behind 340. This does not make the numbering wrong, of course – since it is nominal – but it makes it rather a challenge to find your locker.

OVERVIEW: HOW TO USE NUMBERS

In this chapter, I presented to you an analysis of the relationship between numbers and objects. I showed that if we employ the Representational Theory of Measurement as an umbrella for different kinds of number assignments, we can account for cardinal, ordinal, and nominal number contexts alike. On this basis, I characterised numbers as highly flexible tools that we use in different kinds of number assignments to assess properties of objects as diverse as cardinality, weight, temperature, rank, and identity. What makes these number assignments meaningful is the fact that, in each case, we associate a particular property of numbers with the property we

---

[8] Assuming, of course, that we still use the standard sequence of natural numbers (as mentioned above) for our numerical relational structure in the ordinal number assignment.

want to assess in the empirical objects: we correlate numbers and objects in a pattern of dependent linking.

The analysis of the different ways in which we assign numbers to objects revealed that the different purposes that numbers serve are grounded in only two basic features: in order to do their job, numbers have to be (1) well distinguished from each other, and (2) elements of a progression. Given these two features, numbers can represent all the properties we want to assess in cardinal, ordinal, and nominal number assignments alike. These two features are at the same time powerful enough to cover all the purposes for which we want to use numbers when applying them to objects, and basic enough to make numbers so flexible that they can be used in contexts that are so diverse that on first sight, they hardly seem to have anything in common.

The following paragraphs sum up our analysis of the relationship between numbers and objects, identifying the way we draw on numerical properties in each kind of number assignment, and the features of the number sequence N that are crucial for this task.

A. Cardinal number assignments

In cardinal number assignments, the empirical objects are sets. A number n identifies the cardinality of a set s (n tells us how many elements s has). The numerical statement is meaningful if the number sequence from 1 to n has the same cardinality as the set s, that is, if there is a one-to-one mapping between the numbers from 1 to n and the elements of s. Number assignments including measure units (direct and indirect measurement) can be defined as a special case of cardinal number assignments. The crucial property of numbers is their sequential order within a progression: starting with 1, each element of the number sequence N has a fixed position within N, and therefore terminates a unique initial sequence of N. For a particular number n, the sequence from 1 to n has always a unique cardinality that can be used to identify the cardinality of a set.

B. Ordinal number assignments

In ordinal number assignments, the empirical objects are elements of a progression. A number n identifies the rank of an object a within a progression p. The numerical statement is meaningful if objects receive higher and lower numbers with respect to their higher and lower positions within the progression p. The number assignment is established by correlating sequential positions of numbers with the positions of the empirical objects within *p*. The crucial property of the number sequence N is the sequential order: since the elements of N are ordered sequentially, the relative ranks of numbers can be used to identify the ranks of objects.

C. Nominal number assignments

In nominal number assignments, the empirical objects are elements of a set. A number *n* identifies an object *a* within a set *s*. The numerical statement is meaningful if distinct objects always receive distinct numbers. The crucial property of the number sequence N is the distinctness of its elements: each element of N is well distinguished from all other elements of N. Each number *n* can therefore be used as a label to identify an object.

Table 1 gives a synopsis of the different kinds of number assignments, identifying the relevant empirical property in each case, a linguistic expression that illustrates the number assignment, the type of scale it is based on, and the numerical feature that is crucial for each kind of number assignment, that is, the feature of N that allows us to use numbers for the different cardinal, ordinal and nominal tasks.

Table 1 *Numbers and objects classification of number assignments*

Number assignment	Empirical property	Linguistic expression	Scale	Crucial feature of N
Cardinals				
Cardinality assignments	cardinality	'three pens'	absolute scales	N is a progression (a particular kind of sequence)
Direct measurement	extensive properties (for example weight)	'a 3 kg pumpkin'	rational scales	
Indirect measurement	non-extensive properties (for example temperature)	'bathing water of 3 °C'	interval scales	
Ordinal	rank	'the third runner'	ordinal scales	N is a sequence.
Nominal	identity	'bus #3'	nominal scales	The elements of N are distinct.

CHAPTER 2

What does it mean to be a number?

In the previous chapter, we analysed the relationship between numbers and objects. We encountered numbers as efficient tools in different kinds of 'measurements', that is, tools that we assign to objects in a meaningful way in different contexts. Our discussion has identified the different purposes numbers fulfil in these contexts, and has shown us how we manage to employ them to tell us something about empirical properties. Now that we have an understanding of what we use numbers for, and how we do that, let us explore the philosophical background of our discussion and see what would be a good characterisation of numbers, in order to carve out the area in which our investigation will take place.

What does it mean to be a number? One of the earliest definitions of numbers that have been passed on to us is an analysis that the Greek mathematician Euclid gave in his 'Elements':

1. A unit is that by virtue of which each of the things that exist is called one.
2. A number is a multitude composed of units. (Euclid, Book VII, §§ 1–2)

So, are numbers multitudes? What must a definition of numbers account for? Which characteristics distinguish numbers from other entities? At the end of the nineteenth and beginning of the twentieth centuries, these questions were discussed intensely in the philosophy of mathematics. The results from this discussion are still relevant for our view of numbers today, and can contribute to our understanding of numerical cognition and the meaning of number words.

As I am going to demonstrate in the present chapter, our investigation benefits specifically from three major accounts of natural numbers emerging from this debate: the 'intersective analysis' that goes back to Gottlob Frege, the 'itemising approach' to numbers that is based on an analysis by Bertrand Russell, and the 'relational view' of numbers introduced by Richard Dedekind. Each of these theories approaches numbers from a different direction; the respective definitions they suggest reflect different views of the nature of numbers. By doing so, the three accounts will give us a handle on different aspects of the cognitive number domain.

The view of number assignments we developed in the preceding chapter allows us to integrate these different aspects into a unified framework of numbers and number contexts. Among others, this gives us a new perspective on the question whether numbers are primarily cardinal or ordinal, a topic that has been a controversial issue in the foundations of mathematics as well as in developmental psychology. In view of the results from chapter 1, this 'cardinal/ordinal dichotomy' is not a dichotomy, but reflects two – of three – different aspects of numbers or, rather, of number contexts. Within the approach we developed here, we need not assume that numbers bear on either cardinality or on ordinality per se, but can account for these notions in the context of cardinal and ordinal number *assignments*. Under this perspective, we can also add a third context, namely that of nominal number contexts.

Let me now introduce the three philosophical approaches to numbers in turn, and discuss their relevance for our investigation, that is, their relevance for an ontology of numbers that reflects the way we conceptualise numbers and number assignments. I have summarised the definitions that are crucial for the respective approaches in Appendix 2. As the discussion will show, not all of the theories can account for a common-sense view of numbers to the same degree. This should not come as a surprise, since these approaches are not primarily concerned with the particular way in which numbers are represented in the human mind, but rather set out to define numbers as the primary objects of mathematics. However, as mentioned above, each of the analyses can contribute to our understanding of the cognitive domain of numbers as a whole, as each of them can account for different concepts related to our numerical cognition. In particular, I will show that the intersective and the itemising definitions of number will give us a handle on different aspects of cardinal number contexts, while the relational approach, together with our results from the previous chapter, will provide the basis for a criteria-based view of numbers that will constitute the framework for our further investigation.

THE INTERSECTIVE ANALYSIS OF NUMBERS

This analysis goes back to Gottlob Frege's classic definition of numbers in his 1884 'Grundlagen der Arithmetik' ('Foundations of Arithmetic') and its formalisation in the 'Grundgesetze der Arithmetik' ('Basic Laws of Arithmetic'), published in two volumes in 1893 and 1903. Frege was fascinated by the nature of numbers all his life, and his work has deeply influenced the way we think about numbers today. A mathematician, logician, and philosopher, he invented the predicate calculus and made fundamental contributions to semantics and the philosophy of language as 'by-products' of his main enterprise, the founding of mathematics on purely logical grounds.

It is one of the sad stories in the history of science that shortly after Frege had finished his major work, the 'Grundgesetze', at a time when the second volume of the book was just about to be published, it was brought to his attention in a letter by Bertrand Russell that a contradiction (now known as 'Russell's paradox') can be derived from one of his key axioms.[1] Ultimately, this meant that Frege's system could not serve as a logical foundation of mathematics.

When facing the failure of his life's project, Frege added an appendix to his book where he pointed out the problem in detail and expressed hope that in future work he might be able to modify his axiom in a way that would avoid the antinomy, while keeping the system intact. This hope, however, would not be fulfilled, and Frege never published anything about the foundations of arithmetic again. (In 1931, Kurt Gödel showed that elementary number theory admits no complete axiomatisation, that is, *any* complete axiomatic system that contains at least elementary arithmetic will face antinomies (Gödel 1931).)

Here is something that Russell said about his discussion with Frege later, which I think gives a nice impression of their debate. It is a passage from a 1962 letter that Russell sent to Jean van Heijenoort, who edited an English translation of the Russell–Frege correspondence on the antinomies:

As I think about acts of integrity and grace, I realise that there is nothing in my knowledge to compare with Frege's dedication to truth. His entire life's work was on the verge of completion, much of his work had been ignored to the benefit of men infinitely less capable, his second volume was about to be published, and upon finding that his fundamental assumption was in error, he responded with

---

[1] See Russell (1902, and 1903: ch. 10) and Frege (1902). The contradiction arises from Frege's axiom 5, which allows us to identify for every truth-valued function f the set of objects that satisfy f (that is, the set of all x for which $f(x)$ is true). As Russell pointed out, this unrestricted introduction of sets gives rise to a contradiction of the following kind: consider the function 'is not an element of itself'. According to Frege's axiom 5, this function identifies the elements of a particular set; in this case: the set of all sets that are not an element of themselves. Let us call this set s. An example of an element of s is the set of all stars (which is not a star itself, hence it is not an element of itself), but not the set of all sets (which is a set, and accordingly *is* an element of itself). Now, is s itself an element of s or not? If it is, then it cannot be an element of s, since s was the set of all sets that are *not* an element of themselves. And vice versa, if it is not an element of itself, it must be an element of s. It turns out that s is an element of itself exactly if it is not an element of itself.

intellectual pleasure clearly submerging any feelings of personal disappointment. It was almost superhuman and a telling indication of that of which men are capable if their dedication is to creative work and knowledge instead of cruder efforts to dominate and be known. (Russell 1962)

However, even though Frege did not accomplish the task he set himself – the foundation of mathematics on purely logical grounds – his definition of cardinality as a basic notion of arithmetic is still valid today and has had a major impact on our understanding of numbers. The definition accounts for the fact that cardinality, unlike colour, is not a property of individuals, but of sets. Whereas a colour like 'red' can be perceived of an individual object (for instance of a cherry), cardinality – as emphasised in chapter 1 – does not belong to an object, but to a set of objects, a collection of individuals that we subsume under a common concept (for instance in 'two stars', we assign the number 'two' to a set of objects that fall under the concept 'star').

To understand why Frege's definition is often referred to as 'intersective', one has to be aware of the set–theoretical view of properties. From a set–theoretical point of view we can define a property, say colour, via the set of things that have this property. For instance, the colour 'grey' can be seen as that which all grey things have in common. So, in order to refer to 'grey-ness', we introduce the set of grey things. Similarly, for the property of being a star we introduce the set of all stars. If we now want to identify a combined property like that of being a grey star (hence the property of being a star, and at the same time being grey), we refer to the intersection between the set of grey things and the set of stars, which gives us the set of grey stars.

How does this apply to a property like cardinality now? As mentioned above, cardinality is assigned to sets, not to individuals. Whereas a grey star is something that is grey and is a star, *three stars* is not something that is three

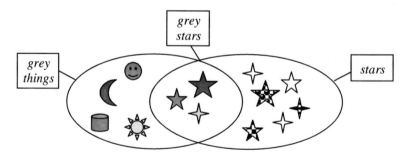

Figure 17   Grey stars in the intersection between grey things and stars

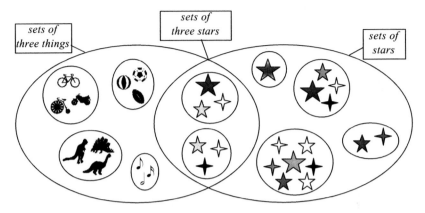

Figure 18 Cardinalities as sets of sets: three stars

and is a star. Rather, the entity 'three stars' is a set that has three elements and whose elements are stars. This means that 'three stars' does not fit into an intersection between two sets of individuals. Rather, it belongs to an intersection of two sets of sets, that is, of two sets whose elements are sets themselves: (1) sets with three elements, and (2) sets of stars.

Above, we regarded the colour 'grey' as that property that grey things have in common, whatever these things might be. In the same way, we can now analyse 'three' as an abstracted cardinality: as that property that sets with three elements have in common, whatever these elements might be – stars, dinosaurs, bikes, tones, or even other sets. Whereas, for 'grey-ness', we identified the set of grey things, we can hence identify for 'three-ness' the set of sets of three things. So according to this approach, a number n can be regarded as the set of sets with n elements.

My reason for this rather elaborate exposition of numbers as sets of sets was to demonstrate that, like most mathematical approaches, the inter-sective approach defines numbers from a *cardinal* perspective. Based on our analysis from the previous chapter, we can characterise the intersective approach as one that focuses on numbers as used in cardinal assignments. Accordingly, in the German original Frege talks about cardinalities ('Anzahlen'), rather than numbers ('Zahlen') (Frege 1884, 1893). Following common practice, I will use the term 'numbers' for abstracted cardinalities when discussing his theory, but you should keep in mind that Frege's definition concentrates on the cardinal aspect of numbers.

The identification of numbers as sets of sets provides the framework for an intersective analysis, but it is only half of the story. It would be circular

Figure 19 Which sets have the same cardinality?

to define, say, 3 as the set of all sets with three elements, so this cannot yet be the complete definition of numbers. What we still need to know is what it means to be a set of three elements in the first place. In other words, what is it that all sets of three elements have in common, how can we define a property like 'three-ness'?

Frege's answer to this question is based on the premise that we know a property when we have a criterion that allows us to recognise it as identical in different entities (Frege 1884: § 62). For instance, we know what a colour is when we can determine whether two objects have the same colour or not. And we know what a number is when we know how to decide whether two sets have the same cardinality or not. So which criterion can we use to find out which sets have the same cardinality? Let us try to do this for some of the sets from Figure 18 above, which I have assembled in Figure 19.

What is important here is to give a criterion to recognise identical cardinalities without using numbers yet. That is, it would not count if you told me that, say, the set of dinosaurs and the set of bikes in Figure 19 have the same cardinality because they both have three elements. What we can do instead (and what you have probably had in mind all along) is link up the elements of two sets and see if we can establish a one-to-one correspondence between all the elements of the first set and all the elements of the other set. For instance, to verify that the set of dinosaurs and the set of bikes have the same cardinality, we could link up the motorbike with the grey dinosaur, the Pennyfarthing (the antique bicycle) with the tyrannosaurus, and the modern bike with the long-necked dinosaur.

It is such a one-to-one correspondence that Frege uses to establish that two sets have the same cardinality. He calls two sets equinumerous (or like-numbered, 'gleichzahlig' in German) if there is a relation that brings about a one-to-one correspondence between all their respective elements (Frege 1884: § 68). With this criterion in hand, he can define a number as a set of equinumerous sets, that is, as a set of sets with the same cardinality (Frege 1893: § 40; I have spelled out Frege's definition in Appendix 2).

This gives us a general notion of numbers, but we still need a definition for individual numbers. It is all very well to know that a number is a set of sets with the same cardinality, but this does not get me very far in my analysis of, say, the number 3, since it does not tell me how to determine particular cardinalities. Hence the next step must be to define these sets of equinumerous sets for individual numbers. For this purpose, Frege introduces something I call 'paradigm sets'. Paradigm sets are particular sets with a fixed cardinality that Frege uses to anchor the definition of equinumerous sets for individual numbers.

The recourse to paradigm sets is an aspect of Frege's definition that has received little attention in discussions of his account of numbers. However – as I hope to convince you in the following discussion – paradigm sets constitute an important aspect of Frege's approach since they provide the underpinnings of his definition of individual numbers. Accordingly, this is an aspect we should be aware of when we want to see how far his theory can contribute to an account of our number concept.

Let us call *pn* the paradigm set for a number *n*. For instance, *p3* would be the paradigm set for 3. Now, if we define our set *p3* such that it has exactly three elements, then obviously every set that is equinumerous with *p3* has three elements, too, and vice versa, every set that has three elements is equinumerous with *p3*. Being equinumerous with *p3* would be a property that gives us exactly all sets with the cardinality 3. Accordingly, the number 3 could be defined as the set of all sets that are equinumerous with *p3*. Figure 20 illustrates the use of paradigm sets in verifying the cardinality of the set of dinosaurs from Figure 19: given a set *p3*, we can determine the cardinality of the set of dinosaurs by finding out whether or not it is equinumerous with *p3*. In accordance with our definition of equinumerous sets, this means that we have to find out whether or not we can set up a one-to-one correspondence between all the dinosaurs and all the elements of *p3*. If this is possible, then the sets are equinumerous, which means that the set of dinosaurs has the same cardinality as *p3*, namely 3.

For the definition of paradigm sets, Frege first defines a set *po*, and then introduces a 'successor' function that yields, for the paradigm set of each number *n*, the corresponding paradigm set for its successor *n + 1*. To

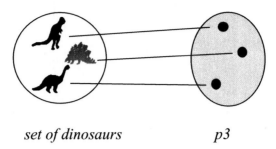

set of dinosaurs   *p3*

Figure 20   Determining particular cardinalities via paradigm sets: '3'

define *po*, Frege needs an empty set: *po* must be a set with zero elements. Because he wants to base his number definition on purely logical grounds, Frege chooses as *po* the set of all entities that are not self-identical. Since everything is identical with itself, this set has no elements. He can now define the number o as the set of all sets that are equinumerous with *po*, making o the set of all sets with zero elements (Frege 1893: § 41; see Appendix 2, p. 301 for a formalisation).

On this basis, Frege defines *p1* as the set of all entities that are identical with o. Since o is already defined as one particular set, there is exactly one entity that is identical with o, namely o itself. This gives us *p1* as a set that has o as its only element. Accordingly, all sets that are equinumerous with *p1* have exactly one element, so 1 can be defined as the set of all sets equinumerous with *p1*, that is as the set of all sets with exactly one element (Frege 1893: § 42).

p2 is then defined as the set consisting of o and 1, which gives us exactly two elements; *p3* has the elements o, 1, and 2, and so forth: the paradigm set for the successor *n + 1* of each number *n* contains as its elements all (and only) the numbers from o to *n*. This gives us exactly *n + 1* elements in each case (Frege 1893: § 46). I have illustrated this for the paradigm sets *po* to *p3* in Figure 21. In accordance with Frege's definition, the digits o, 1, and 2 stand for sets of all those sets that are equinumerous with *po*, *p1* and *p2*, respectively. Arrows with dotted lines indicate the relationship between numbers and their paradigm sets.

Starting with *po*, this procedure renders paradigm sets for the entire (infinite) sequence of natural numbers, and subsequently yields the desired definition of numbers: following Frege's schema, every number *n* is now defined as the set of all sets that are equinumerous with its paradigm set *pn*. The definition of paradigm sets guarantees that each set *pn* has exactly

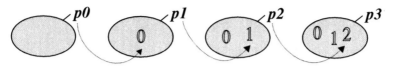

Figure 21 Frege's definition of paradigm sets for numbers: Paradigm sets for 0, 1, 2, and 3

n elements; therefore, a number n is always identified as the set of all sets with the cardinality n.

How far can this definition of numbers shed light on the ontology of our cognitive number domain; how far can it account for the way numbers are represented in the human mind? As I pointed out above, Frege's definition anchors numbers in the cardinality of sets. His notion of numbers as sets of equinumerous sets shows us how to define cardinality as a property of sets. However, the cardinal aspect is only one aspect of numbers. As the discussion in chapter 1 made clear, numbers are not necessarily related to cardinalities: they serve as tools in a wide variety of number assignments, where they represent different relations between empirical objects. Of these number assignments, the assignment of cardinalities is a salient instance, but by no means the only one. If we – unlike Frege – want to relate our analysis to the psychological reality of numbers, we have to account not only for cardinal, but also for ordinal and nominal aspects. Hence the view of numbers we will adopt for our investigation of numbers and the human mind should be less specific in order to capture the whole potential of numerical contexts.

In addition, there are two implications in Frege's definition that we should be aware of when we want to account for numerical cognition. First, Frege introduces specific paradigm sets to determine the cardinality of the sets that constitute a number. In particular, he defines as the primary paradigm set $p0$, the set of all 'entities that are not self-identical'. Following Frege in this respect would lead to problematic assumptions for our approach to numerical cognition: if we based our account of number concepts on this definition, we would have to assume that young children must have the concept of an abstract set of 'not self-identical entities' before they acquire the concepts of 0, 1, 2, and so on.

Second, Frege defines 0 as the basis of his number definition. All numbers from 1 onwards are defined as successors, or successors of . . . of successors of 0. That is, his whole system of natural numbers builds on 0 as its foundation. However, as we will also see later when discussing the emergence of number concepts, 0 evolves late both in human history and in the individual development of humans. Ontogenetically as well as phylogenet-ically, numerical cognition is already developed to a large extent before we grasp the notion of 0.

Frege's definition as it stands can therefore not serve as a basis for our analysis of the way numbers are represented in the human mind. How-ever, in chapter 6, I will employ his central notion of numbers as sets of sets to account for 'individualised numbers', numbers that are denoted by nominalised numerals in contexts like '1 + 2' and form the basis of our arithmetic reasoning. In particular, I will show that these 'individualised numbers' can be derived from cardinalities along the lines that Frege sug-gested: we can define the numbers that occur in mathematical contexts like '1 + 2' by abstraction from concrete cardinalities like 'one star', 'two stars' etc., that is, we can define them as sets of sets with the same cardinality – albeit based on a different analysis of 'one star', 'two stars' etc. than the one Frege used. Hence, even though the account of 'individualised num-bers' I will put forward will not employ Frege's intersective definition of numbers in its specific details, I will follow him in defining numbers in mathematical contexts – the objects of our mathematical reasoning – as sets of equinumerous sets.

THE ITEMISING APPROACH TO NUMBERS

The itemising approach, too, accounts for the cardinal aspect of numbers. Unlike the intersective approach, though, it does not base its definition on paradigm sets and does not define numbers as sets of equinumerous sets. In fact, it does not define numbers per se at all, it defines cardinality assignments: the itemising approach is not concerned with numbers in isolation, it gives us an analysis of number contexts like 'three stars' that identify the cardinality of particular sets of objects.

By focusing on concrete cardinalities, the itemising approach does not need to define numbers as abstract sets. This is in keeping with a tendency in the philosophy of mathematics after the discovery of the set–theoretical antinomies: after Frege, philosophers have been careful not to treat sets or classes[2] as unproblematic abstract entities, but to restrict the definition of classes they introduce for the foundations of mathematics. One way of doing this is to define class symbols as mere abbreviations, as terms that can be eliminated in further analysis. Under this view, there are no classes – and consequently no numbers – per se; a class symbol does not

---

[2] I treat the terms 'set' and 'class' as synonyms, following whatever terminology the respective approaches are using that I discuss here. In particular, I do not distinguish between 'sets' that can be an element of a set, and 'classes' that cannot (as is sometimes done within the philosophy of mathematics).

refer to a particular abstract entity, but disappears under proper analysis and is replaced by a predication that avoids antinomies. Here is a quote from a 1918 paper by Bertrand Russell that emphasises this point:

> all numbers are what I call logical fictions. Numbers are classes of classes, and classes are logical fictions, so that numbers are, as it were, fictions at two removes, fictions of fictions. Therefore you do not have, as part of the ultimate constituents of your world, these queer entities that you are inclined to call numbers. (Russell 1918: 270)

Russell himself was not a proponent of the itemising view,[3] but he lay the grounds for an itemising account of cardinalities with an analysis he suggested for definite descriptions (Russell 1905). Definite descriptions are expressions of the form 'the F', where F denotes a nominal concept, for instance 'the pope'. The itemising approach elaborates Russell's analysis in order to account not only for singletons ('the pope' / 'one pope'), but also for multitudes (sets with more than one element; for instance, two popes, three popes etc.).

Russell accounts for the singularity expressed by a definite description like 'the pope' in the following way. First, he introduces an entity x that fulfils the description 'pope'. This makes sure that there is *at least one* pope. Second, to ensure that there is *at most one* pope, he postulates that any entity that fulfils the description 'pope' must be identical with x. With these two components, an existence condition and a uniqueness condition, Russell can formalise the statement that there is *exactly one* pope. Within this approach, a statement like 'Tom is the pope.' comes out as 'There is an entity x, such that: (a) x is a pope [hence, there is at least one pope, namely x], (b) every entity y that is a pope is identical with x [hence, there is at most one pope, that is, x is the only pope], and (c) Tom is identical with x [hence, Tom is the pope]. (1) renders this analysis within the formalism of predicate logic, where $\exists_x$ is an existential quantifier that binds x (that is, $\exists_x$ reads: 'there is an x, such that: . . .'), $\forall_y$ is a universal quantifier that binds y (read: 'for all y: . . .'), and '$\rightarrow$' stands for the logical implication:

$$(1)\ \exists_x\ (\text{POPE}(x)\ \&\ \forall_y(\text{POPE}(y) \rightarrow y = x))\ \&\ \text{Tom} = x)$$

[This reads as: 'There is an x, such that x is a pope, and for all y: if y is a pope, then y is identical with x, and Tom is identical with x.']

---

[3] Russell followed Frege in defining numbers as classes of classes, but – as the quote above emphasises – unlike Frege, did not assume classes as abstract entities. By introducing a Theory of Types for his logical calculus, he made sure that a formula containing a class symbol can always be replaced by one that is based on propositional functions that avoid the antinomies (cf. Russell 1908 and Russell and Whitehead 1910–13).

The interesting point here is that there is no single component of the formula that represents 'the pope': the definite description seems to vanish into the formula. 'The pope' is what Russell called a syncategorematic expression: an expression that is essentially part of a sentence; it does not refer to an independent constituent of the proposition, but is analysed as a complex symbol that gets its meaning within context.

Russell did not elaborate this formalisation to account for statements about two or more objects, but his analysis has been applied to multitudes by, among others, Alfred Tarski and Willard Van Orman Quine. For his analysis, Tarski – and, following him, Quine – used 'numerically definite quantifiers': quantifiers that indicate an exact cardinality.[4] First, he introduced the quantifier $\exists_{1x}$ to indicate 'exactly one x'. For instance (2) stands for the proposition that there is exactly one pope:

$$(2)\ \exists_{1x}\ (POPE(x)) \quad - \quad \text{'There is exactly one pope.'}$$

[literally: 'There is exactly one x, such that x is a pope.']

As it stands, this formula lacks a definition, since it is not yet clear how the quantifier works. However, if you look again at Russell's analysis above, you can see that the first part of the formula in (1) (the part without Tom) represents precisely what we want for (2). Hence in order to give a definition for $\exists_{1x}$ as our initial numerically definite quantifier, we can identify (2) as an abbreviation for (3):

$$(3)\ \exists_x\ (POPE(x)\ \&\ \forall_y(POPE(y) \rightarrow y = x))$$

To account for higher cardinalities, we now need quantifiers like $\exists_{2x}$, $\exists_{3x}$ etc., that would allow us, for instance, to treat (4) and (5) as translations of 'There are (exactly) two popes' and 'There are (exactly) three popes', respectively:

$$(4)\ \exists_{2x}\ (POPE(x)) \quad - \quad \text{'There are exactly two popes.'}$$

$$(5)\ \exists_{3x}\ (POPE(x)) \quad - \quad \text{'There are exactly three popes.'}$$

Hence we are looking for analyses for formulae containing $\exists_{2x}$, $\exists_{3x}$, etc., along the same lines we used (3) as a definition for (2): if we want to employ Russell's analysis not only for singular definite descriptions, but also for cardinality assignments with numbers > 1, we have to elaborate his procedure from above in such a way that we can apply it to more than one entity, accounting for sets of two, three, four, etc.

---

[4] Cf. Tarski (1936); Quine (1974). I have spelled out the definition of numerically definite quantifiers in Appendix 2, p. 302.

Let us do this for '(exactly) three stars'. First we need three entities x, y, z that satisfy the predicate 'STAR'. Hence, whereas for 'the pope' in (1) above, we introduced an entity x that is a pope, we must now introduce a star x together with two additional stars y and z. That is, in addition to x, we must introduce entities y and z that are different from x and different from each other, and that are stars as well. This gives us *at least* three stars, that is, at least three non-identical entities that are stars:

(6) $\exists_x \exists_y \exists_z$ (STAR(x) & STAR(y) & STAR(z) & $x \neq y$ & $x \neq z$ & $y \neq z$)

Now we have to determine that there are *at most* three stars, hence our second requirement is that there are no more stars, apart from x, y, and z: every entity w that is a star must be identical with either x, or y, or z. (7) gives the formula for this ('$\vee$' stands for non-exclusive 'or'):

(7) $\forall_w$(STAR(w) $\rightarrow$ ($w = x \vee w = y \vee w = z$))

Together, (6) and (7) yield the definition for our numerically definite quantifier: '$\exists_{3x}$ (STAR(x))' can be defined as equivalent to (8) (the three dots in (8) stand for the parts from (6) that I skipped for the sake of readability):

(8) $\exists_x \exists_y \exists_z$ (STAR(x) & ... & $y \neq z$ &
    $\forall_w$ (STAR(w) $\rightarrow$ ($w = x \vee w = y \vee w = z$)))

This gives us an analysis for 'three stars', or generally for 'three Fs', where the Fs are our empirical objects (just replace the predicate STAR in (8) by the predicate characterising the empirical objects in question). For 'four stars', we have to introduce another entity in addition to x, y, z; for instance 'u', which would yield a formula as indicated in (9). For 'five stars', we add another variable to our formula, and so on (a general schema for the derivation of these formulae is sketched in Appendix 2).

(9) $\exists_x \exists_y \exists_z \exists_u$(STAR($x$)& ... STAR($u$)& $x \neq y$ & ... $z \neq u$ &
    $\forall_w$(STAR(w) $\rightarrow$ ($w = x \vee ... w = u$)))

Following this approach, a statement like 'There are (exactly) three stars' is replaced by something like 'There is a star x, and another star y, and another star z, and anything that is a star is identical with x or with y or with z.' Hence within the itemising view, 'three' is a syncategorematic expression; it does not refer to anything (and in particular not to the number 3) in isolation, but is eliminated by further analysis and replaced by an enumeration of elements. I have illustrated this account of cardinalities in

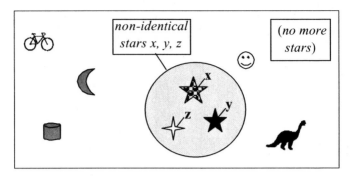

Figure 22 Analysis of 'three stars' within the itemising approach

Figure 22: we have a set consisting of the entities x, y and z, these entities are stars, and they are the only stars around.

This is why I called this approach the 'itemising view of numbers': in this account, the quantification of a set ('three stars') boils down to itemising it, to identifying its elements in turn ('a star, and another star, and another star'). This way, the itemising approach gives us a 'definition by extension' for a set: an enumeration of its elements. This enumeration specifies a particular set, a multitude of objects, rather than a number. The notion of number disappears into the identification of a multitude.

The concept of multitudes as they are defined by the itemising view can support our grasp of cardinality. While the analysis might not capture our concepts of sets with higher cardinalities (imagine an analysis of '612 stars' within the itemising view: 'a star, and another star, and . . .'), it does allow us to account for the concepts we have of small multitudes – sets of two, three, or four objects. Interestingly, the mechanism underlying our grasp of these smaller multitudes seems to differ significantly from the one responsible for higher cardinalities (we will discuss this in more detail in chapters 4 and 5). This mechanism, which has been termed 'subitising' in the psychological literature, allows us to recognise cardinalities of small sets like 'one star', 'two stars', and 'three stars' at a glance, without involving numerical strategies like counting.

When discussing the emergence of numerical thinking in chapters 4 and 5, I will argue that the phenomenon of subitising suggests concepts of 'one-ness', 'two-ness' and 'three-ness' that refer to singletons or small multitudes – sets of one, two, or three elements – rather than to a full-blown concept of number. These concepts are evident in human infants as well as in higher animals; they constitute an early basis for our numerical thinking, and are later integrated into a number concept that goes beyond the limits of perception and leads us up to infinity. The itemising view of number will give us a handle on these early cardinal concepts.

In the previous sections, I discussed two approaches that focus on the cardinal aspect of numbers: the itemising approach, by enumerating objects, presents us multitudes, whereas the intersective analysis defines sets of equinumerous sets as an abstraction from concrete cardinalities. By doing so, the two approaches point to two important areas in our cognitive number domain: the mechanism of subitising that underlies our perception of small multitudes ('a star, another star, and another star') and forms the underpinnings for our comprehension of cardinality, and the elaboration of cardinal number concepts that establishes abstracted 'individualised numbers' ('two Fs, whatever these Fs may be') as the basis for our arithmetic reasoning.

Figure 23 summarises this account of the itemising and the iterative approach, and integrates it into the view of number contexts put forward in chapter 1. Recall that – as the graphic illustrates – this view does not confine numbers to either cardinal, ordinal, or nominal aspects, but characterises them as fundamental entities that can bear on all of these aspects in application, that is, when applied to empirical objects in the different kinds of number assignments we distinguished above. This way, it allows us to integrate the different approaches to number we discussed in the preceding sections as approaches to different aspects of a broader number domain.

What we need now is something for the elementary area, the area I labelled 'numbers' in Figure 23: we need a notion of numbers that enables us to understand the nature of the entities that constitute our 'numerical relational structures' in number assignments, an analysis that can account for the whole range of numerical thinking, including not only cardinal, but also ordinal and nominal aspects of numbers. An approach that can give us a handle on this is the relational view of numbers.

The relational view of numbers was proposed by the mathematician Richard Dedekind. In his 1887 work on 'The Nature and Meaning of Numbers', he analysed the essential properties of numbers. In particular, he investigated which properties numbers need to have as the objects of arithmetic. As a result of his discussion, he identified three conditions that the set N of natural numbers must fulfil:

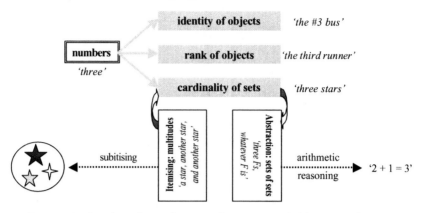

Figure 23 Multitudes and sets of sets as underpinnings and elaborations of cardinal
number concepts, respectively

1. All elements of N must be well distinguished from each other;
2. N must be a progression;
3. N must be infinite.[5]

The first condition is one that comes for free if we require N to be a set: if something is a set, its elements are distinct anyway. To ensure that N is an infinite progression (conditions 2 and 3), Dedekind defined a function that yields us successor numbers, step by step, without end. More precisely, he defined this function as an injective mapping that generates N, a mapping *m* from N onto a proper subset N' of N. He identified 1 as the initial number; 1 is an element of N, but not of N', which makes N' a proper subset of N. This mapping *m* gives us a new number for every number, starting with 1. So, *m* takes 1 and yields the new number *m*(1); it takes *m*(1) and gives us *m*(*m*(1)), and so forth, up to infinity. To make things look more familiar, let us call *m*(1) '2', and let us call *m*(*m*(1)) '3'. In this terminology, *m* takes 1 and gives us 2, it takes 2 and gives us 3, and so on. Hence *m* provides us with an infinite progression N that starts with an initial element 1 (Figure 24).

The crucial point for our investigation is that Dedekind suggested that these properties are all we need in numbers. This means that whenever we have a set that forms an infinite progression of well-distinguished entities, and ignore any additional features its elements might have, then we can regard this set as a number sequence. Thus, the above list from (1) to (3) is *comprehensive*: there are no properties apart from these that a set must

---

[5] More precisely, N must be unbounded; that is, only potential, but no actual infinity is required. I have spelled out Dedekind's definition in Appendix 2, p. 302.

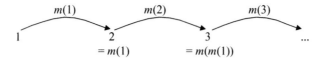

Figure 24 The relational view: *m* as a mapping that yields an infinite progression

possess in order to function as the set N of natural numbers. Following this view, (1) through (3) are the necessary and sufficient conditions for a set to play the role of the number sequence N, or, as Quine put it:

The condition upon all acceptable explications of number (that is, of the natural numbers 0, 1, 2, . . .) [. . .]: any *progression* – i.e., any infinite series each of whose members has only finitely many precursors – will do nicely. (Quine 1960: § 54)[6]

This is particularly interesting in view of our discussion from the previous chapter. In that chapter, we investigated the purposes we use numbers for, and determined the aspects of N that are crucial for the different ways in which we assign numbers to objects. The properties of numbers we found relevant for number assignments were exactly those identified by the conditions (1) and (2): the numerical properties we actually make use of when assigning numbers to objects are that (1) numbers are well distinguished, and (2) they are elements of a progression. Dedekind's other condition (3), which requires that N be infinite, ensures that there are no limitations to the size of the empirical sets that numbers can be assigned to, and lays the grounds for the whole range of mathematical thinking. Hence, the definition of essential numerical features that the relational approach suggests is very much in keeping with what we found out about numbers in the previous chapter.

The fact that Dedekind's definition does not stipulate any additional, distinguishing properties for numbers has, however, caused a certain uneasiness, for instance for Bertrand Russell, who considered the relational definition as too unspecific to identify numbers:

What Dedekind presents to us is not the numbers, but any progression: what he says is true of all progressions alike, and his demonstrations nowhere . . . involve any property distinguishing numbers from other progressions. (Russell 1903: 249)

In the following section I introduce an approach that adapts Dedekind's conditions for a criteria-based view of numbers that gets around this problem. According to this view, there are many sequences that could

---

[6] Note that Quine's definition of a progression differs slightly from the one I have been using (based on the definition I gave in chapter 1; formalised in Appendix 1, p. 299), since Quine requires a progression to be infinite, whereas my definition also includes finite progressions.

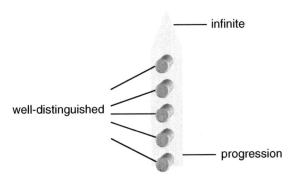

Figure 25 A criteria-based view of numbers: profile for possible number sequences

serve as numbers, but of these some are distinguished from the others as the dedicated sequences that are conventionally used as tools in number assignments.

A CRITERIA-BASED VIEW OF NUMBERS

Let us see what happens when we take Dedekind's approach to its logical end and interpret his three conditions as the criteria that give us a possible number sequence. This would mean that whenever we encounter an infinite progression of well-distinguished entities we can safely use it as a number sequence. Figure 25 illustrates this view of numbers. In order to indicate the reduction of numbers to the three criteria, I tried to give you something like a 'number profile', the mould into which a number sequence must fit. This gives rise to a rather liberal view of numbers. According to this view, we do not need to commit ourselves to a particular set of abstract entities that we call 'numbers'. Rather, 'to be used as a number' (along the lines we discussed in chapter 1) is a job that can be done by the elements of any set that satisfies the above conditions (1) through (3). There are not *the* numbers waiting to be identified by us somewhere out there, but a range of possible number sequences, sequences that we can use as numbers because they fulfil the necessary requirements for this function. According to this view, the entities we assign to empirical objects in the different kinds of number assignments – the entities constituting the basis of our cognitive number domain – are not particular abstract objects; rather, they represent a set of tools with particular functions and many possible instances. (The definitions for the criteria-based approach to numbers are in Appendix 3.)

Do we need abstract numbers for the domain of arithmetic? According to the philosopher Paul Benacerraf, we do not (Benacerraf 1965). Discussing several explications of numbers from the philosophy of mathematics, he argued that, since any infinite progression would be adequate to define numbers as the objects of arithmetic, we cannot identify one particular progression as *the* numbers. He concluded that arithmetic is about the structure that all progressions have in common in virtue of being progressions, and that numbers are accordingly completely defined by the relations that constitute a progression – a conclusion very much in line with the view we developed here.

Hence we are now not looking for *the* numbers anymore, but can take a position according to which some things can be numbers, while others cannot; or, more precisely, some things are elements of a sequence that can fulfil number functions, others are not.

One system that *is* such a sequence is defined within the 'formalistic' approach to numbers, an approach advanced by David Hilbert and Paul Bernays. In their 1928 book on the Foundations of Mathematics ('Die Grundlagen der Mathematik'), they define a system that is based on the arabic numeral 'I' (to indicate that we are talking about the numeral itself here and not about anything it might denote, I will use underlining, as in I). To generate the elements of their system, Hilbert and Bernays introduce a simple concatenation rule that allows us to combine every element with I. Starting with the initial, primitive element I, this yields us II, III, IIII, and so on, as subsequent successors. As an abbreviation, we can use the conventional series of arabic numerals, replacing II by 2, III by 3, IIII by 4, etc.

As Hilbert and Bernays point out, this system can serve as a number system, the characters themselves (I, II, III etc.) can be regarded as the objects of number theory. The concatenation rule together with the initial element I constitutes an infinite progression of well-distinguished entities that have all the properties to function as a number sequence. In particular, one does not have to stipulate any additional 'meaning' for the characters so defined: II does not *stand for* the number 2 or *refer to* the number 2, it *is* the number 2 in this system, since it is used as the second element of the sequence:

These number-signs, which are numbers and which completely make up the numbers, are themselves the object of our consideration, but otherwise they have no *meaning* of any sort. (Hilbert 1922: 1122/163; emphasis in the original)

By regarding the very characters as numbers, Hilbert sees himself in opposition to Dedekind who bases his number theory on an abstract definition of infinity. However, interpreting Dedekind's three conditions on N as a

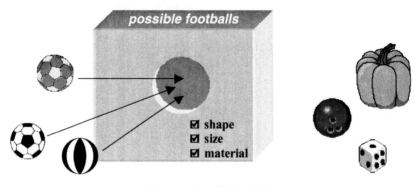

Figure 26 Possible footballs

general paradigm for possible number sequences, we are now in a position to combine the two approaches: according to our criteria-based view, the system of characters that Hilbert and Bernays introduce is a possible number sequence. Being an infinite progression of well-distinguished entities, it meets all the number criteria we set up (in chapter 7, we will discuss arabic numerals as a non-verbal number system in more detail).

Implications of our view: possible number sequences

What implications does our new criteria-based approach to numbers have? What does it tell us about numbers? As an illustration, let us have a look at a non-numerical example first. Imagine that I ask you to play a game of soccer, and we are looking for a suitable ball. In this case, the relevant criteria will be shape, size, and material: our football should be round; it should be, well, football-sized, and it should be made of a material that is not too heavy, and is flexible but firm, so the ball bounces nicely and will not burst if we kick it. These criteria identify the three balls in Figure 26 as possible footballs, while keeping out, among others, objects like the bowling ball, the pumpkin, and the die.

This procedure gives us (at least) three balls, instead of the one football we need for our match. So how do we know which one to take; which one will be identified (or defined) as *the* football? It turns out that this is not a problem at all, for trivial reasons: we can choose just any one of the three footballs, since for our purpose – the soccer match – it is not relevant which ball we actually use. It could be the classic black-and-white ball, the grey one, or the one with the stripes; whichever one you might like better. For the purpose of the game, they all come out the same. It is just important

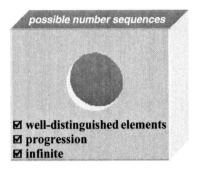

Figure 27 Criteria for possible number sequences

that we end up using the same ball in our match, since if everyone uses a different ball, the match will not make much sense. The ball we choose will then be *the football* in the sense of the rules of the game.

With this in mind, let us do the same procedure for numbers now. Our criteria for a number sequence are the conditions we identified above: a possible number sequence must consist of well-distinguished entities that form a progression, and this progression must have no upper limit (Figure 27). Hence in this criteria-based approach to numbers, we interpret Dedekind's definition as the admission criteria for the number club: we regard the three conditions as a doorkeeper for our investigation that lets in those entities that are possible number sequences, but keeps out the others. As in the case of footballs, our criteria will not identify one particular set of numbers, but different entities that we could use as number sequences. And as in the case of footballs, it is just important we are using the same sequence as our designated number sequence in a particular context, since otherwise our number assignments will not be comprehensible. Basically, any infinite progression will do fine, for the purposes of arithmetic as well as in the various kinds of number assignments. Just like the different balls we considered come out the same for the purpose of the football match, different number sequences come out the same for our numerical purposes.

And given that all qualifying balls serve our purpose for the game equally well, we can base our choice on additional matters that are unrelated to the game itself; for instance, we can base our choice on the question as to which one might be preferable for aesthetic reasons (for example which one has a nicer colour?) or financial reasons (which one is cheaper?) etc. Similarly, since all sequences that fulfil our numerical criteria serve the purpose of numbers equally well, we can choose one that might be preferable for matters unrelated to the numerical function itself; for instance, we can base our choice on efficiency of accessibility. As I am going to argue in the next two chapters, it is exactly this option that enabled humans to develop a systematic concept of numbers in the first place.

In this sense, a certain ball or a certain sequence might be preferable to other ones, not because it would serve our purpose for the game or our purpose for number assignments better than the others, but because it might provide certain advantages in addition to this, that is, it might be better for reasons unrelated to the game or to number assignments proper. From the point of view of number assignments, different sequences that fulfil our number criteria are indistinguishable, that is, they are indistinguishable as numerical tools.

By talking of 'numerical tools' rather than 'numbers', I want to emphasise the functional aspect of our approach: tools are not interesting for their own sake, but with respect to the function they fulfil. For instance, when we need a hammer, we are not so much interested in, say, the different colours it might have, but in its suitability for driving a nail into a wall, and for this purpose it needs to meet certain criteria concerning, say, shape, hardness, and weight. It is these criteria that really characterise a hammer, because a hammer is defined by its purpose as a certain kind of tool, and meeting these criteria qualifies an object to fulfil this purpose. Only with regard to this purpose, an object *is* a hammer in the first place; in the words of the Gestalt psychologist Kurt Koffka:

As long as no need arises for using a hammer, there will not be any hammers, however many suitable T-shaped objects there may be around. (Koffka 1935: 393)

Are we getting arbitrary? The power of convention

Once we regard numbers as tools in number assignments, we see that there is no need to define properties that pick out one and only one particular progression. What makes numbers so powerful is exactly the fact that they relate to a small set of fundamental features for their tasks, and to no more. Rather than making numbers arbitrary, this view acknowledges them as powerful, efficient, and highly flexible devices with many possible instances. If our number assignment is to be intersubjectively comprehensible, it is merely relevant that the sequence we are using is one that is conventionally acknowledged as a number sequence, such that the relations holding in our numerical relational structure are clear.

Let me demonstrate my point with a thought experiment. Imagine me as a really shrewd painter who has invented an ingenious system of mixing colours which gives me as many different, and well-distinguished colours as I ever want – in fact, infinitely many colours – plus an inherent feature (say, darkness) that enables me to order them sequentially, starting with one particular colour (for example black). Let us assume that, based on this system of generating and ordering colours, my colour line would go: 'black' – 'brown' – 'purple' – . . . (infinitely many more colours here, all distinct from each other and neatly ordered).

Given this, according to the account I outlined in the preceding paragraphs I would have a possible number sequence. At first sight, this might look like an undesirable outcome, but the colour sequence can in fact be regarded as a well-behaved number sequence, a sequence that I could use as a tool in all the different kinds of number assignments we described. For instance in cardinal number assignments, I would assign the colour purple to all sets of three, because purple is the endpoint of the initial sequence <black, brown, purple>, which has as many elements as the sets in question (among them, for example, the set of stars in Figure 23 or the three possible footballs from Figure 26). In ordinal assignments, purple is assigned to those empirical objects whose position within a progression is the same as the position that purple occupies in my colour progression (formerly known as 'the third position'). For instance, in our runner example from the previous chapter, Mick (the third runner) would receive purple, while Karen, who came in second, would be assigned the colour brown, and Charles, as the winner, would receive black. And, last but not least, in nominal number assignments I would use colours to distinguish objects, as is actually done for the subway lines in some cities.[7]

However, this use of colours as numbers could be a very private pleasure. As long as I do not introduce my system to you, the assignment of colours to objects would work as a number assignment only for me. As long as you are not aware of the relations holding in the numerical relational structure I am using (for instance, 'darker than'), the number assignment is lost on you. Only for me could colours indicate the intended empirical relationships between the objects; only for me could they identify properties like cardinality, rank, and identity. For anyone else, the assignment would not have this significance; my assignment of colours would not be informative,

---

[7] Admittedly, these tend to be cities with only a few subway lines, since colours do get a bit undistinguishable once you have more – well, as I said above, for my example to work, you have to imagine me as a really shrewd combiner of colours. If you are not happy with the idea of blending infinitely many colours and still keeping them distinct, one could always imagine combining them in a discrete way, for example by introducing a concatenation rule that gives me for any two colours a new colour obtained by painting them side by side. This rule would, for instance, give me blue-purple from blue and purple, and blue-purple- blue from blue-purple and blue, and so on.

because I would be using a non-conventional number sequence, one that is not established as a number sequence in my community.

This is no reason to despair, though. It just means that the use of a particular number sequence gets its intersubjective significance from convention. It is a bit like using a language. Making up your own language all to yourself is not much fun, since, if you are the only speaker, you cannot put it to use properly: you cannot communicate with anyone but yourself in that language. It takes at least two to make it work, but, once we have a community of two speakers, that is of two people who master the linguistic system, we have a functioning language – as for instance in 'twin languages': secret languages sometimes invented by close siblings, mostly twins (using such a language with your twin brother or sister can be great fun, exactly because it is limited to the two of you, and your parents and other people do not understand you).[8]

Along the same lines, in our colour example I could have a fellow painter who shares my obsession with colour mixing and uses the same colour sequence in number assignments. To him, it would make perfect sense if in answer to a question like, 'How many ice cubes do you want in your schnapps?', I would point to this particular shade of purple on my colour palette, instead of saying 'Three'. As soon as we identify the colour progression as our number sequence – and this implies that we are both acquainted with the relations holding in the 'numerical' (read: colour) relational structure – it can fulfil all the number tasks in a significant way for both of us. Just as I was able to employ the colour palette for 'private' number assignments by myself, I can also use it intersubjectively as soon as it is identified as a conventional number sequence in my community.

So, even though our criteria do not pick out one particular progression as the sequence of numbers, we have a working set of numerical tools once we have settled on a progression. This is also in accordance with a requirement Quine pointed out for arithmetic number theory, referring to Russell's criticism of an unrestricted definition of numbers as progressions:

> though Russell was wrong in suggesting that numbers need more than their arithmetical properties, he was right in objecting to the definition of numbers as any things fulfilling arithmetic. The subtle point is that any progression will serve as a version of numbers so long and only so long as we stick to one and the same progression. Arithmetic is, in this sense, all there is to number: there is no saying absolutely what the numbers are; there is only arithmetic. (Quine 1969: 45)

---

[8] An example of such a language is 'Spaka', a language described by Randy Diehl and Katherine Kolodzey. Kolodzey invented Spaka together with her sister in the late fifties, when the two were seven and eleven years old. At the time the article appeared, the two sisters still used Spaka when talking to each other, to the virtual exclusion of English (Diehl and Kolodzey 1981).

This does not mean that we have to restrict ourselves to one progression once and for all – and, as we will see later, we are actually quite happy using several different number sequences in our daily lives, just as we can use more than one language. It just means the sequence we are using should not change arbitrarily, it should be a recognised number sequence, so that the relations holding in our numerical relational structure are intersubjectively clear. (As I will argue in chapter 4, the significance that convention has for numbers as well as for language is not the only feature that links the cognitive number domain to our linguistic faculty.)

So it is mostly a matter of convention which sequence we use as a number sequence. It is not because our designated number sequence is inherently different, and in particular more 'number-like' than other sequences that meet the three numerical criteria we established above. We do not choose a particular sequence because it can do special numerical tricks that the others cannot do; it just happens that we are using this one. So which one do we happen to use? Which sequences can we plausibly regard as the basis of our numerical cognition; which sequences provide the key to our concept of numbers? The exploration of these questions is the topic of the next chapter.

CHAPTER 3

Can words be numbers?

The criteria-based approach characterises numbers as elements of an infinite progression that is used as a tool in cardinal, ordinal, and nominal assignments. This account gives rise to a range of possible number sequences. We are not looking for *the* number sequence anymore, but for sequences that are employed as numbers, sequences that fulfil the function of numbers in our daily lives. In the present chapter we explore the consequences that can be derived from this view. The criteria-based view carves out the principal area of numbers, it gives us the criteria to recognise possible number sequences; with this characterisation in hand, we can now ask which sequences it is that we use for numerical purposes: what are the 'numbers' we employ in number assignments, the entities that constitute the core of our cognitive number domain?

So, what we are looking for now are sequences that fulfil the three 'number' requirements and that are actually used in the different types of number assignments: we want a designated number sequence that can serve as the basis for the cardinal, ordinal, and nominal number concepts we will discuss in chapters 5 and 6. Let us have a look at how we come to grasp numerical tools first: which sequence is it that children initially encounter when they are exposed to numbers which sequence do they employ in numerical routines like counting?

If we study the way numbers are acquired by young children, we find that early in their numerical development, they learn the *counting sequence* of their language, the set of words like ONE, TWO, THREE, etc.[1] that are used for counting objects, but that also appear, in a more basic usage, as part of a recited series of words, as in 'counting up to 10' (a usage that has been called 'rote counting' in the psychological literature).

A counting sequence starts with an initial element, for instance ONE in English, and then goes on step by step, with no upper limit: for any counting

[1] I use SMALL CAPITALS to indicate that I talk about counting words *as words* here (rather than to something they might refer to).

68

word I say, you can always tell me the following word, and what is more, you can also tell me for any two counting words which of them comes earlier and which comes later in the sequence. Hence you cannot only give me new counting words endlessly, but you can also tell their positions relative to each other. Counting words are not represented in a random order, but form a progression. Being words, they are also well distinguished from each other: each counting word has a different phonological representation, which enables us to tell them apart.

Together, this means that counting words fulfil all the requirements we set up for numerical tools: (i) they are well distinguished, (ii) they form a progression, (iii) this progression is non-terminating. Now this opens an interesting perspective: can we identify *counting words* as numerical tools? Can we analyse counting words as words that do not *refer* to numbers, but can be *used* as numbers right away? On grounds of parsimony and simplicity, this notion of counting words and numbers would be a very attractive one. Is it also a plausible one?

In the present chapter, I intend to convince you that it is. I will show that this approach is not only plausible, but can account for a range of unusual properties of counting words which have been observed independently in different domains by linguists, psycholinguists, and developmental psychologists, and which otherwise would have to be considered idiosyncratic. Before we discuss this in more detail, let me outline the argument I am going to pursue.

I will argue for the analysis of counting words as a number sequence from different angles. First, I discuss the status of counting words within the linguistic system. I show that counting words, when considered as lexical items, have several peculiar features that set them apart from other words. I show that this peculiarity of counting words within the linguistic system can be related to their number function, that is, I show that the features that make counting words such an eccentric species within language are the same that make them suitable as numerical tools.

Second, I argue that counting words are non-referential, that they do not denote anything (in contrast to what we would normally expect from linguistic expressions), hence there is *no more* to counting words than being an element of a progression, a progression that can be used as a number sequence. Note that this is a claim about *counting words*, the words we recite in a counting sequence, but not about all numerical expressions that might be derived from them. In particular, it does not apply to cardinal, ordinal, and nominal number words in complex syntactic contexts, like 'three pens', 'the third runner', or 'bus #3'. Drawing on the results from the first chapter,

I will later (in chapters 6 and 8) show that these expressions refer to three different kinds of number assignments, the three different ways we assign 'numbers' (non-referential counting words) to empirical objects.

In the third main section of this chapter, I show that the numerical status of counting words is reflected in first language acquisition, where counting words differ markedly from other words. I argue that this deviation can be attributed to the instrumental and non-referential status of counting words as numerical tools. On this basis, I will then suggest a 'cut with Occam's razor' that leads us to dispense with numbers as the denotations of counting words, and instead regard counting words as numbers right away.

This approach to counting words and numbers will provide the first key to understanding the intimate way in which numbers are connected with language in the human mind: based on the results from this chapter and the preceding chapters, in chapter 4 we will investigate how the human language faculty lays the grounds for the emergence of a systematic number concept.

COUNTING WORDS ARE SPECIAL

The numerical vocabulary is divorced from other parts of language in interesting ways. In what follows, I will argue that in particular there are four main aspects in which counting words differ from other lexical items: they form a progression, this progression is infinite, its elements are well distinguished by their respective phonological representations, and they are non-referential. The first three of these features establish the numerical character of counting words; the last one, their non-referentiality, confines them to the function of numbers.

The elements of a counting sequence are well distinguished

It is a common feature of languages that words that sound the same can have different, unrelated meanings; more precisely, the same phonological representation can be linked to different concepts within our mental lexicon. An example from English is 'bank', which can denote both a financial institution, and the shore of a river. Hence the same phonological representation, /bæŋk/, is used for two different lexical items: 'bank' as in *savings bank*, and 'bank' as in *river bank*. As a result, these lexical items cannot be distinguished by their phonological representation: when you just hear 'bank', it could be either. This can even happen within restricted conceptual domains, as the English noun 'weight' shows, which can refer to a property ('weight' as in 'The pumpkin's weight is 3 kg') as well as to devices that are used to measure this property ('weight' as in "This balance uses lead weights") – something that made it rather tricky for me to discuss the details of measurement in the first chapter, where I had to avoid sentences like 'One can use weights to measure weight'.

German children play a game called 'Teekesselchen' (literally: 'little teapot'), which is based solely on this phenomenon. In this game, two children think of an ambiguous word, the 'teapot', and then describe its two respective meanings to the others. For instance, if the 'teapot' was the word 'bank', then one child would say things like 'My teapot is where you put your money', while the second child could say 'My teapot is part of a river.' The other children in the game then have to guess which word the 'teapot' stands for, that is, they have to come up with the two lexical items (sharing the same phonological representation) that have the two meanings described. Judging from my own childhood experience, there are enough of these cases to fill at least a whole afternoon.

This phenomenon, which is quite common in language, is totally alien to counting words: there are no two counting words that share the same phonological representation; each occurs only once within the counting sequence, and this is exactly because counting words function as numbers. Since it is crucial for numbers to be well distinguished, we must have a way to tell counting words apart unambiguously. Being words, the obvious means for counting words to achieve this distinctness is their phonological representation. Hence, the same representation is never used twice within a counting sequence; you will not come across a word like THIRX, which, for example as a result of language change, could either be 'six' or 'thirteen' (imagine asking 'Do you mean "THIRX" as in "FIVE – THIRX – SEVEN", or "THIRX" as in "TWELVE – THIRX – FOURTEEN"?').[2]

What we can have, though, is two words that are linked to the same position in the counting sequence, like in English THIRTEEN HUNDRED and ONE THOUSAND THREE HUNDRED. Abundance does not hurt; whichever counting word we are using in a given context, will be well distinguished from all other elements of the sequence and will have a unique position among them.

---

[2] This does not mean that there can be no words *outside* the counting sequence with a similar or identical phonological representation as a counting word (examples of this are 'too', 'to' and TWO, or 'for' and FOUR). It is just important that within a counting sequence, all elements are well distinguished.

Counting words form an infinite progression

Being ordered as a progression and being infinite – the two additional features we want for numbers – distinguishes counting sequences from other lexical domains, for example from words for animals. 'Dog', 'cat', 'butterfly', and 'dolphin' are not ordered sequentially like ONE, TWO, THREE, and FOUR, and there is no rule that yields the next animal name for every animal name I can think of, like the rule that tells me that TWO MILLION AND FORTY-TWO has a successor TWO MILLION AND FORTY-THREE, and so on.

The infiniteness of a counting sequence is induced by the recursive rules that govern the generation of counting words. These rules take counting words as their input and generate new counting words as their output; usually they have either an additive character, like the rule that yields SIXTY-FIVE from SIXTY and FIVE; or a multiplicative character, like the rule that combines a counting word like FOUR with a base word like HUNDRED to form FOUR HUNDRED. Hence that counting sequences are infinite does not mean that they consist of infinitely many primitive elements. It means that there are morphosyntactic rules that generate infinitely many counting words, based on a finite set of lexical primitives and a stock of 'bases', elements like -TY, HUNDRED, THOUSAND, etc. that are used in combinations with (primitive and complex) counting words.[3] As a result, counting words form an infinite set, and the elements of this set have an internal structure that forms the basis for their sequential order.

Let me sketch the rules for English as an illustration.[4] To generate the English counting sequence we first introduce the primitive elements ONE to NINE. Since this set is finite (and quite small), we can provide an order for its elements explicitly, by enumeration: <ONE, TWO, THREE, . . . , NINE>. On this basis we define rules that generate complex counting words of different kinds that we can identify as different classes within the counting sequence: elements of the Teen-class (counting words from TEN to NINETEEN), the Ty-class (TWENTY to NINETY-NINE), the Hundred-class

---

[3] A terminological note: as you can see from this reasoning, I treat as one 'counting word' every item that serves as one element of the counting sequence, that is, every item that occupies a particular position within the counting sequence. Accordingly, a counting word can be morphologically primitive (as FIVE), or it can have a complex internal structure (as FIVE HUNDRED AND SIXTY-TWO). Hurford (1975) gives an account of the phrase structure rules underlying the generation of complex counting words within generative grammar.

[4] In Appendix 3, I have spelled out the recursive definition for the English counting sequence that I sketch here. You can find an overview of the structure of counting sequences from a wide range of languages in Menninger (1958).

(ONE HUNDRED to NINE HUNDRED AND NINETY-NINE), the Thousand-class (ONE THOUSAND to NINE HUNDRED AND NINETY-NINE THOUSAND NINE HUNDRED AND NINETY-NINE), the Million-class (from ONE MILLION upwards), and so on.

The classes can now be ordered with respect to each other: the primitive counting words constitute the lowest class, followed by the Teen-class, then the Ty-class, the Hundred-class, the Thousand-class, and the Million-class. For each class we define multiplicative rules that combine a base (-TY, HUNDRED, THOUSAND, MILLION) with a counting word that serves as a *multiplier*. For example in the Hundred-class we have a rule that generates SIX HUNDRED from a base HUNDRED and a multiplier SIX, and similarly for the other classes. An exception is the Teen-class which has a base TEEN, but this base does not serve as a multiplier: we do not have 'oneteen', but instead TEN, and the element that should be 'twoteen' is TWENTY, which is already an element of the next class, namely the Ty-class.

In addition to multiplicative rules, we introduce additive rules that take counting words like SIX HUNDRED as their input and combine them with elements of lower classes, yielding counting words like SIX HUNDRED AND FORTY. Again, the Teen-class deviates somewhat: its first three elements – TEN, ELEVEN, TWELVE – are opaque, that is, they do not display a constituent structure that relates them to other counting words (as opposed to, say, SEVENTEEN which is generated from SEVEN and the base TEEN). Accordingly, these elements can be defined as primitives, that is, by enumeration along the same lines as we defined the elements of the initial class (ONE to NINE).

Elements of the same class are ordered with respect to the ranks of their multipliers (SIXTY comes before NINETY, because SIX comes before NINE), and elements with the same multiplier are ordered with respect to their increments (SIXTY-THREE comes before SIXTY-NINE, because THREE comes before NINE).

For multiplicative elements of the Ty-, Hundred-, and Thousand-class, the multiplier must always be an element of a lower class (for instance, SIX THOUSAND and SIX HUNDRED THOUSAND are allowed, but SIX THOUSAND THOUSAND or SIX MILLION THOUSAND are not). This restriction does not hold for the highest class: this class is open in order to make the sequence infinite. For the sake of brevity, let us ignore classes based on BILLION etc., and treat the Million-class as the highest class of our counting sequence. As an open class the Million-class then includes combinations like FOUR MILLION MILLIONS ($= 4,000,000,000,000$ or 4×10^{12}), or FOUR MILLION MILLION MILLIONS ($= 4 \times 10^{18}$).

This option introduces recursion: basically, the rule yielding multiplicative elements of the Million-class says 'Give me any counting word, and I give you a new counting word by combining it with MILLION.' This word then serves as a basis for a whole new sequence of additive elements. Since the output of our rule is a counting word again and hence qualifies as a new input word, we never run out of such multiplicative elements. This way we never reach a limit with our words; it is this recursivity in their generative rules that makes counting sequences infinite.

The additive and multiplicative character of the rules governing the generation of a counting sequence is not always transparent to the same degree. As a result of language change, a counting sequence can contain more or less opaque elements, too. In our English example the rules we have sketched above give us an idealised version of the counting sequence, generating for instance elements like THREE-TY instead of THIRTY. Accordingly, in the definition of the English counting sequence I have spelled out in Appendix 3, I have included a function that accounts for these idiosyncrasies by replacing idealised elements (THREE-TY) by their actual counterparts (THIRTY) (cf. p. 308).

Since – due to the fact that counting words form a progression – lower counting words are used more often than higher ones, they are also more prone to idiosyncrasies.[5] An example from English are the elements ELEVEN and TWELVE. As mentioned in our sketch of the English counting sequence, these words are opaque today; their is no internal structure accessible that indicates their sequential position in the way that, say, SEVENTEEN fits into a position between SIXTEEN and EIGHTEEN. However, ELEVEN and TWELVE go back to Proto-Germanic words that did have an internal structure, as reflected in the Gothic AIN-LIF and TWA-LIF that translate as something like 'one is left over' and 'two is left over', suggesting an old upper limit of 'ten' in the counting sequence.

A language can also have counting words that are perfectly transparent with respect to their internal structure, but are generated by an idiosyncratic rule that brings in, say, subtraction instead of addition. This happens for instance in Latin, where the two counting words preceding 'twenty' (VIGINTI) come out as 'two of twenty' (DUO-DE-VIGINTI, *eighteen*) and 'one of twenty' (UN-DE-VIGINTI, *nineteen*), whereas, according to the standard additive system that underlies the Latin counting sequence, they should be

---

[5] In general, words that are less frequent tend to be more regular. An irregular word that is seldom used tends to become regularised in the course of language change, because the irregular forms are not encountered often enough to be memorised by new generations learning the language.

characterised as the elements that occur eight and nine positions after ten, respectively (like EIGHTEEN and NINETEEN in English).

A rather confusing system that is a bit similar to the subtraction involved in UNDEVIGINTI is *overcounting*. This term was introduced by Karl Menninger in his comprehensive work on the structure and emergence of number word systems (Menninger 1958). A counting word based on overcounting gives you its position within the next block, as defined by the respective multiplier. For instance in this system 'sixteen' would not be generated as 'the element six positions after ten', but as 'the sixth element within the block ending with twenty'. Menninger describes such a case for Finnish, where 'sixteen' comes out as 'six-second' (KUUSI-TOISTA), being the sixth element within the second decade, the block ending with 'twenty'.

A lot of deviations from the overall building structure of a counting sequence arise from small subsystems of counting words that are generated by non-standard rules. For instance the 'overcounting' rule in Finnish is employed for the sequence from 'eleven' to 'nineteen', but not for counting words up to 'ten' or for words from higher classes. A counting sequence can also involve subsequences that are based on different multipliers than the rest of the system, like in the French QUATRE-VINGTS ('four-twenties', *eighty*) and QUATRE-VINGT-DIX ('four-twenty-ten', *ninety*) which are based on multiples of twenty rather than ten, in opposition to the decimal system that underlies most of the French counting sequence.

In addition, deviating subsystems can be due to rules that determine a non-standard order for the constituents of some complex counting words. An example are the English words from THIRTEEN to NINETEEN – instead of TEN-THREE, . . . , TEN-NINE, which would be parallel to TWENTY-THREE etc., the German and Arabic counting sequences are examples where this subsystem not only consists of the sequence from 'thirteen' to 'nineteen', but covers the whole sequence up to 'ninety-nine'. Additive counting words accordingly come out as something like 'one-and-twenty', 'two-and-twenty', . . . , 'nine-and-ninety', parallel to 'thir-teen', 'four-teen', . . . , 'nine-teen'. Italian, on the other hand, employs this order only for counting words from 'eleven' through 'sixteen' (UN-DICI, DO-DICI, TRE-DICI, QUATTOR-DICI, QUIN-DICI, SE-DICI), but not for 'seventeen', 'eighteen', and 'nineteen' (DICI-ASSETTE, DICI-OTTO, DICI-ANNOVE), that is, the subsystem includes not even all the 'teens'.

Hence, as these examples illustrate, deviations from the overall structure of a counting sequence are a common phenomenon in languages. What is important is that this is confined to a few areas and a finite set of elements, hence these subsequences or individual elements can be memorised as idiosyncratic. So, while a counting sequence might contain its fair share of deviations, there are still general rules that allow us to generate an open set of new elements, and to order them with respect to their internal structure, such that the constitutive structure of the counting sequence provides the basis for infiniteness and sequential order.

The less idiosyncrasies occur within a counting sequence, the easier it is for children to grasp its organisation. This does not only speed up the learning process for the counting sequence, it can also enhance the development of arithmetic concepts by making it easier to see multiplicative and additive relations between numbers. A further advantage for early mathematical learning is the fact that a more transparent counting sequence is also easier to correlate with arabic numerals (we will come back to this correlation in chapter 7). If your counting sequence goes 'ten – ten-one – ten-two – ten-three – . . . – two-ten' instead of 'ten – eleven – twelve – thirteen – . . . – twenty' (to pick out a particularly confusing area in the English counting sequence), you will find it much easier to grasp that, for instance, ten plus two equals twelve, thirteen minus three equals ten, and two times ten is twenty.

A counting sequence that has such a regular, transparently multiplicative and additive structure is the one of Chinese, where counting words follow exactly the pattern sketched above ('ten – ten-one – ten-two – ten-three – . . . – two-ten, two-ten-one', etc.). Related counting sequences that are based on the ancient Chinese sequence are used in Japan and Korea (in addition to indigenous Japanese and Korean sequences). Accordingly, in a number of studies with Asian (Chinese, Korean, and Japanese) versus US-American (English-speaking) and European (French and Swedish) first-graders, Irene Miura and her colleagues found that the Asian group had a significantly better understanding of the base ten structure of their number sequence and – related to that – of the place value system underlying the use of digits in Arabic numerals.[6] As a result of their studies, Miura and her collaborators concluded that structurally different counting sequences may have a significant impact on the way number is represented in children; a correlation that supports our view of counting words as elements of a number sequence:

---

[6] Cf. Miura et al. (1988, 1993); Miura and Okamoto (1989). Similar results have been reported for Chinese and Korean versus British and American kindergarteners (for instance, by Song and Ginsburg 1988; Miller and Zhu 1991; Ho and Fuson 1998). Cf. Towse and Saxton (1998), though, who argue that the Miura and Okamoto results may be partly prompted by the experimental design. I will develop an analysis for the system underlying arabic numerals and their correlation with counting words in chapter 7.

cognitive representation of number may be differentially influenced by the structural characteristics of particular numerical languages and . . . these differences in number representation may contribute to variations in mathematics understanding and performance. (Miura et al. 1993: 28)

The fact that counting sequences can be imported from other languages *in toto* (as mentioned above for the Chinese-based sequence used in Japan and Korea), that is, as something like one huge set of loan words, adds further support to the view advanced here. In particular, we can relate this phenomenon to the special status of counting sequences within the linguistic system: we can interpret it as the importing of a set of numerical tools, words that are closely linked up with each other, forming one complex entity, namely a progression, and – as we will see later in this chapter – these words are furthermore separated from other linguistic domains by their non-referential, instrumental status. From such a perspective it does not come as a surprise that counting sequences can be imported from other languages as wholes, and also that they might coexist with the original, indigenous sequence, as is the case in Japan and Korea, where the indigenous and the Chinese-based sequences tend to be used in different contexts – just as they coexist with other possible number sequences anyway (for instance with arabic numerals, as I will argue in chapter 7).

Is infiniteness necessary?

When we investigated the relationship between numbers and objects in chapter 1, we noticed that infiniteness is actually not a strict prerequisite for our tools in the different types of number assignments. The properties that we identified as crucial for numbers when we assign them to empirical objects were just their distinctness and their sequential ordering. We can manage perfectly well with a limited number sequence as long as we do not have to cope with more extended empirical relational structures and do not want to perform mathematical operations based on higher numbers or on infinity.

Accordingly, there are languages in which the indigenous counting sequence is not based on recursive rules and hence has only finitely many elements – why use an infinite sequence if you only ever need so many numbers?[7] The elements of a finite counting sequence are well distinguished and

---

[7] In a cross-cultural study of traditional societies, William Divale found a relationship between the highest number used in a counting sequence and the need to store food. In general, societies that live in areas of climatic instability tend to use counting sequences with higher numbers that enable them to figure out food storage requirements (Divale 1999).

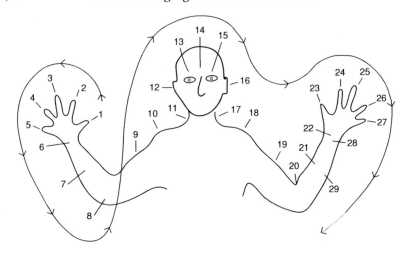

Figure 28 The Oksapmin counting sequence (Saxe 1981: 307)

they are ordered sequentially, starting with a word for 'one', but there are no recursive rules that allow us to go on forever. At some point, the sequence comes to an end. However, as soon as higher numbers are required – for instance, as a result of economic or technological change – recursive rules are introduced into the system, making the sequence a full-blown infinite counting sequence.

Geoffrey Saxe has described such a development for the Oksapmin in Papua New Guinea.[8] The traditional Oksapmin counting sequence consists of a limited number of words that are usually accompanied by gestures connected with body parts. Whenever you utter Oksapmin counting words, you point to parts of your upper body, step by step, starting with the thumb of the right hand for 'one', going via your fingers all the way up your arm, around your head, and via the left arm down to your left hand, ending with your little finger for 'twenty-seven'. If you need more numbers, you can add some more steps, continuing back up to your wrist up to 'twenty-nine' and then upwards on the back of your body (see Figure 28). The connection with body parts introduces a spatial basis into the sequence; this spatial aspect supports the distinctness and the stable sequential order of its elements. Such a system of 'body counting' is common among languages in Papua New Guinea.

This sequence could fulfil all the numerical purposes of Oksapmin everyday life: it was employed for cardinality assignments (for instance, to

---

[8] Cf. Saxe (1981, 2003).

identify how many pigs somebody owns), for the measurement of properties like length, and for ordinal number assignments (for instance, to tell the relative position of different hamlets on a path). However, in the early 1960s Western currency entered the Oksapmin region, brought in by Australian missionaries and patrol officers. With the introduction of money into their culture, people needed to deal with higher numbers, and to perform more abstract arithmetical operations.

Given this need, the Oksapmin counting word sequence developed a base structure, a process that yielded a hybrid system consisting of indigenous Oksapmin counting words and a base POUND ('twenty', from the currency then used in Australia which was divided into 20 shillings). In this new system, the body counting does not go up to 'twenty-seven' (or further) anymore, but stops at the inner elbow of the second arm, indicating 'twenty'. At this point, 'one pound' is recorded, and the counting, rather than continuing with the forearm (which indicates the element 'twenty-one' in the old system), starts with the thumb ('one') on the first hand again.

This procedure can be interpreted as an additive rule which generates complex elements like 'twenty-one' ('one' after the recording of 'one pound') from a base 'twenty' and an element 'one', rather than representing 'twenty-one' as a primitive element, as in the old system. The recording of several 'pound' counts ('six pounds', 'seven pounds' etc.) would then give us higher number words as complex multiplicative elements on a basis of twenty, in a parallel way as we generate multiples of ten by suffixing -TY in English (SIX-TY, SEVEN-TY). Hence the new base structure lays the grounds for a system similar to the one we discussed for English; it transforms a finite sequence into one that is potentially infinite.

COUNTING WORDS ARE NON-REFERENTIAL

In the preceding section I have argued that counting words differ from other words in that they show the features that make them suitable as numerical tools: forming an infinite progression of well-distinguished entities is something that makes counting words fit as numbers, and it is also what discriminates them from other, non-numerical, linguistic domains. In the present section I am going to claim that this is *all* there is to counting words: unlike other words, they do not have any meaning, they do not refer to anything in the outside world. This is because they are not names for numbers, they *are* numbers. Counting words are tools that we use in number assignments, and for this job they do not need any referentiality.

This might make counting words look somewhat wanting from the point of view of language, but it adds to their suitability as numbers, for numbers should be well distinguished, infinite, and sequential – they should have 'number' properties – but nothing else. When we use something as a number sequence, we abstract from its special characteristics, taking into account only those properties that we need for numerical purposes. In the present section I discuss the status of counting words as non-referential elements within the linguistic system; in the next section I will present psychological and psycholinguistic evidence from the acquisition of counting sequences that supports this view.

To get an idea of what it means for counting words to be non-referential, let us employ a common thought experiment and picture yourself stranded on a remote island where you do not understand the local language. In order to find out the meanings of words, you might point to different objects and see what the speakers of that language call them, that is, you could try to learn words by ostension (ignoring for the present the problem to find out which object, object part, or object property it is exactly that is being named in each case; cf. the discussion in Quine 1960). Once you speak some of the language and rudimentary communication is possible, you might support your acquisition of a new word by asking people to describe the entity that it refers to, something along the lines of 'What is a "cat"?' – 'An animal that meows and chases mice'.[9]

This would be quite different with counting words. To figure out the elements of an unfamiliar counting sequence you might start with some cardinality assignments, like pointing to sets of three or four objects and hoping to make out a number word when people name these multitudes. A more straightforward way, though, would be to identify counting words directly when they are employed in a numerical procedure, say in counting. Once you know the first two or three elements of a counting sequence, you can learn more counting words just by reciting them and making people continue with the sequence. This way, you could learn every counting word just by its position within the sequence, with no need to refer to anything in the world.

Whereas you know that CAT translates into French as CHAT because both words refer to the same things, you know that FOUR in English corresponds to QUATRE in French because both words have the same position within their respective counting sequences: if you and I count in step in the two

---

[9] Note though, that this is not meant to stand for a definition of 'cat' (cf. the discussion of Hilary Putnam's thought experiment below).

languages, you get to FOUR just when I say QUATRE. Accordingly, no interpretation problem occurs for counting words from different languages, in contrast to referential words. While you might not be sure whether the French BATEAU should translate as BOAT or rather as SHIP in English, this problem does not arise for counting words at all (imagine someone reasoning, 'Well, "four" in English is actually not quite what you would call "quatre" in French. "Four" always covers some aspect of fiveness, too, whereas "quatre" is more restricted.'). This is because we do not use counting words to denote something in the world, we use them to figure out something; they are well-defined tools, with clean correspondences holding between the respective elements of different instances (different counting sequences).

This is also the reason why our notion of counting words would not change with new knowledge about the world. Hilary Putnam has discussed this possibility for common nouns (Putnam 1975), arguing that words like 'cat' have an *indexical* aspect, that is, their extension depends upon the actual nature of the things that serve as paradigms: a noun like 'cat' refers to the things we commonly know as cats, and is not based on a set of well-defined, predetermined characteristics; 'cat' is not synonymous to a particular description. Imagine that some day it comes out that cats are not the nice pets we always believed them to be, but remote-controlled robots from Mars. In this case, our notion of cats would change, but we would still call them 'cats'. We might say things like 'Cats have turned out not to be animals, but robots', which would not make much sense if 'cats' was synonymous with a description of some kind of animal.

This could not happen to counting words. The counting word FOUR is defined as that element of the counting sequence that is preceded by exactly 'ONE – TWO – THREE' and comes immediately before FIVE, and in cardinal number assignments FOUR is assigned to sets with a cardinality that matches the cardinality of the word sequence from ONE to FOUR. Should it come out that all the multitudes we used to call 'sets of four' are actually sets of five, because mischievous Martians manipulated our perception, we would adjust the number assignment, namely calling these sets 'sets of five' now, while our understanding of a 'set of four' would remain untouched. FOUR would not move up one position within the counting sequence, it would keep its position between THREE and FIVE. Hence nothing in our knowledge of sets can change our understanding of a non-referential counting word like FOUR; it can only change our number assignment, the assignment of FOUR to a set: FOUR is just a (well-defined) tool; if it comes out that it has been misapplied, we will adjust the assignment, not the tool.

But should not counting words denote something numerical? A question that you might have asked yourself is, if we use the words themselves as numbers, what is left to denote cardinalities, ranks, and numerical labels? The answer lies in the distinction between a counting sequence like 'one – two – three – . . .' on the one hand, and number word constructions like 'three stars', 'the third man', and 'bus number three' on the other hand. Counting words, as elements of the counting sequence, do not denote anything; they are non-referential, instrumental items that can be used as tools in the different kinds of number assignments. To *denote* these number assignments, we integrate counting words into complex linguistic structures, where they take the form of cardinals ('three' like in 'three stars'), ordinals ('third' as in 'the third man'), and nominal number words ('three' as in 'bus number three').

The different number word constructions that result from this integration are proper – that is, referential – linguistic elements; they express the concepts of cardinality, rank, and numerical label, so 'three stars' refers to a set with the cardinality 'three', 'the third man' denotes a man with the rank 'three', and 'bus number three' refers to a bus with the label 'three'.[10] Interestingly, the syntactic integration of counting words is not random. Once they enter linguistic constructions, they do not behave as a class of outlaws, but adjust to the local customs: each class of number words (cardinal, ordinal, and nominal number words) goes with a class of non-numerical linguistic items that have a similar semantic structure. I will give an account of this phenomenon in chapter 8 when we discuss in more detail the different linguistic constructions we use in order to denote number assignments.

Where do counting words come from; how can 'words' that do not refer to anything evolve within a language? Counting sequences recruit their members like the Borg from *Star Trek*: they assimilate words from other areas. They strip them of their expressiveness, making them a non-referential, integral part of their system. Unlike in the Borg empire, however, the words are copied into the counting sequence rather than absorbed by it; the original word stays intact and leads its own, referential life.

Many counting words originate from words for specific multitudes. For example, FIVE is presumably related to the Proto-Indo-European word for 'fist' (as an indication of five fingers);[11] the Russian word for forty, SOROK, is believed to originate from the Old Nordic word for furs, SEKR, which

---

[10] I will give an account of the organisation of these concepts and their linguistic expressions in chapters 6 and 8.
[11] Cf. Winter (1992) on the origin of Indo-European number words.

were traded in bundles of forty; and in the West African language Malinke the word for thousand, WÁA, was originally an expression for (standardised) baskets which contain 1,000 cola nuts.

However, once a word enters a counting sequence, it is dissociated from its non-numerical, referential counterpart and is reduced to the status of being an element of a well-ordered set. Due to this dissociation, in the process of language change it undergoes a different development than its non-numerical source, and synchronically the two are often not related anymore. The meaning attached to the original source might motivate the use of a particular counting word, but this reference is eliminated once the word is used as an element of the counting sequence.

The same goes for the building blocks that counting words are made of. Using AND as a constituent of complex additive counting words like TWO HUNDRED AND FORTY does have some plausibility, and surely points to the coordinative meaning of AND we encounter outside counting sequences, like in 'Kay and Mick'. As the examples in (1) through (3) show, a connective like AND can be found in additive counting words cross-linguistically:

(1) Kurdish: sē sad-**u** bist-**u** du   –   'three hundred and twenty and two' (*322*)

(2) German: drei**und**achtzig   –   'three and eighty' (*83*)

(3) Arabic: sittun **wa** ʿišrūna   –   'six and twenty' (*26*)

(4) Malinke: wáa fila **ní** tàn   –   'thousand two and ten' (*2010*)

(5) Swahili: kumi **na** kenda   –   'ten and nine' (*19*)

However, this does not mean we should mistake the counting-word constituent 'and' for an independent word with an additive/coordinative meaning. If 'and' was a full-blown marker of addition in counting words, we should expect it whenever additivity is involved. However, unlike in non-numerical contexts, the usage of 'and' seems to be totally random in additive counting words. Sometimes 'and' is optional (for instance in German, DREIHUNDERT-ACHTZIG, 'three hundred-eighty', works as well as DREIHUNDERT UND ACHTZIG, 'three hundred *and* eighty'); sometimes 'and' is downright banned although we have an additive construction (for instance in English FORTY-TWO, as opposed to the ungrammatical FORTY-AND-TWO), and sometimes 'and' is obligatory in one additive construction but banned in a parallel construction within the same paradigm (for instance French ET, 'and', must occur in each first counting word in the twenties through seventies, i.e. VINGT

ET UN, TRENTE ET UN etc., but is neither used in the eighties, i.e. QUATRE-VINGT-UN, nor in the respective succeeding additive counting words, i.e. VINGT-DEUX etc.).

A further kind of reduction can be seen in German: German UND ('and') can be phonologically reduced to 'N when it occurs as a constituent of complex counting words, but it cannot be reduced outside a counting word. So 'Kay 'n Mick', which works fine in spoken (informal) English, would be ungrammatical in German (spoken or written), whereas DREI-'N-ACHTZIG ('eighty-three', literally: 'three-'n-eighty') is not only grammatical, but actually the default in spoken language.[12]

The dissociation from the referential, non-numerical source can be observed not only in the case of lexical items like 'and', but also for grammatical elements like plural. The plural marker is used in Hebrew and Arabic to generate elements of the Ten-class (namely multiplicative decade words like *sixty*) from the corresponding 'Ones' (for instance from the word for *six*). By doing so, plural in Hebrew and Arabic decade words has a similar function as the English suffix -TY: while SIXTY in English is generated from a counting word SIX and a multiplier -TY, 'sixty' in Arabic (SITTUNA) is a plural form of 'six' (SITTUN). Similar to AND when it is a constituent of English counting words, the plural in Arabic 'Tens' like SITTUNA is dissociated from its source. In particular, it has lost its referential function: in SITTUNA, the plural feature does not indicate 'multitude' – as one might argue for non-numerical contexts (namely, for nominal plural as in 'cats') – but is used as a means to generate new elements of the counting sequence. The plural feature is a non-referential constituent of counting words: SITTUNA does not mean 'several six-es' or 'several instances of six' (whereas 'cats' refers to several instances of 'cat').

The upshot is that the form a counting word takes might be motivated by referential aspects of its (non-numerical) source, but, once a word is part of a counting sequence, these referential aspects become obsolete, leaving the association to wither away. This is how the mathematician Leonard Conant put it in an 1896 work on number word systems:

Deep regret must be felt by every student of philology, that the primitive meanings of simple numerals have been so generally lost. But, just as the pebble on the beach

---

[12] Note that this phenomenon cannot be attributed to general phonological or phonetic processes, as reflected by the fact that the reduction in 'Kai 'n Achim' is ungrammatical (*Kai* and *Achim* are proper names; the grammatical construction is 'Kai *und* Achim'). In this non-numerical example, we have exactly the same phonological context for 'und' as in DREI-UND-ACHTZIG, ('three-and-eighty') where 'und' gets reduced (the respective phonological representations are [kajn̩ʔaxi:m] and [dʁajn̩ ʔaxtsɪç]).

has been worn and rounded by the beating of the waves and by other pebbles, until no trace of its original form is left, and until we can say of it now only that it is quartz, or that it is diotrite, so too the numerals of many languages have suffered from the attrition of the ages, until all semblance of their origin has been lost, and we can say of them only that they are numerals. (Conant 1896: 209f.)

As deplorable as the process of integrating words into the number sequence may sound in Conant's words, *using words as numbers* is in fact an ingenious invention. With counting words we have a surprisingly efficient means to generate a sequence that can be put to use in number assignments. We will discuss this aspect in more detail in chapter 4. In the following section I support the view of counting words as numerical tools by demonstrating the consequences that the special status of counting words has in first language acquisition, that is, by showing how the numerical status of counting words is reflected in first language acquisition and sets them apart from other words.

COUNTING WORDS ARE ACQUIRED DIFFERENTLY

Children face counting words early in their linguistic development, and show productive use of the counting sequence by two years of age. The sequential character of counting words is salient early on. Before children know how to apply the counting sequence correctly in number assignments, they learn it as a pure series of meaningless words, and only later master the application of this sequence in cardinal, ordinal, and nominal assignments to objects. This acquisition order has been shown both for counting sequences like English and for the Oksapmin sequence that is closely linked to body parts.[13]

As a result of several longitudinal studies on the acquisition of number words in English, Karen Fuson and her colleagues identified the first stages in the acquisition of a counting sequence as the 'string level' and the 'unbreakable chain level'.[14] On these levels, learning the counting words is essentially a serial recall task: you learn a list of words (first as a single whole, later as a connected series of words) that have to be recited in a fixed order, apparently for the sake of reciting alone. As Fuson and her colleagues put it: at this stage, the counting sequence is represented 'as an arbitrary, long sequence having a conventional order and which adults and other children seem to love to ask one to recite' (Fuson et al. 1982: 35).

---

[13] Cf. Saxe (1982); Fuson (1988).
[14] Cf. Fuson et al. (1982); Fuson and Hall (1983); Fuson (1988 and 1992). I will come back to the acquisition of counting words in more detail in chapter 5.

Hence the sequential order of counting words is emphasised right from the start in first language acquisition. Unlike object words, children learn counting words as elements of a progression, with initially no further point to them. Counting words have no significance apart from being an element of this conventional progression, and in particular, they have no referential features. This is how Karen Wynn summarises this developmental stage:

The 'meaning' of a number word in this context [the context of a recited sequence, H. W.] is that it comprises part of this sequence; the words have no referents. The evidence for such a stage is that in children's earliest productions of the number word list, they treat the words as an unbreakable string, a sequence of sounds with no intrinsic meaning, recited by rote. (Wynn 1992b: 223f.)

As I argued above, the sequential order is essential for the use of counting words as tools in number assignments. In accordance with this account, parents tend to focus on counting words as elements of a progression, as opposed to other linguistic items, say, nouns. Obviously, whereas you might insist on saying 'one, two, three, . . .' when you try to teach your daughter the counting sequence, you will hardly ever do this with nouns, implying that one should always say 'dog' first and then 'cat', and so on. Here is an illustration from a mother–child interaction:

MOTHER (to Amy, 24 months): One
     AMY: Doo.
     MOTHER: One.
     AMY: Doo.
     MOTHER: Wha' ha'ened to one? What happened to one? One, say one.
     AMY: Two.
     MOTHER: I know two comes after one. Say one. One.
     (Durkin et al. 1986: 282)

Accordingly, for counting words the order of acquisition tends to mirror the order of the sequence. Children learn the initial elements of the counting sequence, ONE to TEN and later ELEVEN to TWENTY, earlier than higher counting words (unlike nouns that naturally do not have an acquisition order to the effect that, say, 'dog' is always learned before 'cat').[15]

A typical context for young children to apply counting words is a 'counting game' where they learn to count objects. These games have been investigated, among others, by Kevin Durkin and his colleagues. They came across counting games in connection with a longitudinal study with 9- to

---

[15] At later stages, when children grasp the rules that organise the sequence, they might know higher multiplicative words, like THIRTY or THREE HUNDRED, before they can produce the whole sequence of words that leads to them (cf. the discussion in chapter 5 below).

36-month-old children and their mothers, originally designed to investigate turn-taking in mother–infant conversations. As it turned out, these
conversations involved a considerable amount of counting games that the
mothers initiated when playing with their children. Counting games are
a great means to pass the time when you are sitting in a psycholinguistic
laboratory with your child, since – as we noted at the very beginning of
our investigation into numbers – anything that is a discrete object can be
counted: in the laboratory, mothers used for their counting games, among
other things, the leaves of office plants, cameras, and their own eyes.

In counting games, the non-referential status of counting words is evident: they do not identify objects, but are used as devices to count them.
When counting, you pair counting words with objects in a similar way as
you pair the 'words' in a nursery rhyme of the 'eenie-meenie'-type with your
friends. When counting the pens on my desk I do not name them 'one',
'two', and 'three', respectively, just as, when reciting a nursery rhyme, you
do not mean to call your friend Charles an 'eenie', Karen a 'meenie', and
so forth. In both nursery rhymes and counting routines the words are not
used as names, but as props in a certain ritual: they are tools in a stylised,
repetitive procedure that involves the systematic correlation of a sequence
of words and a set of objects.

This ritual context emphasises the instrumental status of counting words.
It enables children to distinguish counting words from object names and
to apply different sets of strategies in their acquisition. Ellen Markman
identified two general principles that help children to establish the reference
of object labels in first language acquisition (Markman 1989):

(1) *one label for objects of the same type*   ('Taxonomic Assumption Principle');
(2) *only one label for the same object*   ('Mutual Exclusivity Principle').

The first principle accounts for the fact that objects that share some salient
properties tend to get the same label at early stages of language acquisition.
For instance, if a child sees several pens and hears each of them called 'pen',
the task to figure out what 'pen' means is easier than it would be if the
first pen was called 'pen', the second one 'Karen's favourite writing utensil',
and the third one 'biro'. The second principle, which Markman called the
'Mutual Exclusivity Principle', reflects the tendency to stick with one label
for one object. If you show a pen to a child and say 'pen', you do not
normally some minutes later show her the same pen again and call it 'biro'
then. Even though these principles are, of course, not strict laws (after all,
we *can* call a pen a 'biro' or 'writing utensil' etc.), one can get pretty far if
one wants to establish the reference of new words and assumes that the two
principles will be obeyed as a default. As basic guidelines, they can help

children to figure out the meaning of words at early stages in first language acquisition.

However, both of these principles are systematically violated in the way counting words are used. In counting games, (1) objects of the same type are correlated with different words (instead of calling all pens 'pen', one pen is assigned the word ONE, another pen gets the word TWO, and so on), and (2) the same object may receive different counting words in the course of several counting tasks (you might assign the blue pen the word ONE when counting the pens now, and the word TWO when you count them again, while starting with the red pen). As the following transcript from a mother–child interaction from the Durkin et al. study shows, this can get quite confusing at times: in this conversation, which took place after the mother and daughter had counted the four cameras in the studio, the mother switches directly from *counting* fingers (assigning them counting words non-referentially) to *naming* fingers (assigning them nouns referentially):

MOTHER (to Lucy, 24 months):	One.	(raises thumb)
LUCY:	One.	(waves arm)
MOTHER:	Two.	(raises thumb and index finger)
LUCY:	Two.	(waves arm)
MOTHER:	Three.	(raises thumb, index and middle fingers)
LUCY:	Sree.	(waves arm)
MOTHER:	Four.	(raises thumb, index, middle and ring fingers)
LUCY:	Four.	(hands in lap, smiling)
MOTHER:	What's that?	(raises index finger)
LUCY:	Two.	
MOTHER:	Finger.	
LUCY:	Finger.	
MOTHER:	And what's that?	(raises thumb)
LUCY:	B – one two three ror.	('one' pronounced emphatically)
MOTHER:	Thumb.	

(Durkin et al. 1986: 281)

In spite of the deviation from standard principles of word usage in first language acquisition, the acquisition of counting sequences and the discrimination of counting words and object names does not cause significant problems for young children.[16] This is now no longer surprising, but can be derived from our view of counting words: it is the non-referential, instrumental status of counting words *as numbers* that enables children to accomplish this task; this special status sets them apart from other words in acquisition and representation. Since counting words are used as tools in specific rituals (like counting games), where we want to figure out something about objects rather than denote them, the principles for referential words do not apply to them.

Accordingly, children hardly ever mix up counting words with referential linguistic items. The only intrusions into counting contexts that have been reported in the literature are letters of the alphabet;[17] a telling example, since these, too, form a conventional progression: a sequence of elements starting with 'A' that do not refer to anything, but are used as tools (namely, tools that are employed in order to represent phonological representations of words in script). Hence children learn counting words not in the way they learn object names, as labels for things of a certain kind, but rather like nursery rhymes or letters of the alphabet, as non-referential elements of a conventional sequence.

A CUT WITH OCCAM'S RAZOR

In the preceding sections, we have assessed counting words as candidates for the job of numbers. As it turned out, they passed the test with great success. For one, we found that counting words form an infinite progression of well-distinguished entities. These properties that qualify them as numbers make counting words pretty unusual as linguistic items. An additional – and rather gross – peculiarity arises from the fact that they are non-referential; they do not denote anything. This additional feature strips them down to their instrumental status: counting words are numerical tools, not names for numbers. Finally, we found that this status is reflected in their acquisition, where they deviate from other words in – again – being instrumental, non-referential, and sequentially ordered.

The exceptional status of counting sequences is also reflected on the electrophysiological level. In a study on lexical processing, the neuroscientist Stanislas Dehaene asked people to categorise different kinds of words while he measured the electric activity in their brain. The words could be animal names (for example 'chicken'), action verbs (for example 'whisper'), proper names of famous persons, or counting words (for example 'fifteen'). He

---

[16] Cf. also Wynn (1990, 1992b). [17] Gelman and Gallistel (1978); Fuson et al. (1982).

found specific patterns (that is, specific event-related potentials) for the processing of counting words that were not elicited by other words.[18] This is in accordance with our view of counting words as exceptional – namely numerical – entities whose status sets them apart from other words in their mental representation, in a way that might be reflected neurologically.

And it is counting words that we actually employ as the tools of choice in number assignments: if I ask you to prove to me that the pens on my desk in front of me are actually three, what you are most likely to do is assign every pen a counting word, starting with ONE, and use the last counting word, THREE, to identify the cardinality of the entire set of pens. This is what we defined as a cardinal number assignment in chapter 1: you assign a number n to a set of empirical objects s (the set of pens), such that the sequence from 1 to n has the same cardinality as s; to make sure that this holds, you constitute a one-to-one-mapping between the numbers from 1 to n (counting words from ONE to THREE) and the elements of the counted set (pens). Similarly, when you counted the 20 stars in Figure 5 (on page 20 above), you probably set up a one-to-one mapping between all the stars and the counting words from ONE to TWENTY.

Along the same lines, if you think back to your job as a judge in that race in chapter 1 (see Figure 14 on page 34), it would actually have been counting words you mapped to runners in your ordinal number assignment, assigning ONE to Charles, TWO to Karen, THREE to Mick, and FOUR to Paul (at least these would be the words if you had been a fair judge). Finally, in nominal number assignments counting words readily serve as labels for empirical objects. Being well distinguished by their phonological representations, they can be used to tell apart different elements of an empirical set (for instance, bus lines or members of a football team). Since we habitually use other words – in particular proper names – to distinguish objects this way, this kind of number assignment, which might seem rather peripheral from a numerical standpoint, comes naturally to counting words.

As a result of this discussion, we now find ourselves in a position to regard the sequences of counting words as number sequences. In an 'Occamian'

---

[18] Dehaene (1995). By 250 to 280 ms after the word appeared on the screen, when category-specific differences appeared in the ERPs, counting words were the only category to yield a bilateral parietal positivity, while words of other categories yielded a left temporal negativity, suggesting the activation of a semantic network that seems not to be involved in the processing of counting words. In another experiment, Le Clec'H et al. (2000) showed that counting words and words for body parts activate partially distinct cortical areas in a comparison task (in this study, subjects saw a word for a body part and had to decide whether it identified a body part above or below the shoulders, or they saw a counting word and had to decide whether it identified a number larger or smaller than 12).

spirit, we can do away with numbers, and stick to counting words alone, as an instance of a number sequence – though, of course, not necessarily the only one. Instead of a duplication into words and numbers, we only have to cope with words in our 'number' universe.

So how many sets of 'numbers' are there? Do we have to assume a distinct sequence of numbers for every single language now? Recall that numbers in our account are not particular abstract entities, but the entities we use as tools in cardinal, ordinal, and nominal assignments; and just as you can use different balls for a football game and different things as a hammer if you want to drive a nail into the wall, you can use different sequences as 'numbers' in your number assignments. Which sequence you use can, for instance, depend on the language you are in. So counting sequences of different languages do not constitute distinct 'numbers', they are alternative progressions fulfilling the same numerical purpose.

This is possible because counting sequences from different languages are isomorphic with respect to the ordering of their elements, they have the same structure as progressions and constitute the same numerical relational structures. Due to this isomorphism, they are not only interchangeable (they can fulfil the same purpose), they are also indistinguishable if we only take into account the features that make them suitable for numerical purposes and that are relevant in numerical operations. Stripped down to their numerical features, one could not tell the difference between counting words from different languages. Remember our translation example from above: it was easy to correlate FOUR with QUATRE, because all we had to do was correlating two equivalent positions in the English and French counting sequence, whereas when translating a noun like 'boat' into French, we have to think of possible referents, our concept of boat ('Is this still a boat, or would you rather call it a ship?') and the like. In chapter 7, I will argue that there also systems other than those of counting words that we use for number purposes. In particular, I will discuss arabic numerals as an example of a non-verbal number sequence, and their correlation with counting words.

COUNTING WORDS AS NUMERICAL TOOLS

In the present chapter, I made a case for counting sequences as a key instance of numerical tools. I argued that counting words are not as names for numbers, but tools that fulfil the function of numbers. Since we will come back to this point throughout the following chapters, let me quickly summarise my argument here.

A. Counting sequences fulfil all the criteria for numerical tools

(1) *Distinctness:* Counting words are well distinguished by their phonological representations.

(2) *Infiniteness:* Counting words are generated by recursive rules. This makes the sets of counting words potentially infinite. [*optional*]

(3) *Progression:* Counting words are ordered with respect to the rank of their constituents, based on the order of primitive counting words and the classification of (mostly additive and multiplicative) generative rules. As a result of this, counting words form a progression.

In short, counting words form an infinite progression of well-distinguished elements. In so doing, they differ significantly from other lexical items.

B. Counting sequences are non-referential

Counting words often originate in words associated with quantities or words for body parts, but, once a word enters a counting sequence, it is dissociated from its referential, non-numerical counterpart and reduced to being an element of an infinite progression. The same is true for elements like 'and' and plural markers, when they occur as parts of complex counting words. Counting words from different languages correspond to each other not because they refer to the same number, but because they occupy the same position in their respective sequences. A translation of a counting word from one language into another is based not on a shared prototypical referent, but on the equivalence of two well-defined positions within the respective progressions.

C. Counting sequences are acquired as verbal tools

The non-referential, instrumental status of counting words is reflected in first language acquisition where it distinguishes them from other words. They are encountered as elements of a verbal sequence that does not refer to anything in the world, but fulfils an instrumental function in ritualised procedures like counting games. Like the elements of nursery rhymes and the letters of an alphabet, counting words have to be recited in a conventional order. Their status as elements of a non-referential conventional progression allows children to apply specific strategies in the acquisition of counting words and to distinguish them from other words.

D. Counting sequences can be defined as numbers

As a result, we can regard counting words as entities that do not refer to numbers, but fulfil the function of numbers. The criteria-based approach we developed in chapter 2 characterises numbers as a class of highly efficient, multi-purpose toolkits defined by three basic properties. In the present chapter, we have identified counting sequences as a prime instance of these numerical tools. Enlisting counting words for numerical purposes adds convenience to efficiency: these numbers are easy to generate, and are stored in memory. Using words as numbers means that we have a number sequence that can be reproduced whenever we need it and which can be carried along freely – as opposed to, say, my wonderful infinite colour palette that we encountered in the previous chapter. Using words as numbers also means that language and number concepts are connected in the human mind in an intimate way, since it is language that provides us with the tools for our number assignments. Let us take a closer look into this relationship.

CHAPTER 4

The language legacy

In this chapter, I am going to show that our account of numbers and counting words provides the grounds for a new perspective on the relationship between language and the emergence of numerical thinking in the history of our species. In particular I am going to show that the contribution of language does not end with giving us counting sequences as numerical tools. I will argue that language not only provides us with access to a number sequence, but that it is the human language faculty that enabled us to develop a fully-fledged, systematic number concept in the first place.

Crucially, such a concept enables us to employ numbers – or rather, 'numerical tools' – in a pattern of dependent linking: we can use them to identify empirical properties (like cardinality, rank, or identity) because of the relations they have with other numbers, that is, because of their position within a numerical system and not because they have these properties as individuals in their own standing. In short: it is the system that makes numbers. In the present chapter I am going to show that it is our linguistic capacity that enables us to grasp numbers the way we do: language as a mental faculty laid the grounds for the emergence of a systematic concept of number, a concept of number that builds on a pattern of dependent linking and covers the different numerical relational structures we use in number assignments and mathematical reasoning.

However, not all aspects of our numerical cognition rely on language. Before I make my case for the contribution of language to the emergence of number, I will discuss evidence for early, language-independent sources for our numerical thinking, most notably quantitative concepts that serve as a basis for our understanding of cardinality: mammals and birds can distinguish two from three elements and can also tell apart sizes of larger sets if the difference is big enough; human babies can do it before they utter their first words, and even newborns show some amazing capacities in this area. In the first main part of this chapter, I present experimental evidence for these early quantitative capacities, and also for an early grasp of sequential order. On this basis, I then show how the human language faculty enables us to integrate these underpinnings for our numerical cognition into a systematic concept of number.

BEFORE LANGUAGE: QUANTITATIVE CAPACITIES IN INFANTS AND ANIMALS

Over the last decades, converging evidence coming from developmental psychology, comparative psychology, and cognitive ethology has revealed some striking quantitative capacities that are independent of language. Studies with babies have shown that we do not need language to grasp the cardinality[1] of small sets and to perform simple arithmetic operations on them, and experiments with higher animals suggest that we share these capacities with other species. In the present section I first give a general description of this language-independent ability to grasp cardinalities, and show how it differs from a numerical routine like counting. On this basis, I then discuss the evidence from studies with human infants and from field studies and lab experiments on higher animals.

How to grasp the cardinality of sets: subitising and noisy magnitudes

There are two main sources for our early representation of cardinality: (1) subitising, the capacity to recognise small cardinalities (this is the mechanism I mentioned when we discussed the itemising view of numbers in chapter 2), and (2) noisy magnitudes, a representation of quantities that allows us to estimate the size of sets.

'Subitising', a term originally coined in a paper by Kaufman et al. (1949), refers to a nearly instantaneous process that allows us to discriminate small sets of different sizes.[2] Subitising occurs automatically, accurately, and without conscious attention; it enables us to recognise the cardinality of sets with up to three or four elements, for instance, it enables us to tell two stars from one star and from three stars, without invoking numerical strategies like counting. Remember the 20 stars from chapter 1 that I employed in order to illustrate how we use counting as a basis for cardinal number assignments (Figure 5, p. 20). When I asked you to tell me how many stars there

---

[1] In the psychological literature one often finds the term 'numerosity' in this context. In view of our discussion above, I use 'cardinality' (which we defined as the property that tells us 'how many'), in order to distinguish this property from other properties that can also be identified with numbers, namely, ordinal or nominal properties.

[2] Cf. also the discussion in Mandler and Shebo (1982) and Trick and Pylyshyn (1994).

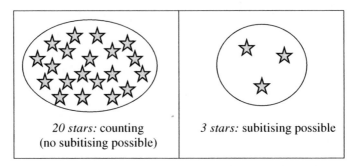

20 *stars:* counting   3 *stars:* subitising possible
(no subitising possible)

Figure 29 Determining the cardinality of sets – counting versus subitising

were, I used a set that was sufficiently large to make sure you actually had to employ counting and could not tell me the cardinality right away. Had I used only three stars, you would have been able to determine the cardinality at a glance, with no counting involved (Figure 29). One can use this capacity to cut short the counting procedure we discussed in chapter 1: instead of tediously applying a number to each single star, you might have grouped two or three stars together, going for instance 'two – four – six – . . . – eighteen – twenty stars'.

Subitising allows us to recognise the cardinality of a small set right away, we just have to look at it. Employing counting, on the other hand – our standard *numerical* procedure for cardinality assessments – means that we have to link up, in a one-to-one manner, the elements of the set with counting words (as our numerical tools). Hence counting, but not subitising, involves reciting a sequence of words, aloud or subvocally. Accordingly our ability to count, but not to subitise, should be disturbed if one has to perform an articulatory task simultaneously with the cardinality assessment, that is, if one has to say something else while trying to find out 'how many'.

In order to test this hypothesis, Graham Hitch and his colleagues showed schoolchildren drawings of houses on a computer screen, and asked them to indicate (by pressing a key on a numeric keyboard), as fast as possible, how many houses they saw, while at the same time, they had to say 'blah, blah, blah'. This articulatory task had a significant effect on both accuracy and speed: the children were significantly slower and made more errors in their cardinality assessments than a control group who did not have to say 'blah, blah' when quantifying the objects. However, this difference occurred only for sets that had more than three elements. For one, two, or three houses no disturbing effect of the 'blah, blah'-task was evident. These results suggest that subitising of small sets does not involve subvocalisation, whereas counting does.[3]

You can test this on yourself, for the two sets of stars in Figure 29 above: try to verify again how many stars are in the large set on the left side, while saying 'blah blah blah' all the time, and compare this to your performance for the stars in the right set. Probably you found the articulatory task rather disturbing when quantifying the large set, while you were not hampered in your cardinality assessment of the small set (at least as long as you pretend not yet to know that it is 20 stars in the large set, of course . . .).

The distinction between subitising and counting is also evident in the time one needs for a cardinality assessment. Subitising, as a rapid and accurate process, works only for the first three cardinalities. To assess the cardinality of sets with up to three elements, we need about 40 ms per item, which probably reflects the time needed to individualise the items in subitising. For more than three items we encounter a dramatic increase in reaction time: for larger sets, reaction time jumps to an average of about 300 ms per item.

In sum, we can tell the cardinality of sets with up to three elements, unlike that of larger sets, nearly instantaneously, apparently effortless, and accurate, without involving counting procedures. Jean-Paul Fischer called this phenomenon the 'discontinuity after three', and interpreted it as evidence for a specific apprehension mechanism for small cardinalities (Fischer 1992).

Krish Sathian and his colleagues showed that the brain areas involved in subitising and counting are at least partly disjoint. This suggests that the distinction of subitising and counting maps onto a distinction of their neurological underpinnings (Sathian et al. 1999). In this study, participants sat in front of a computer monitor where they saw several vertical bars popping up (between one and eight bars). Their task was to tell, as fast as possible, how many bars they saw on the screen each time. While the subjects performed this task, Sathian and his colleagues measured changes in their regional cerebral blood flow, using a PET (positron emission tomography) scan. These changes indicate areas of higher activity in the brain. By comparing the PET images they got during cardinality assessments for five to eight bars with those for one to four bars, Sathian et al. were able to identify specific regions that were activated in the first conditions, but not in the second ones, and vice versa. This contrast suggests that the distinction of

---

[3] Hitch et al. (1987). Similar results were obtained from studies with adult subjects (cf. Logie and Baddeley 1987; Buchner et al. 1998).

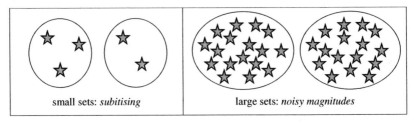

| small sets: *subitising* | large sets: *noisy magnitudes* |

Figure 30 Which is the larger set of each pair? Subitising versus noisy magnitudes

mental processes involved in subitising and counting of visual objects is at least to some degree reflected on the neurological level.

Whereas cardinalities up to three or four can be recognised fast and distinctively, we cannot grasp precise cardinalities of larger sets at a glance. Our representation of larger quantities, as long as it is not based on counting, is not distinct, but rather fuzzy and continuous; it gives us only approximate sizes for sets, so-called 'noisy magnitudes'. If counting is not possible (for instance because the objects are shown for only a very short time) one makes significantly more errors in cardinality assessments for sets with more than three elements, compared to sets of one to three objects. Our estimation for larger sets is less reliable, and it also takes longer: in (non-counting) cardinality assessments for larger sets, both response times and standard deviations increase in direct proportion to the size of sets.[4]

Accordingly, when sets become larger we can discriminate the cardinality of two sets only if the difference is big enough. If counting is not possible, accuracy can be shown to be a function of set size and numerical distance: the larger the sets and the closer their sizes, the less accurate is the comparison of their cardinalities. You can try this out by comparing – without counting! – in Figure 30 the cardinalities of the two small sets of stars on the left side (within the subitising range) and the cardinalities of the two larger sets on the right side (out of the subitising range: 'noisy magnitudes').

Both subitising and our representation of 'noisy magnitudes' provide a notion of cardinality that is independent of language, but they are of different precision. The mechanism of subitising enables us to grasp the cardinality of small sets accurately and nearly instantaneously: without counting, we can discriminate sets of one, two, and three objects confidently at a glance. For sets with more than three elements, however, things get fuzzier when counting is excluded. We cannot grasp precise cardinalities of larger sets at a glance, but have to rely on continuous and approximate

---

[4] Cf. Whalen et al. (1999).

rather than distinct and exact representations of numerical quantities. It is counting that allows us to generalise a concept of precise quantification to sets of any size; it introduces a distinct notion of cardinality that is independent of the size of the quantified set.

This has been employed, anecdotally, in an old piece of hunting advice: to kill a raven that has its nest atop a tower, seven men must go into the tower; six of them must come out of it again while the raven is watching. Since the raven cannot tell six men from seven, it will fly back onto the tower, and can then be shot by the man who stayed behind. If, on the other hand, only three men go into the tower, with two of them coming out of it again, the raven will stay in the air, knowing that one man is still hiding inside the tower. It cannot count the way we do, employing counting words as numerical tools. A raven can only grasp small quantities distinctively, because it does not have the cognitive equipment to systematically assign numbers to objects in order to count sets of any size. To discriminate between different cardinalities, it therefore has to depend on perceptual quantitative differences.

The ability to figure out relationships between small quantities without employing numerical tools has also been observed – with kinder motives – in human infants. Hence, while the language faculty might be crucial for the emergence of a full-blown concept of number (as in fact I hope to convince you in the present chapter), one does not need language to discriminate the cardinality of small sets and to figure out that three minus two is one. Since the early pioneering work of Jean Piaget and his collaborators, when children were believed to have very little understanding of the cardinality of sets before their fourth or fifth year of life,[5] a lot of experimental work has been done not only on pre-schoolers, but also on infants and newborns, revealing a surprisingly sophisticated early grasp of small cardinalities. Let us have a closer look at the experimental evidence for such abilities in preverbal infants and in animals in the following sections.[6]

Before counting: babies know 'How many'

Our capacity to distinguish small cardinalities is probably inborn, or is at least developed by a very early age. Sue Antell and Daniel Keating have

[5] For an exposition of Piaget's account cf. Piaget (1941). A critical discussion of his claims in the light of recent experimental evidence can be found in Dehaene (1997: ch. 2).

[6] Overviews of the grasp of cardinality and quantitative relations by animals and human infants can be found in Wynn (1993); Dehaene (1997: chs. 1 and 2); Carey (1998); and Butterworth (1999: ch. 3). Gallistel (1990) and Davis (1993) review evidence from animal studies.

shown that newborns in their first week of life already discriminate between the cardinalities two and three (Antell and Keating 1983). In their experiments, Antell and Keating used a 'habituation' technique that is based on differences in looking time: babies will look longer at novel stimuli than at stimuli they have got used to. If you show a baby similar objects, say, teddy bears, again and again, after a while she usually loses interest and will look at the next bear for a shorter and shorter time, indicating that she has become 'habituated' to this stimulus. If you then show her a new kind of object, for instance a ball, she will look at it longer again. In studies on infant cognition, this phenomenon can be used in order to find out what counts as a novel stimulus for the baby, that is, what kinds of distinctions are available for her.[7]

Antell and Keating showed babies not teddy bears, but different pictures of two dots (on these pictures the dots were sometimes closer together and sometimes further apart, but there were always two), and measured the time they spent looking at them. After a habituation phase, they presented the babies with pictures of three dots. Infants as young as one to three days of age looked significantly longer now. They looked longer at pictures of three dots after being habituated to two dots, and vice versa: they also looked longer at pictures of two dots after being habituated to three dots. This finding suggests that the babies were able to discriminate small cardinalities, the cardinality of sets with two and sets with three elements, in their first days of life.

Other studies provide evidence for the abstract nature of this ability: it is independent of a specific modality, it is not linked to a particular configuration of the objects, and it is not tied to the objects' identity (that is, the elements of the sets can be exchanged as long as their cardinality stays the same). Infants in their first year of life have been shown to discriminate between sets whose elements could be photographs showing different object of various sizes and in different configurations (Starkey et al. 1990); moving visual objects like patterns on a video screen (van Loosbroek and Smitsman 1990); events like the jumps of a doll (Wynn 1996); sounds like drum beats (Starkey et al. 1990), and even syllables of spoken words (Bijeljac-Babic et al. 1993).

As we discussed in chapter 2, cardinality – unlike, for instance, colour – is not a property of objects, but of sets. And these sets are not just random collections of things, but collections of objects that are subsumed under a certain concept: cardinality depends on a particular classification of objects.

---

[7] For a discussion of differences in looking times and an overview of its impact for studies on infant cognition, cf. Bornstein (1985).

So, for instance, the fruits I have here in a bowl on my desk can count as six fruits, or as two apples, three bananas, and one pear, or as three kinds of fruits, that is, they have the cardinality 6 if the relevant concept is *fruit*, and the cardinality 3 if our concept is *kind of fruit*, and so on. This is how Frege put it:

while I am not in a position, simply by thinking of it differently, to alter the colour or hardness of a thing in the slightest, I am able to think of the Iliad either as one poem, or as 24 books, or as some large number of verses. (Frege 1884: § 22)

For young infants in particular such early salient concepts as *physical object* or *discrete sound* are available for set formation.[8] In addition, as Karen Wynn and her colleagues showed, infants might even be able to employ concepts as sophisticated as *group*. In their study, five-month-olds were shown to discriminate two and four groups of objects (Wynn et al. 2002): the infants distinguished between a presentation where they saw two groups of dots moving on a computer screen, and another one where they saw four moving groups, that is, they distinguished sets whose elements were *groups of objects*, rather than individual objects.

As the discussion from the previous section suggests, our early capacity to distinguish the cardinality of sets precisely is limited to small sets with up to three or four elements. For instance, infants who were shown to discriminate between two and three dots did not react to the difference between four dots and six dots (Starkey and Cooper 1980). However, infants can tell apart sets of higher cardinalities if the difference is large enough: in a study conducted by Fei Xu and Elizabeth Spelke, six-month-old infants who did not discriminate between pictures of eight dots and pictures of twelve dots, did react to the difference between eight and sixteen dots (Xu and Spelke 2000). This suggests an early ability to grasp approximate sizes of larger sets along the lines we discussed above, that is, it suggests an early representation of 'noisy magnitudes'.

Wynn (1992a, 1998) showed that infants as young as five months can also perform simple arithmetic operations on small sets, similar to that of the unfortunate raven from above. In Wynn's experiments an infant was placed in front of an open case with a puppet in it. A small screen then rotated up, concealing the puppet from the baby's view. The experimenter brought a second puppet in full view of the infant, and placed it behind the screen, out of the infant's sight. Then the screen rotated downwards and revealed either two puppets (the expected outcome, since 1 puppet + 1

---

[8] We will discuss the development of cardinality assessments that involve concepts like *kinds of fruits* in chapter 5.

puppet = 2 puppets), or only one puppet (the unexpected outcome). In the second experiment two puppets sat in the case in the beginning. After the screen came up, one puppet was taken out of the case, in view of the infant. When the screen came down, there was either one puppet in the case (the expected outcome, since 2 puppets − 1 puppet = 1 puppet), or there were two puppets (the unexpected outcome).

What is exciting is that the infants looked significantly longer at the stages with the seemingly impossible outcome than at those with the expected outcome. This difference in the amount of time the infants spend in examining the scene has been shown in other, independent, studies to differentiate between expected and unexpected events: infants do not only look longer at novel stimuli (as in Antell and Keating's experiments from above), but also at stimuli that seem to present impossible events, and thus violate their knowledge of the world. Hence, like you and me, the infants were surprised to see one puppet instead of two in the '1 + 1'-case, and two instead of one in the '2 − 1'-case. This suggests that they could not only distinguish sets of one versus two elements, but even perform simple arithmetic operations on them.[9]

Taken together, these findings indicate that babies have a concept of cardinality that provides them with precise representations of smaller sets and forms the basis for addition and subtraction, and is supplemented by a representation of noisy magnitudes for larger sets.

Quantitative and sequential concepts in other species

The evidence discussed in the previous section indicates that our ability to subitise the cardinality of small sets, to perform simple arithmetic operations on them, and to estimate the size of larger sets is present from a very early age and might in fact be inborn. It suggests that humans have a biologically determined concept of cardinality that is independent of the acquisition of language. This does not necessarily imply, though, that this concept is independent of language as a mental faculty. While infants have not acquired a particular language yet, they do possess the human language faculty as part of their (species-specific) mental repertoire.

It is for this reason that the evidence from animal studies is of particular interest for our discussion: it shows that these early numerical capacities

---

[9] These results have been replicated in a number of subsequent studies with different experimental set-ups, among them experiments with moving objects, that is, with objects that were placed on a revolving platform (Koechlin et al. 1997), and even with objects whose identity changed (Simon et al. 1995). Starkey (1992) reports similar results from a study with one- to four-year-olds. For an overview cf. also Wynn (1998).

exist not only in humans, but also in other species, hence species that do not possess the human language faculty as part of their biological heritage. The evidence that I review in the following paragraphs suggests that the emergence of a full-blown number concept in humans could build on pre-existing and language-independent capacities we share with other species, capacities that support our understanding of cardinality and sequential order and our grasp of simple arithmetic operations.

Cardinality of sets
Converging evidence from animal studies suggests that our concept of car-dinality can build on an evolutionarily old capacity that we share with other species, and in particular with other warm-blooded vertebrates. Mammals and birds have been shown to grasp the cardinality of sets of objects pre-sented successively and simultaneously and displayed this capacity not only with concrete objects, but also with sets of sounds and sets of events, like light flashes, suggesting that the comprehension of cardinality in higher an-imals is not restricted to a specific modality (say, to that of visual objects).

For instance, in laboratory studies ravens and crows have been trained to match sets of dots or grains of the same cardinality (Koehler 1941, 1943, 1950; Smirnova et al. 2000). Pigeons learned to discriminate between sequentially presented sounds or lights that varied in frequency (Roberts and Mitchell 1994). A raccoon has been taught to pick, from an array of transparent plastic cubes that contained between one and five objects, always the cube with three items (Davis 1984); and rats learned to eat a fixed number of food pellets (Davis and Bradford 1991), to press a lever for a fixed number of times, and to discriminate sets of two and four items that could be objects or sounds or even mixed sets of objects and sounds (Meck and Church 1983).

In their natural environment, American coots (a kind of rail) lay eggs up to a certain clutch size, using as a clue the number of their own eggs that are already in the nest (ignoring – when they recognise them – 'parasitic' eggs that other coots managed to smuggle into the nest; cf. Lyon 2003). Female lions compare the number of their own group with that of other lions intruding on their territory. Field experiments have shown that they can base their assessment of the intruders' group on the number of different roars they hear – that is, they base it on the cardinality of a set of sounds (McComb et al. 1994).

Some animals also learned to interpret arbitrary objects as an index for different cardinalities. Robert Mitchell and his colleagues trained a captive dolphin named Phoenix to associate different plastic objects (like bowls and trays) with different amounts of fish. In the experiment, Phoenix had to choose between two of these objects and would then get a certain number of fish. For instance she would find a mixing bowl and an ice-cube tray in her training pool. When picking up the bowl she would get two fish, whereas choosing the tray would get her four fish. After an initial training with small amounts of fish, Phoenix learned to associate up to five different plastic objects with different amounts of fish (Mitchell et al. 1985).

After extensive training, some animals that had previously taken part in language studies and hence had some experience in labelling, were able to represent different cardinalities with number words or arabic numerals. Tetsuro Matsuzawa trained his chimpanzee Ai to select one of the arabic numerals 1 to 6 when presented with up to six items on a computer display (Matsuzawa 1985). Ai also learned to arrange arabic numerals according to their conventional order (Biro and Matsuzawa 1999; Kawai and Matsuzawa 2000). This sequential skill was also involved in the performance of Austin, a chimpanzee famous from various language studies conducted by Sue Savage-Rumbaugh and her colleagues (we will discuss more evidence for the grasp of sequential order in animals below). Austin learned to react to an arabic numeral on a computer screen by selecting either individual dots or fixed sequences of numerals with a cursor (Beran et al. 1998). For instance, he would see '3' on the screen, and then either select three dots, one at a time, or select the numerals '1', then '2', and then '3'.

Alex, an African grey parrot trained by Irene Pepperberg, has been taught to answer 'How many?'-questions for sets of objects (Pepperberg 1987, 1999). What is more, his performance suggests that he managed to link cardinality to a classification of objects. As we discussed above, cardinality (unlike colour) belongs to sets of objects that fall under a certain concept, it depends on a particular classification of objects, and this means for instance that the same entity can constitute different sets with different cardinalities. After learning verbal labels like 'toy', 'key', 'cork', 'thimble', and 'wood' and the first six number words of English, Alex showed at least some understanding of this aspect of cardinality. For instance, when presented with two thimbles and four pieces of wood he was able not only to give the cardinality of the whole set ('six'), but also to tell how many thimbles ('two') or how many pieces of wood there were ('four'), suggesting that he could grasp the cardinalities of sets that are based on different classifications of objects.

Arithmetic operations on the cardinality of sets
Animals can not only discriminate different cardinalities, but also perform simple arithmetic operations on them. In a field experiment on the island of

Addition: (0+)1 + 1

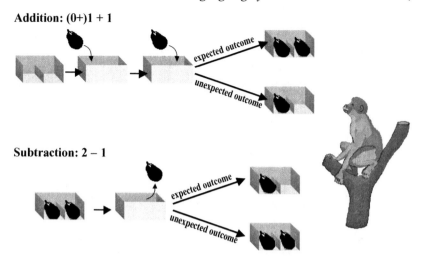

Subtraction: 2 − 1

Figure 31 Testing mental arithmetic in rhesus monkeys (Hauser et al. 1996)

Cayo Santiago in Puerto Rico, Marc Hauser, Pogen MacNeilage, and Molly Ware showed that rhesus monkeys have some understanding of addition and subtraction similar to that of the babies in Karen Wynn's study (Hauser et al. 1996). For their experiment, Hauser and his colleagues used a display box with two compartments and a moveable screen, as in Figure 31. They waited until a monkey watched them and saw the empty box, then they placed the screen in front of the compartments and put first one and then another eggplant into the box, and finally raised the screen again, showing two eggplants.

However, there was a hidden pocket in the back of the screen that enabled them to secretly remove an eggplant from the box before the screen was raised. So sometimes, instead of seeing two eggplants ($1+1 = 2$), the monkeys saw only one after the screen was raised. Hauser and his colleagues found that in these 'impossible' events, the monkeys looked significantly longer at the box, indicating that the outcome violated their expectations.

Similarly, when the experimenters placed two eggplants in the box, raised the screen and then removed one eggplant, the monkeys expected one vegetable to be left over ($2 − 1 = 1$): when Hauser surreptitiously added an eggplant from the hidden pocket, so that there were two vegetables in the box when the screen went down, the monkeys looked longer at these seemingly impossible outcomes than at the expected ones where one eggplant was left in the box. These findings suggest that rhesus monkeys are able to perform some basic mental arithmetic in their natural environment.

Rebecca West and Robert Young observed a similar performance in the '1 + 1'-task for dogs, using doggie treats instead of eggplants (West and Young 2002): in their experiment, the dogs looked significantly longer when they saw one or three treats when the screen came up than when they saw two treats, suggesting that domestic dogs, just like monkeys, can perform '1 + 1'-additions on objects.

In a lab experiment with chimpanzees, Duane M. Rumbaugh, Sue Savage-Rumbaugh, and Mark Hegel presented their subjects with a choice of two trays, each with two piles of chocolates. The chimpanzees could see both trays, but were only allowed to pick one of them. Since chimpanzees like chocolates, too, they would try to get the tray which had more chocolates, that is, the tray with the piles that added up to a greater overall quantity of chocolates.

What made the decision difficult was that the tray with the biggest single pile was not necessarily the tray which held the most chocolates altogether. For instance, on one tray there could be two piles of three chocolates each, and on the other tray a pile of four chocolates together with a single chocolate. In order to pick the tray with most chocolates the chimps had to summate the chocolates, that is, they had to compute 3 + 3 versus 4 + 1. They succeeded at this task without elaborate training, reliably choosing the pair of piles with the greater overall sum, a finding that suggests that they were able to summate the chocolates (Rumbaugh et al. 1987).

A chimpanzee called Sheba, trained by Sarah Boysen, learned not only to label sets of objects (like oranges) with the arabic numerals 1 to 4, but could also perform additions on both the objects *and* on the cardinalities represented by numerals (Boysen 1993). After extensive training on arabic numerals and their association with cardinalities, Sheba first learned to search a cage for different sets of fruits hidden at particular locations. After finding all the fruits, she had to pick from several cards with numerals printed on them the one that presented their overall sum. For instance, she would find two oranges in one location and three in the other location, and then had to select a '5'. At the next stage, she had to transfer this summation to arabic numerals that were substituted for the fruits: now, she would find a '2' in one location and a '3' in the other location, and had to select a '5'. She eventually succeeded even on this latter task, suggesting that she not only learned to represent sets of different cardinalities by labels, but that she could also transfer her knowledge of cardinal relations between sets to the labels that represented these sets.

Serial order

Another gift from our mental heritage is the apprehension of serial order, and – related to this – of an object's position within a progression, a capacity that underlies both our grasp of counting procedures and our concept of numerical rank. Again, this capacity was demonstrated in a number of experiments with different animal species, among them canaries, rats, monkeys, and apes.

In the early 1960s, Nicholas Pastore trained canary birds to identify always the fourth or fifth object in a row (Pastore 1961). In his experiments, the birds learned to pick the fourth or fifth tablet in a series of aspirins, where the tablets were unevenly distributed over several cubicles along a runway (for instance, the first cubicle could contain two tablets, the next one none, the next cubicle would contain one aspirin, and so on), so that the only clue the birds could use for their task was the overall sequence of aspirins they had encountered thus far.

Rats have been trained always to enter a tunnel with a particular rank in a maze (for instance, always the third, the fourth, or the fifth tunnel), or to enter a particular box in an array of boxes.[10] The experiments were set up in a way that the rats could not use clues like a tunnel's absolute location within the maze or a tunnel's relative location within the entire sequence. To account for the first aspect, the distance between tunnels would be varied, so that the fourth tunnel could be closer to the entrance or further down the route. To account for the second point, the total number of tunnels would be varied, so that the fourth tunnel would for instance be closer to the beginning (when there are, say, twenty tunnels altogether), or in the middle (when there are seven tunnels altogether), or closer to the end (when there are only six tunnels altogether).

The rats' success at this task – apart from confirming that rats are rather smart creatures – indicates that they can form a concept of rank that is independent of accidental spatial features. It is this concept of rank that we relate to in ordinal number assignments. It allows us to grasp the empirical property we identify with numbers in ordinal assignments.

The concept of sequential order is also involved when we apply numbers in a numerical subroutine like counting, as a basis for our cardinal number assignments. As we have seen above, counting involves access to a conventionally ordered progression (for instance, a sequence of counting words that we use as numerical tools). The ability to grasp such an ordering

---

[10] Cf. Davis and Bradford (1986). Suzuki and Kobayashi (2000) replicated these results in an extended paradigm.

was evident in the performance of Ai and of Austin, the chimpanzees we encountered above. Remember that both Ai and Austin learned, as part of their training on labelling cardinalities, to arrange arabic numerals in their conventional order.

More evidence for a concept of sequential order in animals comes from studies with monkeys. In a memory task for sequentially presented triplets of pictures, macaque monkeys tended to mix up images that had the same position within their respective triplets; for instance they would mistake the second picture from one triplet with the second picture from another triplet. This type of error suggests that they categorised the images by their sequential positions (Orlov et al. 2000).

Macaques have also been shown to represent cardinalities of sets in an ascending order. Elizabeth Brannon and Herbert Terrace trained rhesus macaques to select sets of one to four pictures in an order of 1-2-3-4, that is, they had to touch the stimulus with one element first, then the one with two elements, then three, and finally the one with four elements. In subsequent experiments, the monkeys were able to extrapolate this ordering rule to sets with up to nine elements. Brannon and Terrace interpreted this as evidence that macaques can represent cardinalities in an ordinal sequence. Monkeys who had been trained on a descending order (4-3-2-1) could not extrapolate the ordering rule, while attempts to train them on a numerically random order (3-1-4-2) failed altogether, suggesting that the monkeys in this study represented the cardinalities indeed not as unrelated individual tokens, but in an ascending order (Brannon and Terrace 1998).

NUMBER SENSE AND BEYOND

The evidence we reviewed in the preceding sections suggests that humans possess a concept of numerical quantities and their interrelations and a concept of sequential order that we share with other species, concepts that are independent of the acquisition of a specific language and independent of the human language faculty in general. Does this mean that our concept of *number* is independent of language? The results from our discussion of numbers indicate that the answer is 'No'. There is more to our concept of number than a grasp of cardinality or of sequential positions.

According to the view I put forward in the preceding chapters, numbers are tools that enable us to assess different properties of objects; they can bear on quantitative aspects (cardinality of sets), ordinal aspects (rank of objects within a sequence), and nominal aspects (identity of objects within a set) *in application*, that is, when employed in the different kinds of number assignments. This approach integrates cardinality and sequential rank into a broader view of the number domain. Under this account, cardinality and sequential position are linked to our number concept as properties that we can identify with numbers, but they are not part of numbers per se. The argument I am going to pursue in the remainder of this chapter is that language contributed to numerical cognition not by providing us with a concept of cardinality (or sequential position), but in a more fundamental way: the emergence of language enabled humans to integrate these concepts into a generalised concept of number.

What the evidence that we reviewed in the preceding sections shows is that our understanding of the empirical properties we assess with numbers – like cardinality or sequential position – has a non-linguistic basis. These properties are represented by concepts that are evident both in pre-verbal infants and in other species and hence presumably have developed independently of and prior to language. In particular, the evidence from studies on quantitative abilities in human infants and animals has received a lot of attention in the discussion of numerical cognition and its basis. This evidence suggests that we are equipped with an early concept of cardinality that is independent of our language faculty and has the following characteristics:

- It involves a mechanism ('subitising') that enables us to discriminate small sets accurately and nearly instantaneously.
- It allows us to grasp the approximate size of larger sets ('noisy magnitudes').
- It represents cardinality as an abstract property of sets that is not restricted to a particular modality.
- It allows us to compare the cardinality of different sets and to grasp quantitative relationships between them.
- It can be associated with arbitrary labels, and these labels can relate cardinality to a specific classification of objects.

These early concepts of (exact and approximate) sizes of sets establish what Stanislas Dehaene called the 'number sense' (Dehaene 1997): a domain-specific ability that we share with higher animals and that provides us with an apprehension of quantities and their interrelations.

The 'number sense' forms an early basis for our understanding of *cardinal number assignments*; however it does not yet involve a systematic concept of number. In view of our discussion above, we can think of Dehaene's number sense as an ability to grasp cardinalities, rather than numbers. It is not surprising that such an ability would be found in different species: the ability to discriminate sets with respect to their cardinality has obvious evolutionary advantages in a wide range of contexts. It provides valuable information for instance in such vital activities as foraging (which tree offers more fruits?), infant care (are none of the offspring missing?), or territorial defence (can we outnumber the intruders?).

Brian Butterworth relates our grasp of cardinality to a mental organ he calls the 'number module': 'The job of the Number Module is to categorize the world in terms of numerosities – the number of things in a collection.' (Butterworth 1999: 7). Again, 'number' in this context refers to cardinality, rather than to the numerical tools we have defined in our account.

In calling our ability to recognise cardinalities (or 'numerosities') a mental module, Butterworth refers to a concept proposed by Jerry Fodor. Fodor identifies three main features that characterise a module: (1) modular mental systems operate fast and mandatorily, (2) they are domain-specific and informationally encapsulated, and (3) they often have a fixed neural architecture, that is, a typical module has a dedicated brain area as its neurological underpinning, and accordingly can show specific breakdown patterns after brain damage.[11]

Hence, modular processing works a bit like a reflex: automatically and with only limited feedback from other systems. This distinguishes modular systems from central cognitive processes, like belief fixation and problem solving. These processes operate on information from input modules; they are non-modular and can make use of a wide range of data. Two of my favourite examples of modular processing come from the domain of visual representation. You can experience your visual input module at work when looking at the two graphics in Figure 32. On the left side you can see two parallel lines. Both lines have exactly the same length, and you can check this for instance by measuring them. However, even though you *know* that they are the same, my guess is that you will still see the top line as shorter than the bottom line, due to the different chevrons attached to their ends. No matter what your higher-level knowledge might tell you, no matter what you believe to be true, your visual system will represent the lines as of different lengths. It works compulsorily and independently of our belief system, with the effect that one cannot help seeing the upper line as shorter. Similarly, on the right side of Figure 32, our visual system construes a white

---

[11] Cf. Fodor (1983). Note, though, that neurological underpinnings do not imply that the emergence of a module is genetically pre-specified and based on innate domain-specific mechanisms (as is often assumed). According to a neuroconstructive approach as put forward by Annette Karmiloff-Smith, we could also regard a mental module as something that develops over time and in interaction with the cognitive environment, that is, it emerges as a result of developmental specialisation from domain-relevant, but initially general (rather than domain-specific) mechanisms (cf. Karmiloff-Smith 1998).

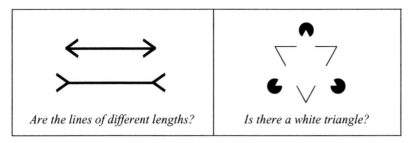

Are the lines of different lengths?	*Is there a white triangle?*

Figure 32 Modularity: the representation of visual information is independent of beliefs

triangle, even though we *know* that there is none.[12] Hence our visual input module works automatically and by itself; it generates visual representations unhampered by any higher-level cognitive processes (like the belief that the two lines are actually of the same length, or that there is no white triangle in front).

Along similar lines, our grasp of small cardinalities has all the virtues of a well-behaved module. The processing of quantitative information we experience in subitising is fast (as we have seen above, it is nearly instantaneous), mandatory (one just cannot help seeing, say, the three stars in Figure 29 above as a set of three), and it is informationally encapsulated and does not access higher-level cognitive processes (independently of what someone might try to make you believe, you will see the three stars as three).

What is more, this mental system seems to have a fixed neural architecture that can be affected by brain damage, hence like a proper module it seems to be 'hard-wired'. Evidence from lesion and brain-imaging studies suggests that a specific brain region, presumably the inferior parietal cortex, is associated with our language-independent ability to recognise cardinalities.[13] Accordingly, our ability to subitise can break down independently of numerical skills like counting. This was the case for Signora Gaddi, a patient discussed by Brian Butterworth (1999: ch. 4). After suffering a stroke that damaged the left parietal lobe of her brain, Signora Gaddi could not subitise small cardinalities anymore. To determine the cardinality of a set, she had to count its elements, no matter how few there were. For instance, to find out that there are three stars on the left side of Figure 29 above, she would have to go 'one, two, three'. Signora Gaddi lost her ability to

[12] This figure is from a 1955 paper on the formation of contours in visual perception by Gaetano Kanizsa (Kanizsa 1955: 16, fig. 11).
[13] Cf. Dehaene (1997) and the overviews in Dehaene et al. (1998, 1999). Brian Butterworth reviews case studies that suggest that subitising might have its neuronal underpinnings specifically in the left inferior lobule (Butterworth 1999: ch. 4).

recognise small cardinalities at a glance, and had to employ the numerical procedure of counting instead.

Hence, the mental module that supports subitising helps us to grasp the cardinality of sets, but it can be dissociated from our ability to employ numerical routines in number assignments. In fact, as I have argued above, cardinality by itself does not imply the assignment of numbers at all. Cardinality is only one of the properties we can assess with numbers, albeit a prominent one. A concept of cardinality neither involves the representation of numerical tools – a potentially infinite progression of well-distinguished entities – nor does it involve the representation of number assignments, that is, the application of these tools by way of dependent linking.

It is this pattern of dependent linking, a mapping between relational structures, that gives us a genuine number assignment. As I have shown above, in cardinal, ordinal, and nominal number assignments alike, a relation between empirical objects is associated with a relation between numbers. In cardinal number assignments we associate the numerical relation '>' with the empirical relation 'has more elements than'; in ordinal number assignments we associate the numerical relation '<' (or '>', respectively) with the relative ranks of objects within a progression; in nominal number assignments we associate the numerical relation '=' (or '≠') with the empirical relation 'is (non-)identical with'. It is this association of relations that constitutes number assignments, and by doing so lays the grounds for systematic numerical cognition.

How did this pattern evolve? In the following section I suggest that the translation of relational structures has its origins in the emergence of language. I will argue that it is the human language faculty that made this pattern available to the human mind, and thus enabled us to develop a systematic number concept; language contributes the mental equipment that allows us to cross the boundaries of these early pre-numerical concepts, bringing together our grasp of different empirical properties in a pattern of dependent linking. I show that this view is supported by a number of structural and material correspondences between language and number which suggest that in the development of our species, the human language faculty played a pivotal role in the evolution of systematic numerical cognition.

My argument will be based on three main pillars: I will show that (1) the emergence of language as a symbolic system provided the basis for the use of numbers as tools, by giving us a cognitive pattern for dependent linking, (2) the linguistic routine of conventional association (associations between linguistic signs and their referents) supports the use of counting words as conventional tools in this linking, and (3) the recursive rules underlying linguistic constructions give us a handle on infinity and can be put to use in our number domain through the medium of counting words.

SYMBOLIC REFERENCE AND THE EVOLUTION OF LANGUAGE

In his 1997 book on language evolution, *The Symbolic Species*, Terrence Deacon argues that the main step in the emergence of human language (as opposed to animal communication systems) is the development of a *symbolic* system, a system of signs that refer to objects due to the relations that hold between them. According to Deacon, in a process of coevolution of language and the brain, the adaptation of our brain to symbolic thinking gave rise to the development of the linguistic capacity we have today. To understand the significance of this view for our investigation into numbers and language, it is crucial to understand what Deacon means by *symbolic reference* here.

Following a semiotic taxonomy introduced by Charles Sanders Peirce,[14] Deacon distinguishes three kinds of signs: icons, indices, and symbols. Let me briefly characterise the different semiotic domains in turn, as a background for our discussion of symbolic thinking and its significance for numerical cognition.

In iconic reference, the sign shares certain features with its referent, which makes it similar to the object it refers to. An example of such a sign is the icon ♿ that refers to a wheel-chair user. You also find examples of icons on traffic signs warning you of animals crossing the road. These signs might show you images of cows or deer, of elks (as in Sweden), or of camels (as in the Arab Emirates). In these cases you can identify the kind of animal that the sign refers to because the picture resembles the animal. Here is an example I found on a road in Scotland (Figure 33). It combines an iconic and a symbolic sign that both refer to squirrels: an image of a squirrel, and the word 'SQUIRRELS'. In order to understand what the icon means, one makes use of the visual similarity between the image and a squirrel: the sign looks like the silhouette of a squirrel, so we can figure out that it is meant to identify these animals. For the symbolic sign no such similarity is available. To understand the word 'squirrel', one has to know a lexical item of a symbolic system, namely the English language.

---

[14] Cf. Peirce (1931: 2.227ff.).

SQUIRRELS CROSSING

Figure 33 How to refer to squirrels: iconic versus symbolic reference

Before we discuss the workings of symbols in more detail, let us have a look at indexical signs. In indexical reference, the sign is related to the object by a physical or temporal relation; it occurs together with its referent. For instance, if I had the habit of performing a somersault whenever I see a dachshund – and only in these cases – then you could take my somersaults as an index for the presence of these dogs. As a more common example, tears could be interpreted as an index for grief.

The alarm calls used by some animal species might also be based on indexical reference. The vervet monkeys from Kenya's Amboseli National Park have become famous among linguists and anthropologists for their different alarm calls. In a number of studies conducted in the late 70s and 80s, the primatologists Robert Seyfarth and Dorothy Cheney and their colleagues systematically distinguished three different calls that the monkeys produced when seeing different kinds of predators: an alarm call for leopards, one for eagles, and another one for snakes.[15]

When hearing the different calls, the members of the monkey group reacted with different – and appropriate – patterns of behaviour: running up into trees (to escape from a leopard), looking into the sky and rushing out of the tree (where an eagle might attack), and peering carefully into the grass around them (to detect a snake). This distinction has been shown to be independent of the intensity of the call and independent of the actual presence of the caller (that is, the monkeys showed the same behaviour

---

[15] Cf. Seyfarth et al. (1980). These calls were first described by Tom Struhsacker (1967). You can find an overview of these and related studies in Cheney's and Seyfarth's work on 'How Monkeys See the World' (Cheney and Seyfarth 1990).

when they heard tape recordings of alarm calls), which suggests an – at least – indexical understanding of these alarm calls in vervet monkeys.

Biochemists discovered a phenomenon in the plant kingdom that looks somewhat similar: chemical information transfer between plants.[16] For instance, when attacked by herbivores like spider mites, lima beans produce chemicals that make their leaves less suitable as food, and emit chemicals into the air that attract natural predators of the attackers, for instance predatory mites. The combination of chemicals the plants emit to their environment is different when they are attacked by different kinds of predators, and when they suffer mechanical damage, for instance when hit by a cow's hoof.

What is interesting now is that other plants in the vicinity of the attacked plant show distinct and – again – appropriate reactions to the different chemicals that the attacked plant emits. In particular, when exposed to the 'mite warning', they produce chemicals that act as a defence against spider mites, whereas in reaction to the chemicals indicating the danger of mechanical damage they do not. This has been interpreted as a plant–plant interaction mediated by specific and differentiated airborne signals, which allows lima beans to prepare defences against spider mites in advance (cf. Arimura et al. 2000; Arimura and Takabayashi 2001) – a pattern that reminds one a bit of the alarm calls we encountered in vervet monkeys. While the similarity might not go too far,[17] it demonstrates that the reactions of plants to danger can show a pattern that allows an indexical semiotic interpretation, too.

In symbolic reference, now, the link between sign and object is established by convention, as in the case of human languages. As Deacon emphasises, the crucial point about symbolic reference is that this link is mediated by relations between the signs: symbols are always part of a system, and they refer to objects not as individual tokens, but with respect to their position in that system. In the case of symbols, reference shifts from individual signs and individual objects to relations between signs and relations between objects; it shifts from the token to the system. Symbols bring in a systematic complexity. In symbolic reference, you can produce not only alarm calls like "Leopard!", but also warnings like "There is a leopard creeping up the tree

---

[16] The journal *Biochemical Systematics and Ecology* has dedicated a special issue to this topic (Dicke and Bruin 2001).

[17] In particular, it seems plausible to assume that the alarm calls of vervet monkeys involve at least first-order intentions in the sense explicated by Daniel Dennett (Dennett 1987: ch. 7) – that is, their calls are not simply a manifestation of their fear, but involve beliefs or wishes; for instance a belief that a certain kind of predator is near, or the wish that other members of the group run up a tree – whereas one might rather hesitate to ascribe such a mental background to lima beans.

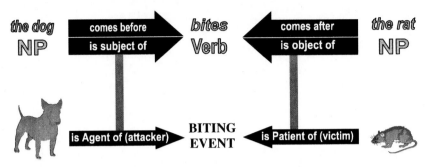

Figure 34 Symbolic and conceptual relations: 'The dog bites the rat'

right behind Sheba!" And those who hear a warning like that, can interpret who crouches up where and behind whom by figuring out the relations between the symbols in that call ('leopard', 'tree', 'Sheba' etc.).

Under this account, symbolic reference as the basis of human languages is crucially a link between relations (sign–sign relations and object–object relations), not between individuals (signs and objects). It is the relations between words that reference is based on. The relevant relations are linear relations like the order of words in a sentence, and hierarchical relations like 'object of' or 'subject of' which mark the relations between a verb and its complements. Let me spell this out for an example from English.

In the English sentence "The dog bites the rat" you know who is the attacker (the dog) and who is the victim (the rat), because the noun phrase 'the dog' comes before the verb, which is the position for the subject in English, and 'the rat' comes after the verb in object position, and the noun phrases in these positions denote the agent (attacker) and the patient (victim) of the 'biting'-action, respectively. So the connection one makes is between (a) symbolic relations like 'The words *the dog* come before the word *bites*' (linear) and 'The noun phrase *the dog* is subject of the verb *bite*' (hierarchical) and (b) relations between referents (that is, conceptual relations: relations between objects as they are represented to us by our conceptual system), namely 'The dog is the agent (attacker) in the biting-event'; and similarly for the rat (Figure 34).

To make clear how this association works, let me sketch a more explicit picture of the human language system in the following paragraphs, as a background for our discussion. The linguistic system involves representations from three subsystems: PHON (for phonetic–phonological structures), SYN (for syntactic structures), and SEM (for semantic

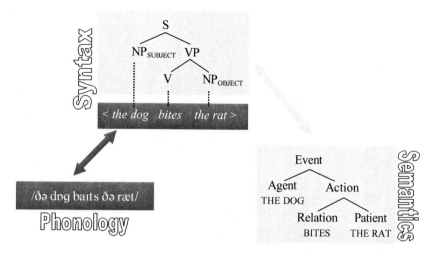

Figure 35 Different levels of representation: 'The dog bites the rat'

structures).[18] The crucial connection we want to make in language is now that between PHON and SEM: ultimately, in language we want to get from sound to meaning and vice versa;[19] we want to make the connection between a sound string like 'the dog bites the rat' and the representation of an event where the dog bites the rat. In human language, this connection is mediated by the syntactic system. This system, SYN, correlates linear order from the phonological system ('comes before / after') with hierarchical order in the semantic-conceptual system ('is agent of / patient of').

Figure 35 gives a simplified overview of the different kinds of representations involved in our example of 'The dog bites the rat': '/ðə dɒg baɪts ðə ræt/' identifies the phonological representation, where empty spaces mark word boundaries; 'NP' stands for 'noun phrase', 'VP' for 'verb phrase', and 'S' for 'sentence'; I use angle brackets, < and >, to indicate the linear order between 'the dog', 'bites', and 'the rat' in the syntactic tree. The phonological representation of 'the dog bites the rat' on the bottom left of Figure 35 gives us a linear order, the succession of the words in the utterance: /ðə dɒg/ comes before /baɪts/, while /ðə ræt/ comes after /baɪts/. This linear order relates to the linear order of nodes in a syntactic tree: the noun phrase

---

[18] A detailed discussion of language as a threefold system can be found in Ray Jackendoff's proposal of a Tripartite Parallel Architecture for the human language faculty (Jackendoff 1997, 2002). In Wiese (2003 a,b) I give an account of linguistic interfaces as the relational structures that are involved in such a framework.

[19] 'Sound' is actually too specific: in sign languages the modality is not acoustic, but visual.

'the dog' is left of the verb 'bites', while the noun phrase 'the rat' is right of 'bites' (this connection between linear order in phonology and in syntax is marked by dark grey background colouring in Figure 35).

The syntactic tree structure itself establishes hierarchical relations between the respective elements: the NP 'the dog' is represented as the subject, it is the sister node of the verb phrase, while the noun phrase 'the rat' is the object of 'bites'; it is inside the VP as the sister node of the verb. Hence, positions in the tree (in our case: the position of an NP inside the VP versus outside the VP) mark syntactic functions ('subject of' versus 'object of').

This hierarchical structure in SYN is linked with a hierarchical representation of an event in the semantic system. This linking relates syntactic functions (subject / object) to thematic roles (agent / patient), based on specifications in the verb's lexical entry (the connection between hierarchical order in syntax and semantics is marked by light grey background colouring in Figure 35). In our example, we get the representation of an event consisting of an agent 'the dog' and its action, which sets up a 'biting'-relation with a patient 'the rat'. In other words: The dog bites the rat.

Hence, the connection between sound and meaning is carried out in language by a pattern of dependent linking, establishing a route from phonological to semantic representations (and vice versa) that goes via syntax and takes into account the relationships that hold between elements of the different subsystems. I summarise these links between relations for our example in (Figure 36). Note that there is no fixed one-to-one connection in syntax between particular linear positions and particular hierarchical positions (this distinction is depicted by the bold vertical line in Figure 36). For instance, in Figure 36 the connections are 'initial position – agent' and 'final position – patient', which is the canonical correspondence in English: the phrase in the initial position ('the dog') is the subject and refers to the agent (the attacker), and the phrase in the final position ('the rat') is the object of the verb and refers to the patient (the victim). However, we can also have just the opposite correspondences, for instance when we look at the same sentence in the passive voice: in 'The rat is bitten by the dog', it is now the final phrase ('the dog') that refers to the agent, and the phrase in initial position ('the rat') that refers to the patient. (a) and (b) bring the two examples together:

(a) active:	The dog	bites	the rat.
	agent		*patient*
(b) passive:	The rat	is bitten by	the dog.
	patient		*agent*

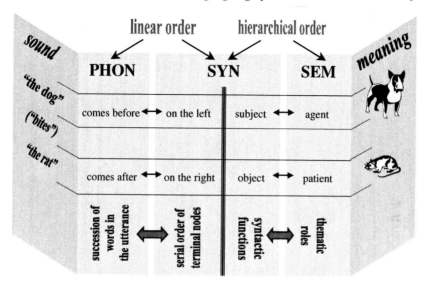

Figure 36 Association of relations from Phonology and Semantics via Syntax

Hence, linear positions and hierarchical positions are mediated by syntactic structures that can involve transformations like active–passive that affect the linear order of the phrases in the sentence. The syntactic system computes different links between the serial order of terminal nodes in a tree and the syntactic functions of the elements that occupy these nodes, and by so doing provides a particular translation from linear relationships like 'comes before / comes after' as established by the phonological representation, into hierarchical relationships like 'agent of / patient of' that are represented in the semantic system.

Another option would be to go straight from linear order in speech to hierarchical structure in the conceptual system, without involving syntactic computations. In this case, we would have an instance of *protolanguage* as described by Derek Bickerton (1990). A central feature of protolanguage is the limitation of syntactic organisation. According to Bickerton, protolanguage evolutionarily precedes modern language, but it can also emerge in modern contexts where a full-blown language is not available or is impaired. Examples of these contexts are early stages in first language acquisition (where the syntactic system of a full language is not yet available), the language of people who have been deprived of linguistic interaction in early years of their childhood (so-called 'feral children'), pidgins (which evolve in contact situations where no common language is available), or agrammatic aphasia (a linguistic impairment that typically occurs after brain damage in Broca's area in the left hemisphere; lesions in this area seem to affect the syntactic system and the interface between syntactic and semantic structures).

In a protolinguistic setting, constructions like passive would not work out anymore. If we only had the linear order of words to tell who bites whom, 'The dog bites the rat' and 'The dog is bitten by the rat' would come out just the same, since in both cases 'the dog' is in initial position and 'the rat' is in final position. Accordingly, sentences like passives are exactly the ones that cause problems for instance in agrammatic aphasia. Patients encounter difficulties with the interpretation of constructions where the correspondence between linear order and thematic roles differs from the canonical correspondence[20] (in English, this canonical correspondence is 'initial position – agent' and 'final position – patient', as in our example in Figure 36). We can interpret this as a problem to access the linear–hierarchical correspondences that are computed by the syntactic system in a full-blown (non-proto-) language.

Discussing possible stages in the evolution of language, Ray Jackendoff argued that language started most likely with these direct relationships between linear order and conceptual structures. In the course of language evolution, direct sound–meaning relationships were later replaced by links that were mediated by complex hierarchical syntax (Jackendoff 1999). Under the view of symbolic reference sketched here, this would mean that the focus of symbolic relationships shifts from linear relations to hierarchical relations: at an early stage in the evolution of language, *linear relations* between symbols as evident in speech ('comes before / after') would directly be associated with hierarchical relations between referents ('agent of / 'patient of'), whereas at a later stage we would have (syntactic) *hierarchical relations* between symbols, like 'subject of / object of', which can be linked up with hierarchical relations between referents.

What is important for our discussion here is that in both cases, it is the relationships that are crucial in this association, rather than individual symbols and individual referents. This is what symbolic reference is ultimately about: it is a connection between sound and meaning that focuses on relationships. How does this pattern relate to our discussion of numerical thinking now?

---

[20] Cf. Grodzinsky et al. (1999) for a detailed discussion of this pattern.

Figure 37 Number assignment as an association of relations (cf. chapter 1)

MATCHING PATTERNS IN SYMBOLIC REFERENCE AND NUMBER ASSIGNMENTS

According to our analysis from the previous section, symbolic reference boils down to a translation of relations: in symbolic reference we regard the signs and their referents only in so far as they are part of a system whose elements stand in specific relations to each other; the association of symbols and their referents is determined by the respective relations that hold between them.

And this, of course, is exactly what we identified as the basis of number assignments. As I pointed out above, number assignments are all about relations, too: in number assignments, we associate relations between numbers (for instance '<') with relations between empirical objects (for instance 'faster than') – just as in language we associate *symbolic* relations with relations between objects. This is what we called "dependent linking" in our discussion of number assignments: a correlation between elements (in our case, numbers and objects) that depends on the relationships in which these elements stand in their respective systems. Figure 37 illustrates this for our Marathon example from chapter 1, the ordinal assignment of numbers to runners according to their respective ranks in the race. Given the similarity between number assignments and symbolic reference, we can give a graphic account analogously to the one that spells out the reference in our linguistic example ('The dog bites the rat.') in Figure 34 (p. 116 above).

In short, when we assign numbers to empirical objects the links we establish are not between individual numbers and individual objects, but between a numerical relational structure and an empirical relational structure. And, similarly, when we assign symbols to their referents, the links we

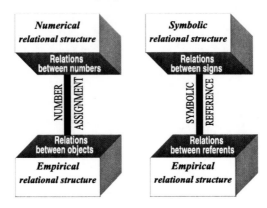

Figure 38 Dependent linking: association of relations in number assignments and symbolic reference

establish are not between individual signs and individual objects, but between a relational structure of signs and a relational structure of the objects that they refer to.

This means that we can identify the same pattern in number assignments and in symbolic reference: in number assignments a numerical relational structure is correlated with an empirical relational structure; in symbolic reference a 'symbolic relational structure' is correlated with an empirical relational structure (constituted by the symbols' referents). In both cases, the links between individual tokens (a number and an object, or a symbol and its referent) rely on the tokens' respective positions in the system, they are system-dependent links that are constituted by associations between relations (numerical relations and empirical relations, or symbolic relations and relations between referents). This puts number assignments in a close association with the symbolic reference that lies at the core of our linguistic capacity. Figure 38 illustrates these parallels. This shows us how systematic numerical cognition could have evolved: in the development of our species, the emergence of language might have enabled us to grasp the logic of number assignments. Once we had passed the symbolic threshold, a paradigm was set for a pattern of dependent linking which prepared the way for systematic numerical cognition. This means that we can account for the capacity to systematically assign numbers to objects by a relatively small evolutionary step. According to this analysis, our capacity to use numerical relational structures did not come out of nowhere – brought about by a really lucky mutation – but could build on already existing cognitive patterns that had evolved as part of symbolic cognition: a re-usage that makes a lot of sense in terms of evolutionary economy.

The important point here is not that our language faculty allows us to develop number *symbols*, but that it allows us to develop numerical tools. These tools are not symbols, because they do not refer. Like symbols, though, their usage is based on dependent linking. The novelty is that the pattern of dependent linking is not employed for reference, but for number assignments: we do not denote with these words, we 'measure' (using 'measurement' in the sense of the Representational Theory we discussed in chapter 1).

If, on the other hand, all that we derived from symbolic reference was the possession of symbols that refer to numbers, we would not be any further in developing a number concept. There would be nothing gained if language gave us not words that are used as numbers, but instead only words that refer to numbers – as little as it helps for our grasp of complex physical concepts (say, quantum gravity) to have a word for them. The development of systematic numerical thinking is triggered by using a special set of words (namely the elements of counting sequences) *not* for reference, but as numerical tools.

The development of systematic numerical tools might have been supported by the requirements of a more complex social environment. Robin Dunbar claims that the emergence of language has enabled humans to form larger social groups, namely groups of about 150, as opposed to the groups of at most 40 individuals that other primates live in (Dunbar 1996).[21] Dunbar argues that gossip works as a human equivalent to primate grooming, but provides us with a more efficient means for social bonding, since grooming is restricted to two individuals, whereas conversation groups usually involve up to four or five people at the same time. This way, language allows humans to build and maintain three times as many close relationships as other primates.

If Dunbar is right, language – as a verbal 'grooming technique' – brought about an environment in which the capacity of complex numerical reasoning is a clear advantage. In larger groups, one has to deal with more individuals, which means higher cardinalities, but it also involves a more elaborate hierarchy, a larger system of social ranks. The development of

---

[21] Dunbar's research suggests that this group size is still manifest in modern societies. While we live in groups much larger than 150 people, those groups that make up our immediate social network, our circle of friends and acquaintances, still have an upper limit of about 150. The same holds for such different groups as church congregations, basic fighting units in a military structure, and Hutterite communes (Dunbar 1996: ch. 4).

bigger groups would hence favour individuals with the ability for more elaborate cardinal, ordinal and nominal reasoning – while the emergence of language as a mental faculty meant that the cognitive lay-out was made for the grasp of a sequence that works as a toolkit in exactly these contexts.

LANGUAGE OPENS THE WAY FOR NUMERICAL COGNITION: FURTHER SUPPORT

Giving us the capacity for dependent linking is not the only way in which language may have contributed to the emergence of systematic numerical thinking. In the following sections, I present additional evidence for my claim that the human language faculty opened the way for numerical cognition. In particular, I show two additional ways in which language supported the emergence of a systematic concept of number: the linguistic system allows us to employ convention when we settle on the tools we use for dependent linking, and its generative rules give us a handle on infinity.

Convention

The power of convention is exploited for a key feature of the human language faculty: the arbitrariness of the sign. As we discussed above, in symbolic reference the sign need not share specific features with its referent (as in iconic reference) and it need not be related to it by a physical or temporal relation (as in indexical reference) – in symbolic reference, the sign-object association is arbitrary. It is convention that determines the association between a particular word and its meaning. There is nothing inherently doggish about a noun like 'dog'; nothing but the lexical convention in English keeps us from calling dogs, say, 'blogs'.[22] As anyone learning a foreign language has painfully experienced, learning its vocabulary is basically a task of brute-force memorisation, of learning by heart conventional correspondences between sound and meaning.

While this might be a source of frustration in language classes, the arbitrariness of individual signs contributes to the richness and flexibility of language. It allows us dramatically to increase the size of the lexicon in symbolic reference; since we can employ convention in order to set up the associations we want, we do not have to find special signs that have

---

[22] A possible counter-example are cases of onomatopoeia, like 'cock-a-doodle-doo'. However, as cross-linguistic comparison shows, even these are convention-based. For instance, 'cock-a-doodle-doo' translates as 'Kikeriki' into German, although cockerels presumably sound the same in Germany and in England.

an inherent association with their referents, but can define any old string of sounds as a lexical item (as long as we observe the phonological rules of our language). Backed up by the routine of system-dependent linking, convention allows us to use arbitrary individual elements without being incomprehensible. The critical similarity, the similarity between symbols and their referents, emerges on a higher level, namely on that of the system. From the system's point of view, there is nothing arbitrary about symbolic reference; as the discussion in the previous sections has shown, the interpretation of, say, the dog as the attacker in the biting episode is not accidental, but based on a structural similarity between two systems (the syntactic and the semantic system), that is, the interpretation is based on a homomorphism: because 'the dog' is the subject in 'The dog bites the rat', its referent (the dog) is interpreted as the agent in the biting event.

Discussing the conventional, rule-based nature of language, Ferdinand de Saussure compared words with the pieces in a chess game.[23] In a chess game, it is not the particular shape of, say, a knight that motivates its function, but the powers conventionally associated with it by the rules of the game. Similarly, in language, it is not the particular form of a word that motivates the link with its referent, but the conventional value assigned to it by the rules governing the linguistic system:

> Consider a knight in chess. Is the piece by itself an element of the game? Certainly not. For as a material object, separated from its square on the board and the other conditions of play, it is of no significance for the player. It becomes a real, concrete element only when it takes on or becomes identified with its value in the game. Suppose that during a game this piece gets destroyed or lost. Can it be replaced? Of course it can. Not only by some other knight, but even by an object of quite a different shape, which can be counted as a knight, provided it is assigned the same value as the missing piece. Thus it can be seen that in semiological systems, such as languages, where the elements keep one another in a state of equilibrium in accordance with fixed rules, the notions of identity and value merge. (Saussure 1916: 153f., quoted from the translation by Harris 1986: 108f.)

And again, we can now state the same for numbers: as our investigation has shown, our use of numerical tools is based on a conventional system; their numerical function is not motivated by their particular form, but by the value associated with them by the rules that define the sequence. A counting word, for instance, can fulfil its numerical function not because of the features it has in isolation, but because of the powers associated with it by the counting sequence, more precisely, because of the position allotted

---

[23] Cf. Saussure (1916). A similar analogy has been used by Ludwig Wittgenstein (Wittgenstein 1953).

to it within a sequence of words that is used for number assignments. In a chess game the rules identify the values of the pieces and tell us how we can move them across the board; in a 'number game' the rules identify the positions for the numbers within the sequence, and tell us how we can apply them to objects.

Accordingly as far as the game is concerned, different sets of chess pieces are interchangeable; with respect to the features that make them suitable for the game and that are relevant in the game, they are indistinguishable. And along the same lines, counting words of different languages are indistinguishable if we only take into account the features that are relevant in numerical operations. So just as different sets of chess pieces do not constitute different 'chesses', but fulfil the same purpose (because they are isomorphic), counting sequences of different languages do not constitute different 'numbers', but fulfil the same numerical purposes (again, because they are isomorphic). As I argued in the previous chapters, there is nothing inherently numerical about counting words anymore than about other sequences that fulfil our number criteria. The elements ONE, TWO, THREE etc. cannot do any special 'number tricks' that elements of other sequences would not be capable of. Not only counting sequences of different languages, but – as I demonstrated above – even my hypothetical colour palette would do fine, as long as there is a convention that identifies the relevant relations between these 'numbers'.

So we can identify another matching pattern in language and numerical cognition: both the assignment of lexical items (elements of a linguistic system) to objects and the assignment of numbers (elements of a number sequence) to objects, are linked to convention. In language we establish associations between a conventional set of words and their referents. For number assignments, we want associations between a conventional series of numbers and empirical objects. Language might hence have made the way for systematic numerical cognition in more than one respect: while the routine of dependent linking in symbolic reference provides a cognitive pattern for the kind of mapping that establishes the very foundations of number assignments, conventional support makes our numerical tools especially user-friendly, setting us free to choose our number sequence in terms of efficiency and convenience.

In connection with this, the linguistic routine of conventional association would particularly support the use of *verbal* entities, such as counting words, as our numerical tools. Whereas language is a conventional verbal tool used for symbolic reference, a counting sequence is a conventional verbal tool used for number assignments. If counting words were our first numbers, we could take advantage of the opportunities convention offers us in just the same way we make use of them within language anyway.

Infinity

There is yet another way in which our language faculty supports the emergence of a full-blown number concept: language as a recursive system gives us a handle on infinity. The phrases we can potentially generate in a language represent a discrete infinity, just as we want it for a number sequence. This is accomplished by combinatorial rules that allow us to generate infinitely many complex constructions from a finite set of basic elements. Here is how Steven Pinker described this property of language:

A finite number of discrete elements (in this case, words) are sampled, combined, and permuted to create larger structures (in this case, sentences) with properties that are quite distinct from those of their elements . . . In a discrete combinatorial system like language, there can be an unlimited number of completely distinct combinations with an infinite range of properties. (Pinker 1994: 84)

As the nineteenth-century linguist Wilhelm von Humboldt pointed out, the infiniteness of language is closely related to the infiniteness of human thought: by making 'infinite use of finite means' (Humboldt 1836) language can capture an unlimited number of possible propositions. In the twentieth-century Noam Chomsky suggested that language, by making available the principle of discrete infinity, might have supported the emergence of our number faculty:

It is possible that the number faculty developed as a by-product of the language faculty . . . Human language has the extremely unusual, possibly unique, property of discrete infinity, and the same is true of the human number faculty. In fact, we might think of the human number faculty as essentially an 'abstraction' from human language, preserving the mechanism of discrete infinity and eliminating the other special features of language. (Chomsky 1988: 169)

The key to the infiniteness of linguistic constructions is recursivity. Let me illustrate this with an example from a non-linguistic domain. A simple non-linguistic instance of recursivity would be an – admittedly rather silly – party game along the following lines (Figure 39). There are three participants, say, Karen, Alexander, and Anne. The rules of the game define different tasks for each of them, to be done under different circumstances. Karen's job is to watch out for someone doing a performance that ends on a dance step. If she sees someone doing that, she has to start her own performance: she is to repeat the one she just saw, and then add a jump to it. Alexander's task

Alexander's task:
jump-act + somersault

Karen's task:
dance-act + jump

Anne's task:
somersault-act + dance

Figure 39　Recursivity in a silly party game

is to repeat any performance ending on a jump and then add a somersault. Anne's performance, finally, starts whenever she sees someone doing an act ending on a somersault. When this happens, she has to perform the same act and add a dance step to it. The game starts with Karen doing a jump.

Once this game starts, our rules will make sure it never stops; if there is nothing from outside to disrupt the procedure (as there would be in real life, namely that our players would get tired of it at some point), it could virtually go on forever, yielding more and more complex performances. This is what recursivity gives us, and it is also exactly what we want in language. More precisely, what we want is an unlimited choice of possible constructions, and constructions from constructions from constructions. This is made possible by combinatorial rules that allow us for instance in (a somewhat simplified version of) English,

1. to generate a verb phrase from a verb and its object;
2. to generate a sentence from a verb phrase and its subject;
3. to generate the object of a verb from a sentence and a complementiser (for example 'that').

For instance, (1) would give us the verb phrase 'bite the rat' from the verb 'bite' and its object 'the rat'. According to (2) we could then combine this verb phrase with a subject, say, 'the dog', and get the sentence 'The dog bites the rat.' So far nothing looks very recursive. But now there is (3), which allows us to combine this sentence with a complementiser like 'that', and to use it then as the object of a verb. Hence, our element – which is now 'that the dogs bites the rat' – can be combined with a verb along the lines of (1) again, for instance with 'know', yielding 'know that the dog bites the rat' – a new verb phrase, which according to (2) gives us a sentence when combined with a subject, say, 'You know that the dog bites the rat', which in turn qualifies as new input for (3), and so on.

We can regard this instance of recursion as a direct counterpart of our party game example, with Karen's task as the twin of the rule in (1), Alexander's as parallel to (2), and Anne's as a match for (3). Karen's performance would then stand for a verb phrase, with the final jump being the verb, and the dance act its object; Alexander's performance stands for a sentence (where the 'subject' is a somersault), and Anne's performance stands for the object of a verb, consisting of a somersault task (the 'sentence') and a dance step (the 'complementiser'). Whereas in our party game we get infinitely many possible acts, in our English example we can generate infinitely many possible linguistic constructions.

As Paul Bloom pointed out, recursivity – as illustrated by these examples – is an integrative property of the whole system; it need not be reflected in single rules, but emerges out of their interaction (Bloom 1994a). A rule like Alexander's 'repeat any jump-act and add a somersault to it' by itself does not suggest recursion. The rules of our party game, taken separately and by themselves, look harmless; it is in combination that they gain their recursive power. And the same applies to our linguistic example: there is nothing in a single one of the generative rules (1) through (3) above that suggests recursivity. Recursivity cannot be extracted from either (1), (2), or (3), but emerges out of the system, as a result of their interaction. Accordingly, recursivity by itself cannot be 'abstracted from language' (as the earlier quote from Chomsky suggests) and passed on to numerical thinking; in Bloom's words:

Being recursive is not the sort of property that can be extracted from a system and passed on. It is, in an explicit sense, a 'holistic property of systems' . . . the notion of generativity itself (and more specifically, recursion), moving out of one system and into another, makes no sense. (Bloom 1994a: 179)

To sum up, recursivity is a property of sets of rules, and, since in the case of language these rules are linguistic rules, we cannot transfer recursivity from language to another system. What, then, are the origins of recursivity in the numerical domain? In the context of first language acquisition, Bloom suggests that 'children 'bootstrap' a generative understanding of number out of the productive syntactic and morphological structures available in the counting system' (1994a: 186). As we have seen in the previous chapter, counting sequences are open-ended because of the generative rules that govern the construction of complex elements. These rules introduce recursion and ultimately constitute the infiniteness of counting sequences:

for every counting word, they allow us to generate a successor, the word that follows it in the counting sequence. Hence when children learn the counting sequence of their first language, the lexical rules that allow them to generate infinitely many counting words might help them to understand the infiniteness of the number sequence.

However, while this means that recursivity might move from language to number, under Bloom's account the only way this could happen is in individual cognitive development, because in this case children encounter an existing sequence of number words, a ready-made sequence that relates linguistic recursivity to a recursivity that already exists in the number system that their culture provides. This can account for the emergence of language-style recursivity in the number domain in individual development, but not in hominid evolution.[24] Hence we are left with the puzzle of how recursivity could have evolved in numerical thinking in the first place. If we do not want to assume that the same pattern of recursivity was invented twice (and totally independently in each domain), how then could this principle have been transferred from language to numerical cognition?

The answer is that *recursivity travelled on words* not only in first language acquisition, but also in the development of our species. As I have argued in the previous chapters, counting words do not denote numbers, but instead are an instance of numbers themselves: they can be used as numerical tools. If this account is correct, we do not have to look for an independent development of recursivity outside the linguistic system anymore. We do not need to assume a recursive system of numbers that exist independently of language and can then be denoted by a recursive system of counting words – without there being any trade of recursivity between these two systems.

Within the approach I have put forward here, the transfer of this principle can be connected to the use of counting words as our numerical tools: if our first numbers were words, it would come naturally to employ the generativity they bring with them as linguistic items – and the recursion it gives us – when we use them as numbers. Recursivity could be passed on from language to number because it did not have to be transferred as an isolated feature, but could be accessed as a property that was already connected to our numerical tools. In order to use, in the numerical domain, the recursivity that language provides, we do not have to move out of the system in the first place, but can use *linguistic* recursivity right away, the

---

[24] Bloom explicitly rejects the latter possibility: 'in the case of language and number . . . generativity also can move *across* domains, not in hominid evolution, but in cognitive development' (Bloom 1994a: 188; emphasis in the original text).

recursivity that counting words bring with them as part of their rightful heritage as lexical items. In contrast to that, if our first numbers were not language-based, we would not have such a connecting element that allows recursivity to be passed on. Without counting words as numerical tools, it would be difficult to see how recursivity emerged in the numerical domain.

This is now a good point at which to summarise our results so far. Before we go on in our investigation, the following list brings together the different ways in which language contributed to the emergence of numerical thinking.

- *Material*: With counting words, language provides us with a set of verbal items as a possible number sequence.
- *Dependent linking*: Language as a symbolic system associates signs with their referents via the relations that hold between them. In language, we correlate a relational structure of linguistic items (symbols) with an empirical relational structure (their referents). This gives us a cognitive pattern for the correlation of a relational structure of linguistic items (counting words) with an empirical relational structure ('measured^{RTM}' objects) in number assignments.
- *Conventional choice*: The linguistic sign is arbitrary, that is, the choice of a particular word for a particular concept can be based on convention. Similarly, the choice of particular elements as numerical tools can be based on convention. Just as different languages can fulfil the same referential function (express the same concepts), different counting sequences – and also non-verbal number sequences – can fulfil the same numerical function (assess the same properties, be the basis for the same arithmetic reasoning).
- *Infiniteness*: Language employs recursive rules to make infinite use of finite means, allowing us to generate an infinite progression. This recursivity could have entered the numerical domain by travelling on counting words.

A POSSIBLE SCENARIO FOR THE EMERGENCE
OF NUMERICAL TOOLS

The upshot from our discussion thus far is, then, that language provided the perfect means to develop a number sequence, and this number sequence should be a sequence of *verbal* entities. Once we adopt a view of counting words as numerical tools, everything links up: using words as numbers means, first, that we can immediately access the cognitive pattern of dependent linking that language provides; second, it means that we benefit from the power of convention (that is, we have a free choice of the individual elements we use for the number sequence); and, finally, using words as numbers means that recursivity is available as a feature of our number system. Hence, over and above providing our numerical tools, and crucially related to the fact that these tools are words (namely counting words), language as a mental faculty supplied us with the cognitive prerequisites to make use of these tools under a generalised and systematic scheme that establishes the foundations for a full-blown number concept: language gives us both the ingredients and the recipe for a systematic notion of number.

Given this picture, we can now ask how this linguistic–numerical enterprise could have started in the first place: what might the way to the emergence of numerical tools look like, and where and how does language come into the picture? Hence, the task is now to describe a plausible scenario of how counting sequences might have evolved as numerical tools in the history of our species. This is what I am going to do in the present section.

Before I begin, let me make clear what I intend to and what I do not intend to show with this scenario. My purpose in describing this scenario is not to say: 'Look here, this is exactly how it happened, this is how counting words evolved as numerical tools', but rather, 'Here is a scenario of how it could have happened, a scenario that demonstrates that a numerical representation of counting words can evolve from early, pre-numerical roots, based on small steps that constitute plausible transitions from one developmental stage to the other.'

My aim is hence to show that there is at least one plausible scenario for the gradual emergence of numerical tools from primitive, pre-numerical representations. Such a scenario supports our view of counting sequences as numerical tools, by showing that it is possible for such tools to evolve via small behavioural adaptations, but it does not – and does not intend to – make definite claims about the way this development actually took place. It shows one way this could have happened, and it shows how a development that starts from pre-numerical representations, which can be grasped by many mammalian and avian species, can lead to the emergence of numerical tools in a species that possesses the capacity to systematically associate relational structures of verbal and non-verbal elements, hence in a species that possesses language as a mental faculty.

In his account of symbolic reference that we discussed above, Terrence Deacon suggests that the emergence of symbolic thinking is supported by repetitive routines that occur in ritual contexts (Deacon 1997: ch. 12). These routines involve the repeated correlation of (vocal or non-vocal) tokens with objects, often accompanied by pointing gestures, which set up a context of indexical relationships. He argues that the redundancy involved in these routines supports an attentional shift from concrete, indexical sign–object associations to abstract symbolic sign–sign relationships. This way, the repetitive context of rituals can support the grasp of symbolic systems.

Interestingly, a very similar point has been made for the origins of counting sequences. One source for counting sequences might be series of words that were recited in a conventional order and associated with objects or persons as part of a ritual activity.[25] These series of words show essential features that we need for counting sequences: they form a progression, they are part of an activity in which they are applied to objects in a conventional order, and they gain their significance from this function. Like in the emergence of symbolic thinking, the repetitive context in which the words appear could bear on the salience of relational structures. Similarly as for symbolic thinking, the existence of ritual recitations may hence have been a supporting factor in the invention of counting sequences as numbers, a pattern that fits into the general picture we have developed of symbolic cognition as a paradigm for numerical thinking.

This does not mean, of course, that we might have come up with a rather pointless sequence of counting words first, and then suddenly realised that, since we were carrying around this deadweight anyway, we could as well put it to use in number assignments. Rather, I want to suggest that in a process of coevolution the gradual emergence of counting sequences and the development of a more and more systematic and comprehensive concept of number supported each other. Ritual contexts might have been one supporting factor in the development of counting sequences, while the option to generate such a sequence with the means that language gives us, enabled us to integrate preexisting concepts of cardinality and sequential order into a systematic notion of number assignments.

We can think of the first stage in the development of numerical thinking as the invention of tallies: simple iconic representations for cardinalities. In order to indicate how many elements a certain set has, for instance in order to indicate how many deer one has killed in a hunt, one might use a set of pebbles or a set of notches as representations for the deer. To make sure that there are as many pebbles or notches as deer, one can set up a

---

[25] A ritual origin of counting sequences has been suggested, for instance, in Seidenberg (1962) and Flegg (1983). Hurford (1987: 102) calls this the 'Eenie-meenie-miny-mo' hypothesis, capitalising on the similarity with nursery rhymes (cf. also the parallels between counting sequences and nursery rhymes we discussed in the previous chapter).

Figure 40 An iconic representation of cardinality from 30,000 years ago
(Absolon 1957: fig. 38)

one-to-one correspondence between the sets, for instance, by putting one pebble aside or cutting one notch into a stick for each kill. Archaeological evidence suggests that this technique goes back probably at least as far as the Stone Age. In 1925, excavations at an ancient mammoth hunters' base in Dolní Věstonice (then in Czechoslovakia) revealed a dagger from the Aurignacian period, carved out of a mammoth rib, which had 21 notches cut into one side. From the same excavation site comes a fossilised radial wolf's bone, which you see in Figure 40. Karel Absolon, who organised the first systematic excavations at Dolní Věstonice starting in the early 1920s, interpreted these finds as 'marques de chasse' (Absolon 1957), suggesting that nearly 30,000 years ago humans used notches to represent the cardinality of sets iconically.[26] As you can see, the notches come in multiples of 5: there are 30 notches on the upper part of the bone (this is on the right side in the picture), and 25 notches on its lower part (on the left side), such that the last notch on the upper part and the first one on the lower part form a double demarcation line. Absolon interpreted the basis 5 for the marks on this and other prehistoric finds as an indication of an early use of fingers in representations of cardinality (Absolon 1957). We will come back to the role of fingers further down. Note, incidentally, that the notches on this bone are not ordered in *groups of five*, contrary to what is sometimes maintained in historical accounts of numeral systems.[27]

The grasp of cardinality – that feature that we want to relate to with our tally representation – is supported by the early, pre-numerical concepts we encountered at the beginning of this chapter: as I have shown above, not only human babies, but also other species possess an abstract concept of cardinality as a feature of sets, suggesting that such a concept is independent of the human language faculty and was present long before systematic numerical thinking evolved.

[26] The excavations at Dolní Věstonice are described in more detail in Absolon (1928, 1938) and Klíma (1995).
[27] This seems to be a scientific myth, perhaps due to a misunderstanding of Absolon's description. Such a grouping of five seems to be assumed for instance in George Ifrah's history of numbers (Ifrah 1985: 104f.) and in the 'Timetable of Science' (Hellemans and Bunch 1988).

The important step at this stage is to use icons in order to represent cardinality, in our example sets of pebbles or sets of notches on a stick. As discussed above, icons – unlike symbols – are associated with their referents by individual similarity, with no recourse to systematic sign–sign relationships. The grasp of iconic representations must have predated our ability for symbolic reference and hence the emergence of the human language faculty. As we have seen above, iconic representations of cardinality can be understood not only by non-human primates, but also by other mammals and by birds (for instance Otto Koehler's raven that I mentioned on page 103 above, learned to treat sets of dots on a container lid as signs for the amount of grains that were inside that container; cf. Koehler 1943).

However, while iconic representations are easy to interpret, they are difficult to produce (understanding that ♿ is an icon for a wheel-chair user is much easier than creating this sign). Archaeological evidence for the emergence of iconic *productions* not only comes from fossilised tallies, but is also supported by non-numerical representations, paintings and sculptures from the early Aurignacian period and before. From the same excavation site as the tally bones comes the 'Věstonice Venus', a tiny female figurine made from ceramic. Examples from an earlier period are the images and small sculptures of humans and animals found in a cave close to Geissenklösterle in Southern Germany (dating back to about 33,000 years B P[28]), or the paintings of Chauvet-Pont-d'Arc, a Palaeolithic cave in the Ardèche area. This cave was discovered in December 1994 by three speleologists who were privately exploring the area (among them Jean-Marie Chauvet after whom the cave was later named). In its large galleries, more than 400 paintings and engravings were found, including pictures of rhinoceroses, felines, bears, owls, and mammoths: iconic representations that were created about 31,000 years ago, long before Magdalenian artists created their famous paintings in the cave of Lascaux (about 15,000 years B P).

The capacity for iconic representation that manifests itself in these paintings provides the cognitive basis for the use of tallies. The lion painting in Figure 41 can represent animals because of a visual similarity: the image looks similar to the silhouettes of two lions. In the case of tallies, the shared feature that makes our tallies an icon is their cardinality: our set of tallies

---

[28] Cf. Richter et al. (2000) for a recent dating of the Geissenklösterle art. While the Upper Palaeolithic art is the earliest evidence for iconic productions we have to date, findings from African sites suggest that the human capacity to produce deliberate depictions might go back even further. Between 1992 and 2000, excavations at the Blombos cave in South Africa revealed not only a range of bone tools, but also several pieces of red ochre that might have been used for body painting serving ritual purposes, as well as an engraved bone fragment and two pieces of ochre with complex geometric motifs that are more than 70,000 years old (cf. Henshilwood et al. 2001; d'Errico et al. 2001).

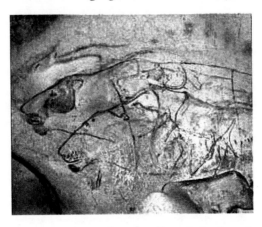

Figure 41 Iconic representations in Stone Age: lion painting from the Chauvet cave

(say, pebbles or notches) has the same cardinality as that of the set we want to represent (say, sheep). Hence, while the cave painting is an iconic representation of lions, our set of notches is an iconic representation of the set of sheep, and, in particular, it is an iconic representation that focuses on cardinality: there are as many sheep as notches.

Due to its iconic character, the use of tallies deviates from a genuine number assignment in two ways: it is restricted to cardinality, and it is not based on dependent linking. We do not need to refer to a system in order to link up tallies and objects: all we need is this one individual set of notches, and the one set of sheep in order to make our representation work, with no reference to other sets necessary. As mentioned earlier, icons are associated with the objects they represent by individual similarity, and this is why they need not relate to a system: the tallies have the property we need – namely, cardinality – themselves, we do not match it up with another property (say, their position in a progression). When using tallies, we represent the cardinality of one set by that of another set, rather than indicating it by a number.

The reason why one would want to employ this kind of representation in the first place is that the objects we use as representatives might be easier to keep and to manipulate than the objects they represent. It is much easier to get an idea of the size of a set of pebbles or notches, or to compare it to other sets, than this task would be for a flock of sheep, or the kills one has made in hunts over the last season. For instance, if I want to know whether I made more kills than you over the last hunting season, it would be easier to compare the notches that each of us recorded on a stick or a bone, than to try and recall our respective achievements on the different hunting occasions.[29]

One kind of objects that make obviously suitable candidates for this kind of representation, because we carry them around in full view all the time, are our fingers. Similarly to pebbles or notches, sets of fingers can be used as iconic representations for sets. For instance, in order to represent a set of three, you could show the index finger, the middle finger, and the ring finger of your right hand, which would give you three fingers as an iconic sign for three objects – a simple and efficient way to generate an iconic cardinality representation which is still in use today. It is a common assumption that the use of fingers in one way or another played a role in the development of number in the history of our species.[30] While agreeing with this assumption, I think that fingers did not just generally support the development of cardinality representations, but rather that they contributed one particular feature that presumably has opened the way for the emergence of a non-iconic system. I would like to draw your attention to a property of fingers that at first sight does not seem to have any significance, but that might have made all the difference for the emergence of number assignments: the fixed positions they occupy on the hand.

When one sets up one-to-one correspondences between fingers and objects for iconic cardinality representations, the fixed order of fingers on each hand emphasises a sequential aspect within our 'finger set'. This supports a routine to link fingers to objects in a sequential, stable order: it would be natural to always start with the same finger and go ahead in a fixed order (Figure 42). For instance, one could start on one hand with the index finger, go on with the middle finger, then the ring finger, the little finger, and finally the thumb; then go on with the other hand in just the same order of fingers and thumb.

This 'stable order' principle is still evident today when we use our fingers (and thumbs) to indicate a cardinality. The culture-dependent differences one can observe show that there is no one 'right' way to do it, but several possible orders. For instance, instead of starting with the index finger, one

---

[29] This is even more pronounced when we want to keep track of sets of events, like days – an ability that has obvious evolutionary advantages since it allows for instance to plan ahead for different seasons of the year. In chapter 6, we will encounter iconic representations for days on a Stone Age calendar.

[30] According to Brian Butterworth, this relation might even be reflected in the organisation of the brain in individual development. Butterworth (1999: ch. 5) suggests that during childhood, our subitising capacity gets connected with our finger representations on a neuronal level: 'as the child grows and develops, the subitizing circuits in the inferior parietal link up with the finger circuits in the intraparietal sulcus. The fingers therefore gain an extended representation by this link: they come to represent the numerosities' (p. 250).

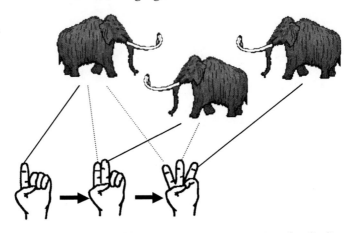

Figure 42 Stable order of fingers in an iconic representation of cardinality:
three mammoths

could start with the thumb, go on with the index finger, and then via middle finger and ring finger to the little finger. Yet another option is to start with the little finger and go via ring finger, middle finger, and index finger to the thumb. In addition, it does not matter which way one singles out fingers – one can start with a closed fist and unbend one finger after the other, or else start with an open hand and bend one finger after the other (as it is done in Japan, for instance).

What is remarkable here is actually not so much that there are all these different ways to use our fingers in this task, but rather what they have in common: in all the cases, the order in which the fingers are used is faithful to the relative positions of the four fingers on the hand (while the thumb gets a special position, for instance before the fingers). Why does nobody use, say, the little finger first, then the index finger, then the middle finger, then the thumb, and finally the ring finger?[31] This might seem a strange question to ask at first, but it demands an answer once one realises that the order in which fingers are singled out does not have any significance here, since in the end one always uses *the whole set of fingers* as a cardinality representation.

Stable order is of no relevance for iconic representations – including finger tallies – but it is an important feature for number assignments. As I have emphasised earlier in our investigation, the fixed order in which our numerical tools, for instance counting words, are linked up with objects

---

[31] In the next chapter, I will show you some answers that children gave to this question.

guarantees that we always end up with the same counting word for sets of the same cardinality; it allows us to use the last counting word as a 'place-holder' for the whole set, making it possible to indicate a cardinality. However, there is no such thing as a cardinal placeholder in our usage of fingers: unlike counting words, fingers are not applied to sets individually; individual fingers do not identify the cardinality of a set (apart from the case where the set is a singleton, of course). Unlike counting words, fingers are not used as numbers, but as representations for the elements of another set – sheep, mammoths, or, in modern contexts for instance, guests at a party: 'How many people will come tonight?' – 'Let me see: Karen, Charles, Mick, . . .' [unbending a different finger for each person named]. When linking up guests and fingers in this way, one would not come up with one finger in the end (the last finger used), but with the whole set of fingers, hence it is of no consequence at all in which order they were unbent (or bent, if you are from Japan).

The stable order is here a matter of convenience: a habit that evolves naturally given the fixed positions of fingers and thumb on each hand. These positions constitute a 'finger sequence' that is visually salient and that is supported by early concepts of serial order, of the kind we encountered earlier – pre-numerical concepts that are part of our mental heritage (cf. the discussion on pp. 107f.). The salient sequential order in which fingers are attached to each hand induces a successive order of (un)bending, but it does not have any implications for the task of cardinality representation, which is purely iconic at this stage, and crucially not based on dependent linking: the relations between fingers are not put into service for a number assignment yet. This comes with the usage of words.

Approaches to language evolution generally agree that the development of language started with – or even triggered – the appearance of *Homo sapiens* (while the roots of language and symbolic thinking might date back as far as 2 million years before present).[32] This means that for instance at the time those mammoth hunters marked their stick in an iconic representation of cardinality, the language faculty was certainly part of the human mental repertoire.

When we link up fingers with objects in an iconic cardinality representation, a natural elaboration is to use the respective names for fingers in addition to the fingers themselves, in order to communicate our results to others. At this stage, then, fingers are accompanied by words when they are linked (in a one-to-one manner) to the objects of a set in a stable order.

---

[32] Cf. Lieberman (1984); Bickerton (1990); Dunbar (1996); Deacon (1997).

Via a gradual shift of focus, these words could eventually replace the use of fingers. Such a shift would be supported by a gain in efficiency: using words instead of fingers frees the fingers of their representational task and enables us to use them for pointing to the objects we want to represent. These pointing gestures help to single out the items of our set for the one-to-one match that ensures both sets (objects and tallies) have the same cardinality.[33] This suggests a transition along the following lines: where initially, we use a sequence of fingers accompanied by their names, we would later use a sequence of names for fingers which are supported by pointing gestures, and finally would just use a sequence of words by itself.

Evidence for such a transition comes from different phenomena that point to a link between fingers and counting words. We find a pattern where sequences of words are supported by pointing gestures for instance in the traditional Oksapmin 'body counting' system that we discussed in chapter 3. Remember that the Oksapmin counting sequence (and other counting sequences from typologically related languages) consists of words for fingers and for other sequentially ordered parts of the body that are usually accompanied by gestures to the respective body parts. In other counting sequences, the original link to fingers is still reflected in the lexical sources of some elements. We came across some examples in the previous chapter when we discussed non-numerical sources of counting words (recall for instance the relation of F I V E to the Proto-Indo-European word for 'fist').

More evidence comes from words that relate to the act of (un-)bending fingers. In his book on number words, Karl Menninger describes such a phenomenon from 'Dene-Dinje', now known as Dëne Sųłiné, a language from the Northern Branch of the Athapaskan family spoken in North America. According to Menninger's account, the words for 'one' to 'five' go back to expressions meaning 'the end is bent' (little finger, *one*), 'it is bent once more' (ring finger, *two*), 'the middle is bent' (middle finger, *three*), 'only one remains' (thumb, *four*), and 'my hand is finished' (*five*).[34] An often-cited example of diachronic links between expressions for fingers and numerical expressions is the English word 'digit' that originates in the Latin word for 'finger' (*digitus*).

Finally, the link between fingers and counting words can also be reflected in the *structure* of a sequence: a well-known phenomenon is the

---

[33] In the next chapter, we will see that pointing gestures of this kind also occur in the individual development of numerical thinking; they help children to single out objects in early cardinality assignments.

[34] Menninger (1958: 46 / 1969: 35). Menninger's account probably goes back to an analysis proposed by Emile Petitot in his 1876 *Dènè-Dindjié* grammar and dictionary (Petitot 1876). Butterworth (1999: 61) describes a similar phenomenon for Zulu number words.

ubiquitousness of base ten structures in counting sequences (or those based on multiples of ten, usually twenty), which are presumably rooted in the use of (ten) fingers.

The shift from fingers to words might have been supported by ritualised sequences along the lines we discussed above. Ritual contexts provide a paradigm for word sequences with an instrumental status; building on this paradigm, the sequence of finger names could evolve into a standardised instrumental sequence: a sequence of words that do not take their usual linguistic meaning (they do not refer to fingers), but fulfil a certain – non-referential – function, namely to represent elements of a set, just like words in a recital fulfil a certain function within a ritual, rather than referring to particular objects. Ritual contexts might hence have supported the use of words as tools, albeit initially these words would not yet have been numerical tools (in the sense we developed here), but tools to represent the cardinality of a set iconically, just like fingers (or notches or pebbles) were used as iconic representations.

Words are realised in speech, where they are not as persistent as notches on a stick or fingers on a hand (the sounds of a word are acoustically gone the instant we hear them, and have to be kept in memory), and because of this, in a given context the last word of a sequence will always be more salient and more accessible than the others. For instance, when people hear a list of words and try to repeat them, they will tend to recall the last word better than those in the middle, and they will also be better at recognising it later. This phenomenon, known as the 'recency effect', might be based on the contribution of a phonological buffer in short-term memory.[35] Another phenomenon suggesting a higher salience and accessibility of final elements is reflected in the preferred order of constituents in a sentence: elements that are in the focus of attention or introduce new information, as well as elements that are grammatically complex, are typically moved towards a sentence-final position.[36]

The last element in a sequence of words will hence have a more prominent status than the others. As a consequence, this word might acquire an indexical connection with the cardinality of the set that is represented by the word sequence. Evidence for such an indexical link comes from counting words that originate in names for sets of a particular cardinality

---

[35] An early work on the relationship between final positions in a list and the accuracy with which a word is recalled is Murdock (1962). For the impact of short-term vs. long-term memory on recency effects cf. Baddeley (1998); the recency effect in recognition is discussed in Neath (1993).

[36] For a discussion of the roles of discourse status and structural complexity for word order, and their interaction, cf. Arnold et al. (2000).

(cf. pp. 82f. above). One example we discussed in chapter 3 was the Russian word for 'forty', which goes probably back to the Old Nordic word for furs that were traded in bundles of forty. Another example was the Malinke word for 'thousand', which was originally an expression for baskets with 1,000 cola nuts.

At this point, then, language comes onto the scene, and with it the liberty of convention and the power of its generative rules. Because counting sequences are sets of words, we are free to choose anything we like when we want to add new elements to them, as long as we obey the phonological rules of the language we are in. Convention allows us to use arbitrary words for our purpose once the tie to fingers is loosened. And because counting words are words, we can generate infinitely many of them (based on a small set of primitive items) by employing the recursive rules our linguistic system provides: language allows us to employ recursion in our system and thereby gives it potential infiniteness. And remember that from their original relation to fingers, counting sequences inherit a stable order, they form a conventional progression. This feature can now be generalised: based on the underlying generative rules, each (complex) counting word is assigned a fixed position within the progression of words.

Since we are in language now, the elements of this progression should be put into service in a routine of dependent linking, suggesting that indexical links between words and sets develop into dependent linking: sequential relations between words are associated with quantitative relations between sets. As I have argued above, because of the linguistic pattern of dependent linking the use of words as numerical tools requires only a slight adjustment of the usage that would be considered appropriate for a normal, referential word. Just like any words, counting words constitute relational structures: sets of words with certain, systematic relations holding between them. In the case of counting words, these are relations like '>' (that is the words' order within the counting sequence), in the case of other, referential words these are relations like 'comes before' and 'subject of'. And just like any words, counting words are mapped onto relational structures that are constituted by empirical objects. In the case of counting words these objects are 'measured^{RTM}', and the relations holding between them are relations like 'has more elements than'; in the case of referential words the objects are denoted, and the relations holding between them are relations like 'agent of'.

The grasp of relations between counting words gets further support from the repetitive, ritualised routines that counting involves: one links up – often rhythmically – first one word and an object, then another word and another object, and so on. Following Deacon's argument from above, this ritualised routine should emphasise word–word relationships and support a focus shift from individual words to the system, hence from individual elements to a relational structure; in our case: the counting routine emphasises sequential relationships between counting words, and by doing so supports a shift from individual counting words to a numerical relational structure.

We now have a potentially infinite progression of verbal elements with an instrumental status in cardinality assignments: a counting sequence is born. Our scenario suggests that counting words are initially used in cardinal number assignments; this usage can then be generalised and transferred to other, non-quantitative contexts, namely to ordinal and nominal number assignments. In these contexts, they keep their instrumental status, and they are also still employed as part of a relational structure, and as such, undergo dependent linking; the only difference is that the dependent links between words and objects focus on other relations. This way, a progression of words that has evolved from names for iconic finger representations could eventually give rise to the whole domain of numerical cognition.

Table 2 summarises the stages I suggested for the emergence of counting sequences (in the left column); the middle column indicates the underpinnings on which the development can build in each case (in italics), and the column on the right lists evidence we discussed for the different stages and their mental basis. Table 2a encompasses the initial, pre-numerical stages, 2b describes the emergence of a systematic number concept once language has come in.

LANGUAGE AND NUMBER AS HUMAN FACULTIES

If the account we developed in this chapter is correct, then the emergence of language gave us all the conceptual and practical ingredients for a fully-fledged and efficient number sequence that can be used in systematic assignments to empirical objects. Once we had language, everything was in place for systematic numerical cognition: the pattern of dependent linking, the power of convention allowing us liberty in the choice of our numerical tools, recursive rules generating an infinite system from finite means, and, as the icing on the cake, a handy way to produce and store the elements of a possible number sequence (namely as lexical entities that can be produced in speech and stored in memory).

Note that it is the possession of the *language faculty*, the emergence of language as a mental faculty in the history of humans, that is crucial here,

Table 2a *A possible scenario for the emergence of numerical thinking: pre-numerical stages*

Non-verbal roots	**Iconic representation of cardinality** Sets of pebbles, notches etc. represent the cardinality of another set iconically.	*Concept of cardinality*	Early concepts of cardinality in animals and pre-verbal human infants
		Capacity to produce iconic representations	Iconic representations in stone age: cave paintings and sculptures; tallies suggesting iconic representations of cardinality
	Sequential order When fingers are used to represent another set, they are singled out successively. This order is induced by their positions on each hand, but does not yet have any further impact.	*Grasp of serial order*	Grasp of serial order in animals; Stable order of fingers as evident in present-day practices of finger counting
Language comes in	**Words as names for fingers** Fingers are accompanied by their names.	*Naming capacity*	**Language provides names.** [emergence of language at least 500,000 years ago]
	Focus shift from fingers to words Fingers are initially supported by words (their names). Later, the focus shifts to words (which can thenx be supported by pointing gestures).	*Ability to use words instrumentally;* *possible support: recital of (other) sequences in ritual contexts*	Body counting systems (for example Oksapmin);
	Words as replacements for fingers Words are used by themselves; in this context they do not refer to fingers, but fulfil the function of fingers. The sequential order is kept: the words form a progression.		Diachronic links of counting words to fingers
	Indexical links to cardinality The salience in speech of the last word of the sequence establishes indexical links between individual words and sets of a certain cardinality.	*Capacity for indexical representation*	Diachronic links of counting words to sets with a certain cardinality

Table 2b *A possible scenario for the emergence of numerical thinking: language supports the development of numerical tools*

SYSTEMATIC NUMBER CONCEPT EMERGES

Emergence of numerical tools Indexical links evolve into dependent links between words and sets: sequential relations between words are associated with quantitative relations between sets. ➤ Counting words are tools in cardinal number assignments.	*Grasp of word–word relations, possibly supported by ritual contexts;* *Capacity to link up relational structures by homomorphic mappings*	**Language provides dependent linking:** an association between a relational structure of words and a relational structure of empirical objects.
Generalised usage of numerical tools The pattern of dependent linking can be generalised and transferred to non-cardinal contexts, constituting ordinal and nominal number assignments. ➤ Counting words can serve as multi-purpose tools in cardinal, ordinal, and nominal number assignments alike.	*Concepts of sequential rank and of (non-)identity*	Concepts of sequential rank in mammals and birds.
Increase of counting words Arbitrary new words can be added to the sequence as long as they are in keeping with the phonological rules of the language.	*Capacity to use arbitrary signs*	**Language provides liberty through convention,** based on the arbitrariness of the linguistic sign.
Infiniteness of the sequence New, complex elements can be created according to generative linguistic rules; they are integrated into the sequence with respect to their constituents.	*Capacity to employ recursion*	**Language provides recursion** through its generative rules.

not the successful and complete acquisition of a particular language in individual development. This means, for instance, that acquired or inborn impairments of language skills do not necessarily affect our ability to grasp number assignments, as long as the basic capacity for linguistic thinking is still intact (including the ability to produce sequences and the grasp of dependent links).

And as our discussion made clear, the claim that language made the way for numerical thinking does not imply that, without language, we would have no concept of properties like cardinality or rank that we identify with numbers, or that we could not grasp quantitative relations between small sets. It does imply that language and numbers, as cognitive capacities, are not disjoint in hominid evolution: in the development of our species a fully-fledged number concept could emerge once symbolic thinking was possible. As the evidence from animal studies and studies with human infants showed, this concept of number could draw on pre-existing capacities we share with other species and that form the basis for our understanding of cardinality, ordinality, and arithmetic operations. Language has been crucial in integrating these early concepts into a systematic number concept; a concept that is based on dependent links, involving a potentially infinite sequence of numerical tools.

Under this notion, numerical cognition as well as language can be regarded as genuinely human – as mental faculties that are not merely of greater complexity (than, say, animal communication systems and cardinality concepts) and grounded in a higher general-purpose intelligence, but qualitatively different and specific to the human mind.

Of course, language conveys information about the world, and so do other communication systems. As honey bees show, a wiggle dance does just fine.[37] But there is much more to language. As we have seen above, language is a generative system with an infinite output, a system that is based on dependent links between phonological, syntactic, and semantic representations. As such, it not only conveys information about the world, but enables us to represent an infinite range of propositions, both actual and hypothetical. By so doing, language provides us with the means for 'off-line thinking': it allows us to create a mental world on its own, to invent different 'What if?'-scenarios as a support for planning and understanding.[38]

---

[37] A detailed account of the wiggle dance is given in Karl von Frisch's classical works on bee communication (Frisch 1927, 1965).

[38] Again, *Star Trek* provides the best illustration. We can think of off-line thinking as something like the simulations on holo-deck: a model of the world that we create *ad libitum*. In his book on 'Language and Species', Derek Bickerton focused on this power of simulation when distinguishing the 'secondary representational system' that language creates from the primary representational systems that are based on sensual data (Bickerton 1990).

And similarly, one can of course use numbers to indicate cardinalities, and cardinality can also be grasped by animals and pre-verbal infants. But there is much more to numbers. As I hope to have convinced you, our number capacity is based on dependent links between numerical tools and empirical objects. As such, our number concept enables us to identify not only cardinal, but also ordinal and nominal relationships between objects in a precise way.

Under this account, then, both the language faculty and systematic numerical thinking can be regarded as species-specific traits, and it is not surprising that both should be specific for the same species, namely humans: given our view that language opened the way for numerical cognition, it is to be expected that the same species that possesses the language faculty as a unique trait, should also be the one that developed a systematic concept of number.

But could it not be just the other way round, namely that it is not our language faculty that made numerical thinking possible, but that instead our concept of numbers made language possible? The reason why I do not believe this to be a possibility is a simple one: there is language without number, but not number without language – that is, as long as 'number' is not confused with cardinality, but refers to the kind of systematic numerical thinking that we investigate here. Let me elaborate this argument.

There are two central aspects that we identified for a systematic notion of number: (1) it is based on the usage of dedicated elements (numerical tools) in a pattern of dependent linking, and (2) these elements can form an infinite sequence based on recursion. In the present chapter, we have identified counterparts for both of these features in language: language is also based on dependent linking, and it employs recursion-based infiniteness.

What is important for our discussion now is that the possession of such a linguistic system is universal among human cultures. In fact as mentioned earlier, the appearance of our species, *Homo sapiens*, seems to be related to the emergence of language. There is not a single culture, however remote and isolated from other cultures, whatever its social organisation and its size, whatever the conditions of its environment, that does not have a full-blown language – a sophisticated symbolic system that employs dependent linking and generates infinitely many possible constructions, based on recursion. As the case of sign languages shows, the emergence of such a system is independent even of the ability to hear and hence to use the auditory modality, and the development of creole languages suggests that in cultures that lack a common language, such a system emerges spontaneously within a single generation.

However, the same is not true for the usage of numbers. While language is presumably the single most important mental faculty that defines our species, systematic numerical thinking does not have such a fundamental status – even though it is unique among humans (but this is exactly because it is triggered by language). What language provides is an option, a licence to employ dependent linking as well as recursion-based infiniteness, but it does not prompt the necessary implementation of these features in a systematic number concept.

Our discussion suggests that it is possible for a culture to manipulate cardinalities by way of iconic representations without employing a systematic notion of numbers, that is, without employing systematic numerical tools of the kind that gets assigned to empirical objects in a pattern of dependent linking. The mammoth hunters we discussed above might have lived in a culture that utilised only iconic representations of cardinality, for instance by notches, while it is reasonable to assume that as humans they had a full linguistic system at their disposal.

Modern evidence for such a possibility comes from some early Australian cultures. The Australian language Aranda seems initially not to have had a counting sequence that was used as a tool in number assignments, but instead had words that identified the cardinality of small sets, namely words denoting sets of one and two elements, respectively.[39] Note that these are cardinalities we can distinguish by subitising, with no counting involved. Related to this, words for these small cardinalities can have a special status and, in particular, they need not be related to the counting sequence of a language (I will come back to this in chapter 8). In addition, there are Aranda words indicating set sizes like 'a few' and 'many' – hence words that refer to set sizes that we can represent as noisy magnitudes, again with no number assignment necessary. In order to identify higher cardinalities, this culture uses iconic representations, namely fingers and lines in the sand. This is how Theodor Strehlow described this practice in his *Aranda Phonetics and Grammar*:[40]

'Seven,' for instance, was normally expressed by putting down in the sand seven strokes side by side, with the words '*njinta ŋaŋa, arbuŋa ŋaŋa, arbuŋa ŋaŋa*, etc. . . . *kalla ŋaŋantma*' (= 'here is one, here is another, here is another, etc. . . . here is

---

[39] Aranda is just one example for this; the same phenomenon has been observed for other Australian languages, too (cf. for instance Dixon's (1980: 108) discussion of Aboriginal number words).

[40] Strehlow (1945). This grammar is the result of extensive fieldwork undertaken by Strehlow in the 1930s as part of his graduate studies in linguistics at the University of Adelaide. Strehlow had been in close contact with the Aranda language and culture from early on, because his father (Carl Strehlow) was a missionary there and had also published several translations of Aranda narratives.

the last'). 'Ten' was expressed by putting up both hands and spreading out all ten fingers and saying '*lakintja*' = 'this many'. (Strehlow 1945: 103)

The same system is employed for ordinal reference: Aranda uses words for the first two ranks (i.e., words for 'the first' and 'the second'), and iconic representations for higher ranks:

'The third', 'the fourth', etc., would all be expressed by continuing with '*wott*' *arbuṇa*' ad infinitum ('*wott*' *arbuṇa*' = 'still another one'): the correct number of strokes in the sand – one for each unit counted – or of fingers raised by the speaker – one for each unit mentioned – would declare the intention of the narrator adequately to his listeners. (Strehlow 1945: 104)

Hence in the Aranda system, one can indicate cardinalities as well as ranks with no recourse to numerical tools. In order to do so, all that is needed is words for small cardinalities and ranks, which can be grasped via subitising,[41] words for noisy magnitudes, and finally a conventional procedure for exact iconic representations of cardinalities and ranks outside the subitising range.

If this account is right, this is an example of a culture that employs recursion-based infiniteness and dependent linking within its linguistic system, but does not put it to use for a number concept. However, the Aranda people – and similarly other Aboriginal Australians – had no difficulties implementing numerical tools into their culture when they first got into contact with Europeans.[42] This makes a lot of sense, given that they had the crucial ingredients for numerical tools at their disposal as part of their language faculty (namely, dependent linking and recursion-based infiniteness).

And while a culture might have a counting sequence that is used in a pattern of dependent linking, this sequence need not necessarily employ recursion and hence be infinite. Recursion is a crucial property of the linguistic system, but it is not indispensable for our number sequence. As the example of the Oksapmin shows, one can do fine with a finite number sequence as long as there is no need to cope with more extended empirical relational structures, and as soon as this need arises one can employ linguistic recursivity to transform this finite sequence into an infinite one (cf. our discussion in chapter 3). The emergence of infinity is an option that counting words bring with them because they are part of a recursive system (namely language). Accordingly, via counting words – used as numerical

---

[41] We will discuss the ordinal counterpart of subitising in more detail in chapter 6.
[42] Cf. for instance Dixon (1980).

tools – language *supports* the implementation of recursivity and hence infiniteness in the numerical domain, but it does not necessarily trigger it. As a result, not all cultures have an infinite, recursive number system, while all have languages that employ recursion and hence allow infinitely many constructions.

To sum up, recursion-based infiniteness and dependent linking are part of language and therefore part of our mental repertoire, and as a result all cultures have the option to develop a recursive, infinite system of numerical tools once they need it, and can implement such a number system when they get into contact with it. Language as a mental faculty is part of our nature as human beings, and it is through this faculty that we develop our systematic concept of number.

CHAPTER 5

Children's route to number: from iconic representations to numerical thinking

As a result of our investigation thus far, we have developed a view of numbers as a set of species-specific mental tools, and we have characterised counting words as verbal manifestations of this toolkit and as the first numbers our species might have grasped. In the previous chapter, I identified language as that human faculty which gave us the mental background to develop a systematic number concept. I suggested a route to number in human evolution which started from iconic representations of cardinality, went via finger tallies and iconic sequences of words, and led to cardinal number assignments as the first context in which counting words might have been used as genuine numerical tools. Let us now have a look at the emergence of number not in human history, but in the individual development of children. What does the picture look like here? What route do children take when they acquire a systematic concept of number?

The present chapter is dedicated to these questions. In particular I will discuss the acquisition of cardinal number assignments, relating our view of counting words and number contexts to the psychological evidence for their representation in individual development. I show what role the numerical status of counting words plays in their acquisition, and how children learn to apply them to empirical objects for the first time. Again, we will find initial stages of iconic cardinality representations, and will see how the development of the language faculty supports the emergence of genuine number assignments. In chapter 6, the results from this discussion will be integrated into a comprehensive view of our cognitive number domain that combines cardinal, ordinal, and nominal aspects of number.

Following Rochel Gelman, I assume that our knowledge of numbers constitutes a natural cognitive domain, where 'a domain . . . can be characterized in terms of a set of interrelated principles that define entities and operations on them' (Gelman 1990: 82). According to Gelman, for a particular cognitive domain children possess a set of initial domain-specific principles that help them to acquire the knowledge that is relevant for this domain. These principles are characterised as a prerequisite for learning; they organise the assimilation of information: guided by domain-specific principles, children can focus on relevant features of the input.

In the linguistic domain, for instance, initial principles would make sure that children take into account who says something and to whom he or she says it, in order to find out the meaning of words like 'I' and 'you' in first language acquisition, whereas they would ignore all kinds of other features of the speech context that could, in principle, also be relevant – for instance, what the speaker wears or what the weather is like while he or she speaks.

The core principles of the human *number domain* that Gelman and her colleagues identify are those that underlie our grasp of cardinality assignments, the 'counting principles'. According to Gelman et al., this is a set of early, innate principles that enable children to distinguish counting words from words for objects and to learn their application in counting procedures.[1]

There are two respects in which the analysis I will put forward deviates from Gelman's. First, I take a broader view of numbers, based on the results from the first chapters: our investigation has emphasised that it is crucial for our understanding of numerical thinking not to focus on cardinality alone, but also to take into account the ordinal and nominal aspects of numbers. These latter aspects will be integrated into the discussion in chapter 6. The second respect in which my account differs from Gelman's pertains to the discussion in the present chapter: I will argue that the basic counting principles, while being relevant in the cardinal subdomain, are not necessarily innate; they do not have to be in place *before* the acquisition of counting words, but arise naturally from the way counting words are introduced as numerical tools in cardinal number assignments.

In our discussion of counting and cardinality and their pre-numerical underpinnings we can build on an extensive body of empirical research. Psychological and psycholinguistic studies from the last two or three decades have given us a clear picture of the acquisition of number words and the representation of counting and cardinality in children; and, as the discussion from the previous chapter showed, developmental psychologists working with pre-verbal infants, and ethologists and comparative psychologists studying higher mammals and birds have gathered evidence for a

---

[1] Cf. Gelman (1978, 1990); Gelman and Gallistel (1978); Gallistel and Gelman (1990); Starkey, Spelke, and Gelman (1991); Gelman and Meck (1992); Gelman and Brenneman (1994). I will come back to these principles below.

protonumerical – or rather, proto-cardinal – module, a cognitive basis for our representation of cardinality and simple arithmetic operations.

THE ACQUISITION OF A COUNTING SEQUENCE

The representation of a counting sequence has to include the features that make counting words suitable as numerical tools: counting words must be represented as (1) phonologically distinct entities, which (2) are ordered as a progression, and (3) constitute an infinite set, due to the rules that underlie the generation of complex elements and that are accessed for their sequential ordering. We identified these properties of counting sequences when discussing their numerical status in chapter 3. In the following paragraphs, I show the impact they have in first language acquisition. A formal definition for our representation of a counting sequence is given in Appendix 3 (starting from p. 304 below) for the example of English, following the analysis I gave in chapter 3.

The acquisition of counting sequences begins before or soon after the age of two. When they enter school, English-speaking children, for instance in North America, have normally mastered the sequence up to the hundreds, in their third school year they count in the thousands, and in their fifth year they can count up to one million and higher (cf. Skwarchuk 1998). This is just the overall picture, of course. As studies on the acquisition of counting words emphasise, there is a large individual variation within all age groups.[2] In addition there can be considerable differences across languages: recall the cross-linguistic data we discussed in chapter 3, which suggested that a counting sequence with a highly transparent structure might be acquired more easily than one with idiosyncrasies and more opaque elements.

As a result of several longitudinal studies on the acquisition of number words by two- to five-year-olds, Karen Fuson and her colleagues[3] distinguished an early acquisition phase in which counting words are learned as part of a connected sequence, and an elaboration phase in which relations between individual words become more salient. On the first level of the acquisition phase – the *string level* – an initial sequence of counting words is represented as a single, unstructured, serial whole ('ONETWOTHREE . . .'). On the next level, which Fuson et al. call the *unbreakable chain level*, individual elements of the sequence are differentiated, but the words are still closely connected ('ONE-TWO-THREE- . . .'). Only later, on the *breakable*

---

[2] Cf. Fischer and Beckey (1990); Fuson et al. (1982), Skwarchuk (1998).
[3] Cf. the studies reported in Fuson (1988, 1992); Fuson et al. (1982); Fuson and Hall (1983), which I have briefly mentioned in chapter 3 above.

chain level, can single elements of the sequence be produced separately. It is not before they reach this developmental level – normally between three-and-a-half and five years of age – that children can produce the successor of a word (for instance, say which word comes after FIVE) without reciting the whole sequence that leads to it ('ONE, TWO, THREE, FOUR, FIVE, SIX').[4] Again, we find parallels in the acquisition of another sequence of verbal tools, namely the letters of the alphabet: just like counting sequences, the alphabet is treated as an uninterrupted whole at the beginning, and children cannot tell which letter follows another without going back to the beginning and reciting the whole sequence that leads to it (cf. Bialystok 1992).

This data underlines our claim from chapter 3 that the sequential character of counting sequences is a prominent feature in first language acquisition: counting words are first and foremost represented as elements of a progression, and initially this progression has to be reproduced every time one wants to identify one of its elements. Indeed, so strong is this feature that in the beginning it comes at the cost of another – and not really irrelevant – property of counting sequences, namely that their elements are well distinguished: Fuson's results suggest that children acquire counting sequences first as one unidirectional whole which is only later, after the *string level*, organised into individual elements.

Additional support for the prominence of sequential features comes from the kind of deviations one finds in children's early counting word sequences, that is, the ways in which they deviate from the adult counting sequence. A typical feature of early counting sequences are what Fuson et al. (1982) called 'stable non-conventional portions': parts that deviate from the conventional sequence, but are used by the child consistently. In the acquisition of the English counting sequence, for instance, children produce such portions at a time roughly before they master counting words above THIRTY. What is interesting for our discussion here is that these subsequences differ from the conventional sequence by leaving out particular counting words, but they do *not* violate its sequential order.[5]

---

[4] Fuson and her colleagues identify two more levels in the acquisition of the counting sequence: (1) the *numerable chain level*, where the elements of the sequence can themselves become objects of numerical procedures like counting, and (2) the *bidirectional chain level*, where words can be produced flexibly in both sequential directions (i.e., not only in the order 'ONE, TWO, THREE, . . .', but also as '. . . , THREE, TWO, ONE').

[5] These 'omission errors' are also known from other (non-numerical) serial recall tasks and, in accordance with our view of counting words, they are known in particular from tasks where people have to recall short sequences of non-referential items, like random letters of the alphabet (cf. for instance McCormack et al. 2000, who discuss the patterns of errors by children and adults).

For instance, a child might consistently go 'ONE, TWO, THREE, FOUR, FIVE, SIX, SEVEN, NINE, THIRTEEN, ...', but she would not be likely to use a stable non-conventional portion like '. . . , NINE, SEVEN, THIRTEEN, SIX, . . .'. These findings are consistent with the counting sequence's status as a progression; they suggest that the sequential order has a psychological reality from early on in acquisition. Our results from the previous chapter suggest that in order to grasp this sequential order children can draw upon an early cognitive capacity that humans share with other species. This basic concept of serial order is independent of numerical thinking and can therefore support its development.

As we discussed in chapter 3, the ordering of higher counting words builds on their internal structure. Complex counting words are ordered with respect to their immediate constituents, and this ordering introduces a repetitive aspect. In English, for instance, the additive counting words that build on a multiplicative element like THIRTY – namely THIRTY-ONE, THIRTY-TWO, THIRTY-THREE etc. – show the same pattern and are ordered in the same way as those that build on TWENTY – namely TWENTY-ONE, TWENTY-TWO, TWENTY-THREE, etc.

The repetitive decade structure of the English counting sequence between TWENTY and ONE HUNDRED becomes evident when words from THIRTY onwards are learned. At about five years of age English-speaking children produce sequences of the form X-TY, X-TY-ONE, X-TY-TWO, ..., Y-TY, Y-TY-ONE, Y-TY-TWO, etc., even though they might not have learned the right order of the decade words 'X-TY' and 'Y-TY' yet; that is, they might be able to produce sequences like 'THIRTY, THIRTY-ONE, THIRTY-TWO', although they do not yet know that TWENTY comes before THIRTY, then FORTY, and so on (cf. Fuson et al. 1982). At this point, the task is no longer to memorise every single element and its sequential position. Rather, complex counting words and their positions can now be derived from primitive ones according to generative rules: the task is now to know the rules underlying the generation of complex counting words and the way the constituents of a counting word determine its position within the sequence, for instance, to know that we can generate THIRTY-TWO from THIRTY and TWO, and that THIRTY-TWO is between THIRTY-ONE and THIRTY-THREE, just like TWO is between ONE and THREE.

The representation of generative rules that is evident at this stage of acquisition contributes to the third criterion that makes counting sequences fit as numbers: their constructive infiniteness. For every counting word, one can always construct a successor, a principle that has been named 'Successor Principle'. Children grasp the Successor Principle by about six to seven years of age. At this time, they are aware of the fact that counting sequences are open-ended, and that this feature is due to the fact that, for every counting word, there is always a word that follows it (even though they might not yet be able to name that word). Here is a passage from an interview with a seven-year-old that illustrates this concept:

INTERVIEWER: Is there a number so big that I couldn't add anymore; I would have to stop?
A.R. (7 years, 3 months): You could always make it bigger and add a number to it.
INTERVIEWER: If I count and count and count, will I ever get to the end of the numbers?
A.R.: Uh, uh.
INTERVIEWER: How can there be no end to the numbers?
A.R.: Because you see people making up numbers. You can keep making them, and it would get higher and higher.
INTERVIEWER: Oh. Well, what if I cheated, and instead of counting from one I count from a really high number? Could I get to the end then?
A.R.: Uh, uh.
INTERVIEWER: You mean there's no last number?
A.R.: Uh, uh. Cause when you get to a really high number, you can just keep on making up letters and adding one to it.

(Hartnett and Gelman 1998: 354)

What I particularly like about this passage is the way A.R. talks of 'people making up numbers' and how they do it: 'when you get to a really high number, you can just keep on making up letters and adding one to it'. This way of putting it emphasises both the man-made status of numbers (numbers are 'made by people'), and their linguistic character (numbers are 'made of letters').[6] This suggests an understanding of numbers as *words* that is very much in keeping with the approach we developed here.

Note that the identification of numbers with words is by no means a natural transition: children, just as adults, do not usually merge words and things this way. To make this clear, take days instead of numbers and let us say that the series of days is just as infinite as the sequence of numbers.[7] When asking a child whether there could be an end to the sequence of days, you are not likely to get an answer to the effect that, 'There is no last day,

---

[6] Although one would normally distinguish the phonological form of words from script and hence talk of 'sounds', rather than of 'letters'.
[7] One might say, of course, that the series of days is not necessarily open-ended, but depends on the sun, and hence might end sometime – for the sake of the argument, let us ignore this and just go by our everyday experience, which tells us that one day always follows the other.

because when you get to a really remote day, you can just keep on making up letters and adding one to it.' However, this is exactly what A.R. above said with respect to numbers. My guess is that you would be rather baffled at such a response in the case of days, whereas the same statement does not sound far-fetched at all when it comes to numbers, but rather like a plausible identification with counting words. And this is exactly because *words can be numbers*, while they cannot be days. The natural transition from numbers to words evidenced in this interview is just another indication for this – a corollary of our account of numbers and counting words.

Let us have a look how these numerical tools are put to use. Before we discuss how children learn to count and how they acquire their first systematic number assignment, let us see what kind of concepts they can build on in this process, which cognitive prerequisites they bring with them when they acquire cardinal number assignments.

PRE-NUMERICAL PROPS FOR NUMBER ASSIGNMENTS

Before children learn to use counting words in cardinal number assignments, they can already distinguish the cardinality of small sets by way of subitising, and estimate the size of larger sets. As we have seen in the previous chapter, this is a capacity that is evident not only in humans, but also in higher animals: young infants as well as monkeys, apes, dolphins, birds, and rats have been shown to discriminate sets of different cardinalities and to perform simple arithmetic operations on them. These sets could be visual objects, sounds, or even combinations of them. And, as Irene Pepperberg's parrot Alex showed, this concept of cardinality can be related to a particular classification of objects, that is, to a concept of sets.[8]

So, when acquiring cardinal number assignments, children can build upon their grasp of properties like 'one-ness', 'two-ness', and 'three-ness', as abstract properties that are independent of a particular modality. By way of subitising, infants can accurately distinguish sets of up to three elements (for instance, distinguish one puppet, two puppets, and three puppets), and grasp the quantitative relations that hold between them (for instance, if we add one puppet to two puppets, they expect there to be three puppets in the end). How can we now account for the mental representations that subitising relates to, what kind of quantitative concepts is this capacity based on?

---

[8] Leaving aside further mathematical implications, this refers to the notion of sets introduced above, where a set is characterised as a complex entity, consisting of elements that fall under a certain concept (for instance, a set of pens consists of objects that fall under the concept 'pen').

As a general approach, we can think of the mechanism underlying subitising as a mental 'object file' activity: when subitising elements of a set, we file mental tokens for these objects in our short-term memory.[9] This allows infants, for instance, to keep a record of the elements a set should have after a transformation, as evidenced in the experiments we discussed in the previous chapter: when seeing two puppets, they would store one mental token for each of them; when another puppet comes onto the scene, they would add another token, and accordingly expect three puppets to be there in the end – namely, as many puppets as represented by the mental tokens (that is, each token should correspond to exactly one puppet).

Based on our discussion of number definitions in chapter 2, we can now account for these early concepts by way of an 'itemising analysis' (cf. pp. 52ff.). Recall that according to this analysis, a notion like 'There are three puppets' is represented as 'There is a puppet x, and another puppet y, and another puppet z, and they are the only puppets around.' In chapter 2, I argued that this way to represent a set does not involve a number assignment, but boils down to itemising the set. Instead of applying numerical tools in order to identify the set's cardinality (for instance, assigning the counting word THREE to the set of puppets), one files its elements (one stores mental tokens x, y, z for the puppets).

However, while this kind of representation does not involve a systematic notion of number yet, it does provide the basis to distinguish sets of different cardinalities and to perform simple arithmetic operations like addition and subtraction on them. For instance, we can distinguish two from three puppets as 'a puppet x and another puppet y' (two puppets) versus 'a puppet x, another puppet y, and another puppet z' (three puppets), and we can identify the difference in cardinality between these two sets as one puppet ('a puppet z'). And, while an itemised representation would not allow us to grasp accurately the size of larger sets (since the enumeration would become too long), it works fine for smaller sets. These are exactly the features we observed for subitising: it allows us to distinguish sets and to grasp additive and subtractive relations between them, but is restricted to small cardinalities.

Hence, in a generalised way we can analyse our early cardinal concepts as representations of distinct items, employing the definitions the itemising approach gives us. Under this account, 'three Fs' (where 'F' describes the objects we quantify, for instance puppets) is represented as 'a set of Fs, consisting of an element x, and another element y, and another element z'.[10] This analysis is in accordance with an object file model; we can think of x, y, and z as our temporary representations of objects. In addition, it introduces a predicate (F) that allows us to include a classification of objects.

In a simple case, 'F' might just be a general object concept (x, y and z are just 'things'), but 'F' can also be a more sophisticated concept like 'group of dots', as the babies in the study by Karen Wynn and her colleagues demonstrated,[11] and the performance of Irene Pepperberg's parrot Alex shows that, in principle, early concepts of cardinality can relate to different classifications of objects. Recall that Alex could identify the same objects either as six toys, or as two thimbles and four pieces of wood.[12] Under the itemising analysis I sketched here, in the first case 'F' is the general concept 'toy', whereas in the second case we get the more specific concepts 'thimble' and 'wood toy' for 'F', respectively. As I argued above, this kind of classification supports the understanding of cardinality as a property of *sets*, that is, of collections of objects that fall under a particular concept.

The early concepts we analysed here give us a precise notion of cardinality for smaller sets. As our discussion in the previous chapter showed, for larger sets we have to rely on approximate representations of quantities: before counting, *noisy magnitudes* support only estimations of set sizes. We can think of the mechanism that underlies these noisy magnitudes as an 'accumulator' that represents the size of sets by means of continuous quantities, rather than distinct object tokens. The accumulator model was initially introduced in order to account for timing and quantification in animals, but it can also give us a handle on our ability to estimate cardinalities.[13] It bases quantification on a 'mental pacemaker' that emits pulses at certain intervals, and can represent either the duration of an event (for timing) or the elements of a set (for cardinality).

To get an idea of how this pacemaker works, imagine putting a handful of sand into a bowl for each element of the set you want to quantify. The overall amount of sand could then represent the set's size for you. When you face a larger set, this representation would not tell you how many elements the set has exactly, because the individual quantities of sand are not distinct anymore (since they are all blended together in the bowl), but the accumulated amount of sand would still give you a rough-and-ready idea of the set's size. Accumulator-based representations would also allow you to distinguish the sizes of larger sets if the difference between them is big enough. This is in accordance with the experimental

---

[10] I provide a formal definition for these concepts in Appendix 4).
[11] Wynn et al. (2002), cf. the discussion on p. 101 above.
[12] See p. 104 above.   [13] Cf. Meck and Church (1983), Broadbent et al. (1993).

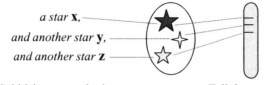

Subitising: mental tokens   Tallying: notches

Figure 43 Iconic representations of cardinality in subitising and tallying

evidence we reviewed in chapter 4: recall that in Fei Xu's and Elizabeth Spelke's study, babies did not seem to distinguish pictures of eight dots from pictures of twelve dots, but they reacted to a difference of eight versus sixteen dots (cf. p. 101 above) – a pattern that fits with an accumulator-like representation.

Note that both accumulator-based concepts and the itemising-based concepts in subitising provide us with iconic representations of cardinality: in both cases, we use something like 'mental tallies' for the elements of the quantified set. In subitising, these tallies are distinct, itemised object tokens, whereas in estimating we rely on accumulated quantities. In particular, subitising, then, can be seen as a mental equivalent to the kind of tallying we encountered in the form of notches in the previous chapter: we produce a distinct representation (a tally) for each object in our set, ending up with exactly as many tallies as objects; accordingly these tallies can serve as an iconic representation of the set's cardinality. I have sketched this kind of iconic representation in Figure 43 for our familiar set of three stars: on the left they are itemised by mental tokens (x,y,z), and on the right they are tallied by notches.

As I emphasised in the previous chapter, this iconic representation does not involve a genuine number concept yet. However, the early concepts we discussed here provide children with a notion of cardinality that enables them to understand what cardinal number assignments are about. These pre-numerical concepts can then be integrated into a concept of numerical quantity: a concept of cardinality that is based on the application of numerical tools.

GATEWAY TO NUMBER

What exactly does a child have to learn when acquiring cardinal number assignments? What does it mean to develop a concept of cardinality as a *numerical* quantity, the quantity of a set as identified by a number? To answer this question, think back to our discussion of numbers and objects in the first chapter, where we defined number assignments as homomorphic mappings between numbers and objects. We showed that these mappings are based on links between numerical and empirical relations, in the case of cardinal number assignments: the '>'-relation between the numbers is associated with the empirical relation 'more', that is, the sequential position of a number (as established by '>') identifies the cardinality of a set – the more elements a set has, the higher the number it receives.

When we analysed how this number assignment works, we identified a numerical subroutine, namely counting, that consists of a one-to-one mapping between the elements of a set and an initial sequence of numbers. The one-to-one mapping ensures that we employ exactly as many numbers as there are objects, that is, it ensures that the counted set and the set of numbers we use in counting have the same cardinality. Since the numbers form a progression and are employed according to their order in this progression, we always end up with the same number for sets of the same cardinality. Hence, this number can be used to identify the cardinality of a set, and it can do so due to its position in the number sequence (cf. our illustration in Figure 7 on p. 22 above).

In view of our analysis of counting words, we can now characterise this mapping as a correlation between the elements of a set and an initial sequence of *counting words*. Counting sequences are represented as a progression starting with 'one', along the lines we discussed earlier in this chapter. In counting games, children learn to apply these sequences as numerical tools in cardinal number assignments: they learn to correlate them (in a one-to-one manner) with objects, and to use the last word in order to indicate how many objects there are. For instance, we can determine how many pens there are on my desk by a one-to-one mapping between the pens and the sequence of counting words <ONE, TWO, THREE>[14] and we can then use the last word, THREE, in order to indicate the cardinality of the whole set. Accordingly, the concept expressed in 'three pens' gives us the cardinality of a set of pens that has as many elements as the counting sequence from ONE to THREE.

We can hence think of our concept of numerical quantity as a relation between sets and our numerical tools. This is the relation I call 'NQ' (numerical quantity) in my illustration in Figure 44. This relation takes into account a one-to-one correlation between the set's elements and an ordered initial sequence of numerical tools, for instance the counting words

---

[14] I use angular brackets to indicate that the counting words come in a fixed order.

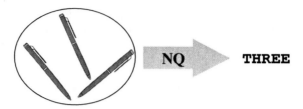

Figure 44 NQ indicates a set's cardinality

from ONE to THREE. NQ then maps the whole set onto the last element in the count, for instance THREE. In Appendix 4(a), I provide a definition for NQ that captures this notion.[15]

In order to account for the acquisition of these cardinality assignments, Rochel Gelman and her colleagues discussed a number of 'counting principles'[16] that children have to adhere to when they learn how to count, that is, when they learn how to apply tags like counting words to objects in order to determine the cardinality of a set. These principles are in accordance with our definition of NQ; they govern not only the counting routine itself, but also its relevance for cardinality assignments. Hence, we might think of them as 'Principles of cardinal number assignment':

(1) *One-One Principle*: Each element of the counted set must receive exactly one tag.
(2) *Stable-Order Principle*: The counting tags must be used in a fixed order.
(3) *Cardinality Principle*: The final tag that is used in the count identifies the cardinality of the counted set.
(4) *Abstraction Principle*: Any collection of things can be counted.
(5) *Order-Irrelevance Principle*: The elements of the counted set can be counted in any order.

The first three principles describe the features a counting routine has to have (Gelman and Gallistel 1978 call them 'how to count' principles): (1) link up exactly one counting word with each of the objects you want to count, (2) use your counting words in a fixed order, and (3) use the final counting word to identify the cardinality. Principles (4) and (5) make clear that there are no restrictions regarding what to count (Abstraction Principle) and in which order (Order-Irrelevance Principle): (4) count any set you like, and (5) tag its elements in any order you like.

---

[15] The definition of NQ relies on the representation of a counting sequence as a progression, as spelled out by our definition in Appendix 3 (in accordance with our discussion in the first section of this chapter). In chapter 7 we will integrate non-verbal progressions, like that of arabic numerals, into our notion of numerical tools.

[16] Cf. our discussion at the beginning of this chapter and the references listed in footnote 1 above.

As Gelman (1978) points out, the tags we use in counting need not be a conventional sequence of counting words, but could also be idiosyncratic sequences that occur before children fully master the counting sequence of their language (for instance, sequences containing stable non-conventional portions), or even non-verbal entities. On this basis one might also think of mental object tokens like the ones we discussed for subitising, as possible candidates for our counting tags. However, these tags do not come in a conventional progression and hence do not provide a basis for an application of the cardinality principle. Crucially, this excludes them from the ranks of numerical tools; they are not elements of a relational structure that is associated with empirical relational structures in genuine number assignments based on dependent linking. In accordance with our criteria-based approach to numbers, we can generalise this requirement in the form of a sixth principle, which states that basically anything can be used as a numerical tool, as long as it fulfils the requirements we set up for numbers:[17]

(6) *Numerical-Tool Principle*: Any progression of well-distinguished entities can be used for counting and cardinal number assignments. Certain progressions can be conventionally identified as dedicated numerical tools.

Gelman et al. regard at least the first three of the counting principles as a priori, that is, as innate principles that have to be present *before* the acquisition of number concepts. According to this view, it is these innate principles that enable children to distinguish counting words from other words and to grasp their application in number assignments. Based on our analysis of counting sequences, we can now relate the understanding of these principles to the special, instrumental, and non-referential behaviour of counting words. Our discussion thus far suggests that counting principles need not be innate; children need not be equipped with these principles right from the start, but can derive them from the use of counting words in procedures like counting games: repetitive, ritualised routines that have a lot in common, for instance, with nursery rhymes of the 'eenie-meenie-miny-mo'-type.

As I emphasised in chapter 3, both counting words and the elements of nursery rhymes are non-referential expressions that we use as devices within ritualised routines, and both kinds of routines are procedures that involve the systematic correlation of a sequence of verbal elements and a set of objects. When this routine is a counting game, the verbal elements

---

[17] I do not include the infiniteness requirement here, since this property of numbers is not necessary for cardinality assignments as long as we remain within a certain finite range (cf. our discussion of the Oksapmin counting sequence in chapter 3).

are counting words like 'one, two, three, . . .'. When we recite a nursery rhyme, the verbal sequence might go 'Eetle, ottle, black bottle; eetle, ottle, out.' In both cases, these 'words' are not employed to name objects. We do not mean to call a pen 'one' or 'two' when counting pens, and we do not name our friends 'eetle' or 'ottle' in this nursery rhyme, any more than we mistake them for a black bottle.

In counting games as well as nursery rhymes, the non-referential nature of the words is evident from the ritualised way they are employed: they are recited in a stable sequence and with a rhythmic intonation that emphasises the repetitive correlation of verbal elements and objects (counting words and elements of a set, or nursery rhyme 'words' and children), and in counting games as well as in nursery rhymes the last word is uttered with a special emphasis that marks its prominent status. This suggests that we do not have to assume innate principles for the acquisition of counting procedures any more than we have to grant children special innate principles for the acquisition of nursery rhymes. The principles governing the application of these verbal elements in counting procedures or in games that use nursery rhymes can be derived naturally from their salient instrumental status in these contexts.

Children begin engaging in counting routines at about two-and-a-half years, shortly after they start to learn the counting words of their language. It then takes about two years before they show a full understanding of counting. By the age of about five, children master cardinal number assignments in such a way that they can even do some meta-reasoning and apply their knowledge to counter-factual situations. This ability was tested, for instance, in a study where a doll, 'Molly', tried to count toys, but left out one toy or counted one toy twice (Freeman et al. 2000). Five-year-old children had no problems telling how many toys there were, without re-counting the set – instead, they figured out the right cardinality from Molly's miscounts – and they were also able to say how many toys Molly (counter-factually) thought were there.

This suggests the acquisition of a fairly sophisticated concept of cardinal number assignments by at least the age of five. In the following sections, let us have a look at the route children take to get there. I will focus on the different counting principles in this acquisition process in turn.

One–One Principle: match counting words and objects

Three processes are involved when we link up words with the elements of a set in a one-to-one correspondence:

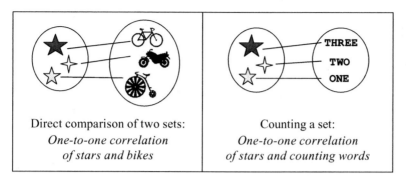

Direct comparison of two sets: | Counting a set:
One-to-one correlation | *One-to-one correlation*
of stars and bikes | *of stars and counting words*

Figure 45 Two kinds of one-to-one correlation: comparing and counting sets

(1) *Itemising:* We have to single out the individual elements of the set we want to count.

(2) *Tagging:* We have to correlate words with the items we single out.

(3) *Partitioning:* We have to distinguish the items that we have already tagged from those that still have to be tagged.

Before they know how to count correctly, children can compare the cardinality of two sets by linking up their elements in a direct one-to-one correlation. This correlation already shows a lot of the features that they will need when matching counting words and objects: it involves both itemising (singling out individual elements of a set) and partitioning (making sure that one deals with each object exactly once). The difference from counting is only that the second set is another set of objects, and not a series of counting words. Hence, instead of linking up objects with counting words ('tagging') one links them up with other objects. Figure 45 illustrates the two kinds of one-to-one correlation for the example of our set of stars. In both cases, the one-to-one correspondence between the elements of the respective sets – either objects and objects, or objects and counting words – tells us that they have the same cardinality (in Frege's words, they are 'like-numbered'; cf. our discussion in chapter 2). Making use of this knowledge, three- and four-year-olds can employ one-to-one correspondences between sets in order to find out the cardinality of a set outside their counting range: when they are told the cardinality of one set and then find out that its elements can be put in a one-to-one correspondence with those of another set, they know that the same number should be applied to both sets.[18]

---

[18] Cf. Sophian (1988); Becker (1989).

Of the three processes mentioned above that are involved in this one-to-one correspondence, the first one, itemising, can build on an early pre-numerical ability: as we saw earlier on, this capacity is also evident when we subitise small cardinalities. Tagging and partitioning emerge later, and at initial stages they are often supported by additional devices, in particular gesturing.

When setting up one-to-one correspondences between counting words and the elements of a set, children often spontaneously point to the objects while counting,[19] just as they will do to support one-to-one correspondences in nursery rhymes. In a study with four- to five-year-olds, Martha Alibali and Alyssa DiRusso showed that gestures support the task of tagging as well as partitioning: gesture helps children both (a) to co-ordinate saying counting words and single out elements of the set, and (b) to keep track of what items have already been counted (Alibali and DiRusso 1999). Gestures support the one-to-one correspondence in particular at earlier acquisition stages: whereas three-year-olds often touch the objects they count, four- and five-year-olds sometimes just point to them, without actually touching, and adults normally gaze at the counted objects in turn – although we also might employ gestures when the counting task gets more complicated (cf. Fuson and Hall 1983).

Sarah Boysen and her colleagues showed that gesturing can also be observed in non-human primates (Boysen et al. 1995). They conducted a study on cardinality with Sheba, the chimpanzee we encountered in the previous chapter (the one who showed those amazing skills on summing up oranges and arabic numerals). Sheba was shown some candies and a set of plastic cards with arabic numerals. She then had to choose the card that indicated the cardinality of the candies. When performing this task, Sheba often pointed to the different candies or touched them. This behaviour might have supported the task of itemising the objects and helped her to set up one-to-one correspondences between objects and tags, similar to the gestures young children employ in counting – although in the case of Sheba, the tags would not be counting words, but mental tokens (these tokens do not enter cardinal number assignments in the sense we developed here, but support the iconic cardinality representations that underlie subitising; cf. our discussion on p. 160 above).

As a result of a study with two- to four-year-old children, Theresa Graham suggested that gesture might serve as a representation for one-to-one correspondences before this principle is mastered for counting words. In her

---

[19] Cf. Saxe and Kaplan (1981); Fuson et al. (1982).

experiments, the younger children often got the one-to-one correspondences between pointing gestures and objects right (they pointed at each object exactly once), while they still made mistakes in matching counting words and objects (they sometimes used two counting words for one object, or no counting word at all). This suggests a command of one-to-one correspondences in gesture prior to speech (Graham 1999).

Stable-Order Principle: counting words have to be sequenced

By 2½ years of age children tend to use stable sequences of words as tags in their counting routines, although at first their sequences might include idiosyncratic portions of the kind we encountered above, that is, sequences like 'ONE-TWO-FOUR-NINE' that deviate from the conventional counting sequence (cf. Gelman and Gallistel 1978). In order to employ such stable sequences, children need not be endowed with an innate principle that requires stable order, though.[20] As we have seen above, the fact that counting words form a progression is a salient feature of our representation of counting sequences right from the start, and the grasp of this feature is further supported by an early capacity to grasp serial order. Before children know how to apply counting words at all, they represent them as elements of a stable (conventional or idiosyncratic) progression. This representation then naturally supports the same stable order for these words when they are employed in counting.

At early stages, children often use fingers along with words when counting, that is, they unbend or bend a finger for every word they say, such that the fingers represent the cardinality iconically (one bends or unbends as many fingers as there are counted objects). As I argued in the context of our evolutionary scenario in the previous chapter, the use of fingers further supports a stable order in counting. Fingers are concrete, visual objects that come in a predetermined sequence, simply due to the way they appear on the hand. This supports a habit to use them in a stable order, which emphasises the stable sequential aspect of counting in individual development.

In a study investigating finger counting in German schoolchildren, we asked eleven- to twelve-year-olds why they unbend their fingers in counting in the order they do (namely, starting with the thumb, and then going from the index finger to the little finger, as is conventional in Germany), and

---

[20] Cf. also the discussion in Fuson et al. (1982); Sophian (1998).

why not, say, start with the little finger, then the index finger, middle finger, then the thumb, and finally unbend the ring finger. In chapter 4, I asked the same question in order to emphasise that there is no reason why we should use our fingers in a stable conventional order, given that the last finger – unlike the last word we use in a count – does not take on any special significance (like indicating the cardinality of a whole set). It is just the salient order of fingers on the hand that suggests such a habit, and this way supports the emergence of a stable progression in counting.

Here are some of the explanations that the children volunteered in answer to our question:[21]

(1) 'This is how my older brother showed me to count with my fingers.'
    'I have seen older kids in kindergarten do it like this.'
(2) 'I do it like this because of the order of fingers.'
    'Otherwise, the fingers would sort of jump.'
    'Otherwise, it would be a mess.'
(3) 'This way I can imagine it better.'
    'So that one does not get confused.'
    'This way I can remember it better.'

Many children pointed out that they counted with their fingers in the conventional order because this was how they learned it from others, as in the examples in (1) (of the 56 children we interviewed, 26 referred to some kind of convention in their answer). Others emphasised the given order of fingers, as in (2) (this feature showed up in 9 of the answers). In addition, several children gave explanations that suggest a mental representation of serial order as a trigger, as illustrated by the answers in (3) (this was the case for 11 of the children). These answers bear on the three key aspects we identified for the representation of cardinality with fingers: (1) the order in which the fingers are used is a matter of convention, (2) it is supported by the order of fingers on the hand, and (3) it reinforces a concept of serial order in counting. The results from our interviews support this account from the perspective of individual development, suggesting that these properties have a reality in children's representation of finger counting.

Order–Irrelevance Principle: counted objects can come in any order

When they are about three years old, children show at least some under-standing of the 'order irrelevance principle' that allows them to introduce the counted objects – unlike the counting words – in any order. For instance,

[21] H. Wiese and I. Wiese (unpublished data); responses translated from German, H. W.

when asked to judge a puppet's counting performance, three- to five-year-olds accepted counts where the puppet did not start at the beginning of a row, or counted every second object first and then went back (Gelman et al. 1986). In the same study children also agreed to count a row of objects from the middle to the end, and then go on from the beginning of the row to the middle.

Knowledge of the order irrelevance principle might not yet be very firmly established at this age, though: in a study that Arthur Baroody conducted in the 1990s, some four-year-olds did not know that when they count the same row of objects twice, but started from different sides, their counts should have the same outcome (Baroody 1993).

Cardinality Principle: use the last counting word to
identify the cardinality of the set

Before about three and a half years of age, children do not always use the last counting word in order to identify the cardinality of a set. So, when you ask a three-year-old how many toys there are in her room, she might just say 'one, two, three, four, five', counting the toys without using the last counting word as an answer. If you ask again, chances are that she will consider you a bit slow on the uptake, and repeat the counting procedure – again without eventually responding with 'five'. Karen Fuson reports that in one study some children re-counted sets of blocks as often as seven times in response to each repeated question of 'How many blocks are there?', rather than giving the final word from the count as an answer (Fuson and Mierkiewicz 1980).

Note that such a response, again, qualifies as an *iconic representation* of cardinality, similar to the iconic representations by tallies and by fingers we discussed earlier, and similar also to the iconic representations by mental tokens that support subitising. Children at this stage produce one counting word for each object by matching a series of counting words with the objects in a one-to-one manner. This means that the counting words can be regarded as verbal tallies, something like a verbal equivalent to notches on a stick. Since the children produce exactly as many counting words as there are objects, the set of these counting words can serve as an iconic representation for the set of objects, a *verbal* icon for its cardinality, just like fingers and notches serve as a *visual* icon (while mental tokens can be regarded as mental icons for cardinality).

Figure 46 illustrates the analogous use of fingers and counting words as iconic cardinality representations, again for our set of stars. In both cases

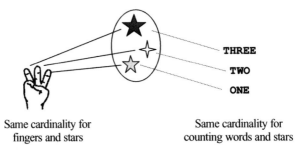

Same cardinality for   Same cardinality for
fingers and stars   counting words and stars

Figure 46   Before the cardinality principle: sets of fingers and sets of counting
words as icons

we have exactly one tally (finger or counting word, respectively) for each
star, hence our icon (the set of fingers or the series of words used in a count)
has the same cardinality as the set of stars that it represents. So, before children master the cardinality principle, they have not yet acquired a genuine
number assignment. They have different means to represent the cardinality
of sets (mental tokens in subitising, fingers or words in counting), but these
representations are still iconic: the mental tokens, fingers, or words have
together the same cardinality as the set they represent. The link between
these representations and the empirical objects (for instance, the stars) is
based on similarity: the representation itself has the property we want to
identify, and this is why it works as a representation.

At about 3½ years children make the step to a non-iconic representation
of cardinality: at this age, they start using the last word from the count
in order to indicate the cardinality of the whole set.[22] For instance a child
might now assign, say, the word NINE to the set of his toys in order to
indicate that he owns as many toys as there are counting words from ONE to
NINE. This establishes a genuine cardinal number assignment; a counting
word is now assigned to a set such that its position in the counting sequence
reflects the set's cardinality. What determines the link between NINE and
the set of toys is not some feature the word has by itself, but the relation
that NINE has to other counting words. Unlike an iconic representation,
NINE does not have the same cardinality as the set of toys (being a single
word, NINE has the cardinality 'one', which does not help a lot when we
want to represent nine toys). Rather, it can indicate a cardinality because
of its position within the system of counting words.

As I have shown above, this way of matching counting words and sets is
based on dependent linking; it associates a relational structure of numbers

---

[22] Cf. Wynn (1990). Jing (1984) reports a similar age for Chinese children.

(namely counting words) and a relational structure of sets (namely sets of different sizes), such that the numerical relation '>' is associated with the empirical relation 'has more elements than'.[23] So, for instance, when the counting word THREE is assigned to the set of tomatoes in your fridge and the counting word TWO to the set of olives, you know that there are more tomatoes than olives (and you might also want to stock up on olives), because THREE comes after TWO in the English counting sequence, that is, THREE > TWO.

The step from iconic representations of cardinality (before the cardinality principle is mastered) to systematic number assignments (adhering to the cardinality principle) is supported from at least three sides. For one, it can draw upon a fundamental linguistic ability: as I argued earlier, our language faculty supports a routine of non-iconic, but system-dependent links between words and objects, and by so doing provides a cognitive pattern for number assignments. We will come back to the developmental impact of language in more detail.

A second source of support comes from the ritual nature of counting. When discussing the evolution of numerical thinking, we saw that ritual contexts emphasise word–word relationships: in ritual contexts, the focus shifts from individual elements to the system, supporting the association of relations. In individual development, children can draw on such a ritual context, too. When counting, one utters words rhythmically, in a ritualised recital of a repetitive character that emphasises their succession. This makes it easier for children to focus on the sequential relationships between counting words, and helps them to link up these relations with the cardinality of sets when they acquire the cardinality principle. Accordingly, children tend to emphasise the rhythmic pattern of intonation when counting.

Third, subitising helps children to understand what property the cardinal number assignment relates to. Since subitising is independent of a genuine number concept, it enables children to grasp the concept of cardinality before they master cardinal number assignments; and, because of the modular nature of subitising, children recognise the cardinality of small sets automatically (cf. our discussion in the previous chapter). Hence, they subitise a small set independently of and along with the counting procedure, before they master the cardinality principle. This pre-numerical support helps them to find out what the number assignment is about; it

---

[23] Remember that in our framework '>' is not a relation between set sizes of any kind (as the paraphrase 'greater than' might suggest), but is just the name we use for the relation that orders our numerical tools.

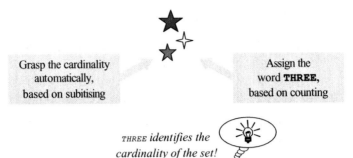

Figure 47 Subitising helps children to figure out what cardinal number assignments are about

enables them to grasp what property the last word in a count is supposed to identify.

Children's early, pre-numerical concepts of cardinality can then be integrated into a concept of numerical quantity, a concept of cardinality that is based on the application of numerical tools and allows children to quantify sets of any size (in Appendix 4, you find a formal account of this integration). For small sets, children now have two ways to find out the cardinality: subitising and counting. Normally children – just like adults – subitise rather than count small sets even after the acquisition of counting, although sometimes they might actually count sets of two or three items: some three- and four-year-olds did that in the Freeman et al. (2000) study that I mentioned above (on p. 164) – although this might have been induced by the experimental situation, which focused on counting skills.

Not surprisingly, this seems to be a cross-cultural phenomenon: in a study that Geoffrey Saxe conducted in Papua New Guinea, Oksapmin children (who use the body count system we discussed in chapter 3) were just as reluctant as European and American children to tediously count sets when they could *see* the cardinality right away: when asked to compare sets of two or three elements, the children would count them only after some probing, and then often just one of the sets, as if to demonstrate that they had put out the correct number (Saxe 1982).

Abstraction Principle: anything counts

Young children are most comfortable counting physical objects, but even three-year-olds are not too bad at counting sounds and events. Karen Wynn asked children between the ages of two-and-a-half and three-and-a-half to help a puppet, Sesame Street's Big Bird, to count toy dinosaurs (i.e. visual objects), elephant roars (sounds), and Big Bird's own jumps (events). Although all children did best on the dinosaurs, most could also count sounds and events to some extent; only some of the youngest children (three out of eight 2½-year-olds) did not know what to do when facing elephant roars or Big Bird's jumps (Wynn 1990).

The ease with which children generalise counting from visual physical objects to sounds and events makes a lot of sense, given the mode-independent nature of our early, pre-numerical concepts of cardinality. Remember that subitising allows babies in their first year of life to distinguish not only two from three dots, but also two versus three drum beats, syllables of words, and jumps of a doll (cf. the experimental evidence we discussed in chapter 4, p. 100). Hence, once children understand that counting is about cardinality, it should be only a small step for them to apply it to elements from different modalities.

It then takes considerably longer before children can apply their counting skills to higher-order concepts like *colours* of things or *kinds* of things, as opposed to the things themselves. In two studies conducted by Elizabeth Shipley and Barbara Shepperson, three- to six-year-old children were shown red, green, and yellow ducks and had to say how many different colours there were; or they would see toy cars and aeroplanes, and had to say how many kinds of toys there were. Only the older children mastered this task, while three- and four-year-olds tended to count individual toys (Shipley and Shepperson 1990).

Numerical-Tool Principle: counting words are just one conventional progression

When do children grasp the principle I called 'Numerical-Tool Principle' above? That is, when do they understand not only that counting words are used for number assignments, but also that they are conventional numerical tools that could as well be replaced by any other progression if the conventions were different? Remember that, at early acquisition stages, children sometimes use letters of the alphabet instead of counting words (cf. our discussion in chapter 3). In so doing, they act in accordance with our criteria-based approach to numbers: for number assignments, any progression will do.

However, at this stage children might just accidentally use one progression instead of the other, given the similarities of the two (both are lists of verbal entities, in both cases the elements of these lists do not refer to anything, and in both cases they have a stable order). This does not mean that they are aware of the principle behind it that allows them to do so with no harm done to the number assignment (except that the assignment does not involve the *conventional* number list anymore).

Geoffrey Saxe and his colleagues asked three- to twelve-year-old children to judge counts with non-standard progressions (Saxe et al. 1989). In the experiments, the children were shown two puppets, Ernie and Bert, and were told that Bert comes from a country where people do not use the words 'ONE, TWO, THREE, . . .', but instead count with the letters of the alphabet. Ernie and Bert then counted some things with their respective count sets and assigned them a number. For instance, on seeing three apples in a shop, Ernie would say: 'There are three', while Bert would say: 'There are C'. Some of the counts were correct within the respective count systems – as in this example – but Ernie and Bert also made some mistakes, for instance they would call three apples 'two' or 'B', respectively. The children were asked to judge, in each case, whose counts were correct.

Only the older children in that study, namely children from eleven years on, consistently accepted correct number assignments that involved the non-standard set of letters. Interestingly, bilingual (French–English) children did much better: six-year-olds already accepted the letters as numerical tools, suggesting that early exposure to different systems makes it easier for children to accept alternatives to their conventional sequence.

An additional problem that might have made it more difficult, at least for the monolingual children to accept letters as counting tools, is the fact that they know them from another context where they are *not* used for counting: letters of the alphabet already have a conventional function, and this is a non-numerical one, namely spelling. This problem was avoided in a follow-up study where the children were told that Bert came from China and used the counting words 'EH, ER, SAN, . . .' (these words are similar to the first three counting words in Mandarin Chinese, YI, ER, SAN). This non-standard set was now readily accepted also by six-year-old monolingual children. This suggests that by the age of six, children show at least some ability to abstract from their standard counting sequence and accept other progressions as numerical tools, too.

LANGUAGE AND THE EMERGENCE OF COUNTING AND CARDINALITY

As we have seen above, children can grasp the cardinality of small sets by way of subitising, before they master cardinal number assignments and independently of language acquisition. When they acquire the counting words of their language, they learn to employ numerical tools in order to determine cardinalities of any size. Since these tools are words, language impairments can slow down the acquisition of number assignments. This seems to be the case, for instance, for children who suffer from Specific Language Impairments (SLI). These children show significant deficits in language development, but are not generally impaired in non-verbal skills. However, they take longer than other children to master counting: four- to five-year-old children with SLI lag considerably behind when it comes to counting objects.[24]

Similarly, for children with Down Syndrome performance in counting tasks seems to be related to their receptive language age. In a comparative study on counting skills, nine-year-old children with Down Syndrome were about as good in counting as four-year-old children who were on the same level in their language acquisition, that is, they showed similar counting skills as a language-matching group but not as an age-matching group.[25]

Hence, counting and cardinal number assignments seem to be initially closely related to linguistic performance, which suggests a reliance on counting words as our numerical tools. This does not mean, though, that linguistic deficits prevent children from acquiring a cardinal number concept altogether. It might take them a bit longer, but as long as their basic symbolic capacity for dependent linking is intact, children will master the use of numerical tools in systematic number assignments. Remember that all we really need from our language faculty is this capacity for dependent linking, that is, the capacity to associate different elements based on the relations that hold between them: we link up relations between objects with relations between words in symbolic reference, and with relations between our numerical tools in number assignments (for instance, we might link up the relations *is agent of* and *is subject of* in symbolic reference, or the relations *has more elements than* and *is greater than* in cardinal number assignments).

That these numerical tools should then be words comes naturally. Using words as numerical tools requires only a slight adjustment to our scheme of dependent linking, namely one that replaces referential, symbolic links between words and objects by non-referential, numerical ones. However, counting words are not the only option we have, and this was exactly the point of our criteria-based approach: any sequence that fulfils our number

---

[24] Cf. Donlan (1998a) for an overview of studies on the numerical development of children with Specific Language Impairments.
[25] Caycho et al. (1991). In this study, the children with Down Syndrome and the four-year-olds had similar scores on the Peabody Picture Vocabulary Test–Revised (PPVT–R).

criteria can be used for numerical tasks. Accordingly, if it is just the acquisition of the verbal counting sequence that causes the problems, children should do better in their acquisition of number assignments when they can use a non-verbal sequence of numerical tools.

Evidence for this comes from an imaginative study that Barbara Fazio conducted with four- to five-year-old children who suffered from Specific Language Impairments (Fazio 1994). Fazio suggested that the difficulties these children have in counting might be based on a deficit in auditory– sequential processing that makes it difficult for them to learn and recite a verbal counting sequence. To get around this problem, she taught the children an invented sequence where one has to point to body parts instead of saying counting words (a bit like the Oksapmin sequence, but without the words). And indeed, when they used this non-verbal sequence, the children's counting skills improved considerably.

Hence, even though the acquisition of number assignments normally builds on the counting sequence, one does not necessarily have to rely on this particular set of numerical tools. The option to use words as numbers is something we get as an extra bonus from our language faculty. It means that we have an efficient and recursion-based sequence of numerical tools at our disposal, but this is not crucial in order to grasp number assignments in individual development (although it might be important for the first appearance of numerical tools in hominid evolution). The crucial ingredient that language provides is our ability to associate relational structures by way of system-dependent links.

This ability manifests itself in first language acquisition when children are about two years old. Between the age of two and three, children's linguistic performance changes dramatically, a change that Derek Bickerton characterised as the step from protolanguage to language (cf. our discussion of protolanguage above). Bickerton proposes that our language faculty might crucially rely on some aspects of our brain that do not develop until after birth and are not completed until children are about two years of age. It is therefore not before this age that children are able to acquire the syntactic structures that mediate symbolic reference in a full-blown language (cf. Bickerton 1990: ch. 5). In other words: by about the age of two, those components of our language faculty mature that enable us to systematically employ the routine of dependent linking.

To get an idea of this development, compare the two samples of utterances in (1) and (2) below. (1) is from a boy of twenty-one months, (2) is from the same boy six months later (examples from Bickerton 1990: pp. 110 and 166).

(1) Rock? (Rocks chair). Rock. Chair. Chair.
(2) Let's get a piece of rock and make it go ding.

Whereas the first example looks like an unstructured, rather repetitive list of words, the second strikes immediately as a much more complex utterance, and in particular as one that suggests a considerable understanding of syntactic structure. For instance, 'a piece of rock' is in the object position of the verb 'get', just as 'it' is the object of 'make', and in both cases these inter-symbolic (sign–sign) relationships indicate a *patient* relation between the respective actions (*getting* and *making*) and the piece of rock. At this stage, then, children begin to anchor linguistic reference in syntactic relations between signs in their speech; they link up conceptual relations like 'patient' with symbolic relations like 'object of': a systematic pattern of dependent linking emerges.

Recall now that not long after this time, namely by about three-and-a-half years of age, children master the cardinality principle. Above, I argued that it is the acquisition of this principle that marks the crucial step from iconic cardinality representations to a genuine number assignment. Before this stage, all one does is to represent elements of one set by the elements of another set (by mental tokens in subitising, or by counting words in counting routines that do not yet involve the cardinality principle). When they master the cardinality principle, children engage in their first non-iconic number assignment, employing counting words as numerical tools: they assign a single counting word (and not a set of words) to a set, based on the relations that hold within the counting sequence.

This acquisitional pattern, then, fits into the picture we have developed here. Between the age of two and three, children make the step from protolanguage to language, applying the symbolic capacity to associate relations between words with relations between objects systematically. And by about three-and-a-half years of age, this capacity is put to use in number assignments: children master the cardinality principle and show an understanding of their first systematic number assignment, an assignment based on dependent links, rather than on iconic similarities.

We have now identified several resources from different cognitive domains that children can draw upon when they acquire their first number assignment. Let me summarise these pre-numerical capacities that help children on their way to number. When children learn counting words, their grasp of serial order lets them perceive the sequential order as a prominent and salient feature. It allows children to represent counting words as elements of a stable progression. Together with the use of fingers, this supports the stable order of counting tags. Their sense of cardinalities (Dehaene's 'number sense', Butterworth's 'number module') enables children to grasp the relevant property in counting, namely the cardinality of sets, and smooths the way for verbal iconic representations of cardinality: representations by counting word lists that emerge before children master the cardinality principle.

It is, then, their language faculty that allows them to make the crucial step to a non-iconic representation of cardinality and, in particular, to one that is based on a pattern of dependent linking. Language as a mental faculty enables children to recognise systematic relationships between words, and to associate them with relationships between objects. This step is further supported by the ritual nature of counting, the rhythmic recitation of counting words emphasises word–word relations and thus makes salient the sequential relations that constitute the numerical relational structure.

Figure 48 summarises children's route to cardinal number assignments, and the impact of language in their acquisition of non-iconic, *numerical* representations of cardinality. This route mirrors in core respects the evolutionary scenario we discussed in the previous chapter. Remember the possible stages we identified for the emergence of numerical tools in the history of our species:

(1) *Early iconic representations of cardinality*
 (a) Notches, pebbles etc. are used as concrete tallies; subitising supports the grasp of cardinality.
 (b) Fingers are used as body tallies; their fixed positions on the hand support a stable order.
 (c) Words are later used as tallies, along with fingers; the stable order (initially induced by fingers) leads to indexical links between particular words and cardinalities.

(2) *Emergence of non-iconic cardinal number assignments*
 Language supports a pattern of dependent linking between words and empirical objects. Sequential relations between counting words are associated with quantitative relations between sets. This transition is further supported by ritual contexts that emphasise word–word relations (namely, the sequential order of counting words).

(3) *Generalised usage of numerical tools*
 The pattern of dependent linking is transferred to non-cardinal contexts, giving rise to ordinal and nominal number assignments.

Some central features of this process are similar to those we observed in individual development. As I have argued in this chapter, children also begin with iconic representations of cardinality and, in particular, they

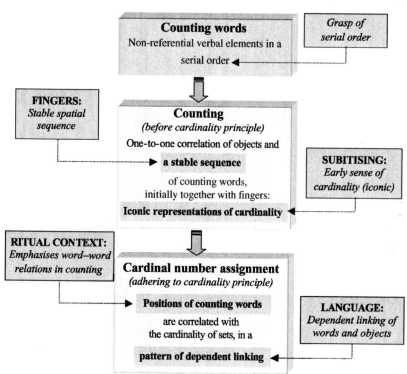

Figure 48 With a little help from outside: the route to cardinal number assignments

initially represent cardinalities by sets of fingers and counting words. Supported by their language faculty, children then make the step to non-iconic representations, when they acquire the cardinality principle and associate sequential positions of counting words with the cardinality of sets. As in our evolutionary scenario, the ritual nature of the counting routine might further support the emergence of relational structures, by emphasising the sequential relations between words.

Of course, the emergence of number need not necessarily go through the same stages in the evolution of our species as in individual cognitive development. However, the parallels suggest that the route I have proposed for the evolution of number is a plausible one; they suggest that our scenario describes a course that is based on possible transitions from simple to more complex representations.

CHAPTER 6

The organisation of our cognitive number domain

Once children grasp the pattern that underlies cardinal number assignments, the way is open for a systematic and generalised concept of number that incorporates not only cardinal, but also ordinal and nominal contexts. In the present chapter, I show how these different contexts can be integrated into a model of our cognitive number domain. The questions that will lead our discussion are: how do children acquire the full range of number contexts? What are the components that make up a unified concept of number, and how do they come together?

Let me sketch a picture of the cognitive number domain as it arises from our results thus far. According to our view of numbers and number assignments, the basis of our numerical concepts is the representation of an infinite progression as provided by counting sequences, and its application in cardinal, ordinal, and nominal number assignments. The representation of these number assignments gives rise to the concepts of (a) numerical quantity and measure, (b) numerical rank, and (c) numerical label. These different numerical concepts constitute different subdomains of the cognitive number domain that are linked up with each other through their association with numerical tools. The acquisition of these concepts is supported by early, pre-numerical cognitive capacities that allow us to grasp the empirical properties we identify with numbers – cardinality, serial order, or identity. These early concepts do not involve the number assignment itself, the systematic association of numbers and objects, they exist prior to and independently of the acquisition of numerical tools.

Following our argument from the previous chapters, our understanding of numerical tools benefits from a cognitive paradigm that is set up by the human language faculty: our natural – and probably species-specific – capacity for symbolic thinking enables us to use words in a mapping of relational structures which we called 'dependent linking', and the same kind of mapping (namely a non-referential instance of dependent linking) is constitutive of systematic number assignments. It is this ability that

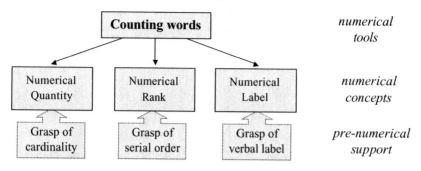

Figure 49 Subdomains of the cognitive number domain and their
pre-numerical underpinnings

ultimately allows children to integrate cardinal, ordinal, and nominal concepts into a comprehensive view of number.

Figure 49 brings together the different areas in a diagram. I will be using this diagram as a signpost throughout this chapter: in the following sections, grey boxes will always tell you which area it is that we are discussing at the moment. As the graphic illustrates, when it comes to numerical tools I will focus on counting words – although, according to our criteria-based approach to numbers, other instances are also possible. Counting sequences are the primary instances of numerical tools when children acquire their first number assignments. In the course of individual development, the representation of counting sequences is later linked up with other instances of numerical tools, and in particular with non-verbal numerals. As mentioned before, we will discuss this issue in more detail for the example of arabic numerals in chapter 7.

REPRESENTATION OF COUNTING WORDS AS NUMERICAL TOOLS

The basis of our number concept is the mental representation of an infinite progression of well-distinguished entities. As we have seen in the previous chapter, children come across such a progression when they learn the counting words of their language. When acquiring a counting sequence, children develop a representation of an infinite progression of words, a verbal manifestation of numerical tools. The representation of these tools constitutes the basis for the other components of our number concept: the conceptual representation of numerical quantity (cardinality of sets, as identified by numbers) and measure, numerical rank (positions in a

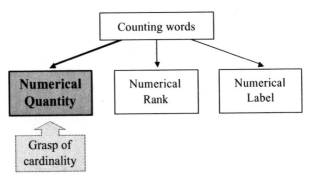

Figure 50   Concepts of numerical quantity within the cognitive number domain

progression, as identified by numbers), and numerical label (objects within a set, as identified by numbers). These concepts reflect the different kinds of number assignments I introduced in chapter 1. On the basis of our results, we can now relate them to the assignments of counting words that serve as numbers. This is what I am going to do in the following sections, where I develop an account of the different kinds of numerical concepts as different applications of counting words, and show how they are acquired. Together, these different concepts constitute a systematic understanding of what numbers are.

CONCEPTS OF NUMERICAL QUANTITY

Children acquire concepts of numerical quantity when they learn to use counting words in cardinal number assignments. In the previous chapter, we described numerical quantity as a relation between sets and our numerical tools. Since we have already discussed the developmental sequence that leads to the acquisition of this concept, together with its pre-numerical underpinnings, we do not need to spell out the details here. Figure 50 identifies these concepts within our diagram from above. This is the application of counting words that we characterised as a 'gateway to number' in the previous chapter. As I argued there, counting itself constitutes an iconic representation of cardinality, because there are as many counting words as elements of the set. The crucial step to a non-iconic, numerical representation of cardinality takes place when a single counting word – the last word from the count – is used to identify the cardinality of the whole set. This word does not have the relevant property (cardinality) by itself, but relies on dependent links: it can identify a cardinality due to its position within a numerical relational structure, the counting sequence. It is at this point that children acquire a systematic concept of numerical quantity, which constitutes the core of the cardinal subdomain of our number domain.

In the following two sections I am going to discuss two kinds of concepts that are integrated into the cardinal subdomain by their association with this core cardinal concept: our concepts of abstract cardinalities that build on numerical quantity, and our concepts of measures which relate numerical quantity to properties like weight, length, or temperature. Later sections will then discuss the acquisition of our concepts of numerical rank and numerical label, and the final section will give an overview of how the different numerical concepts come together within the cognitive number domain.

ABSTRACT CARDINALITIES

Our concepts of numerical quantity allow us to relate the cardinality of a set of objects to a sequence of counting words: when we understand, say, that there are seven pens, we know that there are as many pens as there are counting words from ONE to SEVEN. This concept of cardinality can later be generalised and abstracted from particular sets. Children then do not only understand concrete cardinalities as expressed by 'three pens', but can also grasp 'three' as a cardinality of sets in general. The following interviews with pre-school children illustrate a developmental stage before this abstraction is mastered (Hughes 1984: 9f.):

ADULT:	How many is two and one more?
PATRICK (four years, 1 month):	Four.
ADULT:	Well, how many is two lollipops and one more?
PATRICK:	Three.
ADULT:	How many is two elephants and one more?
PATRICK:	Three.
ADULT:	How many is two giraffes and one more?
PATRICK:	Three.
ADULT:	So how many is two and one more?
PATRICK:	(Looks adult straight in the eye) Six.
ADULT:	How many is two and one?
AMANDA (three years, 11 months):	(Long pause, no response)
ADULT:	Well, how many bricks is two bricks and one brick?
AMANDA:	Three.
ADULT:	OK . . . , so how many is two and one?
AMANDA:	(Pause, then asks hesitatingly) Four?

In this conversation, number words are used in two ways: in constructions like 'two lollipops' the number word is used as a modifier of the noun 'lollipops', while in 'two and one', the number words stand alone, they are used like nominalisations or proper names. Similar constructions are also known from other domains, for instance with words for colours. Here is an illustration:

(1) 'I want the blue lollipop.'

(2) 'I like blue better than yellow.' / 'Blue and yellow together make green.'

In (1), 'blue' is an adjective that is used as a modifier for the noun 'lollipop'. In this construction, 'blue' refers to the colour of a certain object (namely a lollipop). In (2), on the other hand, 'blue' stands by itself. We are not talking about the colour of a particular object here, but use 'blue' as a proper name for a certain colour, abstracting away from particular objects that have that colour (like lollipops, cars etc.). Hence 'blue' can refer to the colour of a particular object as in (1), or abstractly as in (2). This is very similar to the way number words are used in the interview above. 'Two' in the conversation above refers to the cardinality of a particular set in 'two lollipops', and it refers to this cardinality abstractly in 'two and three'.

In any case, then, these number words behave like proper words: both as modifiers and as nominalisations, they refer to something, namely a certain cardinality. In this way they behave fundamentally differently from counting words; they are not used as numerical tools of any kind. When talking about 'two and one', the interviewer does not, say, link up the word 'two' with one lollipop and the word 'one' with the next lollipop (as one would do in a counting routine), but rather he uses these number words in order to denote certain cardinalities.

What does our account say about cardinal number words? So far, not much really. What we have so far is a theory about counting words (as numerical tools), and about cardinal concepts (as mental representations based on cardinal number assignments), but we have not yet analysed in any detail the way we denote these cardinal concepts in language. This will be the topic of chapter 8; for the time being I concentrate on the numerical concepts themselves. In the present chapter, it suffices if we are aware of two distinctions in the context of words and numerical concepts: (1) the distinction between non-referential counting words (for example THREE as a numerical tool) and referential number words (for instance, 'three' in 'three lollipops', or 'three' in 'three plus two'), and (2) the distinction between number words and the concepts they refer to.

Figure 51 summarises the route from counting words via concrete car-dinalities to abstract cardinalities as it emerges from our discussion thus

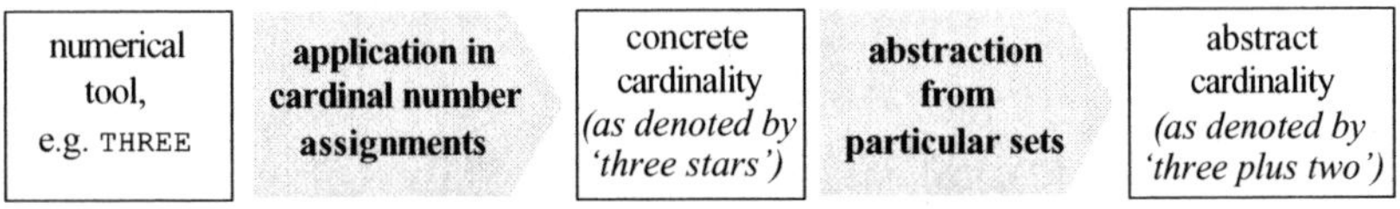

| numerical tool, e.g. THREE | application in cardinal number assignments | concrete cardinality *(as denoted by 'three stars')* | abstraction from particular sets | abstract cardinality *(as denoted by 'three plus two')* |

Figure 51 From counting words to abstract cardinalities

far, and gives illustrations for the different contexts of referential cardinal number words: In order to account for our concept of abstract cardinalities, we can now adopt a set–theoretical approach as sketched in chapter 2 (pp. 46ff.). Remember that set theory gives us a handle on properties. For instance, we can account for a property like the colour blue as the set of all blue things, and we can account for the property of being a star as the set of all stars. In both cases, the set–theoretical approach allows us to account for the property in a generalised way and abstract away from a particular thing that might have this property. We can account for the colour blue in general instead of particular instances of blue things, like the blue pen in front of me or the flower on my windowsill. And we can account for 'star' as an abstract concept, as opposed to our concepts of particular stars, say, the Pole Star or Sirius.

Along the same lines, we can now account for our concepts of abstract cardinalities. We can regard an abstract cardinality like '3' as the property of being a set with three elements, as opposed to particular sets that have this property, for instance the set of pens on my desk, or the set of wishes you are granted if you rub a magic lamp. Under a set–theoretical account, '3' can then be identified as the set of all sets with three elements. And within our approach, this means: the abstract cardinality '3' is the set of all sets that have as many elements as the counting sequence from ONE to THREE (you can find the formal definition for abstract cardinalities in Appendix 4, p. 316).

By abstraction from concrete cardinalities, children acquire a concept of something one might call 'individualised numbers', which serve as the basis for our mathematical thinking. These individualised numbers are objects that can be manipulated, for instance they can be counted themselves and undergo arithmetic operations. So in a way we now have abstract 'numbers' again. Note, though, that these are a far cry from the proverbial Platonic entities – our individualised cardinalities are exactly as abstract as the colour red or the property of being a star; they are not some pure entities that are waiting out there to be discovered, but simply generalisations of cardinality as a property of concrete sets.

Our concept of individualised cardinalities makes it possible to break up the string established by the counting sequence, and lays the grounds

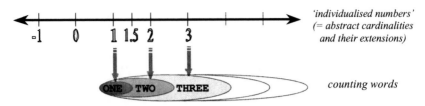

Figure 52 Individualised numbers and counting words

for the various extensions of the number line in mathematical reasoning. Whereas counting words as our numerical tools are defined by their position in a progression (the counting sequence) and only by this position, abstract cardinalities are individuals in their own standing. They form a line with respect to the sets of counting words they relate to, but, unlike the counting sequence, this line is open for the integration of new mathematical entities like 0, negative numbers, rational numbers, and so forth. Figure 52 gives an illustration.   In the illustration, arabic numerals stand for our concepts of individualised numbers (abstract cardinalities and their extensions). The arrows indicate the relations between abstract cardinalities and sets of counting words. Note that, according to our account, this relation is indirect. We did not identify, for instance, the abstract cardinality '3' as the set of counting words 'ONE, TWO, THREE', but rather as the set of all sets *with the same cardinality* as the sequence from ONE to THREE. Due to their link to cardinality, individualised numbers including extensions like rational numbers etc. can be reintegrated into concrete cardinal number assignments (i.e. cardinality assignments or measurements), for instance in contexts like 'This pumpkin weighs 2.3 kg', or 'On average, each family in this village has 2.3 children.'

The definition of abstract cardinalities – or 'individualised numbers' – as sets of like-numbered sets is in accordance with the intersective approach to numbers we encountered in chapter 2. Remember that Frege's account of numbers was based on the insight that cardinality is a property of sets. Accordingly, he identified a number *n* as the set of all sets with the cardinality *n*; for instance he identified the number '3' as the set of all sets with three elements. While our definition hence fits into the general framework set up by the intersective approach to numbers, there are two important deviations from the original intersective definition by Frege.

Firstly, we use different 'paradigm sets' for our definition. Recall that Frege based his account of individual numbers on certain sets that served as a paradigm for a particular cardinality. For instance his paradigm set for 0, which I called '*po*' in chapter 2, is the set of all entities that are not self-identical. Since everything *is* identical to itself, *po* is an empty set, a set with zero elements. Hence when a set has as many elements as *po*, it has zero elements. The paradigm set for 1, *p1*, contains one element, namely *po* (this is the case because *p1* is defined as the set of all entities that are identical with *po*); the paradigm set for 2 has two elements, *po* and *p1*, and so forth. These paradigm sets provide Frege with 'sample cardinalities', they are sets he can relate to in his definition of individual numbers: he needs 0 as the set of all sets with zero elements, hence he defines 0 as the set of all sets with as many elements as *po*; along the same lines, 1 can be defined as the set of all sets that have as many elements as *p1*, and so on.

In our account of individualised cardinalities we need paradigm sets, too – since, like Frege, we define sets of like-numbered sets. However, the paradigm sets we use are not sets like Frege's 'set of all entities that are not self-identical'. Rather, our paradigm sets are *sets of numerical tools*: we use counting words as the elements of our paradigm sets. For instance, the counting sequence from ONE to THREE establishes the paradigm set for '3': within our approach, a set has three elements if we can link up its elements with the counting words <ONE, TWO, THREE> in a one-to-one correlation, that is, a set of three is one that has the same cardinality as the counting sequence from ONE to THREE. The account is hence based on our analysis of counting words as elements of a stable progression and their application in cardinal number assignments, and this allows us to capture the notion of counting in our representation of cardinalities.

The second deviation from Frege's definition is that our analysis does not rely on 0 as the basis for individualised numbers. This accounts for the fact that the concept of 0 develops later than cardinal concepts from 1 onwards. In individual development, children start with a counting sequence and its application to non-empty sets. Only later, based on their grasp of individualised numbers and empty sets, do they acquire a concept of 0. In human history, the number 0 appears late, too. Signs like '0' and related signs in systems other than the arabic numerals were initially introduced as figures that mark an empty space in numeral notations that are based on a place–value system (we will go into more details when we discuss arabic numerals in the next chapter). It was not before the fifteenth century that this figure came into general use in Europe, and at first it was not regarded as a sign for a number at all.

Within the account I developed here, the abstract cardinality 0 can be analysed as the set of all sets with no elements. Regarding 0 as a set of sets is in accordance with the account we gave for individualised numbers from 1. What makes 0 different from positive integers is the fact that a 'set with no elements' cannot be via counting and hence does not relate to our basic numerical toolkit, the counting sequence.[1] Accordingly, o is a later addition to the number domain, an extension that builds on our concept of individualised numbers, with no link to counting. This is why o, and similarly negative numbers, irrational numbers, and so forth are recent inventions in mathematical history: they are not grounded in the counting sequence and they are also not supported by our pre-numerical grasp of cardinality, because they are not related to the cardinality of concrete sets of objects. By endowing us with a concept of mathematical objects as individuals, our abstraction from concrete cardinalities provides a basis for extensions that reach far beyond the limits of our initial numerical intuition.

MEASURE CONCEPTS

Children master measurement procedures when they are about seven years old, that is, at a time when cardinal number assignments are well in place. This makes a lot of sense given the more complex status of measurement. Remember that, in chapter 1, I argued that we can regard measurement as a sophisticated kind of cardinal number assignment, namely one that invokes units of measurement. In number assignments like 'a pumpkin with a weight of 3 kg' and 'bathwater with a temperature of 3 °C', we identify a cardinality. However, this is not the cardinality of the object we are talking about – the pumpkin or the bathwater – but the cardinality of a set of measure items, for instance, metal blocks of the same weight, or length units on a ruler or a thermometer. These measure items are correlated with our measured object in such a way that their cardinality tells us something about the property we are really interested in for our measurement: it tells us how much the pumpkin weighs, or how warm the water is.

Based on this analysis, we can now account for measure concepts (like 'kg', or '°C') as relations between an object (a pumpkin or a bathtub of water) and a set of measure items. These measure items are distinct objects that can undergo a cardinality assignment: they can be related to a counting word, based on our concept of numerical quantity (this is the concept NQ we introduced in the previous chapter).[2] Figure 53 gives an illustration.

Note that it is not the measured object itself (the pumpkin or the bath-water) or some partition of it (pieces of the pumpkin or portions of water)

---

[1] Instead, the definition can be spelled out as 'a set *s* such that there is no entity x that is an element of *s*'; cf. Appendix 4, p. 316.

[2] You find the formal definition of measure concepts in Appendix 4, p. 316.

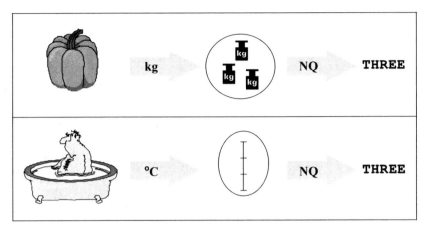

Figure 53 Measure concepts as relations between objects and countable sets of
measure items

that is counted. For the acquisition of measurement, it is crucial that one learns to match the entire object with a set of measure items. We do not cut up the measured object into countable parts, but relate it *as a whole* to countable measure items. The cardinality of this set of measure items then tells us something about the property we want to measure (weight, temperature, etc.). This is also why I used weight instead of, say, length as an example of an extensive property: whereas one might be led to relate the measurement of length to a partition of the measured object into parts of the same length, this seems an unlikely approach to the analysis of weight measurement – and it would obviously not work at all for the measurement of non-additive properties like temperature.[3]

According to this analysis, then, there are two procedures involved in measuring, two subroutines that children must apply when they learn to measure objects:

Subroutines involved in measurement procedures
(1) *Matching*: the object must be matched to an appropriate set of measure items.
(2) *Quantifying* (cardinal number assignment): the set of measure items must be assigned a numerical quantity.

---

[3] However, a partition of an object can initially help children on their way to understanding how measure items work (we will come back to this below).

For the *matching* procedure, children must learn to identify an appropriate set of measure items for the object, and this means they must match the object to a set of measure items whose cardinality identifies the property they want to measure. For this purpose they must (a) choose discrete (and therefore countable) objects as measure items, and (b) make sure that the measure items are identical to each other with respect to the measured property, that is, they must each be of the same length, weight, volume etc.[4] The set of measure items as a whole must then be matched to the measured object, such that the overall length, weight, volume etc. of the measure items is the same as that of the measured object.

Note that this means that our matching procedure is based on an iconic representation: we match the object we want to measure to a set of items that is similar to it, a set of items that represents the object's length, weight, volume etc. iconically. It is then the *quantifying* procedure that brings in a non-iconic number assignment: when we quantify our measure items, we assign them a number by way of dependent linking, namely in the form of a cardinal number assignment.

For properties like temperature, an additional step is included in the procedure, constituting what I called 'indirect measurement' in chapter 1. Recall that the measured object (for example, bathwater) and the measure items are here correlated via a mediating object (for example, a mercury column). In this case, our matching procedure (the correlation of bathwater and the length units on the thermometer) relies on two auxiliary matches. First, the measured object must be matched to the mediating object such that both are identical with respect to the property that is to be measured, for instance they both have the same temperature. Second, the mediating object must be matched to a set of measure items with respect to an additive property, for example length.

So in our example, the cardinality of a set of length units gives us the height of a mercury column, the mercury column's height is linked up with its temperature, and this temperature is the same as that of our bathwater. In this case the correlation between the bathwater (the measured object) and the length units (the measure items) is mediated by the mercury column, such that the number of length units tells us the temperature of the water. The necessary features of measure items and of the mediating object in indirect measurement can be captured by the following two conditions:

---

[4] Cf. our account of measure items in chapter 1, p. 26 above.

Background requirements for measurement

(1) *Requirement for measure items*: the measure items must be identical with respect to an additive property, that is, they must each have the same weight, length etc. This property must either be the property we want to measure (direct measurement), or it must be linked up with this property by a mediating object (indirect measurement).

(2) *Requirement for mediating object* (in indirect measurement): in the mediating object, the property we want to measure ultimately must be linked up with an additive property.

I called these conditions *background requirements*, rather than including them with the subroutines that make up the measurement procedure, because one does not necessarily need to appreciate them in order to apply measurement procedures successfully (albeit mechanically). Being born into a culture that already provides conventionalised techniques for measuring objects, a child can encounter standardised measure devices that fulfil these background requirements implicitly. In principle, one need not know how the mediating object in indirect measurement works in order to use a thermometer successfully, and one need not be aware of the particulars of measure items in order to measure length with a ruler, or weight with a scale.

To find out how warm the bathwater is, one just has to put the thermometer into the water and read the highest number the mercury column reaches. Or if I want to know the length of one of my pens here, I simply lay it side by side with a ruler and read the highest figure it reaches, with no thought wasted on something as tiresome as 'discrete measure items that are identical with respect to an additive property'. And when you need 300 g of marzipan for a cake, you will not bother about the particulars of measure items, either, but rather place the marzipan on your kitchen scale and add to it until the hand reaches the '300' mark.

So when one has a standardised, conventional measure device at hand, one need not go through the background requirements for measurement anymore. It is sufficient to correlate an object with the measure device (thermometer, ruler, scale) in the conventional way: the *matching* procedure, and then to read out the right number: the *quantifying* procedure. In fact, some conventional measure devices can even render the quantifying procedure implicit. Figure 54 gives an example. The figure shows a set of traditional opium weights from Laos. These weights are small bronze figurines that are standardised in a way that each has a particular, different weight and can be used to measure a certain standard amount of opium. Hence, within our account they would not qualify as genuine 'measure items': they differ in

Figure 54   Measuring without quantifying? A Laotian scale

their individual weights, and as a result their cardinality does not indicate their overall weight. You would not want to buy something that weighs as much as, say, three of these buddhas, without knowing which buddhas. However, if you were familiar with these measures, it would help you to know that the white stone (which I used instead of opium for my photo) weighs about as much as the third buddha. This is informative because these objects can be regarded as placeholders for *sets of measure items*. For instance, if we take the smallest buddha to indicate two measure items, then the next buddha, which weighs one and a half times as much, represents three measure items, and so on. Hence we can relate the way these measures work to our notion of measure items, but this relation is implicit and one need not be aware of it when using the balance.

The reason why I discussed in some detail the constraints on measure items and mediating objects in chapter 1 was to demonstrate that there is nothing in the measurement procedure that requires any properties in numbers over and above the properties they need to have for cardinal number assignments (the properties that then went into our criteria-based approach to numbers). These constraints on measure items do not necessarily play

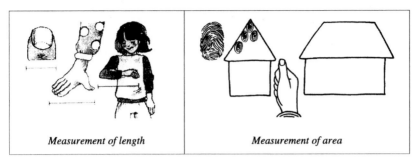

Figure 55 Use of non-standard measure items in maths classes (Radatz et al. 1998: pp. 143, 189)

a central role in the representation of measurement in individual development, and in particular at early stages of acquisition. Unlike for cardinality assignments, there exists a large range of culturally given devices for measurement that do the work for us and spares us the need to bother about the particulars of the measurement procedure.

It is for this reason that school curricula in many countries emphasise the use of non-conventional measure items before children learn to use ready-made devices like rulers and scales.[5] By encouraging children to try out different units of measurement and to invent their own measure devices, one intends to avoid a mechanical application of conventional techniques and to support a conceptual grounding of the background requirements a measurement procedure has to fulfil. Figure 55 shows some graphics I found in a German teachers' handbook, which illustrate the use of body parts as (non-standard) measure items for length and area in mathematics classes with six- to seven-year-olds.

We can distinguish five main stages that children go through on their way to a full concept of measure items:[6]

(1) *Estimating:* At the earliest stage, differences of objects in size, weight, temperature etc. are estimated, based on holistic perception.

(2) *Comparing:* Different objects are compared along a single dimension, at the beginning usually length. To find out whether objects have the

[5] For primary schools in England for instance, Nunes et al. (1993: 47) mention that 'the National Curriculum in England emphasizes the use of non-standard units before the use of rulers in measurement in the classroom'.

[6] This is a general overview that focuses on those features that are relevant for our discussion of the number domain. Different aspects of the acquisition process, in particular for the measurement of length and area, are discussed for instance in Miller (1984), Nunes et al. (1993), Boulton-Lewis et al. (1996), Clements et al. (1997), and Barrett (1998).

same length, they are arranged parallel to each other, starting at the same point.

(3) *Segmenting*: To measure length or area, the object is segmented into different parts which are – more or less – identical with respect to the measured property (as mentioned above, such a partition is difficult to carry out in the case of other additive properties, like weight, and does not work for non-additive properties, like temperature, which we usually assess by indirect measurement). The parts of the object then function as its own measure items; their cardinality can be used as an indicator of the object's length (or area). Hence at this stage the first measure items emerge – although they are not yet independent of the measured object – and the assessment of length and area can be based on a cardinal number assignment.

(4) *Introduction of independent measure items*: Objects that are independent and detached from the measured object are used as measure items. These items could, for instance, be body parts, (as illustrated in Figure 55), but also other idiosyncratic measure items, and in particular, they can include measure items for properties other than length and area.

(5) *Standardisation*: At the final stage, idiosyncratic measure items are replaced by conventional and standardised measure items, as identified by units like 'cm', 'kg', or '°C'.

Note that the first three stages share some characteristic features with those we observed in the acquisition of cardinality assignments. (1) *Estimating* resembles the cardinality estimation that is based on our representations of 'noisy magnitudes': this imprecise, pre-measurement assessment of properties can be regarded as a counterpart of our imprecise assessment of cardinality before counting. (2) What we do in *comparing* the length of objects is similar to comparing the cardinality of sets via one-to-one correspondences between their elements. (3) The routine of *segmenting* (and then counting the segments) can be regarded as a more general notion of the 'itemising' subroutine we described for the One–One Principle in cardinal number assignments (cf. p. 165 above). In itemising, elements of the counted set are singled out one by one, as a basis for the counting procedure. This can be regarded as 'segmenting' a set. Whereas in length measurement the measured object might be a stick, its counterpart in a cardinality assignment would be a set of objects, say, a set of pens. The stick is segmented into parts of the same length, that is, into parts that are identical with respect to the measured property. In counting, the measured property is cardinality, and the set of pens is 'segmented' into parts of the same cardinality, namely its individual elements – each pen has the cardinality 'one'. In the case of the stick, the overall cardinality of the segments tells us something about the property we wanted to measure: knowing how many segments we have allows us to assess the stick's overall length. Trivially, the overall cardinality of the 'segments' in cardinality assignments (in our example, the individual pens) also tells us something about the property we want to assess – simply because this property *is* cardinality.

Hence, on a closer look, the first three stages in the development of measure concepts show a lot of features we know from cardinality assignments: starting from the pre-numerical stages of estimating and comparing, we arrive at a stage where the segments of our object are counted as a basis for a genuine number assignment. In contrast to this, the introduction and standardisation of independent measure items is germane to measurement, with no close counterpart in cardinality assignments. It is the last two stages from our list above, then, that are characteristic for measurement and for measurement only: at these stages a notion of systematic measure items emerges.

This notion of measure items has proved a highly fruitful concept in human history. Measure items have been introduced not only for properties like length, weight, or temperature, but also for a conventional property like value as measured by currencies, and also for a property like time where our measure items are events. What makes these diverse kinds of measurements possible is that, in each case, our measurement units link up the property we want to measure with cardinality, so that we can assess this property via an ordinary cardinal number assignment. Let me illustrate some of the more interesting cases in the following paragraphs.

As the use of such names as 'foot' and 'stone' for length and weight measures indicates, the cultural development of measure items usually goes from idiosyncratic and variable measures to standardised items, similar to the route we observe in individual development. While idiosyncratic measures for length can, for instance, be body parts that are different for different people (leading, for instance, to a length unit like 'foot'), standardised items like metres (or today's 'foot') are usually independent of individual variation.

In some cases, though, a personalised standard might actually be preferable to a general one. An example is the Chinese measurement unit 'cun' (sometimes called 'anatomical inch') which is widely used in acupuncture, and probably goes back at least to the Neolithic cultures of southeast China, in the third millennium BC.[7] One cun identifies the width of the patient's thumb, that is, a cun for you might be longer or shorter than a cun for me, depending on whether your thumb is wider or thinner than mine. However, while such a variation might be unfortunate if one wants to measure, say, cloth – if I sell you 230 cun of silk, do we use your thumb or mine? – it is useful if one wants to measure relative distances that depend on a person's body size. And this is exactly what the cun is used for: this length unit is employed to locate acupuncture points on a person's body. For instance if you go to an acupuncturist and she wants to locate a certain point on your forearm, she might measure a distance of 4 cun upwards from your wrist, such that 1 cun equals the width of your thumb. One wants a different, individualised kind of measure item for everyone here, since generalised measure items would not be related to an individual's body size, and would lead us to different points on the bodies of different people.[8]

An interesting case of standardisation is the way we measure trade value with money. The use of money in a society typically starts with tokens that have their own value, for instance tokens made from a metal like bronze or gold, or rare items like certain kinds of shells. These tokens are measure items that have the property we want to measure intrinsically. Later, they are often replaced by measure items that gain their value by a social contract: in the case of banknotes or modern coins, the property we want to measure with them (value) is conventionally assigned to them. If this convention changes, their value changes, too, and more or less of these measure items have to be applied to the same object in the *matching* routine.

Figure 56 gives some examples: a bronze token that was used as a currency in ancient China, a modern banknote from the People's Republic of China, a Euro coin, and a 5,000,000-Mark note from Germany that was printed at a time of hyper inflation, in 1923. As these examples illustrate, we also find a feature here that we discussed for the Laotian opium weights: we do not necessarily have individual tokens for each measure item, but one token can stand for a whole set of them, making the quantifying procedure implicit. The cardinality of these items can be directly indicated by

---

[7] David N. Keightley discusses archaeological evidence for jade carvings from this period suggesting the first appearance of *cuns* as 'neolithic inches' (Keightley 1995).

[8] In addition to the standardisation of 1 cun as the width of a thumb, this measure system also defines certain multiples of 1 cun via other parts of the body, for instance 3 cun is defined as the width of all four fingers. As Meaghan Coyle and her colleagues showed in Australia, these additional standards can lead to inconsistencies, since at least in modern Western populations the ratio of body parts might deviate from the definitions (cf. Coyle et al. 2000).

Figure 56 Measure items with a conventionally assigned property: money

a number, for instance '1' in the case of the Euro, or 'Fünf Millionen' (*five million*) on the Mark-note. The fact that they receive their value through convention distinguishes currencies from other measures, which have the relevant property intrinsically. However, for the purpose of measurement, this comes out the same: in either case we match an object with a set of measure items, and assign a number to this set.

A further instance of measurement, with yet another kind of measure items, is the measurement of time. When we measure time, our measure items are events that cover a particular time, for instance periodically re-curring events like the rising of the sun that indicates days, or certain movements like the flow of sand in an hour glass or the movements of the hands on a watch.

When children learn to measure time, they often invent their own measure items, along the same lines that they use idiosyncratic measure items in other kinds of measurement. In a study on children's time quantification conducted by Friedrich Wilkening and his colleagues, some five-year-olds used idiosyncratic measure items like rhythmically blowing air out fiercely, repetitively raising and lowering the hand, or uttering a repetitive sound. For six- and seven-year-olds, the dominant strategy was counting out loud (Wilkening et al. 1987). In this strategy, uttering counting words fulfils two functions at the same time. One the hand, each utterance (saying aloud one counting word) is an event of roughly the same duration and accordingly can be employed as a temporal measure item. On the other hand, the se-quence of counting words also gives us a cardinality; hence counting aloud

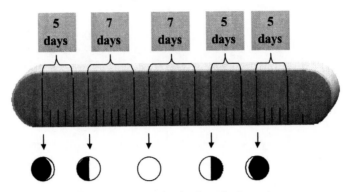

Figure 57 A lunar calendar from the Stone Age

can here be regarded as something like a reflexive counting procedure where the counting words (in their function as counting tags) count themselves (in their function as measure items).

About 25,000 years ago, the mammoth hunters from Dolní Věstonice whom we encountered in chapter 4 probably used *iconic* representations of cardinality when they measured time. On a small rod of marl, they engraved notches in groupings that correspond to the days of characteristic lunar phases, namely waxing moon (5 days), half-moon (7 days), full moon (7 days), half-moon (5 days), and waning moon (5 days).[9] The people who lived at that site might hence have used these notches as iconic cardinal representations for days, in a similar way as they represented the cardinality of physical objects, for instance the animals they had hunted (remember our discussion of the notches on a fossilised wolf's bone on p. 134 above). Figure 57 illustrates this lunar calendar, as described by E. Emmerling and his colleagues (according to Emmerling et al., the small single notch at the right end of the rod indicates the extra day one has to add every other month, since a full lunar circle takes on average twenty-nine-and-a-half days, not twenty-nine).

If this account is right, then this is an intriguing example of a predecessor of our measurement, a kind of 'proto-measurement' that involves measurement units, but does not yet indicate a number assignment. The *matching* procedure is of the same kind as in modern measurement: an event (lunar

[9] This account is based on a reconstruction of the rod from five pieces that were excavated in 1986; cf. Emmerling et al. (1993); Klíma (1995). Cf. also Marshack (1964) who discusses several other examples from the Upper Palaeolithic period where markings on bones and rock walls might indicate lunar calendars.

phase) is matched to a set of temporal units of measurement (days) that are each of the same duration, and together last as long as that event. The cardinality of these measurement units can then tell us the duration of our event. The *quantification* procedure that assesses this cardinality, though, is different from the one we employ in modern measurement. It is iconic rather than numerical, that is, it is not realised by the assignment of a number, but based on an iconic representation of a set's cardinality by notches that stand for its elements: each notch stands for one day, instead of one number representing the whole set of days.

Temporal measure items can also be used in the measurement of distances. This constitutes an interesting case of measurement, which builds on the connection of spatial and temporal concepts in our representations of events. In particular, an event that consists of someone moving from a location A to a location B will cover not only a certain space (the route from A to B), but also a certain amount of time (the time it takes to get from A to B). As a result, our conceptualisation of distances can involve temporal aspects in addition to spatial ones.

So if you ask me how far it is from my apartment to the university, I could tell you the length of the route, for instance: 'My apartment is three kilometres from the university.' This way, I would give you the number (namely, 3) of a set of space-based measure items (kilometres). But I could also tell you the distance by using time-based measure items, that is, I could tell you the time the passage takes: 'My apartment is twenty minutes from the university.' Hence when we want to identify the distance between two places we can do so with reference to space (3 km), but also with reference to time, namely to the amount of time needed to get from one place to the other one (twenty minutes). If one identifies an amount of time to measure a distance, one often specifies the means of travel, for instance 'twenty minutes by bike / by bus / if you walk'. A measure item from physics that falls into this category is the light year, which indicates the distance that light can travel within a year (in this case, a paraphrase analogous to the 'twenty minutes by bike' could be something like: 'one year if you travel by light').

Here is a passage from a travel journal, which gives a vivid picture of the problems that can arise if one is confronted with a measurement unit for distances that has an unfamiliar set-up. It is written by Vita Sackville-West (famous, among other things, for her gardening and as a model for Virginia Woolf's *Orlando*) and describes a journey through the Bakhtiari Mountains in Iran in the early twentieth century:

The way seemed very long indeed that day, and my temper grew correspondingly short . . . It was useless to ask, 'How far?' for Taha's reply would have been given in *farsakhs*, and the Persian *farsakh* is by no means an exact measure of distance, but varies according to the nature of the road; that is to say, a *farsakh* of uphill going, or over a stony road, is longer than a *farsakh* downhill or on a smooth road. Roughly speaking, it means the distance that a mule or horse can cover at a walking-pace in an hour.[10]

Based on our analysis of measure concepts, we can now account for *farsakhs* as time-based measure items for distance. Such measure items can be as exact as those from a space-based system like kilometre or mile, given proper standardisation. For instance one could imagine something like a mechanical mule that would always need exactly the same time to cover a route of the same quality, and would need more or less time depending not only on the length of the way, but also on the incline of the road and the condition of its surface. With reference to this robot mule, we could define exact temporal measure items. The cardinality of a set of these items would be linked up systematically with the property we want to measure, namely the distance of road covered in a certain amount of time, or, from a different perspective: the time needed to cover a certain distance on the road. Hence these measure items would work just as fine as any space-based measures – and might make a lot more sense in terms of practical relevance on a journey.

A modern-day example comes from the domain of public transport. Recently I encountered a bus in Berlin with a sign that I found puzzling at first: the bus was marked as not in regular service, but doing a 'Messfahrt'. My initial thought was that this was an odd way of spelling 'Messe-Fahrt' ('fair tour'). However, it came out that it was indeed a 'Mess-fahrt', a 'measure tour': with this bus, the public transport company tried out a new route, in order to find out how long it takes to cover the distances between the stops. In this context the relevance of temporal features, hence of time-based and not space-based measure items, is pronounced. If you are waiting at a bus stop, it is not so important for you to know how many kilometres it is between certain points on the bus route; what you really want to know is at what time a bus comes to the stop you are waiting at, and how long it will then take to get to the stop you are heading for. It is the time we need to cover the distance that matters, not the actual kilometres.

Similarly, it is the time that matters when one travels on horseback in the Bakhtiari Mountains, and – at least as important – the effort one has

---

[10] Vita Sackville-West, *Twelve Days. An Account of a Journey Across the Bakhtiari Mountains in South-Western Persia* (London: Haag, 1928). pp. 55f.

to put into the journey, depending on the route conditions. Compared to that, the distance in kilometres or miles is of less relevance. Another passage from Sackville-West's book supports this point:

> By our muscles, however, we were made aware that the first stage of our journey lay behind us, and not before. How they ached! It was not so much the actual miles that we had in our legs, as the steepness and roughness of the going. (p. 33)

Similar instances of a temporal-spatial correlation can be observed in the measurement of area in agricultural contexts. For instance the German measurement unit *Morgen* ('morning'), now defined as 0.25 hectares, goes back to a temporal measurement of acres as the area a yoke of oxen could plough in one morning. A reverse example comes from a medieval cookbook. A Middle High German recipe for mead from the fourteenth century gives the instruction: 'Boil for about one acre.'[11] In this case the author makes use of space-based measure items (acres) in order to indicate a certain amount of time, namely the time usually needed to plough a field.

What all these different instances of measurement have in common is that, in each case, we have a set of measure items, and these measure items link up the property we want to measure with cardinality. As the different examples we discussed here have illustrated, the measure items can be concrete physical objects or abstract events, they can possess the property we want to measure intrinsically, or through a social contract – what is important is that they are identical with respect to this property, and that we can match a set of them to the object we want to measure. This notion of measure items and the *matching* routine that correlates them with an object is germane to our conceptualisation of measurement. The second procedure that is involved in measurement, *quantification*, is the part where number comes in. As we have seen in our discussion of proto-measurement above, our ancestors might have done with non-numerical, iconic cardinality representations here. In modern measurement, however, *quantification* is realised as a cardinal number assignment, it is that part that relates measure concepts to our cognitive number domain.

So where have we got to in our investigation of the number domain now? So far, we have discussed the acquisition of counting words as numerical tools, and our concept of numerical quantity that builds on their application in cardinal number assignments; and we have analysed the representation of individualised numbers (as an abstraction from concrete cardinalities), and, finally, the integration of cardinal number assignments into measurement

---

[11] Quoted after Eisenberg (1985: 311); my translation (in the Middle High German original: 'gein eime acker lanc').

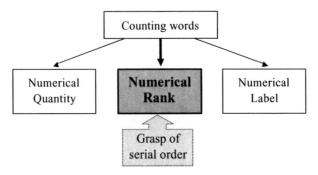

Figure 58 Concepts of numerical rank within the cognitive number domain

procedures. Hence, so far we have focused on the cardinal department of our number domain: our representation of numerical quantity and the concepts related to it. In the following sections, let us explore the two non-cardinal subdomains that contribute to our number concept, namely those based on the acquisition of ordinal and of nominal number assignments.

CONCEPTS OF NUMERICAL RANK

When children learn to employ counting words in ordinal number assign-ments, they acquire a concept of numerical rank. Figure 58 identifies this concept within the diagram (Figure 49) I introduced at the beginning of this chapter. As indicated in this graphic, our concept of numerical rank is supported by mental representations of serial order. Concepts of serial order help children to identify the empirical property that is relevant in ordinal number assignments, namely the position of objects within a progression. The animal data we reviewed in chapter 4 suggests that we share these concepts with other species; the ability to grasp the serial order of objects is independent of and exists prior to a systematic concept of number. This is not surprising since, in order to apply our numerical tools in a certain domain, we first need to grasp empirical relational structure that is relevant there: if we want to associate numerical and empirical relations – and this is what number assignments are about – then of course we need to know what the relevant relation is between the empirical objects. Once this is figured out, we can associate this relation with a relation between our numerical tools, such that the number we assign to an object identifies the property we are interested in.

Similarly to subitising and 'noisy magnitudes', the pre-numerical (and pre-linguistic) underpinnings of our concept of numerical rank allow us to grasp initial positions in a sequence accurately and at a glance, while our representations of higher ranks are fuzzier, and assessments have to be based on estimation as long as we do not employ numerical tools. Imagine a row of trees, lined up at the side of a street starting in front of your house. It would not be difficult to point out (without counting) which tree is the first, second, or third, but one could not tell right away, say, the sixty-fourth tree in the line from the sixty-fifth tree.

The ordinal counterpart of our subitising ability hence provides us with precise representations of small ranks that do not involve numerical tools. We can account for these pre-numerical ordinal concepts in a similar way as for our 'itemising'-based concepts of small cardinalities (cf. our account on pp. 52ff., and the definition in Appendix 4). Whereas for cardinal concepts we itemise the elements of the set we quantify, for ordinal concepts we itemise positions in a progression up to the object whose rank we want to identify. We can think of these representations as 'ordered object files', similar to the mental object files that support our ability to subitise the cardinality of small sets.

Let me spell this out for our row of trees (I provide a formal definition in Appendix 4). The row of trees can be regarded as a progression whose elements are ordered with respect to the proximity to your house, that is, the trees are ordered by a relation 'is closer to the house'. To make things concrete, let us assume that the first tree is an elm tree, the second one an oak, and the third one a birch. Now the elm tree can be defined as that element of the progression that is closest to the house, that is, our representation of ordered object files says that there is no tree that is closer to the house than the elm tree. The oak is then identified as the one that comes directly after the elm, that is, our object files are ordered such that the elm tree is closer to the house than the oak, and there is no tree in-between those two. And, similarly, the birch is the one that comes directly after the second tree, or, to make it explicit: there is a tree right at the beginning of the row (the elm tree), and directly after it there is another tree (the oak), and directly after that one comes the birch tree.

As you can see, this way to represent sequential positions works fine for objects in initial positions, but would become more difficult for trees further down the line, in accordance with our distinction between accurate representations of initial ranks, and fuzzy representations of higher ranks. This kind of representation provides us with pre-numerical ordinal concepts that are similar to the subitising-based concepts of cardinality that we

Figure 59 NR indicates an object's rank within a progression

discussed earlier. And, just like subitising, it does not involve a number assignment.

It is only after the acquisition of ordinal number assignments that these concepts of serial order are integrated into the cognitive number domain. When children acquire a concept of *numerical rank*, they can relate the sequential positions of objects to sequential positions of their numerical tools, for instance to positions of words in the English counting sequence. We can hence account for our representations of numerical rank by a function NR that maps an element of a progression onto a counting word that indicates its rank in that progression (Figure 59).

Building on the results from chapter 1, we can state the following requirements for NR in this mapping: given an empirical object *o* (for instance Mick), which is an element of a progression *p* (for instance the runners in a Marathon race), then NR maps *o* onto a counting word *n*, such that there is an ordered one-to-one mapping between the initial elements of our progression *p* and the counting words from ONE to *n*, and *o* is mapped onto *n* (that is, all runners up to Mick receive a counting word, one after the other, and Mick gets the number *n*).[12] This way NR accounts for the kind of correlation between counting words and empirical objects that constitutes ordinal number assignments.

What do children have to learn when they acquire this concept? Adopting an approach similar to the one described for cardinality assignments, we can account for the assignment of a numerical rank by the following principles:

[12] NR is defined accordingly in Appendix 4.

Principles of ordinal number assignment

(1) *One–One Principle*: Each element of the progression up to the final ranked item must receive exactly one tag.

(2) *Stable-Order Principle*: The tags must be used in a fixed order.

(3) *Order-Relevance Principle*: The tagged items must be elements of a progression, and they must be tagged in the order determined by that progression.

(4) *Ordinality Principle*: Each tag identifies the rank of the item it is matched with.

(5) *Abstraction Principle*: Elements of any progression can be ranked.

(6) *Numerical-Tool Principle*: Any progression of well-distinguished entities can be used for ordinal number assignments.

So far, empirical research on the acquisition of number concepts has mainly concentrated on cardinal aspects.[13] Accordingly, unlike for cardinal number assignments, we do not have enough empirical evidence to identify the different stages in the acquisition of ordinal number assignments, and to see whether the principles I suggest here can be distinguished in the acquisition process – and if so, in which order they are acquired. In the following paragraphs, I give a general description of the different principles and make clear their relation to the principles of cardinal number assignment we discussed in chapter 5 (the 'counting principles').

The first ordinal principle is similar to the One-One Principle that Rochel Gelman and her colleagues proposed for cardinal number assignments (cf. p. 162 above). Both cardinal and ordinal number assignments are based on a routine where we assign exactly one tag (counting word) to one empirical object, and in both cases these objects are elements of a certain set. The difference is that, in ordinal number assignments, this set must be a progression, that is, our empirical objects must be ordered in a certain way. On the other hand, not all elements of this progression need to enter the tagging, but only those leading to the final element we want to rank: we need not assign numbers to each and every runner in the marathon in order to find out that Mick is third. This is because, in the end, numbers are assigned to individual elements of our progression (in our example: to individual runners), not to the progression as a whole, whereas in cardinal number assignments we eventually assign a number to the whole set.

---

[13] A notable exception are the studies conducted by Karen Fuson and her colleagues (as mentioned above), who investigated children's understanding of counting words, and of number words used for cardinal, ordinal, and nominal reference.

The second principle is identical to Gelman's Stable-Order Principle for cardinal number assignments; it ensures that counting words are used in their stable sequential order. My third principle, which I termed 'Order-Relevance Principle', states the same for the empirical objects (in contrast to the Order-Irrelevance Principle Gelman et al. proposed for cardinal number assignments). Together with the fourth principle, which I called the 'Ordinality Principle', this constitutes the main difference between ordinal and cardinal number assignments. As our discussion in chapter 1 made clear, in cardinal number assignments counting is just a prop, a numerical subroutine that we employ for the elements of a set in order to figure out the number we want to assign to the whole set. Accordingly, Gelman's Cardinality Principle states that one of the tags we use in the count, namely the last one, takes on a special significance; it is this tag that identifies the cardinality of the set (cf. our discussion in chapter 5 above).

In ordinal number assignments, on the other hand, the one-to-one correlation of counting words and empirical objects is not a preparation for the number assignment, it *is* the number assignment. Each empirical object gets exactly the number we assign to it in this correlation; it is this number that identifies its rank. This is captured by the Ordinality Principle. As mentioned above, this is also the reason why it is relevant in which order our empirical objects enter the count (Order-Relevance Principle), and why we do not need to count the whole progression, but only that initial subsequence of it that includes the element to which we want to assign a number (as specified as part of the One–One Principle).

The Abstraction Principle restricts our number assignment to empirical objects that are elements of a progression, whereas for cardinal number assignments, the empirical objects have to be sets. Finally, the sixth principle complements the 'Numerical-Tool Principle' I proposed for cardinal number assignments. It extends the domain in which we can use our numerical tools, while keeping up the same standards for them: when we have a progression of well-distinguished entities, we cannot only use it for cardinal, but also for ordinal number assignments.

As our discussion suggests, this generalisation can build on a set of principles that parallel to a large degree those for cardinal number assignments, while introducing some special features that are relevant for ordinality. When children acquire ordinal number assignments, they might hence adjust their usage of counting words in a way that these numerical tools can now indicate ranks of objects. Let us have a closer look at this relationship between cardinal and ordinal number concepts.

At this point, let me emphasise again the distinction between counting words and the words we use to refer to numerical concepts. As I hope to have convinced you in this book, counting words are our numerical tools; they do not refer to anything, but instead can be used in number assignments, and among others we can use them as numbers in ordinal assignments where we identify the rank of objects within a progression. The words we then use to refer to these ranks in linguistic contexts can take different forms, and one option is to employ ordinal number words like English 'first', 'second', 'third' etc. (we will come back to this point in more detail in chapter 8). Not surprisingly, then, it has been noted by some researchers that children (and, one might want to add, adults) use *counting words* in the one-one routine that constitutes ordinal number assignments, and not ordinal number words. For instance, children would say 'One, two, three, four. This one is the fourth (doll, block etc.)' and not 'First, second, third, fourth. This one is the fourth.' It is the counting sequence that is used as our (non-referential) numerical toolkit, and not ordinal number words. It is counting words that are assigned to empirical objects in our numerical routines, while ordinal number words like 'third' etc. refer to the respective numerical ranks we figure out with this routine. Accordingly, children have initially difficulties reciting ordinal number words in an intransitive list ('first, second, third, . . .').[14] Using ordinal number words in such a bare list must seem meaningless to them, as opposed to using them in linguistic contexts where they refer to the numerical rank of a particular object ('the third runner').

Cross-linguistically, cardinal number words usually look very similar to counting words, while ordinal number words might take special forms.[15] This might be a reason why English children, for instance, seem to acquire the ordinal vocabulary later (cf. Fuson and Hall 1983). In addition, the *concepts* denoted by these ordinal number words are probably acquired later, too. In general, knowledge of ordinal number assignments seems to lag behind the acquisition of cardinal number assignments, suggesting that ordinal number principles in fact build on those for cardinal number assignments in individual development.

A study conducted by Florence Fischer and Robert Beckey suggests such a primacy of cardinal over ordinal number concepts for beginning

---

[14] Cf. Beilin (1975: ch. 5), Fuson and Hall (1983).
[15] However, a lot of languages do not have a specialised class of ordinal number words in the first place. In this case, one refers to numerical ranks by a more complex construction (which is also possible in English), namely by something like 'puppet number four' instead of 'the fourth puppet'. We will come back to this phenomenon in chapter 8.

kindergarteners (five-year-olds) in the United States (Fischer and Beckey 1990). In this study children were given, among others, a cardinal task and an ordinal task. In the cardinal task they were asked to identify a set of objects with a certain numerical quantity; for instance, they had to give the experimenter seven blocks from a pile of blocks. In the ordinal task the children were asked to identify an object with a certain numerical rank; for instance, they were asked to point to the third car in an array of cars. Of the 97 children who were tested, 88 succeeded at the cardinal task, but only 30 at the ordinal task.

Melvin Marx found a similar pattern in a study with persons who had been diagnosed as mentally retarded (Marx 1989). He tested different age groups from schoolchildren to adult workers on cardinal and ordinal tasks similar to the ones used by Fischer and Beckey (the schoolchildren were five to seventeen years old, the adult workers nineteen to seventy years). For all age groups, he observed a markedly inferior performance for ordinal compared with cardinal number assignments.

Walter Secada and Karen Fuson investigated children's performance on two conservation tasks. The cardinal task tested whether children knew that the cardinality of a set remains the same when its elements are rearranged, for instance whether they knew that they do not get more when they are spread further apart so that they take up more space (this is the traditional Piagetian conservation task, cf. Piaget 1941). The ordinal task tested whether children knew that the ranks of objects in a progression remain the same when they are rearranged in a way that does not affect their order. Secada and Fuson tested this ordinal knowledge by presenting children with toy animals that were lined up in two queues to go into cages, and then transformed one queue so that it was longer or shorter than the other. They found that children who did well on the cardinal task still had great difficulties with the ordinal conservation task.[16]

So far, there is not enough data available to allow any definite conclusions on the acquisitional sequence for cardinal versus ordinal number assignments, and in particular we do not have enough data from studies that control the influence of ordinal number words in a particular language (in order to identify independent conceptual phenomena).[17] As the studies we discussed here illustrate, though, the evidence thus far points to a primacy of cardinal over ordinal number concepts in individual development, suggesting that number assignments start first and foremost as representations for cardinality. Only later might other applications of these tools

---

[16] Secada and Fuson, unpublished data from a study described in Fuson (1992).
[17] In this respect, it would be interesting, for example, to compare the performance of children whose languages have different means to express numerical rank (cf. also footnote 15 above).

(namely, ordinal and nominal ones) be included in our concept of number, and in particular after the step from iconic to non-iconic representations has been made and counting words have emerged as numerical tools in cardinal number assignments – not only in the phylogenetic evolution of numerical thinking (as discussed in chapter 4), but also in individual development.

The identification of cardinality might hence be a more central task for our numerical tools than the identification of ordinality, and there might also be more emphasis on cardinal as opposed to ordinal number assignments when children learn to apply counting words. Related to this, children and parents do not seem to engage a lot in ritualised games for ordinal number assignments, in contrast to the elaborate counting games that support the acquisition of cardinal number assignments. The crucial step that leads to the understanding of counting words as numerical tools seems to be made when children acquire cardinal number assignments and master the Cardinality Principle. Ordinal number assignments can then be based on a generalisation: they are acquired as an additional domain in which counting words can be used as numerical tools.

Concepts of numerical rank are hence related to concepts of numerical quantity by their common numerical basis, that is, by their mutual relation to numerical tools. In particular at earlier stages, this is the sequence of counting words, a toolkit that enables us to specify both the cardinalities of sets and the ranks of objects in a progression in a precise way. Hence, while empirical properties like rank and quantity are disjoined in non-numerical contexts, they are linked up with each other in the cognitive number domain: they are associated as two kinds of properties that can be assessed with numbers. The third kind of property that joins this group, that is, the third kind of empirical property to which we apply our numerical tools, is the identity and non-identity of objects as represented by our concept of numerical label.

CONCEPTS OF NUMERICAL LABEL

Our concept of numerical label is based on the representation of nominal number assignments. When children learn to use counting words in these number assignments, they can build on their (pre-numerical) grasp of verbal label. Figure 60 identifies the relevant area within our familiar outline of the number domain.

Our grasp of verbal label allows us to identify objects with words. This involves our linguistic naming ability, but we also need a more basic capacity, namely the capacity to individuate and distinguish objects. Studies with

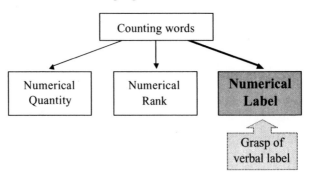

Figure 60 Concepts of numerical label within the cognitive number domain

babies in their first year of life suggest that at least some of this capacity is present at a very early age. In particular, infants seem to possess a (possibly domain-specific) knowledge of physical objects that, among other things, enables them to pick out discrete objects in their environment and to represent some of their properties even when the objects are moved out of their view.[18] In nominal number assignments, this ability provides the pre-numerical underpinnings which enable us to grasp the relevant empirical property, namely in this case the distinction (identity versus non-identity) of objects.

When children acquire nominal number assignments, they learn to employ counting words as labels that distinguish objects within a set, for instance THREE could identify a particular football player in a team. This is illustrated in Figure 61, where 'NL' ('Numerical Label') is a function that links up a football player with the counting word THREE. Drawing on our results from the previous chapters we can analyse NL as a function that establishes dependent links between empirical objects and numerical tools, where counting words feature as our prime example. In particular, NL maps elements of a set onto counting words such that different objects always receive different labels. In other words, NL links up empirical objects and counting words in a way that associates the identity of objects with the '='-relation between the counting words (I have provided the definition for NL in Appendix 4).

Relating our discussion to the analysis of cardinal and ordinal number concepts, we can again identify six principles that govern such a mapping:

---

[18] For a discussion cf. for instance Spelke (1990); Spelke et al. (1992). (Spelke et al. 1992 also provide evidence that babies as young as two-and-a-half months represent hidden objects and their movements in a way that is in accordance with continuity and solidity constraints.)

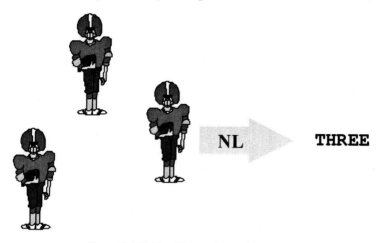

Figure 61 NL identifies an object within a set

Principles of nominal number assignment
(1) *One–One Principle*: Each element of the set must receive a different tag.
(2) *Order-Irrelevance Principle (tags)*: The tags can be used in any order.
(3) *Order-Irrelevance Principle (objects)*: The items can be labelled in any order.
(4) *Nominality Principle*: Each tag identifies the item it is matched with.
(5) *Abstraction Principle*: Elements of any set can be labelled.
(6) *Numerical-Tool Principle*: Any set of well-distinguished entities can be used for nominal number assignments.

These principles are less restrictive than the ones for cardinal and ordinal number assignments in several respects, accounting for the fact that the tags we use in this kind of number assignment do not identify a special property like the cardinality or the rank of the empirical objects, but identify the objects themselves, more precisely: they identify different elements of a set, for instance members of a football team (I called this the 'Nominality Principle' above). Accordingly, in order for this assignment to work we do not need to assign each and every element exactly one tag, but it suffices to make sure that no two objects receive the same tag. Usually, though, each element of a set does receive precisely one tag. In order to account for this pattern, I kept the name 'One–One Principle', parallel to the first principles in cardinal and ordinal number assignments, although strictly speaking, this is a 'One–One- or One–Many-Principle', of course.

Principles (2) and (3) state that both the tags and the labelled items can come in any order, making the routine underlying nominal number assignments the most liberal way we can use our numerical tools. This is because nominal number assignments do not involve sequential order in any way; we do not want to identify a rank of the *empirical* objects (unlike in ordinal number assignments), and we do not make use of the positions of *counting words* either (unlike in both ordinal and cardinal number assignments). The fifth principle, the Abstraction Principle for nominal number assignments, makes clear that we can apply this kind of number assignment to any objects that are elements of a set.

Finally, principle (6) extends the domain of numerical tools to contexts of labelling. Unlike in cardinal and ordinal number assignments, the only requirement here is that the entities we use as numbers are well distinguished from each other, but they need not form a progression. This reflects our results from chapter 1, and it also makes clear that we really do not make high demands of our numerical tools here: all we ask for is that one can tell them apart. Using counting words for this task seems a bit like overkill. After all, these are not just any old items that can be distinguished from each other – they are elements that are meticulously organised within an infinite, well-ordered progression. Enlisting this sophisticated progression for a simple labelling job seems like using my laptop here as a weight to press flowers, instead of using it to write this book: it does work, of course, but it seems like a bit of a waste really.

There are two advantages that come with using counting words as labels, though. On the one hand, counting words come in handy because we can easily generate as many of them as we need, so we do not have to put a lot of thinking into finding new labels when we want to identify more and more objects. On the other hand, since counting words are ordered we can include a secondary ordinal aspect for the labels, which can later help others to figure out which object a particular label identifies (recall our discussion of house numbers in chapter 1). However, for the actual nominal task – that is for the identification of objects – any well-distinguished verbal labels would work well. In fact, for this kind of task it is quite common to use verbal labels other than counting words, namely proper names like 'Karen' or 'Mick'.

This has the effect that nominal number assignments have closer connections with non-numerical domains than the others. As we have seen above, in the acquisition of nominal number assignments children can draw on an early capacity to grasp the relevant empirical property (namely, their capacity to individuate and distinguish objects), in a similar way that they draw on their grasp of cardinality and of serial order in the acquisition of cardinal and ordinal number assignments. And, as in all number assignments, they can draw on their language-based ability for dependent linking. On top of this, though, nominal number assignments have a direct counterpart in the linguistic domain, namely the assignments of verbal labels. In particular, the way we assign proper names to objects is very similar to the way we assign counting words to objects in nominal number assignments – with one important difference: proper names are not ordered sequentially.

And this is exactly what makes nominal number assignments difficult for children at first. What is tricky about the concept of numerical label is not so much the fact that we use words in order to identify particular objects, but that it is counting words, our numerical tools, that we use for this task. This sets up a relation with other number contexts, and at earlier stages of acquisition this relation can lead children to expect that we use counting words for something more sophisticated than a simple naming task here. In particular it might suggest that we employ the sequential order of counting words somehow. This sequential order is not only a key feature in the acquisition and representation of counting words (and other numerical tools), it is also one of the features that is responsible for the exceptional status of counting words within the linguistic system; it is one of the crucial features that distinguishes counting words from other words (cf. our discussion in chapter 3). Nominal contexts fit well for counting words since they are *words*, but it is a difficult transition from the point of view of numerical tools.

Especially at early stages of acquisition, this might suggest a division of labour to the effect that counting words, unlike other words, are used in assignments where we actually make use of this sequential order – that is, in assignments where our numerical relational structure involves sequential order and this order is associated with a property in the empirical relational structure. This expectation fails in the case of nominal number assignments. Concepts of numerical label are therefore less central to our concept of number, and children might initially tend to interpret nominal number assignments as cardinal or ordinal.

Evidence for this comes from a study conducted by Anne Sinclair and Hermine Sinclair with four- to six-year-old Genevan children (Sinclair and Sinclair 1984). They showed the children pictures with numerals in different contexts, among them nominal contexts like labels of runners in a race (in their picture, the runners were children who had numerals printed on their T-shirts), licence plates on cars, and bus numbers. When the children were asked about the meaning of these numerals they often gave answers

Figure 62 Relative salience of numerical concepts

indicating a cardinal understanding; for instance they explained that the numbers in the race tell 'how many runners are there', that the numbers on the licence plate show 'how much the car cost' (cardinal measure), or that the bus number indicates how many routes the bus takes. For the race example – which sets up a context strongly suggestive of ordinality – the children also offered ordinal interpretations for the numbers, suggesting that the number tells 'who wins and who loses', or 'who is to go in front and/or behind'.

THE ARCHITECTURE OF THE NUMBER DOMAIN

Let us now bring together the results from our discussion. What picture emerges of the architecture of our cognitive number domain? Taking a broad perspective, we can distinguish three subdomains that are based on three main ways in which we can assign our numerical tools to empirical objects, and which focus on cardinal, ordinal, and nominal aspects, respectively. The evidence we discussed in the previous sections suggests that the identification of the cardinality of sets might be the prime function of our numerical tools, followed by the identification of ranks, while the nominal identification of objects is presumably the least salient context for numerical tools. This suggests an internal ranking of number concepts as illustrated in Figure 62, where concepts of numerical quantity are at the core, concepts of numerical rank come in the next layer, and concepts of numerical label constitute an outer shell. These concepts are related to each other within the cognitive number domain under the umbrella of number assignments. They are concepts that represent different ways in which we apply numerical tools to empirical objects. Crucially, each kind of number assignment is grounded in a pattern of dependent linking. The application of numerical tools in this kind of linking is the common theme that brings together empirical properties like cardinality, rank, and identity and integrates them into our cognitive number domain.

Taking the 'counting principles' introduced by Rochel Gelman and her colleagues as a starting point, we identified different sets of Number Principles governing the application of numerical tools in each number assignment. We found that the respective principles were overlapping to a large degree; in fact, one might think of the acquisition of each new kind of number assignment as a specific amendment to the principles learned thus far. In a unified approach, our principles of cardinal, ordinal, and nominal number assignments can be regarded as different specifications of the following six parameters:

(1) *One–One Match*: Do numerical tags have to be correlated with objects in a one-to-one manner?

(2) *Stable Order (tags)*: Do the tags have to enter the correlation in a stable order?

(3) *Stable Order (objects)*: Do the objects have to enter the correlation in a stable order?

(4) *Empirical Property*: How does one identify the relevant empirical property?

(5) *Abstraction*: What kinds of elements are allowed for the empirical relational structure?

(6) *Numerical Tools*: What kinds of elements are allowed for the numerical relational structure?

Table 3 summarises the parallels and differences for our three kinds of number assignments with respect to this list. The basis for the cardinal subdomain is our concept of numerical quantity. As our discussion has shown, this concept is the focal point of a network of related numerical concepts that draw on cardinal aspects: our concepts of measure, our concepts of individualised numbers, and their extensions in complex mathematical thinking, including a concept of zero. Our representation of measurement provides a concept of measure items that links up cardinality with properties like length, weight, or temperature. This link allows us to base the assignment of numbers in measurement on two main procedures: (1) *matching* the object we want to measure with a set of measure items, and

Table 3 *Number Principles*

	Number assignments		
Parameters	Cardinal	Ordinal	Nominal
One-One Match	✓	✓	(✓)
Stable Order (tags)	✓	✓	✗
Stable Order (objects)	✗	✓	✗
Empirical Property	the last tag identifies the cardinality of a set	each tag identifies the rank of an object	each tag identifies an object within a set
Abstraction	sets	elements of a progression	elements of a set
Numerical Tools	progression of well-distinguished elements	progression of well-distinguished elements	set of well-distinguished elements

(2) *quantifying* the set of measure items. Ultimately, this allows us to relate the representation of measurement to our concept of numerical quantity, thus integrating it into our cardinal subdomain.

Our concepts of individualised numbers in mathematical reasoning are related to concepts of numerical quantity as an abstraction from concrete sets. Since these concepts are not related to the counting sequence directly, they can integrate a concept of zero that is based on our comprehension of empty sets. In addition, they give rise to various extensions like negative or rational numbers.

The second subdomain of our cognitive number domain is then established by the application of numerical tools in ordinal number assignments, which gives rise to concepts of numerical rank. The third and final subdomain is based on concepts of numerical label and related to our numerical tools by nominal number assignments.

As we have seen in our investigation, each numerical subdomain gets support from a non-numerical domain; each kind of number assignment can build on pre-numerical concepts that enable us to grasp the property that is assessed in our empirical objects: our abilities of subitising, based on mental object files, and of estimating, based on noisy magnitudes, support our grasp of cardinality; ordered object files allow us to grasp ranks in a serial order, and early knowledge of physical objects supports our grasp of (non-)identity, while our ability to use verbal labels contributes to our understanding of numerical labelling. And for all number contexts alike,

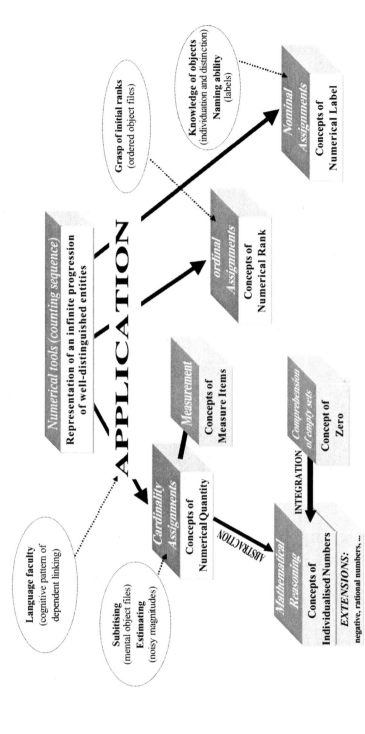

Figure 63 The architecture of our cognitive number domain

our language faculty supports the application of verbal elements in a pattern of dependent linking.

Figure 63 gives an overview of this architecture. White boxes represent the core numerical concepts, grey boxes represent the further concepts that are integrated in the cardinal subdomain, and oval circles indicate cognitive capacities from non-numerical domains that support our grasp of number assignments.

In chapter 8, the results from this chapter will serve as a basis for our understanding of the expressions that denote numerical concepts in language, that is, the different kinds of referential number word constructions and their organisation. Before we come to that, though, let me fulfil my promise and introduce a non-verbal instance of numerical tools into the discussion, namely arabic numerals. In the following chapter, I am going to show how they come into the picture of the cognitive number domain that we developed here.

CHAPTER 7

Non-verbal number systems

What is the status of non-verbal numerals like '5' or 'V'? Obviously they are not linked to a particular language, but used cross-linguistically; for instance, both '5' and 'V' are used in English as well as in French contexts (although they are not used universally). And they are also not part of a particular alphabet: roman numerals are not restricted to contexts where we use, say, the Latin alphabet, but can be used together with the Cyrillic alphabet as well as with Chinese script, and the same is true for arabic or Chinese numerals. Which numeral system is used in the context of a particular script is a cultural phenomenon. The usage is not based on an inherent link between numeral systems and particular alphabets, but rather is due to historical coincidences or to the relative advantages of different numeral systems. And as the case of arabic and roman numerals illustrates, it is also quite common that two (or more) numeral systems are used within the same culture and together with the same script.

The independence of non-verbal numerals from script is particular obvious in Arabic. In contexts where Arabic script is used,[1] one normally finds the East-Arabic numerals, which, like the West-Arabic ones that are used in Europe, originated in the Indian Brahmi-script. This script goes from left to right (hence like Latin, but unlike Arabic script). As a result, complex East-arabic numerals are written from the left to the right, just like the West-Arabic ones, while the Arabic script goes from right to left. So if you read an Arabic text that has a numeral in it, you have to go like this:

---

[1] This script is also used for writing in a number of languages other than Arabic, for instance Persian, Kurdish (in Iraq and Iran), and Urdu. Turkish used to be written in Arabic script before Turkey changed to the Latin alphabet in 1928.

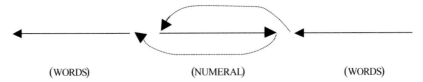

(WORDS)   (NUMERAL)   (WORDS)

Figure 64 How to read non-verbal numerals within Arabic script

If one did this with Latin script (that is, if one wrote from right to left in Latin, while still using arabic numerals), then an English sentence such as 'They invited 192 guests.' would look like this:

.ꙅƚꙅəυɓ 192 bəƚivni γəдT

In the present chapter, I am going to show that non-verbal numerals form independent systems that are neither part of language nor part of script and fulfil all the criteria we set up for numerical tools back in chapter 2. Children learn this sequence when they already have a number system at their disposal, namely a counting sequence. When they acquire arabic numerals, they have to learn that this non-verbal sequence is interchangeable with the existing verbal one (their counting sequence), that is, they have to learn to switch between different kinds of sequences as different instances of numerical tools.

At first sight, this seems to pose a problem for our view of language and number: did we not say that language is crucial for the development of numerical thinking? So how come we can have non-verbal numerical tools just as well, hence we can have number sequences that are totally independent of language? This point offers us an opportunity to further work out what relevance language has for numerical thinking according to the view presented here, and which aspects, on the other hand, might be an accidental surplus, at least from a synchronic point of view.

According to the argument I have pursued in the present book, our language faculty plays a crucial role in the emergence of a systematic concept of number. However, this is the case not so much because language gives us counting words, but rather because it gives us the capacity for dependent linking. Our language faculty allows us to grasp the pattern of system-dependent linking and by so doing lays the grounds for the application of both verbal and non-verbal numerical tools. Nothing in our criteria-based approach confines us to *verbal* elements as numerical tools (hence one example of a possible number sequence was that infinite colour palette

I imagined in chapter 2). Accordingly counting words are one instance of numerical tools, but not the only possible one.

Counting words are a particularly interesting kind of numerical tools because of their verbal character, and according to our discussion in chapter 4 it might be this intimate link to language that set off systematic numerical thinking in the first place. So, from a historical perspective, language might not only have contributed the pattern of system-dependent linking, but also have been crucial to trigger the emergence of our first numerical tools in the form of counting words.

As I argued in chapter 4, it is a small step for a sequence of words to be used as numerical tools because, being words, it would be common for them to undergo some kind of dependent linking anyway, namely the linking we need for symbolic reference. Hence, only a comparatively small adaptation is necessary when we want to use them in the kind of dependent linking that number assignments are based upon. In contrast to that, it is hard to see how a transition from iconic representations of cardinality to dependent linking in number assignments might have been triggered for non-verbal elements – as long as there had not been a number concept already. But this does not confine us to verbal number sequences forever. Once systematic numerical thinking has emerged, the way is open for new sequences that fulfil the number criteria, and in particular our number concept is powerful enough to integrate not only verbal, but also non-verbal sequences, of which arabic numerals are one prominent example.

This chapter is organised in three main sections. In the first section I introduce the system of arabic numerals as an example of a non-verbal number sequence; I show that this system has all the properties we expect for numerical tools. In this context we will see that it is in particular the sequential aspect that is emphasised in their representation, a phenomenon we have also encountered for verbal numerical tools, that is, counting sequences. In the second section we discuss some aspects of how such a non-verbal numerical system develops, which will reveal further parallels with counting sequences. The final section demonstrates how elements of the two sequences can be correlated, for instance when we 'read aloud' arabic numerals in English. I will account for this correlation in a model that brings together verbal and non-verbal numerical tools as two sequences that can fulfil the same numerical functions.

My motivation for introducing arabic numerals into our investigation is twofold. First, the discussion of arabic numerals gives us a chance to apply our criteria-based approach to numbers in a different domain, namely to apply it to a non-verbal sequence. My argument will be that, like counting words, arabic numerals do not denote numbers, but instead can fulfil numerical functions themselves: they are non-verbal elements that can be used as numerical tools, just like counting words are *verbal* elements that we use as numerical tools. The example of arabic numerals will allow us to look from a different perspective at the numerical characteristics we have identified in our investigation, most notably the realisation of our number criteria, but also the non-referential status of numerical tools, and the emergence of a genuine number assignment (which is based on system-dependent links) from iconic representations of cardinality. We will find that these characteristics are not specific to counting words, but analogously can be observed for non-verbal, visual numerals, indicating that our approach to numerical tools is not confined to the verbal modality.

My second reason to introduce arabic numerals into the discussion is that they provide us with a case study for the correlation of alternative number sequences. Remember that back in chapter 3 when I first introduced counting words as numerical tools, I argued that counting sequences from different languages do not constitute different 'numbers', but are different sequences that fulfil the same numerical purposes, and that they can do so due to their isomorphic structures: each counting sequence is a potentially infinite progression, and we can identify corresponding elements in two (or more) sequences based on their respective positions. For instance, we can identify SEPT as the counterpart of SEVEN because both words occupy the same position in their respective counting sequences: SEPT has the same position in the French counting sequence as SEVEN in the English sequence.

Our investigation in the present chapter will give us the opportunity to discuss in more detail how such a correlation works. Using English counting words and arabic numerals as an example, we will spell out such a correlation along the same lines that one would correlate counting sequences from different languages (arabic numerals provide a more interesting case because the differences between a verbal and a non-verbal sequence are potentially more challenging). In particular, this allows us to show that in order to correlate two different instances of numerical tools, we do not have to regard their elements as names for some additional referents 'numbers'.

ARABIC NUMERALS AS A NON-VERBAL NUMBER SEQUENCE

How do we represent and store a sequence of non-verbal numerals? Here is a suggestion by the cartoonist Manfred Hofmann (Figure 65).[2] Hofmann's suggestion is, of course, not meant to be taken seriously. One thing that you

---

[2] From: Manfred Hofmann, *Wo fehlt's uns denn? Dein Körper in gesunden und kranken Tagen* (Frankfurt am Main: Eichborn, 1994), p. 54; my translation, H. W.

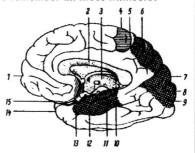

An important question: how can we remember all those numbers?

Scientists have found out that there are specific regions in the brain that are responsible for the numbers from 1 to 15 (cf. figure). How we memorise the numbers from 16 to 435,688 however, is not yet entirely clear. So far it is only sure that other organs come to help. After the removal of his spleen, for instance, a patient forgot the number 51,439!

Figure 65 A way to store arabic numerals?

probably thought of when reading the cartoon is that it would be rather surprising if there were specific brain (and spleen!) regions responsible for individual numerals. As we have seen in the preceding chapters, a crucial feature of a number sequence is its recursive structure: based on a small set of primitive elements (for example, the English counting words from ONE to NINE), we can generate an infinite range of higher elements. So instead of storing individual counting words like, say, FIVE THOUSAND AND SIXTY-TWO in long-term memory, we store the primitive elements of the sequence and the rules of their combination.

The same applies to non-verbal numerals. Like that of counting words, the generation of arabic numerals is governed by recursive rules. These rules are very simple. In order to account for them, all we have to do is introduce the primitive elements 0,1,2,3,4,5,6,7,8,9, and then define a 'string' rule that generates a new numeral from any two numerals by concatenation, that is, by simply placing one next to the other. For instance this rule generates a numeral 17 from 1 and 7, or it yields 171 from 17 and 1, and so forth. This option to generate new numerals makes our set potentially infinite. Its sequential character is established by a function like '<' that tells us the ranks of any two numerals, relative to each other.

The basis for our order is the ordering of the primitive numerals from 0 to 9 (that is, $0 < 1 < 2 < \ldots < 9$). The <-relation can then be defined for complex numerals with reference to their constituents.[3] If two numerals are of different length, the longer numeral is the higher one, for instance $267 < 1354$ because there are more digits in 1354 than in 267. If two numerals are of the same length, their order is determined by a step-by-step

---

[3] I have spelled out the definition for this ordering in Appendix 3, p. 309. Note that, as far as this ordering is concerned, we ignore initial 0s in complex numerals (hence, for instance '007' counts as '7').

comparison of their constituents from left to right, for instance 267 < 315 because 2 < 3, and 267 < 271 because 6 < 7, and 267 < 268 because 7 < 8.

This makes our infinite set of numerals an ordered progression. Since we talk of arabic numerals as visual elements, they are distinct from each other due to their different forms. This means that arabic numerals fulfil all the number criteria: they are well distinguished, they form a potentially infinite set, and this set is ordered as a progression. According to our criteria-based approach, this means that we can regard the sequence of arabic numerals as another instance of numerical tools. In this function, arabic numerals have a non-referential, instrumental status, like counting words. Among others, this leads to merge effects similar to those we observed for counting words. Remember the interview with seven-year-old A.R. we discussed in chapter 5 (p. 156 above). When asked why there is no end to numbers, A.R. explained that one 'can just keep on making up letters', an answer we took as an indication that he does not make a clear distinction between words and numbers, and hence as another piece of support for the numerical status of counting words.

For arabic numerals, this is even more pronounced. Ask several people what their concept of the number 7 is, and you are likely to get at least once an answer that points to a mental image of an arabic numeral: something like 'Well, the number 7 is "7" [writing down a 7]'. This phenomenon is specific to numerals; you do not get this kind of answer in non-numerical contexts. The distinction between signs and what they stand for is not only important for linguistics, it is also something we are pretty good at in everyday life. Nobody ever seems to mistake the word 'dog' for a dog, or – if you want to get abstract – the word 'love' for an emotion. Why, then, do we merge arabic numerals (or counting words) and numbers? Because – to hammer it down just another time – these numerals (just like counting words) do not denote numbers, they *are* numbers.

Not surprisingly, then, the sequential order – a central characteristic for any numerical toolkit – features prominently in our representation of arabic numerals, similar to what we found for counting words. In the following paragraphs, I describe three phenomena that emphasise the sequential representation of numerals: mental number forms, the SNARC effect, and distance effects for arabic numerals.

Number forms

For some people, the sequential character of numerals manifests itself in a mental image, a 'number form' that comes to their mind whenever they

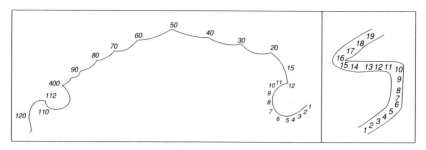

Figure 66 Mental number forms

think of numbers. In these number forms, visual images of numerals are organised in a spatial structure. While these images can have all kinds of different shapes, one can observe one recurring feature, namely a sequential order: typically a number form is some kind of visualised progression of numerals. Figure 66 gives two examples: these are drawings made by people who reported to possess such a mental number form and tried to sketch it on paper (the one on the left is taken from Galton 1880: 253, the one on the right is from Rickmeyer 2001: 56).

Such number forms, or 'visualised numerals', were first described by Francis Galton, a nineteenth-century psychologist and cousin of Charles Darwin (Galton 1880 and 1883: 114ff.). Number forms appear automatically and effortlessly whenever one thinks of a number, and they have a reliable, stable appearance, that is, people who report to have a number form can describe it consistently and in detail.[4] Number forms seem to be more common in women than in men; about every fourth woman possesses a mental number form, while only half as many men seem to have one (these are just tentative figures, though, summarising a tendency that emerges from the studies available thus far).

Number forms are dependent on our visual memory. Accordingly, they can be affected when the visual memory is impaired, for instance as a result of brain damage. One such case, a British soldier who suffered a head injury, is described in Spalding and Zangwill (1950). Before the injury, this man had experienced a distinct number form whenever he thought of numerals. After the brain damage he faced a defect in his visual memory and, as part of this defect, could not evoke his number form very clearly anymore. This impairment also affected his calculation skills, since number forms can

---

[4] Cf. Galton (1883) and Seron et al. (1992) for these charactistics of number forms, as well as of colour associates for arabic numerals (we will discuss colour associates below).

support simple arithmetic operations, which are visualised as a 'journey' along the number line.

Number forms originate at a very early age, probably during infancy. Typically, people report having had this form as long as they can think, and they are often surprised to find that others do not share such an image. Number forms probably emerge together with the acquisition of numerical tools. Most likely the basis for a number form is established when a child first learns counting words, our initial numerical tools (Galton 1880: 125 calls number forms a 'mnemonic diagram' for counting). Later, the development of a detailed visual representation is presumably triggered by the acquisition of a non-verbal number sequence like that of arabic numerals, which are committed to the visual modality.

Accordingly, the organisation of a number form can be influenced by the structure of a counting sequence to some degree, and it can also reflect features that are specific to arabic numerals. For instance, English-speaking people often possess number forms where the first twelve numerals occupy a special area (a point in case is the image on the left in Figure 66 above), which is presumably related to the fact that THIRTEEN, is the first counting word that has a non-opaque complex structure. An example of how form features of *arabic numerals* can influence the shape of a number form comes from a study by Knut Rickmeyer. One of the people in his study reported that in her number form, 'From 100 onwards the numbers stand next to each other from left to right up to 10000, in such a way that illogically, 1000 is in the middle'.[5] Such a spatial distribution, where 1,000 gets situated in the middle between 100 and 10,000, seems to be based on the form of arabic numerals, where '100' has two zeros, '10,000' has four, and '1,000' is just in the middle, with three zeros.

What is interesting for our discussion here is the fact that the shape of number forms can be influenced by accidental features of counting se-quences or non-verbal numerals themselves, by structural characteristics that they have as verbal or visual elements. That in English ONE to TWELVE are non-compound words, or that '1,000' has one zero more than '100' and one less than '10,000' does not reflect intrinsic characteristics of num-bers, but accidental features of the English counting sequence and of the sequence of arabic numerals, respectively. It just so happened that the two sequences developed this way. Nevertheless, it obviously can have a consid-erable influence on mental number forms.

This phenomenon is very much in accordance with our claim that these sequences are non-referential tools: it is these tools that feature in our

⁵ Rickmeyer (2001: 55), original in German; my translation, H. W.

mental representations of numbers, and accordingly it is their characteristics that can influence the shape of a mental image. This would be rather surprising if counting words and arabic numerals were not numerical tools, but instead *names* for numbers, words that identify some additional abstract entities ('numbers'). If there were numbers that are *named* by counting words and arabic numerals, and number forms were an image we have of these abstract numbers, one would not expect the shape of number forms to be influenced by those names. If such phenomena occurred for names (that is, for referential words), this would suggest, for instance, that some people might have a mental image of god that looks like a dog from behind, just because the forms of their names in English mirror each other.

This does not mean, of course, that number forms cannot reflect any general characteristics of numerical tools. Quite the opposite: as mentioned at the beginning of this section, number forms usually have the shape of a visualised progression. This was, in fact, the main motivation for me to introduce these forms into our discussion: the example of number forms shows how the sequential aspect of numerical tools can be emphasised in a mental image. The sequential order is a general feature of numerical tools that can influence the shape of a number form, just like idiosyncratic features of different instances of numerical tools (for instance, English counting words or arabic numerals) can influence it. Sequential order is one of the crucial features we identified for numbers, and it is hence a necessary property of both verbal and non-verbal numerical tools. Unlike the constituent structure of particular elements (that is, of individual counting words or numerals), their sequential order is not negotiable, and it is for this reason that the sequential aspect is so ubiquitous in number forms. As a necessary characteristic of all numerical tools, it is much more apt to influence the shape of a number form than accidental features of different numerical sequences could.

In addition to number forms, some people experience colour associates for arabic numerals: whenever they think of a numeral, they see it in a particular colour. Such colour distinctions emphasise the fact that arabic numerals are well distinguished (another one of our 'number criteria'), but they might also support the sequential aspect. Benny Shanon showed in an investigation of colour associates that there seems to be an intersubjectively stable tendency towards a certain linear order of the colours:[6] the same

---

[6] Shanon (1982). This pattern is confirmed by the colour associates investigated by Seron et al. (1992). As Shanon (1982) argues, the order of colours might also be reflected in their linguistic expressions, namely in the typology of colour terms used in different languages, as proposed by Berlin and Kay (1969).

pattern of colours appears again and again, suggesting that the colour code might access a sequential representation.

This could also explain why colour associates have been reported not only for numerals, but also for non-numerical elements that form sequences, most notably for the letters of the alphabet, for the months of the year, and for days of the week. And these seem to be exactly the cases where we also get spatial–visual representations comparable to number forms: while some people report seeing months of the year etc. in different colours, others see them in an ordered sequence, similar to number forms. Hence, both number forms and colour associates for numerals seem to support a sequential representation: they organise arabic numerals into an ordered sequence and, by so doing, emphasise one of the key features that makes arabic numerals suitable as numerical tools.

The SNARC effect

Stanislas Dehaene and his colleagues found another close association between numerals and space (Dehaene et al. 1993; Dehaene 1997: ch. 3): when people have to answer questions about arabic numerals by pressing a button, they respond to small numerals faster with their left hand and to high numerals faster with their right hand, suggesting that even people who do not have a 'number form' still represent numerals in some kind of spatial order, in a mental number line that goes from left to right. Dehaene termed this phenomenon the 'SNARC effect' (Spatial–Numerical Association of Response Codes), an acronym introduced in tribute to Lewis Carrol's poem 'The Hunting of the Snark'. The SNARC effect occurs in a wide range of contexts where arabic numerals are involved, and in particular it is not restricted to contexts where one has to activate cardinality representations in order to solve the task. For instance, it can be observed when subjects see a digit on a screen and have to decide whether it is odd or even, or whether or not the corresponding counting word starts with a vowel. As Daniel B. Berch and his colleagues showed, children as young as eight years exhibit this effect in odd/even judgments for arabic numerals (Berch et al. 1999).

Like number forms, the SNARC effect suggests a mental representation of arabic numerals that emphasises their serial order. Unlike number forms, this overall spatial distribution in the mental representation of numerals seems to be a general phenomenon and not restricted to only a few people. The orientation of this mental numeral line, however, seems to be culture-specific. In particular, whether one's numeral line goes from left to right or from right to left might depend on the direction of the script that is used in a culture: when Dehaene and his colleagues tested Iranian students, who are familiar with a script that goes from right to left, it turned out that the SNARC effect was reversed (Dehaene et al. 1993). This is probably due to the fact that the direction of a script that is used within a culture influences the direction in which the numeral sequence is arranged in everyday life (for instance on rulers or on computer keyboards, cf. Dehaene 1997: ch. 3).

Distance effects

A third phenomenon that points to a salient sequential representation of arabic numerals occurs in 'numerical judgment tasks'. In these tasks, people see two numerals and have to decide, as fast as possible, which is the higher one. In this situation, reactions are faster the further the numerals are apart. For instance it takes less time to tell which numeral is higher for the pair 9 and 4 than for 5 and 4, a phenomenon that has become known as the 'symbolic distance effect'.[7]

Interestingly, this effect shows a pattern similar to that reported for other, non-numerical series. Distance effects can be observed when people compare physical stimuli directly (for instance they see two lines and are asked to tell which is longer, or they see two sets of dots and have to tell which set has more elements); they can be observed when people have to compare two objects in memory (for instance, they are shown equally sized pictures of animals and have to tell which of the animals is bigger in real life); and they can also be observed when people compare two objects that are named (for instance they see two words for different animals, say, 'ant' and 'cat', and have to tell which one refers to the bigger animal[8]). And distance effects have been observed when the linear order not only is intrinsic to the stimuli that are compared (as in the case of animal sizes), but also when it is conventionally determined, for instance when subjects learn something like 'Charles is faster than Karen, and Karen is faster than Mick', etc., and will then be asked to compare Charles and Karen, or Mick and Charles, etc.[9]

As in the comparison of arabic numerals, the general effect observed in these different paradigms is that the closer two elements of a linear ordering are, the longer it takes to compare them. In the case of numerals, this phenomenon has been interpreted as evidence that numerals activate

---

[7] The original study on this phenomenon was reported in Moyer and Landauer (1967); the term 'symbolic distance effect' was introduced in Moyer and Bayer (1976).
[8] Cf. Johnson (1939); Moyer (1973); Buckley and Gilman (1974).
[9] Cf. Potts (1974); Polich and Potts (1977).

quantity representations which are then compared analogically.[10] While this might be a factor (and we will discuss a close link between arabic numerals and abstract cardinalities below), the 'symbolic distance effect' can also be explained by the pure, sequential representation of the numerals themselves.

Just like the people in our example of 'Charles is faster than Karen, etc.', numerals are elements of a conventionally determined series whose order is stored in memory.[11] Arabic numerals can be accessed as elements of this mental sequence, and positions in this sequence can hence be compared directly, without any additional activation of cardinalities. Analogously to the example of 'Charles is faster than Karen etc.', we would expect distance effects in such a direct sequential comparison: the closer two sequential positions are, the more similar they are and accordingly the more time it takes to compare them; the further two positions are apart, the easier it is to distinguish them. Hence in order to understand distance effects for arabic numerals, we do not need to postulate a mandatory activation of quantity representations; numerical judgment tasks can be based directly on sequential visual representations of numerals.[12]

Recall that there is another conventional progression of non-referential, instrumental elements that hence shares some crucial features with numerical tools: the letters of the alphabet.[13] Not surprisingly, then, a similar distance effect has been observed for letters.[14] As in numerical judgment tasks, people are faster at telling which one of a pair of letters comes later in the alphabet if the distance between the letters is larger, lending further

---

[10] Cf. for instance Moyer and Landauer (1967), Dehaene et al. (1990).

[11] Unlike the people in our marathon example, arabic numerals are not named by signs (for instance by words like 'Charles' and 'Karen'), they are presented directly: arabic numerals *are* those visual elements that are presented on a screen in our experimental set-up (while 'Charles' and 'Karen' are not those words we see on the screen).

[12] This view gets additional support from priming experiments reported in Koechlin et al. (1999). Their results suggest that distance effects do not occur for combinations of arabic numerals with representations of cardinalities (in their set-up, these were sets of dots). I interpret this as an indication that numerical distance effects do not access cardinality representations. In addition, the Koechlin et al. study suggests that under conditions ensuring automatic processing (masked priming), distance effects might not even occur between elements of different numerical sequences (in their set-up, these were combinations of counting words and arabic numerals). This is exactly what we would expect if numerical distance effects are based on sequential representations of numerical tools (rather than on the activation of cardinalities): in this case we should indeed observe distance effects primarily for elements within one sequence (since matching positions within different numerical sequences are correlated, though, distance effects might, in principle, also occur across sequences, albeit to a lesser degree and maybe only under conditions that allow strategic processing).

[13] Remember the parallels between letters of the alphabet and counting words that we discussed in chapter 3 (p. 89 above). The similarities between numerical tools and letters of the alphabet have sometimes led to the use of letters as numerals, for instance in Greek and Hebrew (for a discussion cf. Menninger 1958: vol. II, ch. 3).

[14] Cf. Lovelace and Snodgrass (1971); Hamilton and Sanford (1978).

support to our view that no quantity representations are necessary as a basis for distance effects.

The main difference from numerical judgments is that in order to identify the position of a particular letter, people sometimes run through a portion of the alphabet (for instance when asked to tell which letter of the pair M and P is higher, one might go 'L-M-N-O-P'). This is a pattern that also occurs at early stages in the acquisition of numerical tools. Remember that when children learn the counting sequence, they initially have to recite portions of the sequence when they want to find a certain counting word. For instance, a child might say 'ONE-TWO-THREE-FOUR-FIVE' in order to get to 'FIVE'. This indicates a strong dominance of sequential links in the representation of numerical tools, which is probably the same for verbal ones (counting words) and non-verbal ones (for example, arabic numerals). At an early stage, numerals are represented first and foremost as elements of a non-referential conventional sequence. Later, individual elements can take on additional associations based on their usage in different number contexts, for instance associations with the cardinality of sets.

So if the symbolic distance effect draws on sequential links between numerical tools (rather than on quantitative differences between cardinalities), then we might expect larger effects in early stages of acquisition. This is, in fact, borne out: experiments with different age groups indicate that the symbolic distance effect is more pronounced for younger children than for older children and adults.[15] These findings suggest that, initially, the serial order of arabic numerals by themselves provides the basis for the symbolic distance effect in numerical judgment tasks, while later cardinality associations (among others) might come in.

Another aspect that is interesting for our discussion is that concurrent verbal tasks do not interfere with numerical judgments. We came across such tasks in chapter 4 when we discussed the distinction between subitising and counting (see p. 96 above). In the experiments we reviewed there, people had to indicate how many pictures of houses they saw and at the same time they had to say 'blah blah blah'. This simultaneous verbal task affected the cardinality assessment for larger sets: people got slower and made more errors in experiments where they had to say 'blah blah blah'. However this was not the case for small sets, suggesting that the cardinality of small sets can be grasped by a non-verbal process (namely subitising), while for larger sets we have to activate verbal elements, namely counting words.

[15] Cf. for instance Sekuler and Mierkiewicz (1977) who found steeper distance effects for six- and seven-year-olds than for ten- and thirteen-year-olds and adults.

Along the same lines, we should now expect that tasks where one has to process arabic numerals should not be affected by such a simultaneous verbal task either – if, that is, arabic numerals are indeed elements of a *non-verbal* system. Evidence for this comes from studies that employed concurrent articulation in numerical judgment tasks. In a study conducted by Chris Donlan and his colleagues (Donlan et al. 1998) one group of subjects performed just the standard judgment task, while the other group in addition had to say 'ice-cream ice-cream' all the time. This verbal task did not have a significant effect on the performance in comparing arabic numerals, though – a pattern suggesting that arabic numerals are indeed elements of a non-linguistic system.

Interestingly, this study showed the same pattern for children who suffer from Specific Language Impairments (SLI). In chapter 5 we found that these children lag behind their age peers in the acquisition of number assignments, and that this might be due to a deficit in verbal sequencing which makes it difficult for these children to learn the counting sequence of their language. This account is supported by the fact that they do much better when they are taught to count with a non-verbal sequence, for instance a sequence of body gestures (this was the result of Barbara Fazio's study that we discussed in chapter 5).

It fits well into this picture, then, that these children also do pretty well with arabic numerals, which I claim form a non-verbal number sequence, too, a sequence of non-verbal numerical tools. In the Donlan et al. (1998) study, six- to seven-year-old children diagnosed with Specific Language Impairments showed a normal pattern of responses in the comparison task. What is more, they were significantly faster than a language-matched control group, that is, they were faster than children who were of younger age (namely five years old), but on a similar level of verbal comprehension. Hence performance on arabic numerals seems not to be related to verbal performance: we can regard these numerals as a non-verbal alternative to counting sequences that might circumvent the problems that SLI children have with verbal sequencing.

Arabic numerals as signs for numerical concepts

In our discussion of counting words we have seen that the same elements we use as (non-referential) numerical tools can often also be used as referring signs in complex linguistic constructions. For instance, we can use the English counting sequence in order to figure out how many pens there are on my desk. To this end, we would assign the elements ONE, TWO and

THREE (our numerical tools) to the pens – in this order and in a one-to-one manner – and our last word, in this case THREE, would be the number we assign to the whole set. The same word can then be used to refer to this cardinality in a linguistic construction, for instance in a sentence like 'There are three pens on my desk', where 'three' is a modifier for the noun 'pens'. In addition, a referential number word can also be used by itself, for instance in 'Three plus two equals five'. In this case 'three' is a proper name that refers to the cardinality in a generalised way, abstracting away from concrete sets (like the pens on my desk). In the previous chapter we identified these abstract cardinalities as the 'individualised numbers' we encounter in mathematical contexts.

As in our example, it is often the same word that is used as a counting word (that is, as a non-referential numerical tool) and as a name for the abstract cardinality (that is, as a referential, nominalised number word) and for the cardinality of a set ('three pens'), and we use similar words for our concepts of numerical rank ('the third runner') and numerical label ('bus number three').[16] The same is true for arabic numerals: these non-verbal elements can be used not only as numerical tools, but also as referential signs, that is as names for complex numerical concepts. When used as numerical tools, numerals form a non-referential sequence (1,2,3,4,5, . . .) that can be applied in the different number contexts we identified in our investigation: cardinal, ordinal, and nominal number assignments. When used as referential signs, individual elements of this sequence are employed to denote particular cardinalities, ranks, and labelled objects that are identified in these number assignments, or to denote abstract cardinalities in mathematical contexts.

As a result, arabic numerals can occur in referential linguistic contexts like '3 pens' (cardinal reference: numerical quantity), 'the 3rd century' (ordinal reference: numerical rank), or 'bus #3' (nominal reference: numerical label). Since arabic numerals are confined to the visual modality, they can only occur in written contexts. In spoken language they have to be replaced by verbal counterparts. For instance when reading aloud the examples above, we replace '3' by a cardinal number word ('three'), '3rd' by an ordinal number word ('third'), and '#3' by a nominal construction ('number three').

This is not a big deal in a language like English where the arabic numeral comes out more or less the same in each case, that is, it is replaced by the same verbal element each time we read it aloud (note though the irregular case of 'third' instead of, say, 'threeth'). However, choosing the right number word

---

[16] We will go into more detail in the following chapter, when we have a closer look at the form of these number words and their relation to, on the one hand, counting words, and, on the other, non-numerical words.

can pose more of a challenge in languages where the same numeral, but different words or word forms are used in different grammatical contexts. One such case is Modern Hebrew. In Hebrew, cardinal number words in concrete contexts agree in gender with the noun they precede, and as a result, they can differ from nominalised number words for abstract cardinalities and from counting words. For instance 'three' in Hebrew comes out as 'shalosh' with a feminine noun (for example 'shalosh bananot', three bananas), and as 'shlosha' with a masculine noun (for example 'shlosha tapuchim', three apples). Counting words and number words for abstract cardinalities always look like the feminine form, hence 'three' as a counting word and 'three' in 'three plus two' both translate as 'shalosh'. The distinction is even clearer in the case of 'two', which is 'shtey' as a cardinal number word when it precedes feminine nouns and 'shney' with masculine nouns, but takes a third form, 'shtáyim', when used as a counting word or when it refers to an abstract cardinality.[17]

Drawing on this distinction, Pearla Nesher and Tamar Katriel tested how seven- to nine-year-old Israeli schoolchildren would read aloud constructions like '3 apples', where arabic numerals occur in a concrete cardinal usage (Nesher and Katriel 1986). They found that the children tended to replace arabic numerals by words that are used as counting words or nominalised number words (that is, they overused feminine forms, and used 'shtáyim' in the case of 2), instead of the cardinal number words.

This pattern draws on two sources: it is supported by the close association of arabic numerals with counting words, that is, an association between non-verbal and verbal instances of numerical tools, and it gets further support from the association of arabic numerals with mathematical contexts (for instance, in '3 + 2'), where they are rendered by spoken nominalised number words, our verbal signs for abstract cardinalities.

Arabic numerals are the most familiar elements in mathematical contexts; they are the typical signs for abstract cardinalities. Related to this, people are usually faster and make fewer errors in calculation tasks when the problem

---

[17] This is a simplified description that concentrates on those aspects of the number word paradigm that are relevant for our discussion. In fact, Hebrew cardinal number words from 'three' to 'ten' do not only inflect for gender, they are also different in 'free' and 'construct' contexts: the *free forms* are used with indefinite nouns (as in 'three apples') or when the number word stands alone (as in 'They asked for three.'), the *construct forms* are used with definite nouns (as in 'the three apples'). It is in its 'free' usage that the feminine number word has the same form as the corresponding counting word and the nominalised number word. Compound cardinal number words over 'ten' always come in the free form, while 'two' as a cardinal number word always takes the construct form when preceding nouns (definite or indefinite), which is hence different from the corresponding counting word and the nominalised number word (cf. Glinert 1989 for a description of the number word paradigm in Hebrew).

is presented to them in arabic numerals, as opposed to number words.[18] A study conducted by Marc Brysbaert, Wim Fias, and Marie-Pascale Noël suggests that computations can, in fact, be based entirely on arabic numerals, so that they are independent of language-specific differences (Brysbaert et al. 1998).

Brysbaert and his colleagues tested two groups of Belgian students, whose native language was either French or Dutch, on tasks like '20 + 4 = ?', or '4 + 20 = ?'. By comparing speakers of French and Dutch, they took advantage of a difference between number words in the two languages, namely the different positions of constituents in number words like 'twenty-four'. We came across such a contrast earlier on, for English versus German and Arabic counting words (in our discussion of counting sequences in chapter 3, p. 75 above). Like English, French puts the decade word in the front, for instance 'vingt-quatre' (twenty-four). Dutch, like German and Arabic, has the opposite order: the decade word comes last, for instance 'vierentwintig' (literally: 'four-and-twenty').

In one kind of set-up, Brysbaert et al. showed their subjects calculation problems like '20 + 4' and '4 + 20' on a computer screen and asked them to type in the answer in the form of arabic numerals, as fast as possible. If, for this task, people translated the numerals into number words, one would expect speakers of French to be faster in finding the answer to '20 + 4', whereas Dutch speakers should be faster for '4 + 20'. However, no such differences appeared. Brysbaert et al. interpreted this finding as evidence against the influence of verbal processes on the computation: the calculation was based entirely on arabic numerals, with no influence of number words and their different structures.

Linguistic representations might play a role, though, for memorised mathematical knowledge such as multiplication tables. The retrieval of these arithmetical facts (which are learnt by heart, rather than derived anew each time) seems to be closely linked to the language it was originally learned in.[19] Accordingly, people are better (that is, faster and more accurate) at solving arithmetical problems in their first language than in a second language – while they seem to be best for arabic numerals.[20]

What picture of arabic numerals emerges from our discussion thus far? In the previous sections, we encountered arabic numerals as elements of a non-linguistic system, and in particular as a system of non-verbal numerical

---

[18] Cf. Campbell and Clark (1992), Campbell (1999).
[19] Cf. Dehaene et al. (1999), who also discuss neurological evidence for the networks involved in verbal calculation.
[20] Cf. Frenck-Mestre and Vaid (1993), and references therein.

tools. We found that arabic numerals fulfil all three number criteria, and presented evidence for the prominent role that their sequential character plays in their mental representation, similar to what we found for our *verbal* numerical toolkit – counting sequences. Finally, we had a look at the contexts in which arabic numerals are used as referring expressions, again similar to number words: like number words, arabic numerals can occur in complex linguistic constructions where they refer to numerical concepts (based on the different kinds of number assignments). We saw that, unlike number words, arabic numerals are particularly committed to abstract cardinalities; their most typical usage is in mathematical contexts.

On this basis, let us now have a look at the development of this non-verbal numeral system. This will complement our investigation of counting words by giving us a perspective on the emergence of numerical tools from a different (visual) modality. Accordingly, I do not intend to give a comprehensive overview of the development of numerals in human history and in individual acquisition, but instead will concentrate on those aspects that are relevant for our distinction between pre-numerical iconic representations and systematic numerical tools.[21]

THE DEVELOPMENT OF NON-VERBAL NUMERALS: FROM ICONIC REPRESENTATIONS TO NUMERICAL TOOLS

The development of non-verbal numerals goes back to the same kind of iconic roots as that of counting words. In particular, non-verbal numerals are closely related to visual tallies like notches; unlike counting words, they remain in the written modality. Notches as iconic cardinality representations were available from early on in the development of number, so once counting words had evolved and with them systematic numerical thinking, the development of a non-verbal counterpart for our numerical tools would have been only a small step. This development started with grouping small subsequences of notches together, instead of just lining them up, a grouping we can also observe in modern usages of tallies, like the marks on a board that indicate the number of votes in an election, or the tally that the waiter in a pub uses to keep record of the beers you have to pay for.

The grouping of notches has considerable practical advantages. Remember that subitising only allows us to grasp the cardinality of small sets, whereas the cardinalities of larger sets are represented as noisy magnitudes

---

[21] A detailed historical overview of non-verbal numeral systems can be found, for instance, in Menninger (1958: vol. II).

if counting is excluded. However, when we divide our notches into small, same-sized groups, we can grasp the cardinality of these small sets (the groups of notches), and also the cardinality of the set of groups. The grouping of notches makes it easier to grasp their cardinality, and hence the cardinality of the set they represent.

In the development of non-verbal numerals, such a grouping has probably provided the basis for the next step on our way to a non-iconic system: the invention of specific shapes for particular sets of notches. For instance, instead of tallying |||| for four elements, we could replace this set of notches by a single sign like /\ that then stands for a whole set. Using signs like this, marks the transition to a non-iconic system: in contrast to an icon like ||||, a sign like /\ does not have four elements itself, but represents a set of four by convention.

Traces of such a development can be found, for instance in roman and Chinese numerals. In both numeral systems, the first three elements are still reminiscent of a set of one, two, or three marks (namely I, II and III in Roman, and 一, 二 and 三 in Chinese), while higher elements have forms that are distinct from sets of notches (for instance roman V or the corresponding Chinese 五). Not surprisingly, it is the first three numerals that tend to retain the form of sets: since subitising allows us to grasp sets of up to three elements immediately, it would be superfluous to use special signs for such small sets of notches. With signs like Roman V, though, we introduce non-iconic elements into our system that do not have the relevant cardinality intrinsically: while III could still be regarded as a set of three, V does not have five elements by any stretch.

Once non-iconic elements develop, the sequential order of our signs takes on a special significance. The roots of this order lie in the order of icons: initially the sequence is ordered according to cardinality, that is, | comes first, then || and then |||, and so forth, because they are icons that each consist of one more element than its predecessor in the line. If we replace sets of notches by single signs, these signs will stay in the same positions as the icons. Now that we are talking about non-iconic elements, though, the sequential order becomes a matter of convention. Ultimately this means that we do not need indexical links between individual signs and particular cardinalities, we do not have to regard, say, V as a placeholder for a set with five elements anymore. Rather, V now can indicate a cardinality due to its position in the sequence, in other words: it can indicate a cardinality based on dependent linking.

This establishes a genuine, non-iconic number assignment, where a numerical relational structure (our sequence) is associated with an empirical relational structure (sets of different cardinalities), and this association is based on links between two relations, namely the relation '>' that defines the sequential positions in our numerical system, and the relation 'has more elements than' between empirical sets of different sizes. As we have seen in our discussion in the previous chapters, once we employ a pattern of dependent linking, the connection to cardinality is loosened: we *can* use the elements of our sequence to indicate different cardinalities (and this remains a central function for them), but we can also use them in non-cardinal mappings. In particular, we can use the relations that hold within our number system to indicate ordinal and nominal properties of empirical objects.

Let me sum up the developmental stages we found here. We set out from an iconic cardinal basis, namely icons that are matched to the elements of a set in a one-to-one manner (for instance, the icon ||| can represent the cardinality of the pens on my desk because there are as many lines in this icon as there are pens). These icons form a natural series due to their intrinsic cardinality (for instance, an icon like | comes before ||, then ||| etc.), and this ordering allows us to eventually give up iconicity in favour of sequential order: if we have sequential order anyway, we can indicate a cardinality based on positions in this sequence alone, and do not need an additional intrinsic cardinality for our elements (for instance, V can indicate the cardinality of the pens on my desk because the sequence from I to V has as many elements as the set of pens, and not because V itself consists of five elements). What used to be icons are now elements of a non-referential sequence whose usage is based on dependent linking. This kind of linking can be generalised and allows the implication of non-cardinal contexts, since it is not based on iconic representations, but on relations that hold between numerical tools.

The case of the roman numeral system, with its many iconic allusions, makes clear that it is not so much the absence or presence of an iconic *potential* in its elements that makes a system numerical or iconic, but rather the way these elements constitute the system. Quite a few roman numerals give an iconic impression. For instance, VII is built of V and a set of two 'ones' (namely II), and this goes back to its position two steps after V. And as mentioned above, III is obviously made of three lines, hence we might regard it as a set of three. However, as part of the roman numeral sequence an element like III gets its significance by its position in a conventional sequence and only by this position. The fact that it consists of three lines was presumably the original motivation for its shape, and it might be nice for mnemonic reasons, but it is not relevant for the way the system works.

This becomes evident if we replace a seemingly iconic sign by another, non-iconic element. For instance, if we wanted to introduce a random other element, say *, as the third element of the roman numeral sequence, that would be just fine. The system would not break down or be altered in any way except for the fact that one conventional element is replaced by another one. Since it is not the cardinality of individual signs that is relevant, this change would not have any impact on the system: from the point of view of the system, * is just the same as III, as long as it gets the same position in the sequence and is well distinguished from all other elements. This is a clear indication that we have, in fact, a non-iconic system: a system of elements that we use in a non-iconic way, drawing on the properties of sequential position and (non-)identity in a pattern of dependent linking. Roman numerals form a full-blown numeral system that fulfils all the requirements for a number sequence and is used in a non-iconic way.

While roman numerals form a fully functioning system of numerical tools, they are not as efficient for arithmetical computations as arabic numerals. This numeral system has its origin in northern India about 500 BC and, like so many cultural inventions, came to Europe via the Middle East. The 'West-Arabic' system that made it to Europe is based on the primitive elements 0,1,2,3,4,5,6,7,8,9; their counterparts in the 'East-Arabic' system which is used in most of the Middle East today are ٠, ١, ٢, ٣, ٤, ٥, ٦, ٧, ٨, ٩.

The feature that is responsible for the success of the Hindu–Arabic numerals is the introduction of a marker for an empty space, the element that evolved into 0 and ٠. This allows us to base the sequence on a place-value principle, where the positions in a complex numeral mark different powers of ten. This feature not only provides a simple way to generate new elements, it also reflects transparently the base ten system that underlies arabic numerals and makes them particularly well suited for calculation. The Arabic numeral system allows us to base arithmetical computations on simple algorithms, and it is this advantage that caused their great expansion. In fact, in Europe it was merchants who first promoted this new numeral system, while a large part of the society remained suspicious for quite a while, mainly due to the counter-intuitive element 'o' which has no match in the counting sequence (cf. also our discussion of zero in chapter 6).

The introduction of a place–value principle into a numeral system was of considerable importance for the development of mathematical thinking, but the interesting point for our discussion of numbers lies in a more fundamental feature in the development of our non-verbal tools, namely in the status of iconic cardinality representations in this development. As

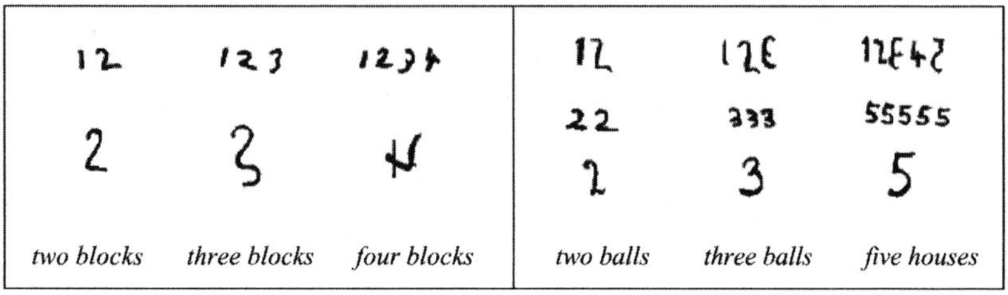

1 2	1 2 3	1 2 3 4	1 2	1 2 3	1 2 3 4 2
			2 2	3 3 3	5 5 5 5 5
2	3	4	2	3	5
two blocks	*three blocks*	*four blocks*	*two balls*	*three balls*	*five houses*

Figure 67 Iconic and non-iconic representations of cardinality with arabic numerals

we have seen in the present section, non-verbal numerals just like counting sequences have their roots in icons for sets of different cardinalities, and these icons later develop into a non-iconic number system that is based on dependent linking and not restricted to cardinality anymore. This pattern hence seems to be characteristic for the development of numerical tools across modalities.

An interesting phenomenon related to the distinction of iconic and numerical stages can be observed in the acquisition of non-verbal numerals in individual development, and again it shows remarkable parallels to the acquisition of counting words: when children start using numerals to indicate a cardinality (usually around four to five years of age), they initially tend to use them in an iconic way, and in particular in a way that resembles early usages of counting words in cardinal number assignments.

For instance, when children are shown some toys on a table and asked to write down how many they see, they often write down a *sequence of numerals* instead of a single numeral, for instance they might write '123' instead of '3', or '1234' instead of '4'. Later, some children also use sets of repeated digits, for instance they write '333' instead of '3', or '55555' instead of '5'. Figure 67 gives examples of iconic and non-iconic (numerical) usages of arabic numerals in cardinality assignments, taken from two studies with pre-schoolchildren (the examples on the left are taken from Munn 1998: 48, the ones on the right from Sinclair et al. 1983: 540). This is a phenomenon similar to what we observed for counting words in chapter 5. Remember that before children master the cardinality principle, they often give a sequence of counting words when asked 'How many?', instead of using the last word from the count to identify the cardinality of the whole set. So, for instance, when asked how many toy houses there were, they might say 'one-two-three-four-five' instead of answering 'five' – just as, in our example, a child wrote down a sequence of numerals, namely '12345' (or a version of it), instead of '5'. The occurrence of numeral sets like '333' or '55555' (as illustrated on the right side of Figure 67) might then mark a transitional stage where the cardinality principle for arabic numerals is about to come in, but is not yet quite mastered. At this stage, the last numeral in the sequence takes on a special significance for the cardinality assignment, but we still have an *iconic* representation of cardinality: the cardinality of one set is represented by another set (for instance a set of three toys is represented by three 3s, namely as '333').

While we did not find such a transitional stage of iconic sets in the case of counting words – presumably because these sets are more likely to occur for visual elements – the occurrence of iconic sequences like '123' or '1234' shows a striking analogy to pre-numerical usages of counting words. Hence, in the acquisition of non-verbal numerals, at least to some degree the same kind of iconic back-up comes in again that supported the acquisition of cardinal number assignments in the verbal domain. Taken together, the results from the present section, then, confirm an early iconic basis for the emergence of both non-verbal and verbal numerical tools, not only in human development, but also in children's acquisition.

How are the elements of these two systems related to each other? Throughout this chapter, I emphasised that arabic numerals and counting words are not different kinds of names or notations for the same abstract referents 'numbers', but different kinds of numerical tools, that is, non-referential sequences that can fulfil the same numerical purposes – just as, say, a hammer made of iron and a hammer made of steel are not different 'names' for some abstract hammer, but *are* different hammers, two instances of what a hammer can be, albeit made of different materials. In the remainder of this chapter I am now going to discuss how arabic numerals and counting words are correlated, for instance when we 'read aloud' arabic numerals or write them to dictation. In particular, I am going to demonstrate that arabic numerals and counting words can be linked up as elements of two alternative systems of numerical tools, rather than with reference to additional 'numbers' as their common denotation.

TWO ALTERNATIVE NUMBER SEQUENCES: THE CORRELATION BETWEEN COUNTING WORDS AND ARABIC NUMERALS

While there are cultures where one can get along knowing only one language, this is very rare for number sequences. Most cultures require children to learn at least two different instances of numerical tools, namely a verbal one (for example the English counting words) and a non-verbal one (for instance arabic numerals), and we are often familiar with more number sequences, both verbal and non-verbal (for instance counting words of another language or roman numerals). Of course, our concept of number does not get multiplied each time we learn a new number sequence. Rather, these sequences are integrated into our cognitive number domain as different instances of numerical tools. The account we give for arabic numerals here can be regarded as an example of how such an integration works.

As a basis for this account, I first discuss in some more detail what it means to link up elements of two non-referential sequences when we 'read aloud' non-verbal numerals, as opposed to reading aloud written words. In particular I am going to discuss some evidence from Japanese that sheds further light on this distinction, supporting our view that the link between non-verbal numerals and counting words is a direct one, a link between numerical elements that is neither based on phonological representations nor on shared referents. In the next step I discuss how this link can work as a correlation between two sequential structures, and distinguish the different aspects involved in this correlation. On this basis, in the final part of this section I sketch an account of this correlation that can be integrated into our model of numerical tools and their applications.

'Reading aloud' non-verbal numerals

Arabic numerals, like roman numerals and other non-verbal numerals, are confined to the visual modality, and this is also why they are the numerical tools that feature in visual representations like mental 'number forms'. Counting words, on the other hand, are first and foremost elements of speech, based on their phonological representation. In addition, though, they can be rendered in script via graphemic representations: written forms allows us to represent words visually. In a system like the Latin alphabet, graphemic representations are correlated with phonological ones in a systematic way (although the relations between graphemic and phonological representations can be more or less transparent, ranging from a highly regular, phonologically oriented spelling system like the one used for Spanish, to a historically based system like the English spelling where correspondences are more in keeping with an earlier stage of the language).

When 'reading aloud' arabic numerals, what we actually do is correlate them with the phonological representations of counting words. However unlike a graphemic representation like 'five', an arabic numeral does not identify one particular phonological representation, but can be correlated with (corresponding) elements from different counting sequences, depending on the context. For instance when '5' occurs in the context of written English, say, 'She has bought 5 pens', we read it (correlate it with): FIVE.

When '5' occurs in a French sentence as in 'Elle a acheté 5 stylos', its counterpart in spoken language is: CINQ.

Reading aloud a non-verbal numeral is not mediated by grapheme-phoneme correspondences, unlike reading a written version of a counting word. When reading the word 'five', we make use of certain correlations between its spelling and its phonological representation,[22] but when we read aloud '5', we do not compute any such links between letters and sounds on our way to the counting word. This is because arabic numerals are not written representations of counting words, but elements of a corresponding system of numerical tools. Children seem to be aware of this non-graphemical and instrumental status from early on. When Anne Sinclair and Hermine Sinclair asked four- to six-year-olds about the meaning of numerals on different pictures, they found that 'many children say that numerals cannot be "read", as they are "for counting", but that they do "tell" something' (Sinclair and Sinclair 1984: 176; this is the study that we also discussed in chapter 6, in connection with nominal number concepts).

As mentioned before, reading aloud arabic numerals is in fact more like translating counting words from one language into another: we link up corresponding positions in two number sequences. Due to this direct link, the correlation of non-verbal numerals and counting words is at least as fast as reading aloud written versions of counting words.[23]

This phenomenon gives rise to an interesting pattern in Japanese. Let me describe this pattern in the following paragraphs and show how it sheds light on two points that are relevant for our discussion in the present section: I am going to argue that the evidence from reading aloud numerals and number words in Japanese suggests that, on the one hand, reading aloud non-verbal numerals is not mediated by grapheme–phoneme correspondences, while, on the other hand, it also is not mediated by common semantic representations of numerals and counting words; in other words:

(1) non-verbal numerals and written counting words are not different ways to render the same phonological representation in script, and

(2) non-verbal numerals and counting words are not different names for the same number.

---

[22] Written versions of words can also be memorised in full. In particular for familiar words, we do not necessarily compute individual letter–sound correlations by piecemeal, but access the phonological representation from the whole written representation or from large chunks of it.

[23] A classic study conducted by Brown (1915) found that counting words are pronounced faster from arabic numerals than from written counting words. Wimmer and Goswami (1994) report the same pattern for seven- to nine-year-olds (as part of a study investigating reading development in English and German), while the adult subjects in Ferrand's (1999) study took about as long to read aloud arabic numerals as they needed for written counting words.

There are two different kinds of script in use in Japan. The script in which most words are conventionally written is *kanji*, a logographic script that is based on Chinese characters. Kanji elements are not related to phonemes or syllables, but identify whole words or morphemes. So for instance the Japanese word for 'hill' is represented by a single kanji sign: 山 (while in Latin script this word would have four elements, namely 'yama'). Since kanji characters identify the meaning of words rather than their phonological representations, there are some characters that are used for words with the same meaning in Japanese and in Chinese, although these are words that have entirely different phonological representations in the two languages. For instance, 山 means 'hill' in Mandarin Chinese as well as in Japanese, although the word for 'hill' is pronounced /shan/ in Mandarin and /yama/ in Japanese.

The non-verbal numerals used in the context of Japanese kanji writing are the same as the Chinese numerals. Like arabic numerals, this numeral system is based on primitive elements for 0 to 9, while higher elements are complex. Unlike arabic numerals, Chinese complex numerals are not based on a positional system. Instead, they are combined in the same way as the Chinese counting words, making Chinese one of the rare contexts where the structure of complex counting words and non-verbal numerals is in a perfect match. For instance, the Chinese counting word corresponding to English FOUR HUNDRED AND TWENTY-SIX has the structure 'four hundred two ten six', and '426' in Chinese numerals comes out as something like '4 H 2 T 6', where 'H' is meant to be the character for 100, and 'T' the character for 10 (and '4', '2', and '6' stand for the respective numerals in Chinese). This structural feature does not have an impact on our present discussion, though: for our purposes the important point is that these are the numerals that are used within kanji script, and that they form a full-blown system of non-verbal counting words.

In contrast to kanji, Japanese *kana* scripts, *katakana* and *hiragana*, are syllabic scripts: individual elements of this script identify different sylla-bles; hence spelling in kana unlike spelling in kanji identifies phonological representations. This is why katakana is conventionally used for writing words that are not lexicalised, for instance for foreign words, while hira-gana is mostly (but not exclusively) used to represent function words and inflectional affixes. In principle, all Japanese words can be spelled in kana, of course, and, in fact, there have been suggestions in Japan to instigate a spelling reform to this effect. For example, the hiragana spelling for 'yama' would be やま ('ya-ma'), but at least at present this is not the conventional way to write this word.

Nevertheless, experimental evidence suggests that people read aloud words written in kana faster than words written in kanji, even if these words that are conventionally written in kanji. This has first been shown for colour words (Feldman and Turvey 1980); a similar effect has later been observed for other common nouns. Generally, people seem to be slower at reading aloud the familiar kanji form than reading the unfamiliar kana form.

In the case of numerals, though, this pattern is reversed: whereas nouns are read faster in kana, numerals are faster in kanji. Jun Yamada showed this in an experiment with undergraduates from Hiroshima university (Yamada 1992). He asked the students to read aloud nouns like the Japanese words for 'hill', 'mouth', or 'tree', and numerals. In each case, they would see either a kana spelling of the word (the unfamiliar form) or its kanji counterpart (the familiar form). When response latencies were measured (that is, the time it took the subjects to start speaking once the probe appeared on the screen), it came out that the students needed more time to say a counting word when they saw a kana spelling of it, than when they saw the corresponding kanji numeral, that is, a Chinese numeral as used within kanji script. Nouns spelled in kana took about as long as counting words spelled in kana, and nouns written in kanji took longest.

It seems, then, that, for colour words and other common nouns, a syllabic script has an advantage for reading over the logographic kanji, but in the numerical domain it does not – even though, in both cases, the task is to speak aloud a word. Why is that so? I think the reason for this pattern is again the special numerical status of counting words, and their relation to arabic numerals. Let me explain this.

In order to read aloud a word, one has to access its phonological representation. This representation is immediately identified by elements of a syllabic script, that is, in kana, but not in kanji. A kanji character identifies the meaning of a lexical entry. For instance when reading the kanji character for 'hill', one activates the meaning of a certain word, namely our concept for 'hill'. For the task of reading aloud one then has to access the phonological representation of that word, in this case /yama/. Hence, when learning Japanese as a foreign language, you might see a kanji character and know what it means, although you might not be able to come up with the right Japanese word for it. In contrast to this, you might be able to pronounce a word written in kana without knowing its meaning, just like you can read aloud 'yama' in Latin script without knowing what it means.

Given this picture, it is not surprising that people read faster when words are spelled in kana script than when they are represented in kanji:

kana, but not kanji, gives us direct access to phonology, and phonology is what we need for reading aloud.[24] Remember that the task we talk about is just pronunciation, hence one is faster if one does not bother too much about the meaning of lexical entries, but makes use of the direct access to phonology that kana provides, based on correspondences between characters and syllables.

Why does this not hold, then, for counting words? The kana part does, in fact. The results in Yamada's study indicated that there is no difference between common nouns and counting words spelled in kana; his subjects were about as fast to read aloud a counting word spelled in kana as they were for common nouns. It is the kanji part where the contrast occurs: whereas people needed longer for common nouns written in kanji compared to kana, they were faster to say aloud counting words when they saw the kanji numerals (that is, the Chinese numerals that go with kanji script), compared to the counting word spelled in kana. This suggests that the effect is due to an advantage of non-verbal numerals (kanji) over written versions of counting words (kana), and not due to the fact that kana spelling slows down the reading of counting words.

And this is where our account of numerical tools comes in: as argued above, numerals are not the written form of counting words, they are their counterparts in another number sequence. A non-verbal numeral like arabic 5 or the corresponding Chinese (kanji) numeral 五 is linked to a counting word like English FIVE or Japanese GO (Japanese for 'five') through a direct numerical correspondence, a link between matching elements in two alternative systems of numerical tools. 'Reading aloud' a non-verbal numeral means in fact identifying its matching element in a counting sequence, and this element is identified by its phonological representation. Accordingly, when we link up a numeral with a counting word we link it up with a phonological representation right away. There is hence no advantage for the unfamiliar kana forms, that is, for written forms of counting words where the phonological representation is accessed via graphemic–phonological correspondences (correspondences between characters and syllables).

And when we link up a numeral with a counting word, we also do not go via a semantic representation, as we would when reading aloud kanji common nouns. Unlike kanji characters for common nouns, a non-verbal

---

[24] This is a somewhat simplified picture, though. On the one hand, for some kanjis, in particular high-frequency kanjis, the phonological representation might also be accessed directly from the written word. On the other hand, for high-frequency kana, experienced readers might not necessarily employ a grapheme–phoneme algorithm, but might directly access the whole word and its meaning (for a detailed discussion and an overview of the experimental evidence cf. Kess and Miyamoto 1999).

numeral is not a referential sign. So in order to identify the right counting word we do not look for a shared referent, but access the counting word directly as a corresponding, non-referential element in another numerical system.

The fast access to the phonological representation of counting words that we observe when people 'read aloud' non-verbal numerals might hence be due to this direct route from elements of one sequence (non-verbal numerals) to elements of the other (spoken counting words), a route that requires neither graphemic computations (like kana) nor a semantic bridge (like kanji common nouns).

Further support for this view comes from a study where people had to perform a comparison task with non-verbal numerals and written versions of counting words. Katsuo Tamaoka and his collaborators showed schoolchildren arabic numerals together with either kanji numerals or counting words written in kana, and asked them to indicate, for each pair, the higher element as fast as possible. The children were faster at comparing arabic numerals with kanji numerals than with written counting words (Tamaoka et al. 1991). This result suggests an advantage for kanji numerals over written words not only when the task involves pronunciation, but also in a context where no 'reading aloud' is required. We can interpret this as further evidence for a direct access to non-verbal numerals, and in this case this means that we can directly access the respective ranks when we compare elements from different non-verbal sequences. For counting words written in kana, we have to compute grapheme/phoneme correspondences, because counting words are first and foremost part of the auditory modality, that is, we access them via phonological representations, even though we might not use these phonological representations for the task of articulation (as in reading aloud). In contrast to this, non-verbal numerals are visual entities and can be compared directly.

Figure 68 illustrates the links between written elements and phonological representations for the examples we discussed here: (a) the Japanese word for 'hill' (pronounced /yama/) written in kanji, (b) the same word written in kana, (c) the Japanese counting word GO ('five') spelled in kana, and (d) the corresponding Chinese/kanji numeral 五, together with its counterpart '5' in the arabic numeral sequence.

The correlation of structures

Let us now have a closer look at how the link between non-verbal numerals and counting words works. We have established that this link is not based

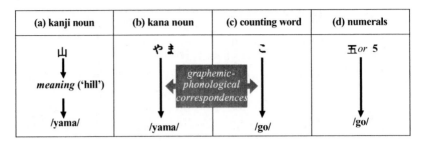

(a) kanji noun	(b) kana noun	(c) counting word	(d) numerals

Figure 68 How to read aloud written nouns, counting words, and non-verbal numerals

on a shared referent and that it does not rely on graphemic–phonological correspondences. 'FIVE' and '5' (just like 'GO' and '五' in Japanese) are not different names for the same number, and they are also not different means of spelling the same word. Rather, counting words and arabic numerals are elements of alternative number sequences: counting sequences and numeral sequences are verbal and non-verbal instances of numerical tools, respectively. This means, then, that their correlation must be a correlation between matching sequential positions, since this is the feature that gives elements of a number sequence their significance: they are well-distinguished elements of a progression.

So what we could do is go through the two sequences simultaneously, starting from the elements ONE and 1, and match in each step a counting word and a numeral, in an ordered one-to-one manner. This works well for a finite and small set, say, the non-verbal numerals 1 to 9 and their verbal matches ONE to NINE. Since the two sequences are open-ended, though, we want a generalised way to achieve this matching, so that we can account for every element we can potentially generate within each sequence. This can be done by a mapping that relates to the rules that generate counting words and arabic numerals, respectively. Such a mapping has to take into account both the primitive elements and the way they make up complex elements, and we want this to work in two directions: when we 'read aloud' arabic numerals, we need to match a numeral to its corresponding counting word; when we write arabic numerals to dictation, we need to get from a counting word to its corresponding numeral.

The points where such a mapping becomes interesting are those areas where the respective rules diverge. Non-verbal and verbal number sequences come out just the same when we only look at their numerical functions, but they do not need to have the same rules of generation, that is, the same kind of make-up for complex elements, and in fact they rarely do. For one, non-verbal numerals can employ a place–value system. While such a place–value system is an extremely efficient way to build up a number sequence, its implementation seems to be confined to the visual modality and does not emerge in verbal counting sequences. Let us look at the effects this has for our example of arabic numerals and English counting words.

As mentioned above, the way we generate complex arabic numerals and integrate them into the sequence is based on such a place–value system. As a result, for instance the digit '4' has a different value in '4', than in '43' and in '403'. In counting words, we use for this purpose the components we called 'bases' in chapter 3, that is, elements like -TY, HUNDRED, THOUSAND, etc. that mark the class a complex counting word belongs to. For instance, we distinguish FOUR from FOURTY and from FOUR HUNDRED.

So, when reading aloud an arabic numeral – that is, when mapping an arabic numeral onto a counting word – one has to introduce bases and skip the os that mark empty positions. Clinical evidence suggests that the capacity to identify the right base for this process can be impaired as a result of brain damage. For instance when asked to read aloud arabic numerals, some patients might say EIGHT THOUSAND NINETY when they see 8,900, or FOUR HUNDRED THOUSAND SEVEN THIRTEEN when they see 407,013.[25]

When writing an arabic numeral to dictation – that is, when mapping a counting word onto an arabic numeral – one has to skip bases and introduce os for empty positions. Since os only mark *empty* positions, there is no one-to-one correspondences between sequences of os and bases. So, while FORTY corresponds to '40' and FOUR HUNDRED corresponds to '400', the base -TY does not come out as 'o' in '43', nor does the base HUNDRED correspond to 'oo' in '435' and '403'. We can account for this by a procedure called 'over-writing': when we write down an arabic numeral in response to a counting word FOUR HUNDRED AND THIRTY-FIVE, we do not write down two constituents '400' and '35', corresponding to the two counting word constituents, but instead over-write part of the first numeral ('400') by replacing its os with the digits of the smaller numeral, starting from the left. In this case, the two os in '400' get over-written by '35', while in the example of '403' only the last o would be over-written.

Children do not master the 'over-writing' procedure right from the start, but have to learn it. So when six- to eight-year-old Italian schoolchildren were asked to write arabic numerals to dictation, they often produced numerals like '40035' instead of '435' (Power and Dal Martello 1990). A

---

[25] Cf. the data reported in Sokol and McCloskey (1988) and McCloskey et al. (1990).

similar pattern has been observed in brain-damaged patients,[26] and also in people who had been diagnosed as mentally retarded.[27]

In addition to differences that result from the place–value system, counting words and non-verbal numerals can differ because – as we have seen in chapter 3 – a counting sequence often contains elements with idiosyncratic features that deviate from the general pattern of the counting sequence and might also constitute morphologically deviating subsystems. The less such idiosyncrasies occur in a counting sequence, the more transparent and regular its structure is and the easier it is to correlate its elements with arabic numerals (recall also the studies of Asian versus American and European children we discussed in chapter 3). Examples of such idiosyncrasies in the English counting sequence are opaque elements like ELEVEN and TWELVE that do not have a constituent structure comparable to that of '11' and '12'.

Another case in point is the constituent order in counting words from THIRTEEN to NINETEEN which deviates from that within the corresponding arabic numerals; for instance, the order of SIX and -TEEN in SIXTEEN is the opposite of the order of '1' and '6' in '16'. In this case, one has to reverse the constituents when writing numerals to dictation or when reading them aloud. The case of a patient reported by Gerhard Blanken and his colleagues suggests that the ability to do this can be affected as a result of brain damage (Blanken et al. 1997). The patient they describe was a speaker of German who produced counting words like ZWEIUNDSECHZIG, literally: 'two-and-sixty', in response to '26' instead of the correct SECHSUNDZWANZIG, literally: 'six-and-twenty' (remember that German – unlike English, but like for example Dutch and Arabic – has the 'ones before tens' constituent order not only for counting words from *thirteen* to *nineteen*, but all the way up to *ninety-nine*).

The examples we discussed thus far were impairments that affect the constituent *structure* of complex elements. The errors that can be observed in these impairments have been called 'syntactic errors' in the psychological literature. In addition, the correlation of counting words and arabic numerals can also suffer from deficits in identifying the right – read: matching – constituent, so-called 'lexical errors'. In this case, patients might get the structure right, but fit the wrong elements into the slots. For instance a patient described by Scott Sokol and Michael McCloskey, when asked to

---

[26] Such cases have been reported, for instance, by Cipolotti et al. (1994) and Delazer and Denes (1998).
[27] For instance Ezawa (1996) provides a detailed single case study of an eighteen-year-old woman, Anne, who made (among others) errors that patterned with those described by Power and Dal Martello (cf. in particular the examples in Ezawa 1996: 77).

read aloud '15', said THIRTEEN in response (Sokol and McCloskey 1988), suggesting that he knew the counting word should consist of a 'one'-word and -TEEN and that he also knew in which order these constituents should come (namely in an order opposite to that of the digits in '15'), but he did not find the right 'one'-word, namely FIVE, to fit into the first constituent slot.

An interesting aspect about impairments resulting from brain lesions is that they can affect separate areas of competence differentially: patients who suffered brain damage – often as a result of a stroke – might face severe problems in one area, while another area remains largely intact, suggesting that the relevant mental processes rely on at least partially distinct neuronal networks.

In our case, brain lesions leading to different numerical impairments can point to different processes in the correlation of counting words and arabic numerals. We have already encountered one kind of dissociation in the preceding paragraphs, namely that between impairments affecting 'lexical' versus 'syntactic' aspects, reflecting the fact that the mapping between elements of different number sequence has to take into account both the primitive elements and the way they make up complex elements. If the association of individual elements is impaired, patients will produce 'lexical errors'; if the generation and/or association of constituent structures is impaired, we will see 'syntactic errors'.

Other dissociations support our view that the correlation of arabic numerals and counting words is based on two kinds of mappings: one that gives us a counting word for each arabic numeral (this is what we need when we read aloud numerals), and one in the other direction, which gives us a numeral for each counting word (this is what we need when we write numerals to dictation). Both mappings can be impaired differentially as a result of brain damage, that is, we can find patients who suffer from problems in reading aloud numerals, but do fine in writing them to dictation, and others who show just the opposite pattern, with impairments for writing numerals to dictation, but a preserved production of counting words in response to numerals.[28]

In addition we find patterns that emphasise the distinction between our two number sequences and their correlation. Lisa Cipolotti presented a case study of a patient 'SF' who seemed to have intact representations of both counting words and arabic numerals, but was impaired in mapping numerals onto counting words (Cipolotti 1995): SF could answer

[28] Cf. McCloskey and Caramazza (1987).

number fact questions verbally (suggesting preserved knowledge of number words) and he could also identify the larger one of a pair of numerals (suggesting preserved knowledge of arabic numerals), but faced problems reading aloud arabic numerals (suggesting impairments in mapping arabic numerals onto counting words). Other patients have a preserved comprehension of counting words, but face errors mapping them onto arabic numerals.[29]

Lesions in the language-dominant hemisphere of the brain can also lead to an overall impairment in arithmetical thinking and in the processing of both arabic numerals and counting words. In some cases, mathematical reasoning and the representation of number sequences are dissociated: these patients show selective deficits for calculation, while the correlation of arabic numerals and counting words is not affected. As two case studies presented by Dehaene and Cohen (1997) showed, these deficits in calculation can be due to deficits in verbal knowledge, or to deficits in the knowledge of numerical quantities. As we have seen above, verbal knowledge is relevant for the retrieval of basic arithmetical facts as stored in multiplication tables, while our knowledge of numerical quantities supports the representation of abstract cardinalities in mathematical contexts.

An impairment of cardinal concepts might also be involved in the cognitive deficits that are sometimes observed as a result of prenatal alcohol exposure. These deficits affect mathematical reasoning, but seem to spare representations of the number sequences that constitute its basis. In a study conducted by Karen Kopera-Frye and her colleagues, patients diagnosed as suffering from Fetal Alcohol Syndrome or Fetal Alcohol Effects faced problems in calculation, but they did fine in mapping arabic numerals onto counting words and vice versa (reading aloud arabic numerals and writing them to dictation), and all but 2 out of 29 performed well in judgment tasks where they had to tell which of two arabic numerals was larger (cf. Kopera-Frye et al. 1996).

Within the account developed here, we can describe this as an impairment that affects the grasp of abstract cardinalities, but does not affect the representation and correlation of verbal and non-verbal sequences of numerical tools. In the opposite case, brain lesions can also affect the ability to map arabic numerals onto counting words, but leave calculation skills intact, in particular when they can be based on arabic numerals.[30] The representation of arabic numerals seems to remain intact here and they can

[29] Cf. for instance the patient 'Chuck' described in Macaruso and Sokol (1998).
[30] This pattern seems to be realised, for instance, in two cases reported in Cohen and Dehaene (1991) and in Macaruso and Sokol (1998) (patient 'YM' and patient 'Rob', respectively).

also be used to identify abstract cardinalities, but patients face problems correlating them with their verbal counterparts.

Taken together, these different patterns give us a clear picture of the different aspects we have to distinguish for the correlation of non-verbal numerals and counting words: (a) the representation of arabic numerals, (b) the representation of counting words, (c) the mapping of arabic numerals onto counting words ('reading aloud' arabic numerals), (d) the mapping of counting words onto arabic numerals (writing arabic numerals 'to dictation'), and (e) the application of arabic numerals or counting words in different numerical contexts (for instance in calculation). We are now in a position to bring together these different aspects in an account of arabic numerals and their relation to counting words.

An account of arabic numerals and their correlation with counting words

Over the last decades, three models have been proposed to account for the processing of arabic numerals and the mechanisms underlying the conversion of arabic numerals into counting words and vice versa: the Modular Model introduced by Michael McCloskey and his colleagues,[31] the Encoding Complex View developed by Jamie Campbell and James Clark,[32] and the Triple-Code Model put forward by Stanislas Dehaene.[33] Let us have a look at these models in turn. On this basis I will introduce an account that integrates arabic numerals into our model of the cognitive number domain as a non-verbal sequence of numerical tools.

The Modular Model
Within the Modular Model, counting words and arabic numerals are correlated via central representations which McCloskey et al. (see references in note 31) call 'semantic representations of number'. These semantic representations are accessed by different comprehension and production mechanisms, and also serve as a basis for calculation procedures. They have the form of abstract quantities that come in a decade structure, that is, they are structured by powers of 10. For instance when we want to get from

---

[31] Cf. McCloskey et al. (1985) and discussions of different theoretical aspects and empirical evidence in McCloskey et al. (1986, 1992); Sokol and McCloskey (1988), McCloskey (1992), Macaruso et al. (1993).

[32] Cf. Campbell and Clark (1988) and further discussions in Clark and Campbell (1991); Campbell and Clark (1992); Campbell (1999).

[33] Cf. Dehaene (1992); further empirical evidence in support of the model is discussed in Dehaene and Cohen (1997).

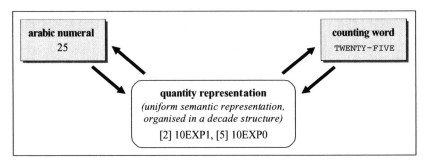

Figure 69   Correlation of arabic numerals and counting words within the Modular Model

the numeral '325' to its corresponding counting word within this model, we access a semantic representation of the form '{3} 10EXP2, {2} 10EXP1, {5} 10EXP0'. This representation identifies three different quantities corresponding to the three digits in the arabic numeral (3, 2, and 5), and indicates the powers of 10 in which these quantities come: 3 times 10^2, 2 times 10^1, and 5 times 10^0.

The graphic in Figure 69 shows how a central, uniform quantity representation mediates the correlation of arabic numerals and counting words in the Modular Model. For the illustration, I used the arabic numeral '25' and the English counting word TWENTY-FIVE as examples. The four separate arrows in this graphic identify different, modularly organised comprehension and production mechanisms for both arabic numerals and counting words, leading to different routes when we map arabic numerals onto counting words (for instance, when reading aloud numerals) and when we map counting words onto arabic numerals (for instance, when writing numerals to dictation). This is in accordance with the evidence that we discussed in the preceding section. As some of the cases of brain damage showed, each of these routes can be affected independently, such that some patients might suffer from deficits in reading aloud arabic numerals, while others have problems writing them to dictation.

The arrow leading from the semantic representation to the counting word includes the generation of a syntactic frame. This syntactic frame links up the semantic representation with the phonological (or graphemic) representation of a counting word. Syntactic frames are made of two kinds of elements: 'number-lexical classes' and 'multipliers'. According to McCloskey et al. (see note 31 above) the number-lexical classes in English are (a) Ones: counting words from ONE to NINE; (b) Teens: counting words from TEN to NINETEEN, and (c) Tens: decade words ending on -TY (that is,

TWENTY, THIRTY, . . . , NINETY). For higher counting words, 'multipliers' identify elements like HUNDRED, THOUSAND, etc.[34]

The class labels in a syntactic frame come with open slots that are filled by a quantity (computed from the quantities in the semantic representation); this quantity identifies a position within that class. For instance, the position {3} in the Ones class identifies the counting word T H R E E, whereas in the Teens class, {3} identifies the word THIRTEEN, and in the Tens class it gets us THIRTY. This distinction of a syntactic frame and the slots it provides allows the model, among others, to account for the patterns of 'syntactic' versus 'lexical' errors we discussed in the previous section. Finally, the filled syntactic frame is used for the phonological representation that underlies the production of the counting word.

Let us spell this out for our example from above. Getting from the arabic numeral '325' to its corresponding counting word would involve the following steps in this model:

(1) *Input*: 325 (arabic numeral)

(2) *Comprehension mechanism.* The numeral is mapped onto a semantic representation:

$$\{3\} \text{ 10EXP2}, \{2\} \text{ 10EXP1}, \{5\} \text{ 10EXP0}$$

(3) *Production mechanism.* The semantic representation is mapped onto a syntactic frame, and the slots in this frame are filled with quantities:

$$[[\text{Ones: } \{3\}] \text{ MULTIPLIER:H} \quad \text{Tens: } \{2\} \quad \text{Ones: } \{5\}]]$$

(4) *Output*: /three hundred twenty-five/ (counting word)

As this example illustrates, the semantic representation has a crucial function in this correlation. It is via this representation that non-verbal numerals and counting words come together; comprehension and production mechanisms for arabic numerals and counting words alike access the same central quantity representation. Hence the Modular Model does not allow direct links between non-verbal numerals and counting words. In this model arabic numerals and counting words are regarded as different names for the same abstract numbers, in accordance with the traditional approach to

---

[34] Note that this account of complex counting words differs from the one I sketched in chapter 3 and formalised in Appendix 3. In particular, my account gives a unified treatment for counting words ending on -TY and those that involve elements like HUNDRED: according to the analysis I suggested, each counting word – and each counting word constituent – belongs to one of the classes Ones, Teens, Tys, Hundreds, Thousands etc., and each class above the Ones and Teens involves an element that serves as a multiplier, namely -TY, HUNDRED etc. In addition, some counting words can undergo transformations that account for idiosyncratic forms that deviate from the overall pattern.

numerals and number words; these 'numbers' are identified by the semantic representations. These semantic representations consist of quantities; hence they restrict numbers to a quantitative/cardinal aspect and cannot account for ordinal and nominal contexts.

An additional problem in this context might arise from the fact that semantic representations specify a certain base structure. In the examples McCloskey and his collaborators discuss, semantic representations are based on powers of 10, corresponding to the base ten structure of arabic numerals and the decade structure underlying most of the English counting sequence. This makes these central representations less independent of particular number sequences than might be desirable. While McCloskey et al. (1992) characterise the base structure as culture-specific and suggest that in other cultures the semantic representations might have for instance a base five structure, it is always one base we have to settle upon, because a semantic representation is characterised as a single, central representation via which the different mechanisms communicate. Since we obligatorily have to go via semantic representations in this model, we might face problems when we want to account for the correlation of two sequences with different bases or even for subsequences, as in the case of French, where we have an idiosyncratic subsystem of counting words that displays a base twenty structure, going from SOIXANTE-DIX ('seventy', literally 'sixty-ten') to QUATRE-VINGT-DIX-NEUF ('ninety-nine', literally 'four-twenty-nineteen').

The Encoding Complex View
The Encoding Complex View has been put forward by Jamie Campbell and James Clark as an alternative to the Modular Model (see references in note 32 above). In opposition to the Modular Model, Campbell and Clark assume that arabic numerals and counting words (among others) can activate different kinds of representations, namely format- and modality-specific codes, rather than a uniform and amodal semantic representation. They distinguish different verbal and non-verbal codes. Verbal codes are activated by counting words (articulatory and auditory codes in the representation of spoken words, visual codes in the representation of written words), non-verbal codes are activated by arabic numerals (these are visual codes), but also by quantities (these are analogue codes) and in activities like finger counting (visual-motor codes).

In support of their view, Campbell and Clark draw on studies indicating format-specific effects in the processing of numerals and in the retrieval of arithmetic facts. For instance, people seem to be faster and to make less

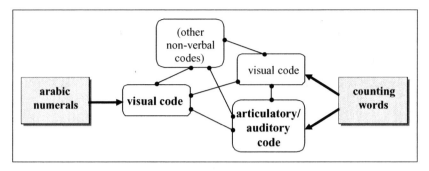

Figure 70 Associations for arabic numerals and counting words within
the Encoding Complex View

errors in calculation tasks when the problem is presented to them in arabic
numerals, as opposed to number words (cf. our discussion on pp. 234f.
above). Campbell and Clark argue that these kinds of effects should not be
observed if calculation was based on uniform and modality-independent
semantic representations, which are the same for non-verbal numerals and
number words.

According to this approach, the different mental codes can activate
each other within an associative representational structure, the 'encoding
complex'. Figure 70 gives an idea of the links within this complex that can
be involved in the correlation of arabic numerals and counting words. As
the graphic illustrates, this model does not assume an abstract quantity representation for our concept of numbers, in accordance with the approach
we developed in the present book. Rather, the encoding complex includes a
visual code for arabic numerals and an articulatory/auditory one for spoken
counting words (I marked these two codes by bold font in Figure 70). The
different components of this encoding complex have not yet been spelled
out within an explicit model, though, and in particular the Encoding Complex View does not specify what the internal codes look like and how they
are involved when we link up non-verbal numerals and counting words.
That they are characterised as 'codes' suggests that they encode something,
that is, it suggests that they stand for something else. Would that be abstract 'numbers' or cardinalities, in accordance with the traditional view?
Alternatively, and drawing on our 'numerical tools' approach, one might
assume that the different codes simply encode counting words and arabic
numerals. In this case, one could regard them as codes for sequences that
have a numerical status on their own. Before we spell out an account that
is in accordance with this suggestion, let me sketch a third model, the

Triple-Code Model, which combines some features of the Modular Model and the Encoding Complex View.

The Triple-Code Model

Like the Encoding Complex View, Stanislas Dehaene's Triple-Code Model allows asemantic transcoding routes between arabic numerals and counting words. These routes link up a visual arabic code and an auditory verbal code. In addition, Dehaene includes a third code in his architecture, an 'analogue magnitude code'. This code represents numerical quantities on an oriented number line (hence it includes a sequential aspect). The three different codes are characterised as three different means to mentally represent numbers. The input for the arabic code and the verbal code are strings of digits and counting words, respectively; the analogue magnitude code receives input from subitising and estimation procedures.

All three codes are interconnected, so that the correlation of arabic numerals and counting words can go either via asemantic routes or semantic routes, using either a direct link between arabic code and verbal code or one that goes via analogue quantity representations, respectively. Different codes might be accessed for different kinds of tasks, and the codes can also activate each other. For instance, for numerical judgment tasks, Dehaene assumes the automatic activation of a quantity code: according to this account, in order to compare arabic numerals we first transform them into mental quantities and then perform the comparison on these quantities (cf. Dehaene 1997: ch. 3).[35] Figure 71 gives a sketch of the three codes and their connections with arabic numerals and counting words.

This model can account for both direct links between representations of arabic numerals and counting words and their relation to numerical quantities. However, again the focus of 'semantic' links is on quantitative contexts only. If we want to account not only for cardinal aspects of numbers, our architecture should include a richer network of representations. Our discussion thus far suggests that, on the one hand, this architecture should integrate ordinal and nominal contexts into the network; on the other hand, it should permit arabic numerals and counting words a status as numerical tools in their own standing. As proposed above, within such a

---

[35] It is not clear to me, though, whether this transformation is one between the visual arabic code and the analogue magnitude code, or whether a fourth kind of representation is assumed for these quantities (or maybe is included within the arabic code?). The reason for this is that, according to Dehaene (1992: 32), the analogue magnitude code provides only approximations and not precise cardinalities (and hence can get its input among others from estimation procedures). If comparisons between arabic numerals were based on quantity representations, though, one might want these representations to be exact and not approximate.

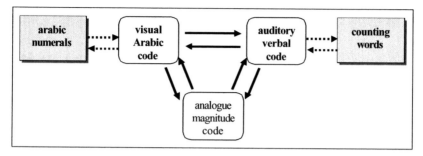

Figure 71 Codes for arabic numerals and counting words within the Triple-Code Model

model we could also account for the comparison of arabic numerals as a task that does not require the mandatory activation of quantity representations, but can be based on sequential visual representations (cf. our discussion of distance effects on pp. 229ff. above).

A model for the correlation of numerical tools
So what do we want our model to account for? The following points recall four major findings from our investigation, and indicate their implications for our approach to arabic numerals and their relation to counting words.
(1) Counting words and arabic numerals are not different names for the same numbers, but elements of different systems.
  Hence, we want direct links between our representations of counting words and arabic numerals that are not negotiated by abstract 'numbers'.
(2) These systems are systems of numerical tools.
  Hence, our representations of counting words and of arabic numerals should provide infinite progressions of well-distinguished elements.
(3) Different sequences of numerical tools do not constitute different 'numbers', but can fulfil the same numerical purposes, based on their sequential character.
  Hence, the links between our representations of counting words and of arabic numerals should be links between verbal and non-verbal elements that occupy corresponding sequential positions in their respective systems.
(4) As numerical tools, counting words and arabic numerals are used in cardinal, ordinal, and nominal number assignments.
  Hence, our representations of counting words and of arabic numerals should have associative links to concepts of numerical quantity, numerical rank, and numerical label.

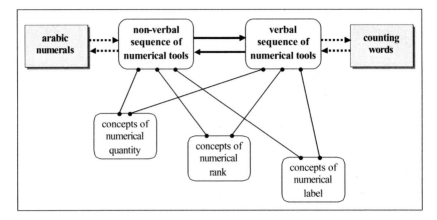

Figure 72 Arabic numerals and counting words within the Numerical Tool Model

Our model should thus be based on the representation of arabic numerals and counting words as two sequences of numerical tools: a non-verbal one that is based on visual representations of numerals, and a verbal one that is based on phonological representations of counting words. These sequences form potentially infinite and isomorphic progressions. Equivalent positions in these progressions are linked up with each other; this establishes direct ('non-semantic') mappings from arabic numerals onto counting words and vice versa. In addition, elements of both numerical sequences are associated with concepts that are based on their application in cardinal, ordinal, and nominal number assignments. This mutual link with complex numerical concepts establishes indirect ('semantic') routes between non-verbal and verbal numerical tools. Figure 72 outlines an architecture for the correlation of arabic numerals and counting words as it emerges from these considerations.

To sum up, this model interprets the correlation of counting words and arabic numerals as the correlation of two alternative sequences that can be used independently as tools in number assignments. What distinguishes the two sequences is their non-linguistic versus linguistic status: arabic numerals are represented as elements of a non-verbal sequence of numerical tools that is based on visual representations, while counting words are represented as a verbal sequence of numerical tools, based on phonological representations.[36]

---

[36] I regard written versions of counting words as a secondary representation that identifies the phonological representation in script via graphemic–phonological correspondences of the kind we discussed

Both sequences can be applied in cardinal, ordinal, and nominal number assignments, which leads to associations with numerical concepts as marked by connecting lines in Figure 72. These concepts have other relationships that I ignored in the graphic for the sake of readability. In particular, I am thinking of relations to the pre-numerical concepts we discussed in the previous chapters, that is, concepts that support our grasp of the empirical properties we identify with numbers, among them our early concepts of cardinality based on subitising. Furthermore, a full picture would also include the complex cardinal concepts that are related to our concepts of numerical quantity, namely abstract cardinalities in mathematical contexts and concepts of measurement.

As became clear from the empirical evidence we discussed above, the ability to identify a counting word for a given arabic numeral, and the ability to identify an arabic numeral for a given counting word can be impaired independently. Hence, the links correlating arabic numerals and counting words are constituted by separate mappings in both directions (marked by separate arrows in our graphic). These mappings are interpreted as links between sequential positions. Accordingly, in our model the correlation of counting words and arabic numerals is based on the same rules that are also the basis for the sequential ordering, namely the recursive rules that govern the generation of counting words and non-verbal numerals.[37] This allows us to account for the internal structure of complex elements from both number sequences, and to account for possible deficits in the correlation of constituent structures ('syntactic errors') as well as for deficits in the correlation of constituents or primitive elements ('lexical errors'), similar to the Modular Model.

Unlike the Modular Model, we do not commit ourselves to the assumption of a mediating quantity representation for this correlation, though. In accordance with the Encoding Complex View, the correlation establishes direct links between number sequences of different formats. Within this 'numerical tool' model, visual representations of arabic numerals and verbal representations of counting words are linked up by a direct, non-semantic route not only for tasks like reading aloud arabic numerals or writing them to dictation, but also on a more general level, namely as different instances of numerical tools.

above. Some counting sequences have a *primary*, phonological, representation in the visual modality, namely counting sequences in sign languages.

[37] A definition for this correlation is spelled out for the example of arabic numerals and English counting words in Appendix 3).

Related to this, our model also provides quantitative representations, namely the concepts of numerical quantity, and our representations of both counting words and arabic numerals have associative links with these concepts. As mentioned above, this allows indirect, 'semantic' routes between numerical tools of different formats, which are mediated by quantitative concepts. For instance, when we perform calculations based on arabic numerals, this will activate our concept of cardinality (at least as long as the calculation has a conceptual grounding, that is, it is neither a purely mechanical application of algorithmic routines nor does it exclusively rely on stored knowledge like memorised multiplication tables). When we then say aloud the results, we will access phonological representations of counting words, and these representations can be activated by their association with the cardinal concepts. The important point is that a detour via quantitative concepts is an additional option, which is not necessary for the connection, since the model provides direct correlations between numerical tools.

While this is similar to the two options we get in the Triple-Code Model, note that in the 'numerical tool' model the associations of number sequences are not confined to quantity. Non-verbal numerals and counting words are characterised as numerical sequences in their own standing, and our representations of these sequences are associated with cardinal as well as ordinal and nominal concepts.

In accordance with our results from the previous chapter, I assume that cardinal concepts are closest to our representations of number sequences, followed by ordinal and then nominal concepts. Furthermore, some sequences of numerical tools might have privileged access to certain number contexts with the result that the connections between different numerical sequences and particular numerical concepts are of different associative strength. In extreme cases, a connection might even become indirect, that is, a particular numerical sequence might be linked to certain numerical concepts only via its link to other sequences. An example is the sequence of roman numerals, which today seems to have lost most of its direct associations with cardinal concepts, and in particular with the abstract cardinalities of mathematical contexts. As we have seen above, the roman numerals' loss is the arabic numerals' gain: they are that sequence of numerical tools that is most at home in mathematical contexts, suggesting strong associations with our concepts of abstract cardinalities.

As a result of our discussion, we have now integrated these non-verbal numerical tools into our account of the cognitive number domain: we have characterised them as a non-linguistic alternative to our primary numerical tools, the counting sequences, and have shown how this alternative sequence – and other non-verbal number sequences – can come into the picture, based on our notion of numbers as conventional tools. In the final chapter, we now come back to an exclusively linguistic domain: the expression of numerical concepts in language. As I hope to convince you the way these expressions are integrated into grammatical structures is not only interesting from a linguistic point of view, but can also contribute to our view of counting words as numerical tools and their relation to language.

CHAPTER 8

Numbers in language: the grammatical integration of numerical tools

In the present chapter – the final chapter of this book – I want to discuss in more detail the expressions that denote number concepts. The reason why these expressions appeared in our discussion thus far was mainly that we had to make clear the distinction between non-referential counting words (our numerical tools) and referential number words (expressions for numerical concepts). In the first part of this chapter, I work out this distinction in some more detail. On this basis, the other sections will then be dedicated to the question of what referential number word constructions can tell us about the relationship between numbers and language.

In the second section we will investigate how the organisation of number word constructions relates to the organisation of numerical concepts. In this context we will see that some constructions can be used for ordinal and nominal reference alike. I show that our account of number contexts allows us to relate this overlap to structural similarities between ordinal and nominal number assignments.

In the third section of this chapter, I look into the grammatical status of referential number words. I show that cardinals ('*four* pens'), ordinals ('the *fourth* runner') and '#'-constructions (constructions like 'bus *number four*') share grammatical features with different kinds of non-numerical expressions, namely with quantifiers like 'few' and 'many', with superlatives like 'the fastest', and with proper names like 'Karen', respectively. We will see that these parallels are not random, but go together with conceptual parallels, suggesting that the correspondences reflect systematic interdependencies of linguistic and conceptual phenomena.

On this basis, in the fourth and final section we ask what these interdependencies can tell us about the relation between referential number words and numerical tools. We will see that the different kinds of number word constructions can be regarded as the shape in which our verbal numerical tools – starting as non-referential outcasts – enter grammatical structures as a result of integrating non-referential counting words into referential

264

linguistic contexts. This integration can hence be characterised as the 'return of the counting words': under this perspective referential number words, as the grammatical cousins of the counting words, close the circle from language to number and back to language.

COUNTING WORDS AND THEIR REFERENTIAL COUSINS

Counting sequences are located on the borderline between the language faculty and numerical cognition. On the one hand, the elements of a counting sequence are words with phonological representations and part of a particular language. This feature distinguishes counting words from non-verbal elements like arabic numerals. On the other hand, counting words (like arabic numerals) form a sequence that can be employed in number assignments and forms the basis of complex numerical concepts. This feature makes counting sequences special within the linguistic system, it distinguishes counting words from referential words: unlike proper words, counting words do not refer to anything; instead, they serve as tools when we figure out numerical quantities, ranks, and labels. When we want to denote these quantities, ranks, and labels, we use expressions like 'three stars', 'the third runner', or 'bus number three'. These expressions contain number words that are closely related to counting words, with the important difference that they are referential, not instrumental.

We can think of these number words as the referential cousins of our counting words. While counting words are something like the black sheep of the linguistic system, these close relations are fully integrated into grammatical structures, as proper words with a suitable reference. In the case of referential number words, we have a division of labour between words and concepts. These are not words that fulfil a numerical function (they do not serve as numerical tools, like counting words do); these are words that refer to something: we have words on the one hand, and numerical concepts on the other hand, and the words are used to refer to these concepts – just as one would expect from ordinary linguistic items.

Take cardinality as an example. In a phrase like 'two stars', the cardinal number word ('two') is referential. It refers to a cardinality, but it does not serve as some kind of cardinality itself. In contrast to this, the counting word TWO is instrumental; it is part of a numerical sequence, and this is why it is at home in both worlds, language and number. It is a verbal entity (a word with a phonological representation), but one that is used as a tool in numerical routines like counting – a counting word is a tool that happens to be a verbal entity. In a cardinal number assignment, we assign a set the

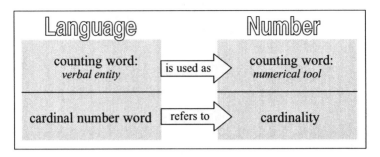

Figure 73 Relations between words and concepts: counting words and cardinals

counting word TWO when it has as many elements as the counting sequence from ONE to TWO. When we then *refer* to the cardinality of this set, we can do so with a cardinal number word construction, for instance 'two stars'.

Similarly, when we assign the counting word T w o to a runner in a race in an ordinal number assignment, we link the position of T w o in the counting sequence to the position of our runner within the race. When we then call this person 'the second runner', we use the ordinal number word 'second' to *refer* to this position. And when we talk about 'bus number two', we use the '#'-construction 'number two' to *refer* to a certain bus line, namely that line that we assigned, as its numerical label, the counting word T w o (or the corresponding element of another sequence of numerical tools, for instance the arabic numeral 2).

In sum, counting words are words that are used as numbers (based on the cardinal, ordinal, and nominal relationships that hold within the counting sequence), but they do not refer to numbers and this distinguishes them from referential number words which are not used as numbers, but refer to numerical concepts. I have sketched the different relations between the linguistic and the numerical domain in Figure 73, using cardinals as an illustration for referential number words.

We have to make a distinction, then, between counting words and the referential number words that are integrated into linguistic constructions. Often these two kinds of words seem to be based on the very same elements, though. Taking our examples from above, this gives us, for instance, at least three options for 'two':

1. the **counting word** 'two': non-referential (instrumental) element of a progression that occurs in recitations like 'ONE, TWO, THREE, . . .' and can be applied to empirical objects in numerical subroutines like counting and in different kinds of number assignments;

2. the **cardinal number word** 'two': number word that occurs in constructions like 'two stars', where it refers to the cardinality of a set;

3. 'two' in a **'#'-construction**: number word that is combined with the lexical item 'number' and occurs in constructions like 'bus number two', which have a nominal meaning.[1]

Hence the same word 'two' – or at least elements with the same phonological representation – can be related to at least three different numerical concepts. This might look a bit confusing at first. However, as the examples illustrate, the different functions that a word like 'two' can fulfil are distinguished by the different contexts in which it occurs: numerical contexts like counting identify counting words, while different linguistic contexts identify different kinds of referential number words. In some languages, the different functions are also distinguished on the word level. In particular, when it comes to smaller numbers, there is sometimes a distinction between counting words and referential number words.

One example comes from Cantonese. The Cantonese counting sequence goes 'YĀHT, YIH, SĀAM, . . .', that is, the Cantonese equivalent to the English counting word TWO is YIH. However, the cardinal number word 'two' is 'léuhng' in Cantonese. For instance, 'two cakes of tofu' translates as 'dauhfuh léuhng gauh' (literally: *tofu two cake*).[2] Hence Cantonese makes a lexical distinction between the counting word 'two' (YIH) and the cardinal number word 'two' (léuhng) that occurs as a modifier of nouns. As we have seen in the previous chapter, a similar case is 'two' in Hebrew: Hebrew distinguishes the modifying cardinal number words 'shney' (with masculine nouns) and 'shtey' (with feminine nouns) that occur in constructions like 'shney tapuchim' (*two apples*) or 'shtey bananot' (*two bananas*), from the counting word SHTÁYIM (which can also be used as a nominalised number word).

Figure 74 illustrates the relations between counting words and cardinal number words for the example of English 'two' and its counterparts in Cantonese. The distinction of YIH versus 'léuhng' in Cantonese, and of SHTÁYIM versus 'shney' and 'shtey' in Hebrew is a special case, of course, and other cardinal number words have the same form as counting words, or at least forms that are very similar to those of counting words, in Cantonese and in Hebrew just as in English.

If a language has different kinds of referential number words, and in particular if it has different cardinal and ordinal number words, the form

---

[1] We will see below that '#'-constructions can sometimes also get an ordinal interpretation.
[2] Cf. Matthews and Yip (1994: ch. 21).

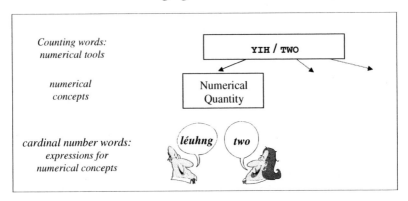

Figure 74 The distinction between counting words, and cardinals: Cantonese counterparts for English 'two'

of cardinal number words is often closer to that of counting words.[3] However the forms are not necessarily identical, not only because there can be such idiosyncratic distinctions as Cantonese YIH (counting word 'two') versus 'léuhng' (cardinal number word 'two'), but also because, in a lot of languages, cardinal number words in contrast to counting words come in different inflectional forms depending on the noun phrases in which they occur, as in our Hebrew examples.

The reason why cardinal number words have such a privileged relationship with counting words in the first place is probably that the numerical concepts they refer to have a privileged position within the cognitive number domain. As we have seen in chapters 5 and 6, cardinal number assignments are a prime context for our numerical tools, and cardinality seems to be first among the concepts we associate with them. Hence, when it comes to linguistic expressions for numerical concepts, it is no surprise that we use lexical items that look very similar to counting words in order to refer to cardinal concepts, while the expressions for ordinal and nominal concepts are usually based on derivations (for example suffixation with '-th', as in 'four-th', for ordinal number words in English), or include additional lexical elements (for example 'number' in English '#'-constructions like 'bus number three').

In any case, though, we have a close relationship between the form of counting words and that of referential number words. This makes a lot of sense. Since our numerical tools are verbal entities anyway, we might as well

---

[3] Greenberg (1966) notes that universally, cardinal number words are the unmarked class compared to ordinal number words.

use words with the same form, or with closely related forms, when we need expressions for our different numerical concepts, rather than inventing new words from scratch. This establishes a transparent relation between individual referential number words and individual counting words which makes it easy to determine the reference of a number word: the cardinal number word 'four' refers to a cardinality that matches that of the counting sequence up to FOUR and not to THREE or SIX, and the ordinal number word 'fourth' refers to a rank that matches that of FOUR in the counting sequence and not that of TWO or SEVEN, and 'bus number four' is that one with the label FOUR rather than NINE.

This is not just a neat way to indicate the link between number words and the numerical tools they relate to. Since a full-blown number sequence has infinitely many elements, it is crucial to have a transparent, generalised relationship between its elements – read: counting words – and referential number words, rather than idiosyncratic correspondences which would have to be memorised one by one. In restricted areas, of course, one can always introduce idiosyncratic items to refer to particular numerical concepts. Such irregular forms can be tolerated as long as there are not too many and as long as they are used frequently enough to be memorised.

The fact that it is small numbers where we can get different forms for counting words and cardinal number words (as in our Cantonese example above) is no accident, but related to a phenomenon we encountered earlier in our investigation: the special status of small cardinalities. As became clear from our discussion of cardinal number assignments in chapter 5, we can identify the cardinality of small sets not only by counting – that is, via a numerical routine – but also by subitising. In the case of subitising we grasp the cardinality of a set right away, without involving numerical tools. Accordingly small cardinalities need not necessarily be related to our numerical tools. This can have the effect that the words that refer to cardinalities of small sets are sometimes not lexically related to the respective counting words. Languages can have suppletive forms for cardinals, that is, special words that are not derived from counting words (like 'léuhng' vs. YIH in Cantonese), and they can also have special words for sets of a particular cardinality (for example words like 'pair' or 'couple' in English), sometimes specified for sets of certain objects (for example English 'twins' or 'brace (of oxen)').

A similar phenomenon can be observed in the ordinal domain. Remember that our early concepts of small ranks are also independent of numerical concepts. They are based on pre-numerical capacities that allow us to grasp initial positions in a sequence at a glance, without applying numerical tools (recall the example with trees by the side of a street on p. 203 above). In chapter 6, we characterised these pre-numerical concepts as an ordinal counterpart to our early concepts of cardinality. Whereas subitising allows us to itemise the elements of small sets, its counterpart in the ordinal domain enables us to itemise the positions in a short sequence.

As in the cardinal domain, the special status of small ranks is sometimes reflected on the linguistic level, that is, it can lead to idiosyncratic forms for small ordinal number words. Just as words for small cardinalities are not always derived from counting words, words for small ranks can take suppletive forms, too. One example from English is the words 'first' and 'second', which are not lexically related to the counting sequence. There is nothing in these words that indicates their relation to their counting word partners ONE and TWO, similar to the Chinese example where the cardinal number word 'léuhng' and the counting word YIH were not lexically related either. The 'second runner' in a race is the person with the same rank in a sequence of runners as the rank of TWO in the counting sequence. Similarly, if we used the words 'léuhng' and YIH instead of 'two' in English, we would have cardinal number constructions like 'léuhng pens', meaning 'a set of pens with as many elements as the counting sequence from ONE to YIH'.

There seem to be no parallel examples of suppletive words within the nominal area. Since nominal number assignments are not based on the sequential order of counting words, small number words do not have a special semantic status in this case. What is more, a reason why there are no special suppletive forms for nominal number words might be that there seem to be no particular (say, morphologically derived) nominal number words in the first place. Rather, languages use complex constructions in order to refer to nominal number concepts, which often involve additional lexical items like 'number' in the English '(bus) *number* three'. In the following discussion I will refer to a lexical item like this – that is, to the item a language uses in '#'-constructions in this way – as a '*#*'-*item*.

HOW TO EXPRESS NUMERICAL CONCEPTS: THE ORGANISATION OF NUMBER WORD CONSTRUCTIONS

Now that we have worked out the distinction between counting words and their referential cousins, let us have a closer look at the relation between the different kinds of referential number words and the numerical concepts they refer to. What means do we use in order to denote number assignments in language? Here is an illustration for English, using examples from our discussion in the preceding paragraphs:

(1) construction with a cardinal number word: 'four pens'

(2) construction with an ordinal number word: 'the fourth runner'

(3) '#'-construction: 'bus number four'.

How do these three kinds of constructions go together with the tripartition of our number domain, the distinction of cardinal, ordinal, and nominal number concepts? For cardinal and ordinal number words, the correspondence is clear: cardinal constructions like 'four pens' express concepts of numerical quantity, while ordinal constructions like 'the fourth runner' denote numerical ranks. '#'-Constructions, however, are more promiscuous – and this is why I avoided calling them 'nominal constructions': they can express concepts of numerical label, as in the case of 'bus number four', but they can also refer to numerical ranks. (4) gives examples of '#'-constructions of the second kind:

(4) '#'-constructions referring to nominal ranks:
You are the number one in my life.
She is the number one tennis player in the world.

These sentences suggest ordinal, rather than nominal interpretations; they mean something along the lines of 'You have the first rank among the persons in my life' and 'She has the first rank among the world's tennis players.' Or, in the pedantic version: 'Your rank among the persons in my life, or her rank among the tennis players in the world, is the same as the rank of ONE within the number sequence.'

This refers to an ordinal number assignment and accordingly statements as in (4) will usually be understood as a compliment, while the corresponding nominal interpretation might come across as a bit of an insult: under a nominal interpretation, the first sentence in (4) for instance would mean something like 'I label you 'one' in order to keep track of you among the other persons in my life.' Normally this is not the way one would want to be understood. However, it is a possible interpretation for a '#'-construction in English (and also in a lot of other languages), and it is exactly the way we interpret such a construction in examples like 'bus number one'. In a sentence like 'This runner was the number four in the marathon' this ambiguity is even clearer, and we have to refer to the broader context in which this sentence is uttered in order to find out whether this runner got the label 'four' (and arrived, say, as the sixteenth) or rather made it fourth in this race (while he might have had the label 'twenty-five').

There is hence no one-to-one relation between concepts and their expressions in the ordinal and nominal areas: '#'-constructions are underspecified between ordinal and nominal interpretations, so we have to make use of contextual information in order to find out which interpretation is intended. This seems a bit careless on first sight – after all, it leaves such an important distinction open to interpretation as the distinction between ranking and mere identification.

However, while ordinal and nominal number assignments differ with respect to the empirical properties they relate to (namely, rank versus identity), on a closer look they show substantial parallels in the way numbers are assigned to objects. In particular, they share a crucial property which distinguishes them from cardinal number assignments: in ordinal as well as in nominal number assignments we assign numbers to *elements* of a set, whereas in cardinal number assignments the empirical objects are themselves sets (in the case of measurement, they are linked up with numbers via sets, namely sets of measure items).

Recall our analysis of number assignments in the first chapter, and the principles of number assignments we proposed in chapter 6. If we link up numbers with individual objects in counting, this is just an iconic prop for the cardinal number assignment: the actual number assignment is established when we link up the last number in our count with the whole set of objects. If we link up numbers with individual objects in ordinal or nominal contexts, for instance in a marathon race or when numbering bus lines, then this linking *is* the number assignment: each individual number identifies the rank of a runner within the race, or identifies a bus line within a public transport system. As we have seen in chapter 1, these parallels between ordinal and nominal number assignments can also lead to a certain merge of ordinal and nominal aspects, more precisely: they can lead to the introduction of a secondary ordinal aspect in nominal number assignments, for instance in the case of house numbers.

What distinguishes ordinal and nominal number assignments from cardinal ones is not only that we treat the empirical objects as individual elements here, but also that we treat them as individual elements *of a certain set* (in ordinal number assignments this set must form a progression, while in nominal assignments any kind of set will do). We do not assign ranks and labels to objects just so, out of the blue, but always with respect to a certain set that they belong to. For instance the numbers we assign in our examples above distinguish ranks within a certain progression of runners or they distinguish lines within a certain bus system. If we look at the same object as an element of a different set, the number assignment might come out totally differently. For instance, Mick might have made it only second in this marathon, but for you he is the number one – meant ordinally here – that is, among the persons in your life he occupies the first rank. Similarly, a bus might have the number four within the public transport system, but it probably got a totally different numerical label among the vehicles built by the same motor company (its vehicle number).

This last aspect is in fact similar to what we found for cardinal number assignments: as Frege pointed out, the same collection of objects can have different cardinalities depending on how we look at it, for instance a collection of physical objects might be perceived as six toys, but also as two thimbles and four wood toys (a distinction that Irene Pepperberg's parrot Alex seemed to grasp, cf. our discussion in chapter 4 above). The crucial difference between cardinal number assignments as opposed to ordinal and nominal ones is that in cardinal number assignments it is the empirical objects themselves that we perceive differently: for instance, a certain collection can be regarded as a set of six toys, or as a set of two thimbles plus a set of four wood toys. In contrast to this, in ordinal and nominal number assignments the empirical objects do not change in so far as we perceive them as different sets, but rather as *elements of different sets*.

Accordingly I defined the functions NR and NL which account for our concepts of numerical rank and numerical label, respectively, as functions with three arguments:[4] an object a (for example a runner or a bus line) which is an element of a set s (a progression of runners in a race, or a set of bus lines within a public transport system) and gets assigned a number n. In contrast to that, we have only two arguments for the function NQ that accounts for our concepts of numerical quantity:[5] a set s (for instance, the set of pens on my desk) and the number we assign to it.

Hence, while ordinal and nominal number assignments identify different empirical properties and therefore fulfil quite different purposes, they are based on very similar procedures. This leads to substantial parallels in the way numbers are assigned to empirical objects in each case. And it is this conceptual similarity that lays the grounds for the overlap on the linguistic level: the similarity between ordinal and nominal number assignments provides a basis for using '#'-constructions for ordinal as well as nominal reference, while a different kind of construction refers to cardinal concepts.

Apart from these two kinds of expressions, we also find number word constructions that are specialised for ordinal but not nominal reference. In English, these are constructions like 'the fourth runner', which include

---

[4] See the definitions in Appendix 4, relating to our discussion in chapter 6.
[5] Cf. the definition in Appendix 4 and the discussion in chapter 5.

Table 4 *Relations between number words and the numerical concepts they denote*

Number assignment	Numerical concept	Linguistic expressions	
		type	example
cardinal	numerical quantity	cardinal number words	'three pens'
ordinal	numerical rank	ordinal number words	'the fourth runner'
nominal	numerical label	number words in '#'-constructions	'the number one player'

a special class of ordinal number words. Cantonese is an example of a language that does not have such a class of number words, but instead has two kinds of '#'-constructions, one for ordinal and one for nominal reference. Cantonese ordinal '#'-constructions are composed of a '#'-item 'daih' and the number word, for instance 'daih luhk' ('number six'). Unlike in English, no nominal interpretation is possible here; hence 'daih luhk' translates as 'the sixth', or as 'number six' with an ordinal meaning. For nominal reference Cantonese employs a '#'-item 'hou' which comes after the number word, so that for instance 'luhk hou' means 'number six' as in the nominal reading (for instance in 'bus number six').

Table 4 summarises the relationships between linguistic expressions and numerical concepts for the example of English, showing how the distinction of different linguistic expressions relates to the distinction of the different numerical concepts they denote, and which overlaps we have in the ordinal and nominal domain. In Appendix 5 I give a formalisation for these relationships, accounting for the way the different kinds of numerical concepts we identified in our investigation are integrated into semantic representations for cardinal, ordinal and '#'-constructions.

REFERENTIAL NUMBER WORDS ARE NOT OUTCASTS

Thus far, we have identified conceptual motivations for two aspects in the organisation of numerical expressions. In the preceding section we found that ordinal and nominal reference overlaps in the case of '#'-constructions, and we showed that this is related to conceptual similarities between ordinal and nominal number assignments. Earlier in this chapter, we noted that cardinal number words usually look more similar to counting words than ordinal number words do. We related this to the closer association of counting words with cardinal as compared to ordinal number assignments.[6]

How about the grammatical structure of the different number word constructions themselves? Why do the different kinds of number word constructions look the way they do? Is this just another case of linguistic arbitrariness, or is there also a motivation behind it? In the remainder of this chapter I am going to argue that there is in fact such a motivation. In order to do so, I will first show that the grammatical properties of referential number word constructions are by no means idiosyncratic: number words are not alone within the grammatical system, but exhibit striking parallels to some non-numerical expressions. A closer look at these non-numerical expressions will then reveal that these grammatical parallels are accompanied by parallels in the conceptual domain: when it comes to grammatical behaviour, our number words tend to go with those expressions that have similar referents. In the final section of this chapter, I will discuss what this means for our view of numbers and language. Let us now have a look at the grammatical and conceptual parallels in turn.[7]

Grammatical parallels between numerical and non-numerical domains

Cardinal number words behave similarly to quantifier expressions like 'many' or 'few', as illustrated by the English examples in (1) where the quantifier 'many' and the cardinal number word 'four' are combined with the same noun 'apples':

(1) 'many apples' / 'four apples'

Similarly, this noun could also be preceded by an adjective, as in 'red apples'. In view of such parallels, it is sometimes suggested that cardinal number words show an adjective-like behaviour.[8] However, this is only an approximation. Cardinal number words do share some features with adjectives, and so do quantifiers. But quantifiers differ from adjectives in a number of grammatical respects cross-linguistically, and interestingly, they

---

[6] Recall our discussion on p. 268 above: in particular, we related the close association of counting words and cardinal number words to the fact that the identification of cardinality is the prime task for our numerical tools, while their other applications – namely, those in ordinal or nominal assignments – emerge later, based on a generalisation of the 'dependent linking' scheme that makes cardinal number assignments possible.

[7] For the purpose of the present discussion, I give a general overview of the grammatical parallels. I develop a detailed formal account of the grammar of number word constructions and their non-numerical counterparts in Wiese (1997a), where I propose syntactic (and semantic) analyses of the different kinds of constructions (also including an analysis of measure constructions).

[8] For instance by Corbett (1978); Hurford (1987).

share these features with cardinal number words.[9] This holds for quantifier expressions in general, but it is pronounced in the case of quantifiers like 'many' and 'few' (which occur in constructions with plural nouns like (1) above, in contrast to expressions like 'much'). Let me give you some examples.

One obvious parallel is that quantifiers and cardinal number words occupy the same position within the noun phrase, as illustrated in (2):

(2) '*many* small red apples' / '*four* small red apples'

Both the quantifier ('many') and the cardinal number word ('four') stand in a position in front of the adjectives ('small red'), which line up right before the noun. This is an instance of a general pattern: cross-linguistically, adjectives tend to stand closer to the noun than quantifiers and cardinal number words. So, if in a language the adjectives precede the noun, then cardinal number words and quantifiers come before the adjectives (as in the English example (2) above). When a language has the order 'noun – adjectives', then cardinal number words or quantifiers will tend to be in the final position, rather than stand between the noun and the adjectives.[10]

Both quantifiers and cardinal number words can also occur in partitive constructions like (3), whereas adjectives cannot (the star * marks an ungrammatical construction):

(3) ♠ cardinal number word: '*four* of the apples'
     ♠ quantifier: '*many* of the apples'
     ♥ adjective: * '*red* of the apples'

And both quantifiers and cardinal number words can often stand in a position isolated from the noun phrase, a phenomenon sometimes discussed as 'quantifier floating'. In English, such a construction often has a poetic flavour to it, as in 'Sorrows I have many', or 'Flowers I brought four'. While these constructions are marginal in English, they are common in various other, typologically different languages (for instance in French, in German, and in Japanese).

---

[9] Accordingly, in generative grammar quantifiers are usually analysed as heads of a functional projection QP ('Quantifier Phrase') above NP (the noun phrase), an analysis that can also be applied to cardinal number words, whereas adjectives (as heads of an adjective phrase AP) are integrated into the NP (see for instance, Abney 1987; Giusti 1991; Watanabe 1992; Wiese 1997a). Alternatively, one could maintain the classification of quantifiers as adjectives by defining them as elements of an adjectival subclass with special properties. What is important is that quantifiers go together with cardinal number words, either as elements of a syntactic category separate from adjectives, or as elements of a special subclass of adjectives.

[10] Cf. the discussion of preferred word orders among the languages of the world in Greenberg (1963).

Cardinal number words are not only combined with plural nouns like 'apples', but also with nouns like 'cattle'. In such a case the cardinal number word is followed by a numeral classifier, for instance 'head' as in 'four head of cattle'. Classifier constructions are an exception in English, but they are the rule in many languages of the world (in particular in Southeast-Asian languages, but also in some Indo-European languages, for instance in Persian). These classifier constructions are yet another indication that cardinal number words fall into one class with quantifiers rather than with adjectives: if a language has numeral classifiers, their occurrence is triggered by cardinal number words and also by quantifiers, but usually not by adjectives. What is more, if adjectives occur within constructions with quantifiers or cardinals and numeral classifiers, they go with the noun, while quantifiers and cardinal number words stand in a position adjacent to the classifier, that is, they come either right before the classifier (as in English) or right behind it. (4) illustrates this for our English example:

(4) ☣ cardinal number word: '*four* head of cattle'
    ☣ quantifier: '*many* head of cattle'
    ☞ adjective: * '*red* head of cattle'
                      (instead: 'four head of red cattle')

Similarly in constructions like 'four litres of wine', which refer to measurement concepts, cardinal number words as well as quantifiers stand in front of the measure noun ('litres'), while adjectives go together with the noun that denotes the empirical object ('wine' in our example):[11]

(5) ☣ cardinal number word: '*four* litres of wine'
    ☣ quantifier: '*many* litres of wine'
    ☞ adjective: * '*red* litres of wine'
                      (instead: 'four litres of red wine')

Higher cardinal number words sometimes tend towards a more noun-like behaviour, as in '*millions* of apples'.[12] This again has a match in the domain

---

[11] Note that, although 'four litres of wine' and 'four head of cattle' look very similar, the first one is a cardinal measure construction, while the second one is a cardinal *counting* construction: 'four litres of wine' refers to the measurement of wine, while 'four head of cattle' refers to the numerical quantity of a set of cattle, it tells us how many individual animals there are. In the first case, the measure noun 'litres' is informative; it indicates that we measure volume, and accordingly it could be replaced by another measure noun, say 'kg', with the result that we refer to a different property (in this case weight). In contrast to this, 'head' does not add any information; rather, it is a numeral classifier, which is syntactically required when we want to refer to individual instances of cattle and cannot be replaced by another classifier.

[12] Cf. Menninger (1958: vol. 1, ch. 1. 1.2c). Corbett (1978) gives a cross-linguistic overview suggesting that the higher a cardinal number word is, the more likely it is to show some nominal features.

of quantificational expressions, where we can get nominal constructions like in '*a huge amount* of apples'. According to Hurford (1987), the difference between smaller and higher cardinal number words might be related to a different focus on the conceptual side: smaller cardinal number words might behave more like modifiers because they can be associated with concrete cardinalities of sets (and these sets are denoted by the nouns that the number word modifies), whereas higher cardinal number words are initially introduced as names for abstract cardinalities and might therefore tend towards a nominal behaviour (since abstract cardinalities are denoted by nominalisations).

The important point for our discussion is that cardinal number words are not unique within the grammatical system: their grammatical behaviour is not idiosyncratic, but resembles that of other linguistic items, and in particular they fall into one class with quantifiers like 'few' and 'many'.

If a language has ordinal number words, they can sometimes form a unique class of grammatical items. However, in general they share at least some features with other expressions, and in particular they often show grammatical features that are similar to those of superlative adjectives. Like superlatives, ordinal number words occur usually in definite noun phrases, where they are in front of other modifiers:

(6) ordinal number word: 'the *third* Japanese runner in this race'
    superlative: 'the *youngest* Japanese runner in this race'

Ordinal number words often also share morphological features with superlatives. In languages with adjectival declension, ordinal number words usually display this inflectional pattern, just like superlatives.[13] By the same token, ordinals tend to show a fuller adjectival inflectional paradigm than cardinal number words (cf. Greenberg 1966); for instance in Spanish and Italian, adjectives and ordinals, but not cardinals, inflect for gender.

An interesting case is Proto-Indo-European, which seems to have employed the same derivational suffix for superlatives and some ordinal number words (namely, for the decades and possibly also for some smaller number words).[14] Hence these ordinal number words were derived from the numeral stem in just the same way as superlatives were derived from the adjectival stem. We can still find traces of this pattern today in some languages from the Indo-European family, for instance in German, where the superlative 'schönst' (*prettiest*) is derived from the adjectival stem 'schön'

---

[13] If there are further distinctions within the adjectival paradigm, ordinals might fall into one class with superlatives, as for instance in Greek, where superlatives and ordinals alike follow the declension of adjectives ending on -ος (cf. for instance Holton et al. 1997).

[14] Cf. the discussion in Schmidt (1992).

(*pretty*) by the same suffix as the ordinal number word 'dreißigst' (*thirtieth*) from the numeral stem 'dreißig' (*thirty*).

In some languages ordinal number words are not derived by morphological means (like suffixation with '-th'), but are identified by syntactic means: they are definite constructions of number words, hence 'the fourth runner' comes out as something like 'the four runner'. Again, the same pattern can be observed for superlatives, which are then definite forms of comparative adjectives, that is, 'the youngest runner' translates as something like 'the younger runner'. Hence definite constructions can be employed to indicate ordinality in a similar way as superlativity.[15]

In sum, we find a similar grammatical integration as for cardinal number words: from the point of view of the grammatical system there is nothing special about ordinal number words either. Referential number words are not linguistic outcasts, but behave similarly to some other class of expressions, and in the case of ordinal number words these expressions are superlative adjectives. The parallels might not be as obvious and as far-reaching as those between cardinal number words and quantifiers, but they are definitely there. Before we discuss the basis for these grammatical parallels, let us see whether the same also holds for our third class of number words, namely the ones that occur in '#'-constructions.

We can indeed identify a non-numerical partner for these constructions, too: '#'-constructions tend to have a similar structure as those with proper names. In constructions like 'bus number four', the '#'-item ('number') and the number word ('four') together behave like a proper name:

(7) '#' + number word: 'bus *number four*'
    proper name: 'my friend *Karen*'

These constructions can stand in an appositive position after the noun, as in the examples in (7), but the combination of '#'-item and number word, as well as the proper name, works also without a noun, as in 'the number four' or 'Karen'. Within the complex of '#' + number word, the '#'-item again behaves like a noun that is combined with a proper name (namely the number word). As a result, in our example 'bus number four' we can skip the noun 'bus', and similarly we can also skip 'number'. This gives

[15] Examples of this come from Semitic languages like Arabic, where superlatives are definite forms of comparative adjectives, while ordinal number words are definite constructions derived from bare numerals. Similarly, Romance superlatives are usually formed by combining a definite article or a demonstrative with (analytical or synthetic) comparatives and the same pattern can be employed for ordinals, for instance in Spanish where constructions like 'la cien representación' are possible (*the one hundredth performance*; lit. 'the hundred performance'; cf. de Bruyne 1995: 135), or in Albanian where ordinals are derived from bare numerals by a derivational suffix (*-të*) that is historically related to a definite or demonstrative article (cf. for instance Demiraj 1993 and Newmark et al. 1981).

us a choice of constructions like 'bus number four', or 'the number four bus' (all elements present), 'the number four' (noun skipped), 'bus four' ('#'-item skipped), and 'the four' (noun and '#'-item skipped).

If there is a noun, proper names as well as '#' + number word stand in an adjacent position to it and cannot be modified in this construction (and, similarly, the number word cannot be modified separately when it is combined with the '#'-item). We can say 'a strange number' in general, and we can also say things like 'I never take the unpunctual #4 when I go to the cinema'. Once we introduce a head noun, though ('*bus* #4'), this is not possible anymore: no modifier is allowed to go between the noun and the '#'-item, hence the only kind of modification we get in this construction is the modification of the noun. As (8) illustrates, this is once again exactly as in constructions with proper names:

(8) '#' + number word: 'the unpunctual *number four*'
* '(the) bus unpunctual *number four*'
(instead: 'the unpunctual bus number four')
proper name: 'the unpunctual *Karen*'
* 'my friend unpunctual *Karen*'
(instead: 'my unpunctual friend Karen')

Whereas cardinal number words can have different patterns of inflection which distinguish them from counting words, and ordinal number words might have special endings like English '-th' (as in 'fourth' etc.), the number words in '#'-constructions take the form of the bare, original counting word. This becomes particularly obvious in cases where we have a lexical distinction between a counting word and a referential number word. One such case that we discussed earlier in this chapter is 'two' in Cantonese, which is YIH as a counting word, but 'léuhng' as a cardinal number word. In '#'-constructions with 'two' the number word then has the form of the counting word and not that of the cardinal number word: 'number two' is 'yih hou' and not 'léuhng hou' in Cantonese (and similarly for the ordinal '#'-constructions that Cantonese has: 'number two' in its ordinal meaning is 'daih yih', and not 'daih léuhng'). The number word in a '#'-construction does not take a special form, but keeps its original counting word guise.

This makes a lot of sense if one thinks of the way counting words are used in nominal number assignments. Remember that in these usages, counting words serve as labels for objects in a similar way as proper names. Given this task, it is not surprising that we should integrate counting words into '#'-constructions as they are, without any further derivations – just as we also use proper names within linguistic constructions. We will come back to this parallel further on in our discussion, when we analyse the relationship between the concepts denoted by proper names and '#'-constructions.

We have now identified 'grammatical role models' for our three kinds of referential number word constructions: we showed that cardinals, ordinals, and '#'-constructions show cross-linguistic similarities to quantifiers, superlatives, and proper names, respectively. Why exactly these ones? Is there a reason why cardinal number words should look like quantifiers, ordinal number words resemble superlatives, and '#'-constructions behave like proper names? I think there is. In the following paragraphs, I am going to show that the grammatical parallels between number word constructions and constructions from other domains are accompanied by conceptual parallels, that is by parallels between the different kinds of number concepts and the concepts these non-numerical expressions refer to; in the final section of this chapter I will then show how this pattern relates to the status of counting words as numerical tools, on the one hand, and as the lexical basis for referential number words, on the other hand.

Conceptual parallels between numerical and non-numerical domains

Let us start with quantifiers and cardinal number words again. The conceptual parallels are particularly obvious here: quantifiers as well as cardinal number words refer to quantities. In the case of cardinal number words, this quantity identifies the size of a set, for instance the size of the set of pens on my desk, as in 'three pens'. In the case of quantifiers, we can refer to a set size, as in 'many pens' or 'few pens', or to the amount of a mass entity, as in 'much water'. It is, hence, in particular quantifiers such as 'many' and 'few' that are semantically close to cardinal number words, and these were also the ones we found to be close to cardinal number words grammatically.

The special feature of cardinal number words is that they denote a cardinality precisely, which allows us to distinguish exactly between sets of different sizes. In contrast to that, quantifiers like 'few' and 'many' refer to noisy magnitudes, which gives us only approximate differences between sets. In particular, 'few' and 'many' tell us whether the size of a set is above ('many') or below ('few') a certain *norm value*, that is above or below of the size we would normally expect for this set.

For instance, if I say that there are 'many pens' on my desk, you do not know how many there are exactly, but you know that there are more than one would normally expect. So if it turns out that there are three pens you might be a bit surprised, since this is a rather small, or at best a medium, set size for pens on a desk. On the other hand, if I said that I have many dogs, a set size of three would fit with my statement. This example also shows that the norm value is not only influenced by the kind of elements a set has – three pens are few, but three dogs are many – but that it is also influenced by the cultural context in which this set occurs – if you and I were mushers in Alaska, we would consider three dogs not as many, but as few.

Such a recourse to a norm value is also known from dimensional adjectives like 'long' and 'short', or 'big' and 'small'.[16] Again, what counts as 'big' and what counts as 'small' depends on the norm value for the objects in question: a big mouse is still smaller than a small elephant. The difference compared to quantifiers like 'few' and 'many', and also to cardinal number words, is that in the case of big mice or small elephants we are talking about properties of objects, and not sizes of sets. Whereas the properties denoted by adjectives usually apply to individuals and only seldom to sets, it is essential for quantifiers like 'few' and 'many' as well as for cardinal number words like 'three' that they refer to a property that applies to sets, and only to sets.

Recall our discussion of 'grey stars' versus 'three stars' in chapter 2: 'grey stars' refers to a set of stars and each of these stars is grey, hence the property of 'greyness' applies to each individual element of this set. The same is true for our example of 'big', as in 'big mice': each of the mice that we denote here has the property of being big. In contrast to this, 'three stars' refers to a set of stars, but none of its elements is three. Rather, the property of 'threeness' applies to the set as a whole, and this is because cardinality is a property of sets, not of individuals. The same applies to our quantifier examples: the difference between 'grey stars' (or, similarly, 'big stars') and 'many stars' is that in 'many stars' the whole set has the property 'many', but not a single one of its elements – again, we refer to the property of a set, not to a property of individuals.

Hence, as in the grammatical discussion above, we find some similarities between cardinal number words and quantifiers with adjectives (all three kinds of expressions refer to properties), but even closer parallels between cardinal number words and quantifiers, and in particular quantifiers like 'many' and 'few': like cardinal number words, and unlike most adjectives, these quantifiers refer to the size of sets; they denote a property that applies to sets and to sets only.

The difference between cardinal number words and quantifiers is that cardinal number words identify the size of sets numerically, whereas quan-

---

[16] A detailed analysis of the status of norm values and the semantic representation of dimensional adjectives is given in Bierwisch (1987) and Lang (1987).

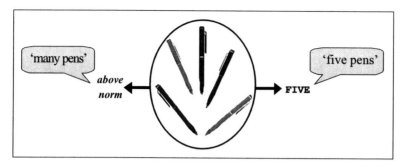

Figure 75 Non-numerical and numerical identification of set sizes

tifiers identify the size of sets non-numerically. A cardinal number word construction like 'five pens' refers to a set of pens that has the *numerical* quantity 'five', that is, to a set of pens that has exactly as many elements as the counting sequence from ONE to FIVE. A quantifier construction like 'many pens' refers to a set of pens with a quantity that is higher than the relevant norm value, that is, to a set of pens that has more elements than we would usually expect in this context.

In sum, the conceptual basis for an expression like 'five pens' is a cardinal number assignment, whereas the conceptual basis for an expression like 'many pens' is the assignment of a quantity above the norm value.[17] Figure 75 gives an illustration of these conceptual parallels, by bringing together 'five pens' and 'many pens' as two ways to refer to the size of a set, a numerical one and a non-numerical one.

This pattern, then, suggests that the grammatical parallels between cardinal number words and quantifiers are grounded in conceptual parallels between the kinds of entities they denote. It suggests that the morpho-syntactic similarities we observed above are motivated by similarities on the conceptual side. Let us see whether we can find more evidence for this in the case of our other cases.

For superlatives and ordinal number words, the parallels are subtler than for the quantifier/cardinal pair, just as their grammatical parallels were not as pervasive either – however, again they are clearly there. Like ordinal number words, superlatives refer to the rank of an element in a sequence: 'the fastest runner' and 'the third runner' both pick out one specific person, according to his or her rank in a sequence of runners. And in both cases the sequence must have an initial element, in our example: that runner

---

[17] You can find a formal account of this parallelism in Appendix 5, where I introduce a non-numerical counterpart for our function NQ ('numerical quantity').

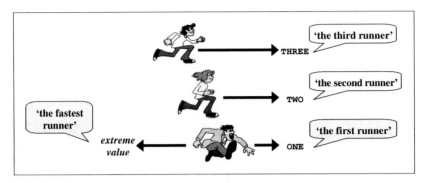

Figure 76 Non-numerical and numerical identification of ranks within a sequence

who arrives before all the others. For the sake of convenience, let us say this runner is Charles, as in our Marathon example from earlier on.

If you find the description I gave for Charles – 'the runner who arrives before all the others' – a bit clumsy, this is because I am trying hard to avoid calling him either 'the first runner' or 'the fastest runner'. The reason I do so is because these are exactly the options I want to distinguish: we can identify Charles's rank either numerically as in 'Charles is the *first* runner', or non-numerically as in 'Charles is the *fastest* runner'. We can either assign him a number in an ordinal number assignment, for instance we can assign him the English counting word ONE, and then refer to him with an ordinal number word construction, 'the first runner'; or we can pick him out as the initial element in our progression of runners ('the-one-who-arrives-before-all-the-others'), and then refer to him with a superlative construction, 'the fastest runner'. In the latter case, we do not assign him a particular number, but something one could characterise as the 'extreme value': that value that identifies the initial rank within a progression (you can find a formal account of this assignment in Appendix 5).

This means that we can again identify a close non-numerical counterpart for our number assignment: whereas an ordinal number word refers to a rank that is identified *numerically* (namely, by a number assignment), a superlative refers to a rank that is identified *non-numerically* (namely, by an assignment of the 'extreme value' to the initial element). Figure 76 gives an illustration. As the graphic illustrates, superlatives identify a particular rank precisely, just as ordinal number words. Hence, while in our previous pair the quantifier construction ('many pens') is less precise than its numerical analogue ('five pens'), a superlative is just as precise as its numerical counterpart. However, it is less powerful: the assignment of an extreme value is limited to a single rank, restricting the reference of superlatives to one particular element (namely the initial one) in a given sequence, whereas ordinal number words can refer to an unlimited range of ranks. This is because ordinal number words are derived from elements of an infinite sequence, namely counting words (whereas superlatives are derived from adjectives).

This comparison is a bit unfair, though: after all, it is not the same ordinal number word that refers to all those ranks, whereas we have only one superlative for each ordering. Accordingly superlatives are somewhat lacking in terms of ranking range – the choice of ranks they can refer to – but their adjectival basis allows us to identify explicitly the ordering relation that constitutes the sequence. If we are talking about 'the fastest runner', it is clear that we refer to a progression of runners who are ordered by speed, that is, they are ordered by the relation 'is faster than'. If we are talking about 'the youngest runner', we refer to a progression of runners ordered by the relation 'is younger than'. These ordering relations remain implicit in ordinal number word constructions or are contributed by additional phrases, as in 'the first runner to arrive at the finish line' (and in fact, in our examples thus far I did not make this explicit; I just assumed that when we are talking about runners in a race, the most obvious interpretation for ordinal number words would suggest an order with respect to speed).

These differences do not affect the basic parallelism, though: while there are differences in the way superlatives and ordinal number words identify ranks, both kinds of expressions crucially denote specific ranks within sequences. This suggests that once again the grammatical parallels we observed are not random, but relate to parallels in the conceptual domain.

Let us have a look at our final pair now, proper names and '#'-constructions. Here the parallels are pretty obvious, particularly when you recall our analysis of nominal number assignments. We characterised these number assignments as contexts where we use our numerical tools as labels that identify elements within a set, for instance bus lines within a city. As we emphasised, this is exactly what we do when we use proper names: in 'my friend Karen', the proper name 'Karen' identifies one of my friends in pretty much the same way as 'four' can identify a certain bus in 'bus number four'. And if Karen played in a football team I could call her 'the player named Karen' just as well as, say, 'the player number six'.

In the first case I would identify her non-numerically by a proper name, in the second case I would identify her numerically, by a counting word. In both cases we distinguish players within a team by the labels we assign

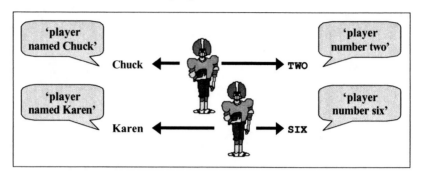

Figure 77 Non-numerical and numerical identification of elements within a set

them. The difference between the two kinds of assignments boils down to
the source of our labels: in the non-numerical case we draw our labels from
a supply of words that are conventionally used as proper names, whereas
in the numerical case our labels come from a sequence of numerical tools.
Figure 77 brings the two kinds of labelling together.

As we noted in our discussion of number assignments in chapter 1,
this labelling does not rely on a sequential order, but only on relations of
(non-)identity between our labels as well as between the empirical objects.
Accordingly, the choice of labels need not be restricted to one kind of
tag. Counting words can be combined with other, non-numerical words,
and if we use non-verbal numerals for labelling we can use elements of
different numerical sequences (for instance arabic and roman numerals, as
in 'vii.2'), and can also combine them with non-numerical elements like
Latin or Greek letters (as in a house number like '5a').

In addition, we can combine different elements of one numerical sequence by putting them together in a simple juxtaposition, that is, as a
mere list, as opposed to generating complex elements from them. Take, for
instance, a number like '6349123'. If this numeral were to indicate a numerical quantity, we would correlate it with the number word 'six million
three hundred and forty-nine thousand one hundred and twenty-three'
when reading aloud, that is, we would treat it as one complex element that
relates to a particular, high position within a sequence of numerical tools.
However, if '6349123' were to indicate a telephone number, we would have
different choices when correlating it with a number word, depending on
how we decide to split up the list. For instance, we could say 'six three four
nine one two three', or – as is common in some countries – 'sixty-three

forty-nine twelve three', or 'six hundred and thirty-four, nine hundred and twelve, three', and so on.

Hence we would treat the numeral not as one element, but as a list of elements. This is specific to nominal contexts, so if this numeral was to identify, say, the rank of a Marathon runner (well, a really slow person in an exceptionally well-attended Marathon), then the corresponding number word would again be a single, complex element: one could imagine saying something like 'It is unbelievable how slow he is – he was number six million three hundred forty-nine thousand one hundred twenty-three in that race', but one would never identify this rank by something like 'number sixty-three forty-nine twelve three'.

We can, in fact, regard nominal number assignments as a special instance of a general naming relation, a relation between objects and the labels that identify them. What makes nominal number assignments a *numerical* instance of naming is the fact that the labels we use here are numerical tools, that is, elements of a progression that is also used in other contexts of dependent linking where no naming is involved. Since our primary numerical tools are verbal items (namely counting words), it comes naturally to use numerical tools also in this kind of assignment.

The far-reaching similarities between the labelling we do with proper names and the labelling we do with counting words make a strong conceptual motivation for the grammatical similarities we found above between '#'-constructions and constructions with proper names. Although this is in particular true for '#'-constructions with a nominal interpretation, the close conceptual parallels we found between nominal and ordinal number assignments suggest that this parallelism can be generalised to include ordinal reference as well.

Taken together, then, the results from our discussion offer us conceptual motivations for the grammatical classification of our three kinds of referential number words. We showed that cardinal number assignments have a counterpart in the non-numerical quantification of sets, as expressed by quantifiers; ordinal number assignments find their partners in the non-numerical assignment of a rank in a sequence, as expressed by superlatives, and nominal number assignments were shown to instantiate the assignment of identificational labels, with proper names as a non-numerical instance. Figure 78 summarises our results. What does this correlation of conceptual and grammatical parallels mean for the relation between numbers and language; how does the behaviour of referential number words relate to counting words and their status as numerical tools? Let us tackle this question in the remainder of this chapter.

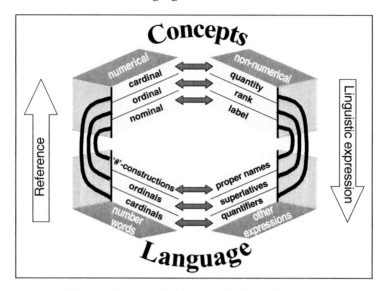

Figure 78 Conceptual and grammatical parallels between
numerical and non-numerical domains

THE RETURN OF THE COUNTING WORDS

The results from the previous section imply that, unlike counting words, referential number words are not a unique class of linguistic items. They are fully integrated into the grammatical system, and, what is more, they are integrated in a way that can be motivated from a conceptual point of view. This is a phenomenon not unheard of within the linguistic system. In particular in the case of syntactic categories, we often find a core domain of elements that share not only syntactic, but also semantic features. For instance, a typical verb phrase together with its subject will refer to an event of some kind, as in 'she sings', while a typical noun phrase will refer to a thing, as in 'the bus'. Among noun phrases we have some that refer to objects, while others refer to non-individuated substances, and in some languages – English being one of them – this conceptual distinction can be reflected by a morpho-syntactic distinction: count nouns refer to objects, have plural forms, and can be combined with the indefinite article, as in 'I bought a cow / cows', while mass nouns refer to substances and can occur in their bare form, as in 'I bought beef'.

Of course, languages, being symbolic systems, can and do include grammatical classifications that are arbitrary from a conceptual point of view as well. For instance, while there might be a considerable number of nouns that identify things, it is also perfectly feasible to denote events with noun phrases, as in 'the singer's performance'; and, similarly, we can have nouns that behave like mass nouns syntactically, but refer to objects rather than substances, for instance 'cattle'.[18]

This being said, the correspondences between syntactic categories like 'verb', 'count noun', and 'mass noun', and conceptual domains like 'event', 'object', and 'substance', which we find for so many other nouns and verbs, seem to be salient enough to trigger syntax–semantics mappings, for instance in first language acquisition, where young children can use syntactic clues in order to find out what a new word means. So, if you show a four-year-old a new plush toy and tell her that this is 'a sib' (hence you use an unknown word with a count noun syntax) she will probably interpret 'sib' as a name for the object, whereas when you tell her 'this is some sib' (mass noun syntax) she will tend to take 'sib' to denote the material. And when you make the toy fly through the air in a strange way and tell her that 'this is sibbing' (verb syntax), she will tend to interpret 'sib' as a kind of action.[19]

Hence, correspondences of grammatical and conceptual aspects like the ones we discussed in the previous section are not restricted to number words and their non-numerical counterparts. Given this picture, the grammatical features of referential number words are not arbitrary, but reflect a general pattern in the relationship between grammatical and conceptual structures.

This correspondence triggers the differences between referential number words and constitutes the three different grammatical classes. Each kind of number word construction refers to a different kind of number assignment and therefore to a different kind of empirical property. And, in each case, this property can be identified not only in a number assignment (the property cannot only be 'measured ^{RTM}'), but also by non-numerical means: the size of a set can be identified by a cardinal number assignment, but it can also be represented as a size below or above a norm value; the rank of an object within a sequence can be identified by an ordinal number assignment, but, if it is the first rank, it can also be represented as that rank that comes before all others; finally, objects can be identified within a set by numerical labels in a nominal number assignment, but they can also be identified

---

[18] Cf. Wiese (2003b: chs. 3–5) for a detailed discussion. In Wiese and Piñango (2001) we discuss evidence from language comprehension suggesting that the discrimination of the two kinds of features (syntactic category versus conceptual domain) for the mass/count distinction has a psychological reality.

[19] The classic study on this phenomenon is reported in Brown (1957). Bloom (1994b,c) discusses evidence from first language acquisition for syntax–semantics mappings in the nominal domain.

by non-numerical verbal labels. The expressions that refer to these non-numerical concepts – namely, quantifiers, superlatives, and proper names, respectively – accordingly provide natural grammatical partners for our referential number words.

These partnerships lead to more specific parallels than in the case of, say, conceptual domains like substances, objects, and events, and syntactic categories like mass nouns, count nouns, and verbs. For one, we are talking about the particular empirical properties that are focused on in number assignments here, and as a result we get rather complex conceptual parallels – pertaining to features like 'rank-within-a-sequence' and so on. What is more, the expressions that refer to these concepts might be simple as well as complex, and as a result we get grammatical parallels, for instance, with morphologically derived expressions like superlative adjectives, rather than with elements of a basic syntactic category.

While referential number words hence fall into different complex grammatical classes, they are lexically closely related: the words we use in cardinal constructions, ordinal constructions, and '#'-constructions look very similar to each other. As our discussion suggests, counting words not only are the common semantic basis for all referential number words, but – being verbal elements – they also provide the *lexical* basis for referential number words (with the exception of suppletive forms for small number words).

As I emphasised in the first section of this chapter, this does not mean that referential number words are identical with counting words. Unlike counting words, referential number words can show different inflectional patterns, like the cardinal number words in our Hebrew examples; they can be derived from counting words by morphological means like suffixation with '-th', as in the case of ordinal number words in English; and they can be combined with an additional lexical item like 'number' or 'daih', in English or Cantonese '#'-constructions, respectively.

However, the differentiation of numbers words is syntactically rather than lexically evident – after all, I had a hard time finding suppletive forms as illustrations for *lexical* distinctions at all, like 'léuhng' versus YIH in Cantonese, or 'second' versus TWO in English. In the normal case, the different kinds of referential number words are distinguished from each other and from counting words by the different morpho-syntactic constructions in which they occur, while their lexical basis identifies the same counting words, as in our example of FOUR as in 'four pens', 'the fourth runner', and 'bus number four'.

This pattern makes a lot of sense given our analysis of counting words as non-referential numerical tools: since counting words are 'linguistic outcasts', they have to be integrated into the grammatical system by different morpho-syntactic means if they are to be employed in expressions that refer to numerical concepts. Under this perspective, we can characterise referential number word constructions as the shape in which counting words are integrated into complex linguistic constructions, that is, as the packaging they must get in order to enter referential contexts.

Our discussion from the previous section now suggests that, in the course of this linguistic integration, number words adapt morpho-syntactic features from different kinds of expressions of non-numerical domains and, by so doing, systematically employ conceptual parallels. These correspondences with non-numerical expressions indicate that the integration of counting words into grammatical structures works pretty much in the same way as the integration of a new product into the market. Let us assume you have created a new kind of chocolate bar that you want to sell in the shops. The packet you are going to use for it will most likely have a form that resembles that of other chocolate bars: it will probably be a paper wrapper, and not, say, a rubber ball. If, on the other hand, you are looking for a package for a chocolate *drink*, you will probably choose a bottle rather than a square glass box.

The same happens with counting words: when entering grammatical structures, they take a 'package' that resembles expressions with a similar denotation. This has the effect that referential number words make use of two kinds of relationships. On the one hand, they are conceptually and lexically related to counting words. On the other hand, they are grammatically related to quantifiers, superlatives, or proper names.

Figure 79 illustrates the two kinds of associations that are established by the grammatical integration of our numerical tools. The grammatical parallels between referential number words and non-numerical expressions are indicated by different shapes (rectangles, triangles, and ellipses), their relation to counting words is indicated by little stars that form the content.

In sum, we can regard referential number word constructions as the result of a particular kind of linguistic integration, an integration of counting words into grammatical structures that is based on their verbal–numerical status and reflects upon their application in different kinds of number assignments: verbal elements that initially serve as non-referential numerical tools are integrated into grammatical structures in the form of number words that refer to numerical concepts.

In this book, then, I have described something like a voyage of counting words in and out of language and back again. We started with proper, referential words, for instance words that refer to fingers or to sets of a certain

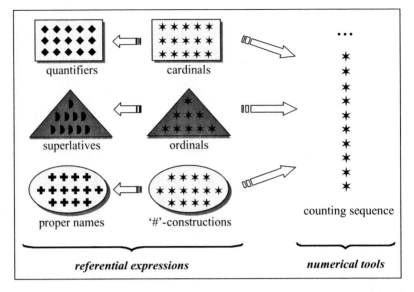

Figure 79 Referential number words and the grammatical integration of numerical tools

cardinality. When these words become part of a counting sequence, they lose their referential power and take on an instrumental status that alienates them from language: we use them as tools in number assignments to assess empirical properties of objects, instead of using them, say, as names for these objects. In order to refer to the results of these number assignments, we then employ the very same verbal elements, our numerical tools, to generate referential number words: counting words return to referential linguistic contexts in the form of cardinals, ordinals, and '#'-constructions. They are now no longer unique, but fall into different grammatical classes, with parallels to other linguistic items.

In fact, we can look at our investigation of numbers and language as an account of this counting word enterprise, an enterprise that builds on their verbal background, their emergence as numerical tools, and their usage in different kinds of number assignments. Let me summarise what I consider to be the five main pillars of the model of language and numbers that I have developed in this book:

1. *A unified view of numerical tools*: Numbers are flexible mental tools that can be employed in a wide range of contexts, based on a pattern of dependent linking.

2. *The tripartition of number contexts*: Numbers can be assigned to objects in different instances of dependent linking, which focus on cardinal relations (as expressed in 'three pens'), ordinal relations ('the third runner'), or nominal relations ('bus #3'). These contexts constitute different subdomains of our cognitive domain of numbers.

3. *A criteria-based approach to numbers*: Numbers are characterised by three crucial properties; these can be regarded as the criteria a sequence must meet in order to be used as a numerical toolkit. Different instances of such a toolkit are the counting sequences of different languages as well as different non-verbal numeral sequences (for instance, arabic numerals). These different sequences do not constitute different 'numbers', but isomorphic systems that can fulfil the same purposes.

4. *The special status of counting words*: Counting words can be used as numerical tools; they are non-referential, instrumental elements that have a special status within the linguistic system. At the same time, they serve as a lexical basis for referential number words that are integrated into the grammatical system and denote cardinal, ordinal, and nominal concepts.

5. *The linguistic foundation of number*: Language plays a crucial role in the emergence of a systematic number concept. Language as a mental faculty enables us to grasp the pattern of dependent linking, and our linguistic system allows us to develop a potentially infinite sequence of words that can be used as numerical tools.

Whereas the first two points give us the characteristics of numbers, the third one allows us to identify different number sequences. On this basis the final two points, then, summarise our results on the relationship between numbers and language. As I hope to have convinced you in this book, this relationship is a special one. Language is not only the most important mental faculty we have as humans, the capacity that might have led to the emergence of our species; it also lies at the heart of what makes us – in Dedekind's words – 'numerical beings'. It is this faculty that enables us to grasp numbers the way we do; it allows us to develop mental tools powerful enough to serve in all kinds of number assignments, tools that open the way to infinity and lay the ground for complex mathematical cognition.

Appendices

In the following definitions, 'iff' is used as a shorthand for 'if and only if'.

Number assignments

MEASUREMENT AS A UNIFIED NOTION FOR NUMBER ASSIGNMENTS: THE REPRESENTATIONAL THEORY OF MEASUREMENT

(cf. Stevens 1946; Suppes and Zinnes 1963; Krantz et al. 1971; Roberts 1979; Narens 1985)

- **Measurement^{RTM}** is a homomorphic mapping f: A $\rightarrow$ B, where
  - A is an empirical relational structure and B is a numerical relational structure; A $=$ $<E_a, R_a>$, B $=$ $<E_b, R_b>$, where E_x is a set of entities and R_x is a set of relations on E_x for x $\in$ $\{a,b\}$, and
  - for all a $\in$ E_a: f(a) $\in$ E_b, and
  - for each i: if R_i is an n-ary relation and $a_1, \ldots, a_n$ are in E_a, then
  - $R_i(a_1, \ldots, a_n)$ $\Leftrightarrow$ $S_i(f(a_1), \ldots, f(a_n))$.
- Different **kinds of measurement^{RTM}** are distinguished by the type of the scale they are based on, where:
  - a **scale** is a homomorphism from A into B;
  - the **type of a scale** is defined by the admissible transformations;
  - a transformation from a scale s_1 into a scale s_2 is **admissible** iff s_1 and s_2 are homomorphic mappings into the same numerical relational structure.
- A numerical statement is **meaningful** if and only if its truth (or falsity) is constant under admissible scale transformations of any of its numerical assignments, that is, any of its numerical functions expressing the result of measurement^{RTM}.

CARDINAL, ORDINAL, AND NOMINAL NUMBER ASSIGNMENTS

In the following analyses:
- for any set x: |x| is the cardinality of x;
- N is the sequence of positive integers;

– a is the object of measurement^{RTM} (hence a is an element of the empirical relational structure);

– f is the homomorphism from A into B that establishes the measurement^{RTM};

– g is an admissible transformation on f

– n is the number onto which a is mapped (hence n is an element of the numerical relational structure, and $f(a) = n$)

– P is the measured^{RTM} property.

Cardinal number assignments: Numerical quantification and measurement
('measurement' in the familiar sense)

Numerical quantification.

- a is a set; $P(a)$ is the cardinality of a, so: $P(a) = |a|$.
- n identifies how many elements a has.
- $P(a) = P(\mathbf{N}^n)$, where $\mathbf{N}^n$ is the smallest subset of $\mathbf{N}$ which contains n and all predecessors of n.
- based on absolute scales: $g(f(a)) = f(a)$ for all admissible transformations from f to $g(f)$.

Measurement

. We distinguish two kinds of measurement: 'direct measurement' (for example measurement of weight by kg) and 'indirect measurement' (for example measurement of temperature by $^\circ$C); for both cases:

- a is an object; $P(a)$ is a property of a.
- n identifies the cardinality of a set m of measure items with a *relevant* property π, i.e.:

π is an additive property, and $\pi(\mu)$ is the same for all $\mu \in m$ (that is, all $\mu \in m$ are identical with respect to π), hence $\pi(m)$ is monotonically covarying with $|m|$.

Direct measurement.

- The relevant property of the measure items is P.
- $P(m) = P(a)$, and $|m| = |\mathbf{N}^n|$.
- for instance, $P(a)$ could be the weight of a pumpkin a and m a set of weights;
- based on rational scales: $g(f(a)) = v \times f(a)$ for some positive real number v.

Indirect measurement.
- The relevant property of the measure items is a property Q which is different from P, such that:
  - there is a mediating object o such that $Q(o)$ is positively covarying with $P(o)$;
  - $P(o) = P(a)$, and $Q(o) = Q(m)$;
  - $|m| = |N^n|$.
- for instance, $P(a)$ could be the temperature of bathwater a; m could be a set of length units on a thermometer, and o a mercury column; $Q(o)$ would then be the height/length of the mercury column, and $Q(m)$ the aggregate height/length of the measure items (i.e., of the length units on the thermometer);
- based on interval scales: $g(f(a)) = v_1 \times f(a) + v_2$ for some real numbers v_1 and v_2, with $v_1 > 0$.

Ordinal number assignments

- a is an object; $P(a)$ is the rank of a.
- n identifies the rank of a in a given progression p.
- $P(a)_p = P(n)_{N'}$ where $P(x)_y$ is the rank of an object x in a progression y, $N' \subset N$, and N' is ordered by $<$.
- based on ordinal scales: $g(f(a)) = h(f(a))$; where h is a monotone increasing function, hence: if $f(a) < f(b)$, then $h(f(a)) < h(f(b))$.
- For any set α: α is a **progression** iff α is totally ordered by a relation R, such that
  - R is asymmetric, antireflexive, and transitive,
  - there is an element e of α, such that: $\neg\exists_{x \in \alpha} R(x,e)$,
  - for every element x of α: s^x is finite, where $s^x = \{y \mid y \in \alpha \text{ and } R(y,x)\}$ (that is, s^x is the set of all predecessors of x in α)

Nominal number assignments

- a is an object; $P(a) = a$ [$P(a)$ is the identity of a; $P(a_1) = P(a_2) \Leftrightarrow a_1 = a_2$].
- n identifies a in a given set s: n serves as the label of a in s.
- $P(a)_s = P(n)_{N'}$, where $P(x)_y$ is the identity of an object x in a set y, and $N' \subset N$.
- based on nominal scales: $g(f(a)) = h(f(a))$ for some injective function h.

The philosophical background: approaches to numbers in the philosophy of mathematics

THE INTERSECTIVE APPROACH: NUMBERS AS SETS OF SETS
(FREGE 1884, 1893)

Definition of properties via 'same-ness'

The number definition is based on a concept of 'sameness' ("Gleichheit") that is attained by abstraction in the 'Grundlagen der Arithmetik' (Frege 1884), where Frege develops a schema based on two examples from geometry, namely direction and shape (Frege 1884: §§ 64–68):

(i) The equivalence of (1) and (2) yields the definition of the direction of a line *a*:

   (1) 'The direction of a line *a* is the same as the direction of a line *b*.'

   (2) '*a* is parallel to *b*.'

→ The direction of *a* is defined as the set of all entities that are parallel to *a*.

(ii) The equivalence of (3) and (4) yields the definition of the shape of a triangle *a*:

   (3) 'The shape ("Gestalt") of a triangle *a* is the same as the shape of a triangle *b*.'

   (4) '*a* is similar ("ähnlich") to *b*.'

→ The shape of *a* is defined as the set of all entities that are similar to *a*.

Schema used for the definitions

(5) $[(F(a) = F(b)) \leftrightarrow G(a,b)] \vdash F(a) = \{x \mid G(a,x)\}$

[in example (i): F = *direction*, G = *parallel*; in example (ii): F = *shape*; G = *similar*]

Definition of cardinality as an instance of this schema

The cardinality of a set u is the same as the cardinality of a set v iff u and v are equinumerous. Hence, according to (5) the cardinality of u is the set of all sets that are equinumerous to u (Frege 1884: § 68): we get (6) as an instance of (5), where $\textbf{R}$ is cardinality ('Anzahl'), and EQ is the relation of equinumerosity:

(6) $[\ (\textbf{R}(u) = \textbf{R}(v)) \leftrightarrow EQ(u,v)\ ] \vdash \textbf{R}(u) = \{x \mid EQ(u,x)\}$

Formalisation of the definition in 'Grundgesetze der Arithmetik'
(Frege 1893: § 40)

(7) $\Vdash \grave{e} \underset{\displaystyle \raise2pt\hbox{} }{} \overset{q}{\frown} \underset{u \cap (e \cap) \textbf{U}q)}{\vdash e \cap (u \cap) q)} \quad = \textbf{R}\, u$

read: 'The cardinality of u is the set of all sets e, such that there is a one-to-one mapping between the objects in e and those in u', i.e.: 'The cardinality of u is the set of all sets that are equinumerous with u'. [$\grave{e}$ is the set of all e, $\textbf{U}q$ is the converse of q, '$e \cap (u \cap)\ q)$' states that there is a function (with an extension q that constitutes a one-to-one-mapping between the elements of e and those of u; a formula $\underset{\displaystyle \vdash A}{\frown}\overset{q}{}\vdash B$ can in modern notation be rendered as: $\neg \forall q\, (A \rightarrow \neg B)$.]

Definition of 0 and 1 via paradigm sets (Frege 1893: §§ 41–42)

(7) gives the general form for cardinality definitions. For the definition of individual numbers, Frege determines for each number n a paradigm set pn. For the definition of 0, he introduces po as the set of all elements that are not self-identical; the definition of 1 makes use of a paradigm set $p1$ that is the set of all elements that are identical to 0:

(8) $\Vdash \textbf{R}\grave{e}\, (\neg\, e = e) = \quad o$

(9) $\Vdash \textbf{R}\grave{e}\, (e = o) \quad = \quad 1$

Definition of Successor (Frege 1893: § 46)

On this basis, all other numbers are defined as successors via their paradigm sets: if n is a natural number, then $n + 1$ is defined as the set of all sets that are equinumerous to the paradigm set p_{n+1} which is the set of all entities that belong to the number sequence ending with n (since 0 belongs to the number sequence, a sequence ending with n contains always $n + 1$ elements).

THE ITEMISING ANALYSIS: MULTITUDES

A multitude of the form 'n Fs' (for instance, *six dogs*, for $n = 6$, and F = 'dog') is represented with the help of numerically definite quantifiers: 'There are n Fs' is analysed as '$\exists_{nx}$ Fx'.

Definition of numerically definite quantifiers in Quine (1974: § 30)

- $\exists_{0x}$ Fx $\Leftrightarrow$ $\neg\exists_x$ Fx
- $\exists_{1x}$ Fx $\Leftrightarrow$ $\exists_x$ (Fx $\wedge$ $\exists_{0y}$ (Fy $\wedge$ $\neg$ (y = x)))
- $\exists_{2x}$ Fx $\Leftrightarrow$ $\exists_x$ (Fx $\wedge$ $\exists_{1y}$ (Fy $\wedge$ $\neg$ (y = x)))

General form (definition of Successor)

- $\exists_{(n+1)x}$ Fx $\Leftrightarrow$ $\exists_x$ (Fx $\wedge$ $\exists_{ny}$ (Fy $\wedge$ $\neg$ (y = x)))

THE RELATIONAL VIEW: CONDITIONS ON THE SEQUENCE N OF NATURAL NUMBERS

Necessary and sufficient conditions for the set N of natural numbers (Dedekind 1887)

a. N is a set.
b. There is a one-to-one mapping φ, such that $\varphi(N) = N'$.
c. $N' \subseteq N$.
d. $N = 1_0$, where
  - given a mapping ψ, a chain of ψ is a set k for which $\psi(k) \subseteq k$, and
  - 1_0 is the intersection of all the chains of φ which contain 1.
  - $1 \notin N'$.

These conditions define N as an infinite progression of well-distinguished elements with an initial element 1 and successors $\varphi(1)$, $\varphi(\varphi(1))$, $\varphi(\varphi(\varphi(1)))$, . . . , yielded by a successor function φ.

(a) ensures that all $x \in$ N are well-distinguished (since a set consists of well-distinguished elements). Condition (b) ensures that all successors are distinct (these successors are the elements of N′). In order to achieve this, φ maps elements of N onto elements of N′ such that different elements of N are always mapped onto different elements of N′ (hence no elements of N′ are shared). According to condition (c), φ maps N onto a subset of itself, that is, all elements of N′ are also elements of N. This ensures that all successors are in N, so one can keep applying φ onto elements of N open-endedly and still remain within N. Condition (d) ensures that 1 is an element of N, and that nothing other than the progression '1, $\varphi(1)$, $\varphi(\varphi(1))$, . . .' is in N. Condition (e), taken together with (b), ensures that each element of this progression is distinct from all others, guaranteeing that there can be no loops (where φ maps elements of N′ back onto 1 or onto elements of N that are already successors of other elements of N′), such that the sequence starts all over again.

Numerical tools

A CRITERIA-BASED APPROACH TO NUMBERS

Criteria for possible number sequences N

(i) All $x \in$ N must be well distinguished.

(ii) N must be a progression.

(iii) N must be infinite.

Definition of numbers as numerical tools, based on these criteria

Any sequence that fulfils these criteria can fulfil numerical purposes, that is, it can be used as a sequence N of numerical tools. As long as this sequence is only used in number assignments for finite sets and does not serve as a basis for complex mathematics, the third feature (infiniteness) is optional.

A POSSIBLE SET N DRAWN FROM VERBAL ENTITIES: THE ENGLISH COUNTING SEQUENCE C

Generation of the elements of C by inductive definition

Elements of C are defined via their phonological representations. I define six classes of C: 'Ones' (ONE to NINE), 'Teens' (TEN to NINETEEN), 'Tys' (TWENTY to NINETY-NINE), 'Hundreds' (ONE HUNDRED to NINE HUNDRED AND NINETY-NINE), 'Thousands' (ONE THOUSAND to NINE HUNDRED AND NINETY-NINE THOUSAND NINE HUNDRED AND NINETY-NINE), and 'Millions' (open-ended, from ONE MILLION). Elements of the initial class of primitive counting words, Ones, are defined as a list, that is, by enumeration.

Apart from the two initial classes, each class consists of two subclasses: (1) the m-class of elements whose immediate constituents are combined by a

rule of a multiplicative character (for example SIX-TY, TWO HUNDRED), and
(2) the *a*-class of elements whose immediate constituents are combined by
a rule of an additive character (for example SIXTY-THREE, TWO HUNDRED
AND TEN).

Elements of *m*-classes are generated by rules **C1–C4** that take elements
of a lower class (in the case of the highest class: elements of any class of **C**)
as their input and combine them with the respective multiplier elements
(-TY, HUNDRED, THOUSAND, MILLION).

Elements of *a*-classes are generated by a concatenation rule **CC** that takes
elements of the respective *m*-classes and elements of a lower class as its input
and combines them by concatenation (for example it yields SIXTY-THREE
from SIXTY and THREE; for elements of the 'Hundred'-class **CC** inserts
'AND', for instance it yields TWO HUNDRED AND TEN from TWO HUNDRED
TEN).

The class of Teens has a special status. Given the decade structure of the
English counting sequence, one would expect the 'Teens' to be elements
of the 'Tys'-class, that is, it should not be TEN, but rather ONE-TY, not
ELEVEN, but ONETY-ONE etc. Instead, the first three elements of the 'Teen'-
class (ONE, ELEVEN, TWELVE) are opaque and accordingly they are defined
by enumeration like the Ones. The other Teens are defined as complex
additive elements with a basis TEEN.

$C = C_O \cup C_T \cup C_Y \cup C_H \cup C_K \cup C_M$ ('Ones', 'Teens', 'Tys', 'Hundreds',
'Thousands', 'Millions')

for all $\alpha \in (Y, H, K, M: C_\alpha = C_{\alpha m} \cup C_{\alpha a}$ ('multiplicative' and 'additive'
    counting words)

$C_T = C_{T_o} \cup C_{T_a}$ ('opaque' and 'additive' elements of the 'Teens'-class)

Abbreviations:
'$C_O{}^2$' stands for "C_O without /wʌn/";
'$C_O{}^3$' stands for "C_O without /wʌn/ and /tu:/"

- $C_O = \{/w\Lambda n/, /tu:/, /\theta ri:/, /f\mathfrak{o}:/, /fa\textsc{i}v/, /s\textsc{i}ks/, /sevn/, /e\textsc{i}t/, /na\textsc{i}n/\}$
- For all $\alpha, \beta \in C$: $CC(\alpha, \beta) = \gamma$, with
  - $\gamma = \alpha$-/and/-β iff $\alpha \in C_{Hm} \cup C_{Km} \cup C_{Mm}$ and $\beta \in C_O \cup C_T \cup C_Y$;
  - $\gamma = \alpha\beta$ otherwise.
- $C_{T_o} = \{/ten/, /\textsc{i}levn/, /twelv/\}$
- If $\alpha \in C_O{}^3$, then $CC(\alpha, /ti:n/) \in C_{Ta}$.
- If $\alpha \in C_O{}^2$, then $C1(\alpha) \in C_{Ym}$, where $C1(\alpha) = \alpha$-/ti:/.
- If $\alpha \in C_{Ym}$ and $\beta \in C_O$, then $CC(\alpha, \beta) \in C_{Ya}$.
- If $\alpha \in C_O$, then $C2(\alpha) \in C_{Hm}$, where $C2(\alpha) = \alpha$-/h\Lambda ndrəd/.

- If $\alpha \in C_{Hm}$ and $\beta \in C_O \cup C_T \cup C_Y$, then $CC(\alpha,\beta) \in C_{Ha}$.
- If $\alpha \in C_O \cup C_T \cup C_Y \cup C_H$, then $C3(\alpha) \in C_{Km}$, where $C3(\alpha) = \alpha\text{-}/\theta a \upsilon znd/$.
- If $\alpha \in C_{Km}$ and $\beta \in C_O \cup C_T \cup C_Y \cup C_H$, then $CC(\alpha,\beta) \in C_{Ka}$.
- If $\alpha \in C$, then $C4(\alpha) \in C_{Mm}$, where $C4(\alpha) = \alpha\text{-}/m\iota l\imath \partial n/$.
- If $\alpha \in C_{Mm}$; $\beta \in C_O \cup C_T \cup C_Y \cup C_H \cup C_K$, then $CC(\alpha,\beta) \in C_{Ma}$.

Sequential ordering of C by a relation (C;<)

The elements of **C** are ordered with respect to the class they belong to, and with reference to their internal structure as constituted by the multiplicative (**C1** to **C4**) and additive (**CC**) generation rules. This yields the following ordering:

(a) order of classes: $<C_O, C_T, C_Y, C_H, C_K, C_M>$

(b) order of elements of the initial class: <ONE, TWO, THREE, FOUR, FIVE, SIX, SEVEN, EIGHT, NINE>

(c) order of opaque Teens: <TEN, ELEVEN, TWELVE>

(d) order of elements of higher classes based on the ordering of multiplicative and additive elements, referring to their immediate constituents: multiplicative elements are ordered with respect to the order of their bases (for example SIXTY < NINETY, because SIX < NINE); additive elements are always higher than the respective multiplicative elements they are based on (for example SIXTY < SIXTY-FOUR; defined via introduction of a Ø-element and the extension of the generative rules accordingly; in the case of Teens: additive elements are higher than the opaque elements), and are ordered with respect to the order of their immediate constituents, with priority given to higher constituents (for example SIXTY-FIVE < SEVENTY-THREE, because SIXTY < SEVENTY, and SIXTY-THREE < SIXTY-NINE, because THREE < NINE).

Keeping with convention, I call the numerical relation '>' here. However, in our framework '>' is just the name we use for the relation that orders our numerical tools, and not a relation between sets of different sizes (as the paraphrase 'greater than' might suggest). Hence, '*a* > *b*' translates simply as '*a* comes after *b* in the sequence of numerical tools'; for instance, 'THREE > TWO' reads as 'THREE comes after TWO in the English counting sequence'. Accordingly, I define the relation '>' directly for counting words, as (non-referential) verbal elements.

We give the following background specifications to account for cases where the definition of '$<$' might include empty elements:
- $\emptyset < \alpha$ for all $\alpha \in$ **C**;
- $CC(\alpha,\beta) = \beta$, if $\alpha = \emptyset$ and $\beta \in$ **C** $\cup \emptyset$;
- for all **C**v, where $v \in \{1,2,3,4\}$: **C**$v(\alpha) = \emptyset$, if $\alpha = \emptyset$.

We distinguish different possible cases for $\alpha, \beta \in$ **C** (where $\alpha \neq \beta$):
- $\alpha \in$ **C**$_O$
  - $\beta \in$ **C**$_O$
    - $\alpha = $ /wʌn/: $\alpha < \beta$
    - $\alpha = $ /tuː/: $\alpha < \beta$ iff $\beta \in \{$/θriː/, /fɔː/, /faɪv/, /sɪks/, /sevn/, /eɪt/, /naɪn/$\}$
    - $\alpha = $ /θriː/: $\alpha < \beta$ iff $\beta \in \{$/fɔː/, /faɪv/, /sɪks/, /sevn/, /eɪt/, /naɪn/$\}$
    - $\alpha = $ /fɔː/: $\alpha < \beta$ iff $\beta \in \{$/faɪv/, /sɪks/, /sevn/, /eɪt/, /naɪn/$\}$
    - $\alpha = $ /faɪv/: $\alpha < \beta$ iff $\beta \in \{$/sɪks/, /sevn/, /eɪt/, /naɪn/$\}$
    - $\alpha = $ /sɪks/: $\alpha < \beta$ iff $\beta \in \{$/sevn/, /eɪt/, /naɪn/$\}$
    - $\alpha = $ /sevn/: $\alpha < \beta$ iff $\beta \in \{$/eɪt/, /naɪn/$\}$
    - $\alpha = $ /eɪt/: $\alpha < \beta$ iff $\beta \in \{$/naɪn/$\}$
    - $\alpha = $ /naɪn/: $\alpha \nless \beta$
  - $\beta \notin$ **C**$_O$: $\alpha < \beta$
- $\alpha \in$ **C**$_{To}$
  - $\beta \in$ **C**$_O$: $\alpha \nless \beta$.
  - $\beta \in$ **C**$_{To}$
    - $\alpha = $ /ten/: $\alpha < \beta$
    - $\alpha = $ /ɪlevn/: $\alpha < \beta$ iff $\beta = $ /twelv/
    - $\alpha = $ /twelv/: $\alpha < \beta$
  - $\beta \in$ **C**-(**C**$_O \cup$ **C**$_{To}$): $\alpha < \beta$
- $\alpha \in$ **C**$_{Ta}$, hence: $\alpha = CC(x, $/tiːn/$)$, where $x \in$ **C**$_O{}^3$
  - $\beta \in$ **C**$_O \cup$ **C**$_{To}$: $\alpha \nless \beta$.
  - $\beta \in$ **C**$_{Ta}$, hence: $\beta = CC(v, $/tiːn/$)$, where $v \in$ **C**$_O{}^3$
    - $x < v$: $\alpha < \beta$
    - $v < x$: $\alpha \nless \beta$
- $\alpha \in$ **C**$_Y$, hence: $\alpha = CC(C1(x),y)$, where $x \in$ **C**$_O{}^2$ and $y \in$ **C**$_O \cup \{\emptyset\}$
  - $\beta \in$ **C**$_O \cup$ **C**$_T$: $\alpha \nless \beta$.
  - $\beta \in$ **C**$_Y$, hence: $\beta = CC(C1(v), w)$, where $v \in$ **C**$_O{}^2$ and $w \in$ **C**$_O \cup \{\emptyset\}$
    - $x < v$: $\alpha < \beta$
    - $v < x$: $\alpha \nless \beta$
    - $x = v$: $\alpha < \beta$ iff $y < w$
  - $\beta \in$ **C**-(**C**$_O \cup$ **C**$_T \cup$ **C**$_Y$): $\alpha < \beta$

- $\alpha \in C_H$, hence: $\alpha = CC(C2(x),y)$, where $x \in C_O$ and $y \in C_O \cup C_T \cup C_Y \cup \{\emptyset\}$
  - $\beta \in C_O \cup C_T \cup C_Y$: $\alpha < \beta$
  - $\beta \in C_H$, hence: $\beta = CC(C2(v),w)$, where $v \in C_O$ and $w \in C_O \cup C_T \cup C_Y \cup \{\emptyset\}$
    - $x < v$: $\alpha < \beta$
    - $v < x$: $\alpha \nless \beta$
    - $x = v$: $\alpha < \beta$ iff $y < w$
  - $\beta \in C\text{-}(C_O \cup C_T \cup C_Y \cup C_H)$: $\alpha < \beta$
- $\alpha \in C_K$, hence: $\alpha = CC(C3(x),y)$, where $x \in C_O \cup C_T \cup C_Y \cup C_H$ and $y \in C_O \cup C_T \cup C_Y \cup C_H \cup \{\emptyset\}$
  - $\beta \in C_O \cup C_T \cup C_Y \cup C_H$: $\alpha < \beta$
  - $\beta \in C_K$, hence: $\beta = CC(C3(v),w)$, where $v \in C_O \cup C_T \cup C_Y \cup C_H$ and $w \in C_O \cup C_T \cup C_Y \cup C_H \cup \{\emptyset\}$
    - $x < v$: $\alpha < \beta$
    - $v < x$: $\alpha \nless \beta$
    - $x = v$: $\alpha < \beta$ iff $y < w$
  - $\beta \in C\text{-}C_O \cup C_T \cup C_Y \cup C_H \cup C_K$: $\alpha < \beta$
- $\alpha \in C_M$, hence: $\alpha = CC(C4(x),y)$, where $x \in C$ and $y \in C_O \cup C_T \cup C_Y \cup C_H \cup C_K \cup \{\emptyset\}$
  - $\beta \in C_O \cup C_T \cup C_Y \cup C_H \cup C_K$: $\alpha < \beta$
  - $\beta \in C_M$, hence: $\beta = CC(C4(v), w)$, where $v \in C$ and $w \in C_O \cup C_T \cup C_Y \cup C_H \cup C_K \cup \{\emptyset\}$
    - $x < v$: $\alpha < \beta$
    - $v < x$: $\alpha \nless \beta$
    - $x = v$: $\alpha < \beta$ iff $y < w$

Derivation of actual counting words from the 'idealised' words in C by a function $\rho : C \to \mathbb{C}$

The definition of ρ accounts for idiosyncrasies in the counting sequences; the concatenation rule CC is extended for the elements generated by ρ.

- If $\alpha \in C_O \cup C_{T_o} \cup C_{Hm} \cup C_{Km} \cup C_{Mm}$, then $\rho(\alpha) = \alpha$.
- If $\alpha \in C_{Ta}$, where $\alpha = CC(\beta, /tiːn/)$, then $\rho(\alpha) = \alpha'$, with $\alpha' =$
  - $\theta_3tiːn/$, if $\beta = /\theta riː/$;
  - /fiftiːn/, if $\beta = /faɪv/$;
  - /eɪtiːn/, if $\beta = /eɪt/$;
  - α otherwise.
- If $\alpha \in C_{Ym}$, where $\alpha = C1(\beta)$, then $\rho(\alpha) = \alpha'$, with $\alpha' =$
  - /twentɪ/, if $\beta = /tuː/$;

- /θɜtɪ/,   if β = /θriː/;
- /fɪftɪ/,   if β = /faɪv/;
- /eɪtɪ/,   if β = /eɪt/;
- α   otherwise.
- If α ∈ C_{Ha} ∪ C_{Ka} ∪ C_{Ma}, where α = CC(β,γ), ρ(β) = β′, ρ(γ) = γ′, then ρ(α) = α′, with α′ = CC(β′, γ′).

A POSSIBLE SET N DRAWN FROM NON-VERBAL ENTITIES: THE SEQUENCE OF ARABIC NUMERALS A

Generation of the elements of A *by inductive definition*

I define a set of set of primitive elements, namely the digits 0 to 9, which form the subset A_D of A. On this basis, I define a 'String Rule' that generates new (complex) elements of A by simple concatenation.
- Basis: A_D = {0,1,2,3,4,5,6,7,8,9}; A_D ⊂ A.
- String Rule: For all x, y ∈ A: S(x,y) ∈ A, where S(x,y) = xy.

Sequential ordering of A *by a relation (*A*;<)*

The order of primitive elements of A (the digits) is given explicitly. The order of complex elements is determined with respect to their constituents (ignoring possible initial occurrences of 0 in a complex numeral; for instance '0012', which can be generated by the String Rule, is treated as '12'). If two numerals are of different length, the longer numeral is the higher one. If two numerals are of the same length, we compare the relative order of constituents. In order to do so, we isolate the respective final (right-most) digits in both numerals and see whether the numerals that are left over are identical or not. If they are identical, their order is determined by the relative order of those final digits. If they are not identical, we repeat our last step, that is, we again isolate the final digits and compare the leftover numerals. We do this until we come to identical leftovers, or to leftovers that are single digits and hence ordered. Hence, this definition of '<' for numerals of the same length is equivalent to a step-by-step comparison of their constituents from left to right. For instance, for 317 and 315 we get the order 315 < 317, because the left constituent '31' is identical in both numerals, and 5 < 7. For 2865 and 3754, we get the order 2865 < 3754, because 286 < 375, and this is the case because their left constituents are ordered '28 < 37', and this is because their respective left-most digits are ordered '2 < 3'.

For all x,y,z,v,w∈ **A**:

- x $\nless$ o;
- x < 1 iff x = o;
- x < 2 iff x ∈ {o,1};
- x < 3 iff x ∈ {o,1,2};
- x < 4 iff x ∈ {o,1,2,3};
- x < 5 iff x ∈ {o,1,2,3,4};
- x < 6 iff x ∈ {o,1,2,3,4,5};
- x < 7 iff x ∈ {o,1,2,3,4,5,6};
- x < 8 iff x ∈ {o,1,2,3,4,5,6,7};
- x < 9 iff x ∈ {o,1,2,3,4,5,6,7,8}
- vx < wy for x,y ∈ **A**$_D$ iff (v = w and x < y) or (v < w), where:
  - all initial occurrences of o are ignored in v and w;
  - if v = Ø and w ≠ Ø, then v < w.

CORRELATION OF ENGLISH COUNTING WORDS AND ARABIC NUMERALS

The correlation of **A** and **C** is defined by a relation μ: **C** ↔ **A**. This relation consists of two parts that account for distinct links in both directions: (1) the mapping from arabic numerals to counting words (that is, from **A** to **C**), and (2) the mapping from counting words to arabic numerals (that is, from **C** to **A**)

Mapping from A to C

The mapping between the primitive elements 1 to 9 and /wʌn/ to /naɪ n/, as well as between 10 to 12 and the opaque elements /ten/ to /twelv/ is defined by enumeration. A special rule for o is introduced, to account for the phonological representation /zɪ ər əʊ/ if o occurs by itself (this phonological representation is introduced separately, since is not part of the counting sequence **C**), and for the over-writing procedure if o occurs within complex numerals.

For all z ∈ **A**$_D$:

- μ(z) = /wʌn/ iff z = 1
- μ(z) = /tuː/ iff z = 2
- μ(z) = /θriː/ iff z = 3
- μ(z) = /fɔː/ iff z = 4
- μ(z) = /faɪ v/ iff z = 5
- μ(z) = /sɪ k s/ iff z = 6
- μ(z) = /sevn/ iff z = 7

- $\mu(z) = $ /eɪt/   iff $z = 8$
- $\mu(z) = $ /naɪn/   iff $z = 9$
- If $z = 0$:
  - $\mu(z) = $ /zɪərəʊ/ if z is not part of a complex numeral z_k
  - $\mu(z) = \varnothing$ otherwise.
  For all $z \in A$:
- $\mu(z) = $ /ten/   iff $z = 10$
- $\mu(z) = $ /ɪlevn/   iff $z = 11$
- $\mu(z) = $ /twelv/   iff $z = 12$

I define further subclasses of **A** parallel to those of **C**; the mapping then makes use of the internal structure of elements of the respective classes. The recourse to generative rules of **C** allows us, among others, to account for the introduction of verbal bases (multiplier elements like 'hundred' etc.); the base '-teen' is introduced directly, since it is not productive in the decades (instead, higher decades are generated with the base '-ty', that is, there is no 'two-teen', but instead 'twenty' etc.). In the following, the abbreviation: 'A_D' stands for 'A_D without 1 and 2'.

For all for all $z \in A$, where $z = S(\alpha,\beta)$:
- $z \in A_T$ iff $\alpha = 1$ and $\beta \in A_D^3$; $A_T \subset A$
- $z \in A_Y$ iff $\alpha,\beta \in A_D$; $A_Y \subset A$
- $z \in A_H$ iff $\alpha \in A_D, \beta \in A_Y$; $A_H \subset A$
- $z \in A_K$ iff $\alpha \in A_D \cup A_Y \cup A_H, \beta \in A_H$; $A_K \subset A$
- $z \in A_M$ iff $\beta = S(\gamma,\delta)$ and $\alpha \in A, \gamma \in A_H, \delta \in A_H$; $A_M \subset A$.

- For all $z \in A_T$, i.e. $z = S(1,y)$, with $y \in A_D^3$: $\mu(z) = \alpha$, with $\alpha = CC(\mu(y),$ /tiːn/).
- For all $z \in A_Y$, i.e. $z = S(x,y)$, with $x,y \in A_D$: $\mu(z) = \alpha$, with $\alpha = CC(C1(\mu(x)),\mu(y))$.
- For all $z \in A_H$, i.e. $z = S(x,y)$, with $x \in A_D, y \in A_Y$: $\mu(z) = \alpha$, with $\alpha = CC(C2(\mu(x)), \mu(y))$.
- For all $z \in A_K$, i.e. $z = S(x,y)$, with $x \in A_D \cup A_Y \cup A_H, y \in A_H$: $\mu(z) = \alpha$, with $\alpha = CC(C3(\mu(x)), \mu(y))$.
- For all $z \in A_M$, i.e. $z = S(x,y)$, where $y = S(v,w)$ and $x \in A, v \in A_H, w \in A_H$: $\mu(z) = \alpha$, with $\alpha = CC(C4(\mu(x)), \mu(y))$.

Mapping from C to A

Again, the mapping between the primitive elements 1 to 9 and /wʌn/ to /naɪn/ as well as between 10 to 12 and the opaque elements /ten/ to /twelv/ is defined by enumeration.

For all $\alpha \in C_O \cup C_{To}$:

- $\mu(\alpha) = 1$ iff $\alpha = /w\Lambda n/$;
- $\mu(\alpha) = 2$ iff $\alpha = /tu{:}/$;
- $\mu(\alpha) = 3$ iff $\alpha = /\theta ri{:}/$;
- $\mu(\alpha) = 4$ iff $\alpha = /fɔ{:}/$;
- $\mu(\alpha) = 5$ iff $\alpha = /fa{:}v/$;
- $\mu(\alpha) = 6$ iff $\alpha = /sɪ k s/$;
- $\mu(\alpha) = 7$ iff $\alpha = /sevn/$;
- $\mu(\alpha) = 8$ iff $\alpha = /eɪ t/$;
- $\mu(\alpha) = 9$ iff $\alpha = /naɪ n/$;
- $\mu(\alpha) = 10$ iff $\alpha = /ten/$;
- $\mu(\alpha) = 11$ iff $\alpha = /ɪ levn/$;
- $\mu(\alpha) = 12$ iff $\alpha = /twelv/$.

The mapping relates to the subclasses of **A** we defined above, for the link from **A** to **C**. The definition then makes use of the internal structure of elements of the respective classes, and accounts for the introduction of 0 as a marker of empty positions within complex numerals.

- For all α, where $\alpha \in C_{Ta}$, hence: $\alpha = CC(x, /ti{:}n/)$, where $x \in C_O{}^3$: $\mu(\alpha) = z$, where $z = ab$, with $a = 1$ and $b = \mu(x)$.
- For all α, where $\alpha \in C_Y$, hence: $\alpha = CC(C1(x),y)$, with $x \in C_O{}^2$ and $y \in C_O \cup \{\varnothing\}$: $\mu(\alpha) = z$, where $z = ab$, with $a = \mu(x)$ and $b =$
  - 0,   if $y = \varnothing$;
  - $\mu(y)$ otherwise.
- For all α, where $\alpha \in C_H$, hence: $\alpha = CC(C2(x),y)$, with $x \in C_O$ and $y \in C_O \cup C_T \cup C_Y \cup \{\varnothing\}$: $\mu(\alpha) = z$, where $z = ab$, with $a = \mu(x)$ and $b =$
  - 00,   if $y = \varnothing$;
  - $0\mu(y)$,   if $\mu(y) \in A_D$;
  - $\mu(y)$ otherwise.
- For all α, where $\alpha \in C_K$, hence: $\alpha = CC(C3(x),y)$, with $x \in C_O \cup C_T \cup C_Y \cup C_H$ and $y \in C_O \cup C_T \cup C_Y \cup C_H \cup \{\varnothing\}$: $\mu(\alpha) = z$, with $z = ab$, where $a = \mu(x)$ and $b =$
  - 000,   if $y = \varnothing$;
  - $00\mu(y)$,   if $\mu(y) \in A_D$;
  - $0\mu(y)$,   if $\mu(y) \in A_2$;
  - $\mu(y)$ otherwise.
- For all α, where $\alpha \in C_M$, hence: $\alpha = CC(C4(x),y)$, with $x \in C$ and $y \in C_O \cup C_T \cup C_Y \cup C_H \cup C_K \cup \{\varnothing\}$: $\mu(\alpha) = z$, where $z = ab$, with $a = \mu(x)$ and $b =$

- oooooo,   if $y = \varnothing$;
- oooooμ(y),   if $\mu(y) \in A_D$;
- ooooμ(y),   if $\mu(y) \in A_2$;
- oooμ(y),   if $\mu(y) \in A_3$;
- ooμ(y),   if $\mu(y) \in A_4$;
- oμ(y),   if $\mu(y) \in A_5$;
- μ(y)   otherwise.

Conceptualisation of number assignments

*A note on the definitions of the functions NQ, NR, and NL, which account
for our concepts of numerical quantity, numerical rank, and numerical label,
respectively:*
In what follows, I introduce an ontology for our conceptualisation of number contexts that is grounded in the representation of numerical tools. In order to keep things simple, I focus on counting sequences as our primary numerical tools. However, according to our criteria-based approach there are also other progressions that can serve as numerical tools. When we acquire these progressions, their representation is integrated into our concept of 'number sequence'.

The definitions are hence generalised in order to cover all sequences that are introduced as number sequences: instead of 'counting sequence' I use the general term 'numerical sequence' for any sequence that fulfils the number criteria and is conventionally used as a set of numerical tools (where the above-defined sequence C is one instance for such a sequence).

As shown in chapter 7 non-verbal numerals can also play this role. In this case, the final argument of NQ, NR, and NL, respectively (the argument identified as 'α' in the definitions) is not an element of a counting sequence C, but for instance an element of the sequence A of arabic numerals whose initial element in these mappings is then the element corresponding to 'one', namely '1'.

CARDINAL CONCEPTS: NUMERICAL QUANTITY AND MEASURE

The pre-numerical basis: early concepts of cardinality

Our grasp of cardinalities of small sets as reflected in subitising can be represented by an enumeration of non-identical objects falling under a concept F. In accordance with the itemising approach to numbers we analyse this with the help of numerically (or rather 'cardinally') definite quantifiers $\exists_1 x$, $\exists_2 x$, $\exists_3 x$; these quantifiers get the following definitions:

$$\exists_1 x \ (Fx) =_{df} \exists x \ (Fx \wedge \forall y(Fy \rightarrow y = x));$$

$$\exists_2 x \ (Fx) =_{df} \exists x \ \exists y \ (Fx \wedge Fy \wedge x \neq y \wedge \forall z(Fz \rightarrow (z = x \vee z = y)));$$

$$\exists_3 x \ (Fx) =_{df} \exists x \ \exists y \ \exists z \ (Fx \wedge Fy \wedge Fz \wedge x \neq y \wedge x \neq z \wedge y \neq z$$
$$\wedge \ \forall w \ (Fw \rightarrow (w = x \vee w = y \vee w = z))).$$

Concepts of numerical quantity: cardinality identified by numerical tools

These concepts are represented by a function NQ ('Numerical Quantity') that maps a set s onto its cardinality α: NQ(s,α) is true iff s has the same numerical quantity as the sequence of numerical tools up to α.

If:
- **N** is a numerical sequence, and $\alpha \in$ **N**;
- s is a set;
- $\mathbf{N}^\alpha$ is the smallest subset of **N** which contains α and all predecessors of α ($\mathbf{N}^\alpha \subset \mathbf{N}$, and for all $x \in \mathbf{N}$: $x \in \mathbf{N}^\alpha$ iff $x \leq \alpha$);

then **NQ(s,α)** is true iff there is a one-to-one mapping f from the elements of s onto those of $\mathbf{N}^\alpha$.

Integration of pre-numerical itemising concepts:
   For all $n \in \{1,2,3\}$ and $m \in \{$/wʌn/, /tuː/, /θriː/$\}$, respectively:

$$\exists_n x(F(x)) \Leftrightarrow \exists s(NQ(s,m) \wedge \forall x((x \in s) \rightarrow F(x)))$$

This definition relates pre-numerical concepts, as defined via numerically definite quantifiers, to the first three numerical quantities as defined via NQ. Take for instance a set of pens with two elements (in the definition, the predicate 'pen' then stands in the place of 'F'). This set can be identified via subitising, namely as a set consisting of a pen x and another pen y, and based on the definitions above we can account for this as '$\exists_2 x(PEN(x))$'. Alternatively, the same set can be defined via a cardinal number assignment, namely as a set of pens with the numerical quantity /tuː/ (using the English counting word 'two' as an example of an element of a number sequence). Based on the definition of NQ, we can account for this as: $\exists s(NQ(s, $ /tuː/$) \wedge \forall x((x \in s) \rightarrow PEN(x)))$. The definition above now brings together these two ways to identify the cardinality of our set.

Concepts of individualised numbers

- Generation of individualised numbers by abstraction from concrete cardinalities:
For all $\alpha \in$ N: $\{s \mid NQ(s, \alpha)\}$ is an individualised number.
[Individualised numbers are defined as sets of sets with a certain numerical quantity. For instance, according to this definition we can identifiy as an individualised number (namely, as the individualised number *2*) the set of all sets *s* such that the numerical quantity of *s* is /tuː/.]
- Integration of *0* as an individualised number smaller *1*:
$0 = \{s \mid \neg\exists x \, (x \in s)\}$; $0 < 1$.
[In this definition, italicised numerals stand for individualised numbers. *0* is defined as the set of all sets *s* such there is no entity *x* that is an element of *s*, that is, *0* is defined as the set of all sets with no elements. The definition integrates *0* into the number line, but grants it a special status in comparison to the individualised numbers from *1*, since the definition of *0* as an abstract cardinality is not based on numerical tools.]
- Individualised numbers as arguments of NQ:
For all individualised numbers γ: $NQ(s,\gamma)$ is true iff $s \in \gamma$.

Concepts of direct and indirect measures

If:
- *a* is an object;
- *P* is a property of *a*;
then
- **M$_d$** is a **direct measure function** for *a* with respect to *P* iff
- M$_d$ maps *a* onto a set *m* of measure items with the relevant property *P*, such that
- $P(m) = P(a)$.
- **M$_i$** is an **indirect measure function** for *a* with respect to *P* iff
- M$_i$ maps *a* onto a set *m* of measure items with a relevant property *Q*, such that
- there is an object *o*, such that $Q(o) = Q(m)$, and
- $Q(o)$ is positively covarying with $P(o)$, and
- $P(o) = P(a)$.

ORDINAL CONCEPTS: NUMERICAL RANK

The pre-numerical basis: early concepts of ordinality

Our grasp of initial ordinal positions can be represented by an enumeration of objects falling under a concept F, which are ranked within a progression. We analyse this with ordinally definite quantifiers $\exists_{1st}x$, $\exists_{2nd}x$, $\exists_{3rd}x$. These quantifiers get the following definitions, where p_R is a progression ordered by a relation R:

$$\exists_{1st}x \in p_R(Fx) \;=\;_{df} \exists x \in p_R \,(Fx \wedge \neg \exists y \in p_R \,(Fy \wedge yRx));$$

$$\exists_{2nd}x \in p_R(Fx) \;=\;_{df} \exists x \in p_R \,\exists_{1st}y \in p_R \,(Fx \wedge Fy \wedge yRx$$
$$\wedge \neg \exists z \in p_R \,(Fz \wedge zRx \wedge yRz));$$

$$\exists_{3rd}x \in p_R(Fx) \;=\;_{df} \exists x \in p_R \,\exists_{2nd}y \in p_R \,(Fx \wedge Fy \wedge yRx$$
$$\wedge \neg \exists z \in p_R \,(Fz \wedge zRx \wedge yRz)).$$

These definitions render the element in the initial position ('the first F', as formalised by '$\exists_{1st}x \in p_R(Fx)$') as an element x of the progression p such that no element of p comes before x. The next element ('the second F', as formalised by '$\exists_{2nd} x \in p_R(Fx)$') is an element x that comes after the initial element such that no element of p is in-between these two; analogously the element in the following position ('the third F', as formalised by '$\exists_{3rd} x \in p_R(Fx)$') comes directly after the second element such that no element of p is in-between these two.

Concepts of numerical rank: ordinality identified by numerical tools

These concepts are represented by a function NR ('Numerical Rank') that maps an element a of a progression p onto its rank α in p: NR(a,p,α) is true iff the rank of a in p is the same as the rank of α in a sequence of numerical tools N with respect to the ordering of N by $<$.
If:
- N is a numerical sequence, and $\alpha \in$ N;
- p is a progression ordered by a relation R, and $a \in p$;

then **NR(a,p,α)** is true iff
- N^α is the smallest subset of N which contains α and all predecessors of α, and
- there is a one-to-one mapping f from p onto N^α such that: R(x,y) iff $f(x) < f(y)$ for all x,y $\in p$, and $f(a) = \alpha$.

NOMINAL CONCEPTS: NUMERICAL LABEL

These concepts are represented by a function NL ('Numerical Label') that maps an element *a* of a set *s* onto its label α: NL(a,s,α) is true iff α identifies *a* in *s* (α is the label for *a* with respect to *s*).
If:
• N is a numerical sequence, and α ∈ N;
• *s* is a set, and *a* ∈ *s*;
then **NL(a,s,α)** is true iff there is an injective function *f* from *s* to N, and $f(a) = \alpha$.

Semantic representations for number word constructions

CARDINAL, ORDINAL, AND '#'-CONSTRUCTIONS

Cardinal, ordinal, and '#'-constructions express concepts of cardinality, numerical rank, and numerical label. Cardinal *measure* constructions (as opposed to cardinal counting constructions) include concepts of measure functions as part of their meaning. The different numerical concepts are integrated in the semantic representation of complex number word constructions. In the following representations, *a* is an empirical object (in the case of cardinal constructions the empirical object *a* is a set), *p* is a progression, *s* is a set, and /θriː/ is an element of the English counting sequence **C** (that is, /θriː/ is an element of a set of numerical tools).

Semantic representations for the different classes of number word constructions

- Cardinal counting construction: *three pens*: εa[PEN⊕(a) ∧ **NQ**(a, /θriː/)]
- Cardinal measure construction: *a pumpkin of 3 kg*:
  εa[PUMPKIN¹(a) ∧ **NQ**(KG(a), /θriː/)]
- Ordinal construction: *the third player*:
  ιa ∃p[PLAYER¹(a) ∧ **NR**(a, p, /θriː/)]
- '#'-construction (ordinal): *player #3*:
  ιa ∃p[PLAYER¹(a) ∧ **NR**(a, p, /θriː/)]
- '#'-construction (nominal): *player #3*:
  ιa ∃s[PLAYER¹(a) ∧ **NL**(a, s, /θriː/)]

Explanations of the elements used in the formulae

ε: The 'ε'-operator is used to model nominal terms: F(εx(G(x))) =df. ∃x(G(x) ∧ F(x)).

ι: The 'ι'-operator is used to model definite terms: 'ιx(F(a))' stands for the most salient F, that is, the most salient realisation of a concept F.

$\mathbf{F^I}$: 'ϵa(F^I(a))' stands for 'one F', that is, F^I(a) is true iff a is a singleton of realisations of F; a singleton of realisations of F is defined as a set of Fs with the numerical quantity 'one';

hence, employing our definition of NQ and of English words as an instance of numerical tools, we can state that F^I(a) is true iff NQ(a, /wʌn/) is true.

$\mathbf{F^{\oplus}}$: $F^{\oplus}$(a) is true iff a is a non-singleton of F-realisations.

(cf. Wiese 1997b for a detailed discussion of semantic representations for singular and plural nominals)

CONCEPTUAL PARALLELS WITH NON-NUMERICAL
CONSTRUCTIONS

Cardinals and natural language quantifiers: assignment of a quantity

The constitutive function in the representation of quantifiers works in a similar way as the function NQ in the representation of cardinal number words. I identify this function for quantifiers as QUANT. This function QUANT assigns a quantity to an empirical object, just as NQ assigns a numerical quantity to an empirical object (namely, a set). In the case of 'many' or 'few', QUANT assigns set sizes above a norm value or below a norm value, respectively.

• **QUANT(a, v $\pm$ c)** maps an object a onto its quantity $v \pm c$, where v identifies the norm value, and c is a degree by which a deviates from v [cf. Bierwisch 1987 for a discussion of v and c];

in the semantic representation of 'many' and 'few', a is a set, and v ranges over set sizes; $v \pm c$ is specified for 'many' as: QUANT(a, v $+$ c); for 'few' as: QUANT(a, v $-$ c).

Ordinals and superlatives: assignment of a rank within a progression

The constitutive function in the representation of superlatives works in a similar way as the function NR in the representation of ordinal number words. I identify this function for superlatives as SUP. This function SUP assigns a rank to a particular element of a progression, just as NR assigns numerical ranks to elements of a progression. In particular, SUP assigns the extreme value ('XT') to the highest element of a progression. For instance, in the case of 'biggest', SUP assigns the extreme value to the biggest element of the progression, that is, to that object a for which there is no other element in the progression that is bigger than a. Hence, SUP picks out always the same element in a progression, and assigns it the same value 'xt', whereas NR can pick out any element within a given progression, and assigns different values (namely different counting words, or elements of other numerical sequences) to elements with different ranks.

- **SUP(a,p,xt)** maps an element *a* of a progression *p* onto the extreme value xt; *p* is ordered by a relation R (R is identified by the adjectival stem, for example R = BIG for a superlative 'biggest'):
  If *p* is a progression that is ordered by a relation R, and $a \in p$, then **SUP(a,p,xt)** **is true iff** $\neg \exists x ((x \in p) \wedge R(x,a))$.

'#'-constructions and proper names: assignment of an identificational label within a set

The constitutive function in the representation of proper names works in a similar way as the function NL in the representation of nominal '#'-constructions. I identify this function for proper names as NOM. This function NOM assigns identificational labels to elements of a set, just as NL assigns numerical identificational labels to elements of a set. The labels that NOM assigns can for instance be phonologically represented entities (for example when naming people, these entities could be labels like /tʃɑːls/, /mɪk/, or /kærən/, for the proper names 'Charles', 'Mick', and 'Karen', respectively). Since NL assigns phonologically represented labels, too – for instance, elements of the English counting sequence – NOM can be seen as a generalisation of NL.

- **NOM(a, s, *l*)** maps an element *a* of a set *s* onto a (phonologically or graphemically represented) label *l*:
  If
  - L is a set of labels (for example phonologically represented entities), and $l \in L$;
  - *s* is a set, and $a \in s$,
  - then **Nom(a, s, *l*)** is true iff there is an injective function *f* from *s* onto L, and $f(a) = l$.

References

Abney, Steven. 1987. *The English Noun Phrase in its Sentential Aspect*. Ph.D. thesis, MIT (Cambridge, MA: MIT Working Papers in Linguistics).

Absolon, Karel. 1928. Über die große Aurignac-Station bei Unter-Wisternitz in Mähren, *Tagungsberichte der deutschen Anthropologischen Gesellschaft*; Bericht über die 49. Versammlung in Köln. Leipzig. pp. 57–61.

1938. *Die Erforschung der diluvialen Mammutjäger-Station von Unter-Wisternitz in den Pollauer Bergen in Mähren*. Studien aus dem Gebiete der allgemeinen Karstforschung, wissenschaftlicher Höhlenkunde und den Nachbargebieten (Brno: Barvic & Novotným).

1957. Dokumente und Beweise der Fähigkeiten des fossilen Menschen zu zählen im mährischen Paläolithikum, *Artibus Asiae* (Institute of Fine Arts, New York University) 20(2/3): 123–50.

Alibali, Martha Wagner and DiRusso, Alyssa A. 1999. The function of gesture in learning to count: more than keeping track, *Cognitive Development* 14(1): 37–56.

Antell, Sue Ellen and Keating, Daniel P. 1983. Perception of numerical invariance in neonates, *Child Development* 54: 695–701.

Arimura, Gen-Ichiro and Takabayashi, Junji. 2001. Do plants communicate with each other via airborne signals? *AgBiotechNet* 3.

Arimura, Gen-Ichiro, Ozawa, Rika, Shimoda, Takeshi, Nishioka, Takaaki, Boland, Wilhelm, and Takabayashi, Junji 2000. Herbivory-induced volatiles elicit defence genes in lima bean leaves, *Nature* 406: 512–15.

Arnold, Jenniger E., Wasow, Thomas, Losongco, Anthony, and Ginstrom, Ryan. 2000. Heaviness vs. newness: the effects of structural complexity and discourse status on constituent ordering, *Language* 76(1): 28–55.

Baddeley, Alan D. 1998. *Human Memory: Theory and Practice*, revised edition (Hove: Psychology Press).

Baroody, Arthur J. 1993. The relationship between the order-irrelevance principle and counting skill, *Journal for Research in Mathematics Education* 24(5): 415–27.

Barrett, Jeffrey Edward. 1998. Representing, connecting and restructuring knowledge: the growth of children's understanding of length in two-dimensional space. Ph.D. thesis, University of Michigan, Ann Arbor.

Becker, Joseph. 1989. Preschoolers' use of number words to denote one-to-one correspondence, *Child Development* 60(5): 1147–57.

Beilin, H. 1975. *Studies in the Cognitive Basis of Language Development* (New York: Academic Press).

Benacerraf, Paul. 1965. What numbers could not be, *Philosophical Review* 74(1): 47–73.

Beran, Michael J., Rumbaugh, Duane M., and Savage-Rumbaugh, Sue. 1998. Chimpanzee (*Pan troglodytes*) counting in a computerized testing paradigm, *Psychological Record* 48(1): 3–19.

Berch, Daniel B., Foley, Elizabeth J., Hill, Rebecca J., and Ryan, Patricia Mc-Donough. 1999. Extracting parity and magnitude from Arabic numerals: developmental changes in number processing and mental representation, *Journal of Experimental Child Psychology* 74(4): 286–308.

Berlin, Brent and Kay, Paul. 1969. *Basic Color Terms: Their Universality and Evolution* (Berkeley: University of California Press).

Bialystok, Ellen. 1992. Symbolic representation of letters and numbers, *Cognitive Development* 7(3): 301–16.

Bickerton, Derek. 1990. *Language and Species* (University of Chicago Press).

Bideaud, Jacqueline, Meljac, Claire, and Fischer, Jean-Paul (eds.) 1992. *Pathways to Number: Children's Developing Numerical Abilities* (Hillsdale, NJ: Erlbaum).

Bierwisch, Manfred. 1987. The semantics of gradation, in: M. Bierwisch and E. Lang (eds.), *Dimensional Adjectives: Grammatical Structure and Conceptual Interpretation* (Berlin, New York: Springer), pp. 71–261. [German original: Semantik der Graduierung, in: M. Bierwisch and E. Lang (eds.) 1987. *Grammatische und konzeptuelle Aspekte von Dimensionsadjektiven* (Berlin: Akademie-Verlag), pp. 91–283.]

Bijeljac-Babic, Ranka, Bertoncini, Josiane, and Mehler, Jacques. 1993. How do fourday-old infants categorize multisyllabic utterances? *Developmental Psychology* 29(4): 711–21.

Biro, Dora and Matsuzawa, Tetsuro. 1999. Numerical ordering in a chimpanzee (*Pan troglodytes*): planning, executing, and monitoring, *Journal of Comparative Psychology* 113(2): 178–185.

Blanken, Gerhard, Dorn, M., and Sinn, H. 1997. Inversion errors in Arabic number reading: is there a nonsemantic route? *Brain and Cognition* 34(3): 404–23.

Bloom, Paul. 1994a. Generativity within language and other cognitive domains, *Cognition* 51: 177–89.

1994b. Syntax-semantics mappings as an explanation for some transitions in language development, in: Y. Levy (ed.), *Other Children, Other Languages: Theoretical Issues in Language Development* (Hillsdale, NJ: Erlbaum), pp. 41–75.

1994c. Possible names: the role of syntax-semantics mappings in the acquisition of nominals, *Lingua* 92: 297–329.

Bornstein, Marc H. 1985. Habituation of attention as a measure of visual information processing in human infants: summary, systematization, and synthesis, in: G. Gottlieb and N. Krasnegor (eds.), *Measurement of Audition and Vision in the First Year of Postnatal Life* (Norwood, NJ: Ablex), pp. 253–300.

Boulton-Lewis, G. M., Wilss, L. A., and Mutch, S. L. 1996. An analysis of young children's strategies for length measurement, *Journal of Mathematical Behavior* 15: 329–47.

Boysen, Sarah T. 1993. Counting in chimpanzees: nonhuman principles and emergent properties of number, in: S. T. Boysen and E. J. Capaldi (eds.), *The Development of Numerical Competence: Animal and Human Models. Comparative Cognition and Neuroscience* (Hillsdale, NJ: Erlbaum), pp. 39–59.

Boysen, Sarah T., Berntson, G. G., Shreyer, T. A., and Hannan, M. B. 1995. Indicating acts during counting by a chimpanzee (*pan troglodytes*), *Journal of Comparative Psychology* 109: 47–51.

Brannon, Elizabeth and Terrace, Herbert. 1998. Ordering of the numerosities 1 to 9 by monkeys, *Science* 282: 746–9.

Broadbent, Hilary A., Church, Russell M., Meck, Warren H., and Rakitin, B. 1993. Quantitative relationships between timing and counting, in: S. T. Boysen and E. J. Capaldi (eds.), *The Development of Numerical Competence: Animal and Human Models. Comparative Cognition and Neuroscience* (Hillsdale, NJ: Erlbaum), pp. 171–87.

Brown, Roger W. 1957. Linguistic determinism and the parts of speech, *Journal of Abnormal and Social Psychology* 55: 1–5.

Brown, Warner. 1915. Practice in associating number-names with number-symbols, *Psychological Review* 22: 77–80.

Bruyne, Jacques de. 1995. *A Comprehensive Spanish Grammar* (Oxford: Blackwell).

Brysbaert, Marc, Fias, Wim, and Noël, Marie-Pascale. 1998. The Whorfian hypothesis and numerical cognition: is "twenty-four" processed in the same way as "four-and-twenty"? *Cognition* 66(1): 51–77.

Buchner, Axel, Steffens, Melanie C., Irmen, Lisa, and Wender, Karl F. 1998. Irrelevant auditory material affects counting, *Journal of Experimental Psychology: Learning, Memory, and Cognition* 24(1): 48–67.

Buckley, P. B. and Gilman, C. B. 1974. Comparison of digits and dot patterns, *Journal of Experimental Psychology* 103: 1131–6.

Butterworth, Brian. 1999. *The Mathematical Brain* (London: Macmillan).

Campbell, Jamie I. D. 1992 (ed.). *The Nature and Origins of Mathematical Skills*, Stelmach, G. E. and Vroon, P. A. (eds.), Advances in Psychology 91 (North Holland: Amsterdam).

1999. The surface form * problem size interaction in cognitive arithmetic: evidence against an encoding locus, *Cognition* 70(2): B25–B33.

Campbell, Jamie I. D. and Clark, James M. 1988. An encoding complex view of cognitive number processing: comment on McCloskey, Sokol, and Goodman (1986), *Journal of Experimental Psychology* 117: 204–14.

1992. Cognitive number processing: an encoding-complex perspective, in: J. Campbell (ed.) (1992), pp. 457–91.

Carey, Susan. 1998. Knowledge of number: its evolution and ontogeny, *Science* 282(5389): 641–42.

2001. Cognitive foundations of arithmetic: evolution and ontogenesis, *Mind & Language* 16(1): 37–55.

Caycho, Liliana, Gunn, Patricia, and Siegal, Michael. 1991. Counting by children with Down syndrome, *American Journal on Mental Retardation* 95(5): 575–83.

Cheney, Dorothy L. and Seyfarth, Robert M. 1990. *How Monkeys See the World* (University of Chicago Press).

Chomsky, Noam. 1988. *Language and Problems of Knowledge. The Managua Lectures* (Cambridge, MA: MIT Press).

Cipolotti, Lisa. 1995. Multiple routes for reading words, why not numbers? Evidence from a case of arabic numeral dyslexia, *Cognitive Neuropsychology* 12: 313–42.

Cipolotti, Lisa, Butterworth, Brian, and Warrington, Elizabeth K. 1994. From "one thousand nine hundred and forty-five" to 1000,945, *Neuropsychologia* 32(4): 503–9.

Clark, James M. and Campbell, Jamie I. D. 1991. Integrated versus modular theories of number skills and acalculia, *Brain and Cognition* 17: 204–39.

Clements, Douglas H., Battista, Michael T., Sarama, Julie, Swaminathan, Sudha, and McMillen, Sue. 1997. Students' development of length concepts in a logo-based unit on geometric paths, *Journal for Research in Mathematics Education* 28(1): 70–95.

Cohen, Laurent and Dehaene, Stanislas. 1991. Neglect dyslexia for numbers? A case report, *Cognitive Neuropsychology* 8(1): 39–58.

Conant, Levi Leonard. 1896. *The Number Concept, Its Origin and Development*.

Corbett, Greville G. 1978. Universals in the syntax of cardinal numbers, *Lingua* 46: 61–74.

Coyle, Meaghan, Aird, Mark, Cobbin, D. M., and Zaslawski, C. 2000. The *cun* measurement system: an investigation into its suitability in current practice, *Acupuncture in Medicine* 18(1): 10–14.

Davis, Hank. 1984. Discrimination of the number three by a raccoon (Procyon lotor), *Animal Learning and Behavior* 12(4): 409–413.

1993. Numerical competence in animals: life beyond Clever Hans, in: S. T. Boysen and E. J. Capaldi (eds.), *The Development of Numerical Competence: Animal and Human Models. Comparative Cognition and Neuroscience* (Hillsdale, NJ: Erlbaum), pp. 109–25.

Davis, Hank and Bradford, S. A. 1986. Counting behavior by rats in a simulated natural environment, *Ethology* 73: 265–80.

1991. Numerically restricted food intake in the rat in a free-feeding situation, *Animal Learning and Behavior* 19: 215–22.

Deacon, Terrence W. 1997. *The Symbolic Species. The Co-evolution of Language and the Brain* (New York: Norton & Co).

Dedekind, Richard. 1887. The nature and meaning of numbers, in: W. Ewald (1996), vol. 2, pp. 790–833. German original: *Was sind und was sollen die Zahlen?* (Braunschweig: Viehweg 1887).

Dehaene, Stanislas. 1992. Varieties of numerical abilities, *Cognition* 44: 1–42.

1995. Electrophysiological evidence for category-specific word processing in the normal human brain, *Neuroreport* 6(16): 2153–7.

1997. *The Number Sense: How the Mind Creates Mathematics* (Oxford University Press).

Dehaene, Stanislas and Cohen, Laurent. 1997. Cerebral pathways for calculation: double dissociation between rote verbal and quantitative knowledge of arithmetic, *Cortex* 33(2): 219–50.

Dehaene, Stanislas, Dupoux, Emmanuel, and Mehler, Jacques. 1990. Is numerical comparison digital? Analogical and symbolic effects in two-digit number comparison, *Journal of Experimental Psychology: Human Perception and Performance* 16(3): 626–41.

Dehaene, Stanislas, Bossini, Serge, and Giraux, Pascal. 1993. The mental representation of parity and number magnitude, *Journal of Experimental Psychology* 122(3): 371–96.

Dehaene, Stanislas, Dehaene-Lambertz, Ghislaine, and Cohen, Laurent. 1998. Abstract representations of numbers in the animal and human brain, *Trends in Neurosciences* 21(8): 355–61.

Dehaene, Stanislas, Spelke, Elizabeth, Pinel, Philippe, Stanescu, R., and Tsivkin, S. 1999. Sources of mathematical thinking: behavioral and brain-imaging evidence, *Science* 2: 970–4.

Delazer, Margarete and Denes, Gianfranco. 1998. Writing Arabic numerals in an agraphic patient. *Brain and Language* 64(2): 257–66.

Demiraj, Shaban. 1993. *Historische Grammatik der albanischen Sprache* (Wien: Verlag der österreichischen Wissenschaften).

Dennett, Daniel C. 1987. *The Intentional Stance* (Cambridge, MA: MIT / Bradford Books).

d'Errico, Francesco E., Henshilwood, Christopher S., and Nilssen, Peter. 2001. An engraved bone fragment from c. 70,000-year-old Middle Stone Age levels at Blombos Cave, South Africa: implications for the origin of symbolism and language. *Antiquity* 75(288): 309–18.

Dicke, Marcel and Bruin, Jan (eds.) 2001. *Biochemical Systematics and Ecology Reports on Plant-to-Plant Communication: back to the future*, special issue of *Biochemical Systematics and Ecology* (10).

Diehl, Randy L. and Kolodzey, Katherine F. 1981. Spaka: a private language, *Language* 57(2): 406–24.

Divale, William. 1999. Climatic instability, food storage, and the development of numerical counting: a cross-cultural study, *Cross-Cultural Research: The Journal of Comparative Social Science* 33(4): 341–68.

Dixon, Robert M. W. 1980. *The Languages of Australia* (Cambridge: Cambridge University Press).

Donlan, Chris. 1998a. Number without language? Studies of children with specific language impairments, in: C. Donlan (ed.) (1998b), pp. 255–74.

Donlan, Chris 1998b (ed.). *The Development of Mathematical Skills* (Hove: Psychology Press).

Donlan, Chris, Bishop, D. V. M., and Hitch, G. J. 1998. Magnitude comparisons by children with Specific Language Impairments: Evidence of unimpaired symbolic processing, *International Journal of Language and Communication Disorders* 33(2): 149–60.

Dunbar, Robin. 1996. *Grooming, Gossip, and the Evolution of Language* (Cambridge, MA: Harvard University Press).

Durkin, Kevin, Shire, Beatrice, Riem, Roland, Crowther, Robert D., and Ruttner, D. R. 1986. The social and linguistic context of early number word use, *British Journal of Developmental Psychology* 4(3): 269–88.

Eisenberg, Peter. 1985. Maß und Zahl. Zur syntaktischen Deutung einer ungefestigten Konstruktion im Deutschen, in: T. Ballmer and R. Posner (eds.), *Nach-Chomskysche Linguistik* (Berlin: de Gruyter), pp. 311–20.

Emmerling, E., Geer, H., and Klíma, Bohuslav, Ein Mondkalenderstab aus Dolni Vestonice, *Quartär* 43/44 (1993): 151–62.

Euclid, *Elements*, translated from the text of Heiberg, with introduction and commentary by Thomas L. Heath (Cambridge University Press, 1909).

Ewald, William. 1996. *From Kant to Hilbert: A Source Book in the Foundations of Mathematics*, 2 vols. (Oxford: Clarendon).

Ezawa, Barbara. 1996. *Zählen und Rechnen bei geistig behinderten Schülern* (Frankfurt am Main: Lang).

Fazio, Barbara B. 1994. The counting abilities of children with specific language impairment: a comparison of oral and gestural tasks, *Journal of Speech and Hearing Research* 37(2): 358–68.

Fechner, Gustav Theodor. 1858. Das psychische Maß, *Zeitschrift für Philosophie und philosophische Kritik* 33: 1–24.

Feldman, Laurie B. and Turvey, Michael T. 1980. Words written in kana are named faster than the same words written in kanji, *Language and Speech* 23: 141–7.

Ferrand, Ludovic. 1999. Why naming takes longer than reading? The special case of Arabic numbers, *Acta Psychologica* 100(3): 253–66.

Fischer, Florence E. and Beckey, Robert D. 1990. Beginning kindergartners' perception of number, *Perceptual and Motor Skills* 70(2): 419–25.

Fischer, Jean-Paul. 1992. Subitizing: the discontinuity after three, in: Bideaud et al. (eds.) (1992), pp. 191–208.

Flegg, Graham. 1983. *Numbers: Their History and Meaning* (London).

Fodor, Jerry A. 1983. *The Modularity of Mind. An Essay on Faculty Psychology* (Cambridge, MA: MIT Press).

Freeman, Norman H., Antonucci, Cristina, and Lewis, Charles. 2000. Representation of the cardinality principle: early conception of error in a counterfactual test, *Cognition* 74: 74–89.

Frege, Gottlob. 1884. *The Foundations of Arithmetic. A Logic-Mathematical Enquiry into the Concept of Number*, trans. by John L. Austin (Oxford: Blackwell, 1950). German original: *Die Grundlagen der Arithmetik. Eine logisch mathematische Untersuchung über den Begriff der Zahl* (Breslau: Wilhelm Koebner, 1884).

1893 and 1903. *The Basic Laws of Arithmetic*, trans. by Montgomery Furth (Berkeley: University of California Press, 1964). German original:

Grundgesetze der Arithmetik. Begriffsschriftlich abgeleitet, 2 vols. (Jena: Pohle, 1893 and 1903).

1902. Letter to Russell, in: J. van Heijenoort (ed.) (1967), pp. 127–8. German original in: Gabriel et al. (1976), pp. 212–15.

Frenck-Mestre, Cheryl and Vaid, Jyotsna. 1993. Activation of number facts in bilinguals, *Memory and Cognition* 21(6): 809–18.

Frisch, Karl von. 1927. *The Dancing Bees – An Account of the Life and Senses of the Honey Bee*, trans. by Dora Isle (New York: Brace, 1955). German original: *Aus dem Leben der Bienen* (Berlin: Springer, 1927).

1965. *The Dance Language and Orientation of Bees*, trans. by Leigh E. Chadwick (Cambridge, MA: Belknap Press of Harvard University Press, 1967). German original: *Tanzsprache und Orientierung der Bienen* (Berlin et al.: Springer, 1965).

Fuson, Karen C. 1988. *Children's Counting and Concepts of Numbers* (Berlin: Springer).

1992. Relationships between counting and cardinality from age 2 to age 8, in: Bideaud, Meljac, and Fischer (eds.) (1992), pp. 127–149.

Fuson, Karen C. and Hall, James W. 1983. The acquisition of early number word meanings: a conceptual analysis and review, in: H. P. Ginsburg (ed.), *The Development of Mathematical Thinking* (New York: Academic Press), pp. 49–107.

Fuson, Karen C. and Mierkiewicz, D. A. 1980. A detailed analysis of the act of counting. Unpublished paper, presented at the Annual Meeting of the American Educational Research Association, Boston, April 1980 (quoted after K. Fuson and J. W. Hall 1983).

Fuson, Karen C., Richards, John, and Briars, Diane J. 1982. The acquisition and elaboration of the number word sequence, in: C. J. Brainerd (ed.), *Children's Logical and Mathematical Cognition* (New York: Springer), pp. 33–92.

Gabriel, G., Hermes, H., Kambartel, F., Thiel, C., and Veraart, A. (eds.), 1976. *Gottlob Frege: Wissenschaftlicher Briefwechsel* (Hamburg: Meiner).

Gallistel, Charles R. 1990. *The Organization of Learning* (Cambridge, MA: MIT Press).

Gallistel, Charles R. and Gelman, Rochel. 1990. The what and how of counting, *Cognition* 34(2): 197–9.

Galton, Francis. 1880. Visualised numerals, *Nature* 21: 252–6 and 494–5.

1883. *Inquiries into Human Faculty and its Development* (London: Macmillan).

Gelman, Rochel. 1978. Counting in the preschooler: what does and does not develop, in: R. S. Siegler (ed.), *Children's Thinking: What Develops?* (Hillsdale, NJ: Erlbaum), pp. 213–41.

1990. First principles organize attention to and learning about relevant data: number and the animate–inanimate distinction as examples, *Cognitive Science* 14(1): 79–106.

Gelman, Rochel and Brenneman, Kimberley. 1994. First principles can support both universal and culture-specific learning about number and music, in: R. Gelman and L. A. Hirschfeld (eds.), *Mapping the Mind: Domain Specificity in Cognition and Culture* (Cambridge University Press), pp. 369–90.

Gelman, Rochel and Gallistel, Charles R. 1978. *The Child's Understanding of Number* (Cambridge, MA: Harvard University Press).

Gelman, Rochel and Meck, Elizabeth. 1992. Early principles aid initial but not later conceptions of number, in Bideaud, Meljac, and Fischer (eds.) (1992), pp. 171–89.

Gelman, Rochel, Meck, Elizabeth and Merkin, Susan. 1986. Young children's numerical competence, *Cognitive Development* 1(1): 1–29.

Giusti, Giuliana. 1991. The categorial status of quantified nominals, *Linguistische Berichte* 136: 438–54.

Glinert, Lewis. 1989. *The Grammar of Modern Hebrew* (Cambridge University Press).

Gödel, Kurt. 1931. On formally undecidable propositions in Principia Mathematica and related systems, in: J. van Heijenoort (ed.) (1967), pp. 596–616. German original: Über formal unentscheidbare Sätze der Principia Mathematica und verwandter Systeme, *Monatshefte für Mathematik und Physik* 38 (1931), 173–98.

Graham, Theresa A. 1999. The role of gesture in children's learning to count, *Journal of Experimental Child Psychology* 74(4): 333–55.

Greenberg, Joseph H. 1963. Some universals of grammar with particular reference to the order of meaningful elements, in: J. H. Greenberg (ed.), *Universals of Language. Report of a Conference Held at Dobbs Ferry, New York, April 13–15, 1961* (Cambridge, MA: MIT Press), pp. 73–113. 1966. *Language Universals* (The Hague: Mouton).

Grodzinsky, Yosef, Piñango, Maria Mercedes, Zurif, Edgar, and Drai, Dan. 1999. The critical role of group studies in neuropsychology: comprehension regularities in Broca's aphasia. *Brain and Language* 76: 134–47.

Hamilton, J. M. E. and Sanford, A. J. 1978. The symbolic distance effect for alphabetic order judgement: A subjective report and reaction time analysis, *Quarterly Journal of Experimental Psychology* 30: 33–43.

Hartnett, Patrice and Gelman, Rochel. 1998. Early understandings of numbers: paths or barriers to the construction of new understandings? *Learning and Instruction* 8(4): 341–74.

Hauser, Marc D., MacNeilage, Pogen, and Ware, Molly. 1996. Numerical representations in primates, *Proceedings of the National Academy of Sciences* 93(4): 1514–17.

Heijenoort, Jean van 1967 (ed.). *From Frege to Gödel. A Source Book in Mathematical Logic* (Cambridge, MA: Harvard University Press).

Hellemans, Alexander and Bunch, Bryan. 1988. *The Timetable of Science* (New York: Simon Schuster).

Helmholtz, Hermann von. 1887. An epistemological analysis of counting and measurement, in: R. Kahl (ed.), *Selected Writings of Hermann von Helmholtz* (Middletown, CT: Wesleyan University Press, 1971), pp. 437–65. [German original: Zählen und Messen, erkenntnistheoretisch betrachtet, in: F. Krischer (ed.), *Philosophische Aufsätze. Eduard Zeller zu seinem fünfzigjährigen Doctorjubiläum gewidmet* (Leipzig: Fues, 1887), pp. 17–52.]

Henshilwood, Christopher S., Sealy, J. S., and Yates, R., et al. 2001. Blombos Cave, Southern Cape, South Africa: preliminary report on the 1992–1999 excavations of the Middle Stone Age levels, *Journal of Archaeological Science* 28: 421–48.

Hilbert, David. 1922. The new grounding of mathematics, in: W. Ewald (1996), vol. 2, pp. 1117–34. [German original: Neubegründung der Mathematik, *Abhandlungen aus dem Mathematischen Seminar der Hamburger Universität* 1 (1922): 157–77.]

Hilbert, David and Bernays, Paul. 1928. *Die Grundlagen der Mathematik* (Leipzig: Teubner).

Hitch, Graham, Cundick, Jill, Haughey, Maeve, Pugh, Rachel, and Wright, Hilary. 1987. Aspects of counting in children's arithmetic, in: J. A. Sloboda and D. Rogers (eds.), *Cognitive Processes in Mathematics*, Keele Cognition Seminars 1 (Oxford: Clarendon), pp. 26–41.

Ho, Connie Suk Han and Fuson, Karen C. 1998. Children's knowledge of teen quantities as tens and ones: comparisons of Chinese, British, and American kindergartners, *Journal of Educational Psychology* 90(3): 536–44.

Hölder, O. 1901. Die Axiome der Quantität und die Lehre vom Mass, *Berichte über die Verhandlungen der Königlich Sächsischen Gesellschaft der Wissenschaften zu Leipzig, Mathematisch-Physische Klasse* 53: 1–64.

Holton, David, Mackridge, Peter, and Philippaki-Warburton, Irene. 1997. *Greek: A Comprehensive Grammar of the Modern Language* (London: Routledge).

Hughes, Martin. 1984. Learning about number, *ESRC Newsletter* 52: 9–11.

Humboldt, Wilhelm von. 1836. *Linguistic Variability and Intellectual Development*, trans. by George C. Buck and Frithjof A. Raven (Coral Gables, Florida: University of Miami Press, 1971). German original: *Über die Verschiedenheit des menschlichen Sprachbaus und ihren Einfluss auf die geistige Entwicklung des Menschengeschlechts*, edited by Eduard Buschmann (Berlin: Königliche Akadamie der Wissenschaften, 1836).

Hurford, James R. 1975. *The Linguistic Theory of Numerals* (Cambridge University Press).

1987. *Language and Number: The Emergence of a Cognitive System* (Oxford: Blackwell).

Ifrah, Georges. 1985. *Les chiffres, ou l'histoire d'une grande invention* (Paris: Robert Laffont).

Jackendoff, Ray S. 1997. *The Architecture of the Language Faculty* (Cambridge, MA: MIT Press).

1999. Possible stages in the evolution of the language capacity, Trends in the Cognitive Sciences 3(7): 272–279.

2002. *Foundations of Language: Brain, Meaning, Grammar, Evolution* (Oxford University Press).

Jing, Lü. 1984. A study of development of number notion in young children (English abstract), *Xinli-kexue-tongxun / Information on Psychological Sciences* 3: 1–7, 64.

Johnson, D. M. 1939. Confidence and speed in the two-category judgment, *Archives of Psychology* 241: 1–52.

Kahneman, Daniel and Treisman, Anne. 1984. Changing views of attention and automaticity, in: R. Parasuraman and D. A. Davies (eds.), *Varieties of Attention* (New York: Academic Press), pp. 29–61.

Kahneman, Daniel, Treisman, Anne, and Gibbs, Brian J. 1992. The reviewing of object files: object-specific integration of information, *Cognitive Psychology* 24: 175–219.

Kanizsa, Gaetano. 1955. Margini quasi-percettivi in campi con stimolazione omagenea, *Rivista di Psicologia* 49: 7–30.

Karmiloff-Smith, Annette. 1998. Development itself is the key to understanding developmental disorders, *Trends in the Cognitive Sciences* 2(10): 389–98.

Kaufman, E. L., Lord, M. W., Reese, T. W., and Vokman, J. 1949. The discrimination of visual number, *American Journal for Psychology* 62: 498–525.

Kawai, Nobuyuki and Matsuzawa, Tetsuro. 2000. Numerical memory span in a chimpanzee, *Nature* 403(6765): 39–40.

Keightley, David N. 1995. A measure of man in early China: in search of the neolithic inch, *Chinese Science* 12: 18–40.

Kess, Jospeh F. and Miyamoto, Tadao. 1999. *The Japanese Mental Lexicon: Psycholinguistic Studies of Kana and Kanji Processing*. (Amsterdam: John Benjamins).

Klíma, Bohuslav. 1995. *Dolní Věstonice II: ein Mammutjägerrastplatz und seine Bestattungen* (Liège: Université de Liège, Service de Préhistoire).

Koechlin, Etienne, Dehaene, Stanislas, and Mehler, Jacques. 1997. Numerical transformations in five-month-old human infants, *Mathematical Cognition* 3: 89–104.

Koechlin, Etienne, Naccache, Lionel, Block, Eliza, and Dehaene, Stanislas. 1999. Primed numbers: exploring the modularity of numerical representations with masked and unmasked semantic priming, *Journal of Experimental Psychology: Human Perception and Performance* 25(6): 1882–905.

Koehler, Otto. 1941. Vom Erlernen unbenannter Anzahlen bei Vögeln, *Naturwissenschaft* 29: 201–18.

1943. "Zähl"-Versuche an einem Kolkraben und Vergleichsversuche am Menschen, *Zeitschrift für Tierpsychologie* 5: 575–721.

1950. The ability of birds to "count", *Bulletin of Animal Behavior* 9: 41–45.

Koffka, Kurt. 1935. *Principles of Gestalt Psychology* (New York: Harcourt & Brace).

Kopera-Frye, Karen, Dehaene, Stanislas, and Streissguth, Ann P. 1996. Impairments of number processing induced by prenatal alcohol exposure, *Neuropsychologia* 34(12): 1187–96.

Krantz, David H., Luce, R. Duncan, Suppes, Patrick, and Tversky, Amos. 1971. *Foundations of Measurement*, 3 vols. (New York: Academic Press).

Lang, Ewald. 1987. The semantics of dimensional designation of spatial objects, in: M. Bierwisch and E. Lang (eds.), *Dimensional Adjectives: Grammatical Structure and Conceptual Interpretation* (Berlin, New York: Springer, 1989), pp. 263–417. [German original: Semantik der Dimensionsauszeichnung räumlicher Objekte, in: M. Bierwisch and E. Lang (eds.), *Grammatische und konzeptuelle Aspekte von Dimensionsadjektiven* (Berlin: Akademie-Verlag, 1987), pp. 287–458.]

Le Clec'H, G., Dehaene, Stanislas, and Cohen, Laurent, et al. 2000. Distinct cortical areas for names of numbers and body parts independent of language and input modality, *NeuroImage* 12: 381–91.

Leibniz, Gottfried Wilhelm. 1703/05. On number, in: *New Essays on Human Understanding*, trans. and ed. P. Remnant and J. Bennett (Cambridge University Press, 1981), Book II, ch. XVI. French original: Du Nombre, in: *Nouveaux essais sur l'entendement humaine*, ed. the Leibniz-Forschungsstelle der Universität Münster. Gottfried Wilhelm Leibniz. Philosophische Schriften, vol. 6 (Berlin: Akademie-Verlag, 1962).

Lieberman, Philip. 1984. *The Biology and Evolution of Language* (Cambridge, MA: Harvard University Press).

Locke, John. 1690. Of number, in: *Essay Concerning Human Understanding* (Oxford: Clarendon Press, 1975), Book II, Ch. XVI.

Logie, Robert H. and Baddeley, Alan D. 1987. Cognitive processes in counting, *Journal of Experimental Psychology, Learning, Memory and Cognition* 13(2): 310–26.

Loosbroek, E. van and Smitsman, A. 1990. Visual perception of numerosity in infancy, *Developmental Psychology* 26: 916–22.

Lovelace, Eugene A. and Snodgrass, Robert D. 1971. Decision times for alphabetic order of letter pairs, *Journal of Experimental Psychology* 88(2): 258–64.

Lyon, Bruce E. 2003. Egg recognition and counting reduce costs of avian conspecific brood parasitism, *Nature* 422: 495–9.

Macaruso, Paul, McCloskey, Michael, and Aliminosa, Donna. 1993. The functional architecture of the cognitive numerical-processing system: evidence from a patient with multiple impairments, *Cognitive Neuropsychology* 10(4): 341–76.

Macaruso, Paul and Sokol, Scott M. 1998. Cognitive neuropsychology and developmental dyscalcula, in: C. Donlan (ed.) (1998b), pp. 201–25.

Mach, Ernst. 1896. *Die Principien der Wärmelehre* (Leipzig: Barth).

Mandler, G. and Shebo, B. J. 1982. Subitizing: an analysis of its component processes, *Journal of Experimental Psychology: General* 111(1): 1–21.

Markman, Ellen M. 1989. *Categorization and Naming in Children* (Cambridge, MA: MIT Press).

Marshack, Alexander. 1964. Lunar notation on Upper Palaeolithic remains. *Science* 146(6): 743–5.

Marx, Melvin H. 1989. Elementary counting of cardinal and ordinal numbers by persons with mental retardation, *Perceptual and Motor Skills* 68(3/2), 1176–8.

Matsuzawa, Tetsuro. 1985. Use of numbers by a chimpanzee, *Nature* 315: 57–9.

Matthews, Stephen and Yip, Virginia. 1994. *Cantonese. A Comprehensive Grammar* (London: Routledge).

McCloskey, Michael. 1992. Cognitive mechanisms in numerical processing: evidence from acquired dyscalculia. *Cognition* 44: 107–57.

McCloskey, Michael and Caramazza, Alfonso. 1987. Cognitive mechanisms involved in normal and impaired number processing, in: G. Deloche and X. Seron (eds.), *Mathematical Disabilities: A Cognitive Neuropsychological Perspective* (Hillsdale, NJ: Erlbaum), pp. 210–19.

McCloskey, Michael, Caramazza, Alfonso, and Basili, Annamaria G. 1985. Cognitive mechanisms in number processing and calculation: evidence from dyscalculia, *Brain and Cognition* 4: 171–96.

McCloskey, Michael, Sokol, Scott M., and Goodman, Roberta Ann. 1986. Cognitive processes in verbal-number production: inferences from brain damaged subjects, *Journal of Experimental Psychology* 115: 307–30.

McCloskey, Michael, Sokol, Scott M., Caramazza, Alfonso, Goodman-Schulman, Roberta Ann. 1990. Cognitive representations and processes in number production: evidence from cases of acquired dyscalculia, in: A. Caramazza (ed.), *Cognitive Neuropsychology and Neurolinguistics: Advances in Models of Cognitive Function and Impairment* (Hove and London: Erlbaum), pp. 1–32.

McCloskey, Michael, Macaruso, Paul, and Whetstone, Tony. 1992. The functional architecture of numerical processing mechanisms: defending the modular model, in: J. Campbell (ed.) (1992), pp. 493–537.

McComb, Karen, Packer, C., and Pusey, A. 1994. Roaring and numerical assessment in contests between groups of female lions, *Panthera leo, Animal Behaviour* 47: 379–87.

McCormack, Teresa, Brown, Gordon D. A., Vouseden, Janet I., and Henson, Richard N. A. 2000. Children's serial recall errors: implications for theories of short-term memory development, *Journal of Experimental Child Psychology* 76: 222–52.

Meck, Warren H. and Church, Russell M. 1983. A mode control model of counting and timing processes, *Journal of Experimental Psychology: Animal Behavior Processes* 9: 320–34.

Menninger, Karl. 1958. *Number Words and Number Symbols: A Cultural History of Numbers*, trans. by Paul Broneer from the revised German edition (Cambridge, MA: MIT Press, 1969). German original: *Zahlwort und Ziffer. Eine Kulturgeschichte der Zahl*, 2 vols. (Göttingen: Vandenhoeck and Ruprecht, 1958, 2nd, extended and revised edition).

Miller, Kevin F. 1984. Child as the measurer of all things: measurement procedures and the development of quantitative concepts, in: C. S. Sophian (ed.), *Origins of Cognitive Skills* (Hillsdale, NJ: Erlbaum), pp. 193–228.

Miller, Kevin F. and Zhu, Jianjun. 1991. The trouble with teens: accessing the structure of number names, *Journal of Memory and Language* 30: 48–68.

Mitchell, Robert W., Yao, Pearl, Sherman, Peter T., and O'Reagan, Mary (1985). Discriminative responding of a dolphin (*Tursiops truncatus*) to differentially rewarded stimuli, *Journal of Comparative Psychology* 99(2): 218–25.

Miura, Irene T., Kim, Chungsoon C., Chang, Chih-Mei, and Okamoto, Yukari. 1988. Effects of language characteristics on children's cognitive representation of number: cross-national comparisons, *Child Development* 59: 1445–50.

Miura, Irene T. and Okamoto, Yukari. 1989. Comparisons of U.S. and Japanese first graders' cognitive representation of number and understanding place value, *Journal of Educational Psychology* 81(1): 109–13.

Miura, Irene T., Okamoto, Yukari, Kim, Chungsoon C., Steere, Marcia, and Fayol, Michel. 1993. First graders' cognitive representation of number and understanding of place value: cross-national comparisons: France, Japan, Korea, Sweden, and the United States, *Journal of Educational Psychology* 85(1): 24–30.

Mix, Kelly. 1999. Preschoolers' recognition of numerical equivalence: sequential sets, *Journal of Experimental Child Psychology* 74(4): 309–32.

Moyer Robert S. 1973. Comparing objects in memory: evidence suggesting an internal psychophysics, *Perception & Psychophysics* 13(2): 180–4.

Moyer, Robert S. and Landauer, Thomas K. 1967. Time required for judgements of numerical inequality, *Nature* 215: 1519–20.

Moyer, Robert S. and Bayer, Richard H. 1976. Mental comparison and the symbolic distance effect, *Cognitive Psychology* 8: 228–46.

Munn, Penny. 1998. Symbolic function in pre-schoolers, in: C. Donlan (ed.) (1998b), pp. 47–71.

Murdock, Bennet B. 1962. The serial position effect in free recall, *Journal of Experimental Psychology* 64: 462–88.

Narens, Louis. 1985. *Abstract Measurement Theory* (Cambridge, MA: MIT Press).

Neath, Ian. 1993. Distinctiveness and serial position effects in recognition, *Memory and Cognition* 21: 183–95.

Nesher, Pearla and Katriel, Tamar. 1986. Learning numbers: a linguistic perspective, *Journal for Research in Mathematics Education* 17(2): 100–11.

Newmark, Leonard, Hubbard, Philip, and Prifti, Peter. 1981. *Standard Albanian. A Reference Grammar for Students* (Stanford University Press).

Nunes, T., Light, P., and Mason, J. 1993. Tools for thought: the measurement of length and area, *Learning and Instruction* 3: 39–54.

Orlov, Tanya, Yakovlev, Volodya, Hochstein, Shaul, and Zohary, Ehud. 2000. Macaque monkeys categorize images by their ordinal number, *Nature* 404(6773): 77–80.

Pastore, Nicholas. 1961. Number sense and 'counting' ability in the canary, *Zeitschrift für Tierpsychologie* 18: 561–73.

Peirce, Charles Sanders. 1931. *Collected Papers*, ed. by C. Hartshorne and P. Weiss. Vol. 1–2 (Cambridge, MA: Harvard University Press).

Pepperberg, Irene M. 1987. Evidence for conceptual quantitative abilities in the African grey parrot: labeling of cardinal sets, *Ethology* 75: 317–61.

1999. *The Alex Studies* (Cambridge, MA: Harvard University Press).

Petitot, Emile Fortune S. 1876. *Dictionnaire de la langue Dènè-Dindjié, dialectes Montagnais ou Chippeway an, peaux de Lièvre et Loucheux, Précédé d'une monographie des Dènè-Dindjié, d'une grammaire et de tableaux synoptiques des conjugaisons* (Paris: Bibliothèque de linguistique et d'ethnographie Américaine, vol. II).

Piaget, Jean. 1941. *The Child's Conception of Number* (Routledge & Kegan Paul: London, 1952). French original: La genèse du nombre chez l'enfant (Neuchâtel: Delachaux et Niestlé, 1941).

Pinker, Steven. 1994. *The Language Instinct* (New York: Morrow).

Polich, John M. and Potts, George R. 1977. Retrieval strategies for linearly ordered information, *Journal of Experimental Psychology: Human Learning and Memory* 3(1): 10–17.

Potts, George R. 1974. Storing and retrieving information about ordered relationships, *Journal of Experimental Psychology* 103: 431–9.

Power, R. J. D. and Dal Martello, M. F. 1990. The dictation of Italian numerals, *Language and Cognitive Processes* 5(3): 237–54.

Putnam, Hilary. 1975. The meaning of meaning, in: H. Putnam, *Mind, Language and Reality. Philosophical Papers* (Cambridge: Cambridge University Press), vol. II, pp. 215–71.

Quine, Willard Van Orman. 1960. *Word and Object* (Cambridge, MA: MIT Press).

1969. Ontological relativity, in: W. V. O. Quine, *Ontological Relativity and Other Essays* (New York: Columbia University Press), pp. 26–68.

1974. *The Roots of Reference* (La Salle, IL: Open Court Publishing Company), section 30 (pp. 115–20): Identity and number.

Radatz, Hendrik, Schipper, Wilhelm, Dröge, Rotraut, and Ebeling, Astrid. 1998. *Handbuch für den Mathematikunterricht, 2. Schuljahr* (Hannover: Schroedel).

Richter, D., Waiblinger J., Rink, W. J., and Wagner, G. A. 2000. Thermoluminescence, electron spin resonance and C-14-dating of the Late Middle and Early Upper Palaeolithic site of Geissenklosterle Cave in southern Germany. *Journal of Archaeological Science* 27(1): 71–89.

Rickmeyer, Knut. 2001. 'Die Zwölf liegt hinter der nächsten Kurve und die Sieben ist pinkrot': Zahlenraumbilder und bunte Zahlen, *Journal für Mathematik-Didaktik* 22(1): 51–71.

Roberts, Fred S. 1979. *Measurement Theory* (Reading: Addison-Wesley). Rota, Gian-Carlo (ed.), *Encyclopedia of Mathematics and its Application*, vol. VII.

Roberts, William A. and Mitchell, S. 1994. Can a pigeon simultaneously process temporal and numerical information? *Journal of Experimental Psychology: Animal Behavior Processes* 29: 66–78.

Rumbaugh, Duane M., Savage-Rumbaugh, Sue, and Hegel, Mark T. 1987. Summation in the chimpanzee (*Pan troglodytes*), *Journal of Experimental Psychology: Animal Behavior Processes* 13(2): 107–15.

Russell, Bertrand. 1902. Letter to Frege, in: J. van Heijenoort (ed.) (1967), pp. 124–5. German original in: Gabriel et al. (1976), pp. 211–12.

1903. *The Principles of Mathematics* (Cambridge University Press).

1905. On denoting, *Mind* 14: 479–93.

1908. Mathematical logic based on the theory of types, in: R. C. Marsh (ed.), *Bertrand Russell: Logic and Knowledge. Essays 1901–1950* (London: Allen & Unwin, 1956), pp. 59–102.

1918. The philosophy of logical atomism, in: J. G. Slater (ed.), *Bertrand Russell: The Philosophy of Logical Atomism and Other Essays. 1914–1919*, Collected Papers of Bertrand Russell 8 (London: George Allen & Unwin, 1983), pp. 157–244.

1962. Letter to Heijenoort, in: J. van Heijenoort (ed.) (1967), p. 127.

Russell, Bertrand and Whitehead, Alfred North. 1910–13. *Principia Mathematica*, 3 vols. (Cambridge University Press).

Sathian, Krish, Simon, Tony J., and Peterson, Scott et al. 1999. Neural evidence linking visual object enumeration and attention, *Journal of Cognitive Neuroscience* 11(1): 36–51.

Saussure, Ferdinand de. 1916. *Course in General Linguistics*, trans. Roy Harris, ed. C. Bally and A. Sechehaye (La Salle, IL: Open Court, 1986). [French original: *Cours de linguistique général* (Paris, 1916).]

Saxe, Geoffrey B. 1981. Body parts as numerals: a developmental analysis of numeration among the Oksapmin in Papua New Guinea, *Child Development* 52: 306–16.

—— 1982. Culture and the development of numerical cognition: studies among the Oksapmin of Papua New Guinea, in: C. J. Brainerd (ed.), *Children's Logical and Mathematical Cognition* (Berlin: Springer), pp. 157–76.

—— 2003. Culture change and cognitive development: cognition, development, and cultural practices, in: E. Turiel (ed.), *Culture and Development* (San Francisco: Jossey-Bass).

Saxe, Geoffrey B. and Kaplan, R. G. 1981. Gesture in early counting: a developmental analysis, *Perceptual and Motor Skills* 53: 851–4.

Saxe, Geoffrey B., Becker, Joseph, Sadeghpour, Mojdeh, and Sicilian, Steven. 1989. Developmental differences in children's understanding of number word conventions, *Journal for Research in Mathematics Education* 20(5): 468–88.

Schmidt, Gernot. 1992. Indogermanische Ordinalzahlen, *Indogermanische Forschungen* 97: 197–235.

Seidenberg, Abraham. 1962. The ritual origin of counting, *Archive for History of Exact Sciences* 2: 1–40.

Sekuler, Robert and Mierkiewicz, Diane. 1977. Children's judgements of numerical inequality, *Child Development* 48: 630–3.

Seron, Xavier, Pesenti, Mauro, Noël, Marie-Pascale, Deloche, Gérard, and Cornet, Jacques-André. 1992. Images of numbers: or 'When 98 is upper left and 6 sky blue', *Cognition* 44(1/2): 159–96.

Seyfarth, Robert M., Cheney, Dorothy L., and Marler, Peter. 1980. Monkey responses to three different alarm calls: evidence of predator classification and semantic communication, *Science* 210: 801–3.

Shanon, Benny. 1982. Colour associates to semantic linear orders, *Psychological Research* 44: 75–83.

Shipley, Elizabeth F. and Shepperson, Barbara. 1990. Countable entities: developmental changes, *Cognition* 34: 109–36.

Simon, Tony J., Hespos, Susan J., and Rochat, Philippe. 1995. Do infants understand simple arithmetic? A replication of Wynn (1992), *Cognitive Development* 10(2): 253–69.

Sinclair, Anne and Sinclair, Hermine. 1984. Preschool children's interpretation of written numbers, *Human Learning* 3: 173–84.

Sinclair, Anne, Siegrist, F., and Sinclair, Hermine. 1983. Young children's ideas about the written number system, in: D. R. Rogers and J. A. Sloboda (eds.), *The Acquisition of Symbolic Skills* (New York: Plenums), pp. 535–42.

Skwarchuk, Sheri Lynn. 1998. Children's acquisition of the English cardinal number words: a special case of vocabulary development (Ph.D. thesis, University of Waterloo).

Smirnova, A. A., Lazareva, O. F., and Zorina, Z. A. 2000. Use of number by crows: investigation by matching and oddity learning, *Journal of the Experimental Analysis of Behavior* 73: 163–76.

Sokol, Scott M. and McCloskey, Michael. 1988. Levels of representation in verbal number production, *Applied Psycholinguistics* 9(3): 267–81.

Song, Myung Ja and Ginsburg, H. P. 1988. The effect of the Korean number system on young children's counting: a natural experiment in numerical bilingualism, *International Journal of Psychology* 2: 319–32.

Sophian, Catherine. 1988. Early developments in children's understanding of number: inferences about numerosity and one-to-one correspondence, *Child Development* 59(5): 1397–414.

1998. A developmental perspective on children's counting, in: C. Donlan (ed.) (1998b), pp. 27–46.

Spalding, J. M. K. and Zangwill, O. L. 1950. Disturbance of number-form in a case of brain injury. *Journal of Neurology, Neurosurgery and Psychiatry* 13: 24–9.

Spelke, Elizabeth S. 1990. Principles of object perception, *Cognitive Science* 14: 29–56.

Spelke, Elizabeth S., Breinlinger, Karen, Macomber, Janet, and Jacobson, Kristen. 1992. Origins of knowledge, *Psychological Review* 99(4): 605–32.

Starkey, Prentice. 1992. The early development of numerical reasoning, *Cognition* 43: 93–126.

Starkey, Prentice and Cooper Jr., Robert G. 1980. Perception of numbers by human infants, *Science* 210(4473): 1033–5.

Starkey, Prentice, Spelke, Elizabeth S., and Gelman, Rochel. 1990. Numerical abstraction by human Infants, *Cognition* 36(2): 97–127.

1991. Toward a comparative psychology of number, *Cognition* 39(2): 171–2.

Stevens, Stanley S. 1946. On the theory of scales of measurement, *Science* 103: 677–80.

Strehlow, Theodor Georg Heinrich. 1945. *Aranda Phonetics and Grammar*, The Oceania Monographs 7 (Sidney: Australian National Research Council).

Struhsacker, Thomas T. 1967. Auditory communication among vervet monkeys (Cercopithecus aethiops), in: S. A. Altmann (ed.), *Social Communication Among Primates* (University of Chicago Press), pp. 281–324.

Suppes, Patrick and Zinnes, Joseph L. 1963. Basic measurement theory, in: R. D. Luce, R. R. Bush, and E. Galanter (eds.), *Handbook of Mathematical Psychology* (New York, London: Wiley), vol. 1, pp. 1–76.

Suzuki, Kotaro and Kobayashi, Tessei. 2000. Numerical competence in rats (*Rattus norvegicus*): Davis and Bradford (1986) extended, *Journal of Comparative Psychology* 114(1): 73–85.

Tamaoka, Katsuo, Leong, Che Kan, and Hatta, Takeshi. 1991. Processing numerals in Arabic, kanji, hiragana and katakana by skilled and less skilled Japanese readers in Grades 4–6, *Psychologia: An International Journal of Psychology in the Orient* 34(3): 200–6.

Tarski, Alfred. 1936. *Introduction to Logic and to the Methodology of Deductive Sciences* (Oxford University Press, 1941). Polish Original: *O logice matematycznej i metodizie dedukcyjnej* (Warsaw, 1936).

Towse, John N. and Saxton, Matthew. 1998. Mathematics across national boundaries: cultural and linguistic perspectives on numerical competence, in: C. Donlan (ed.) (1998b), pp. 129–50.

Trick, Lana M. and Pylyshyn, Zenon W. 1994. Why are small and large numbers enumerated differently? A limited-capacity preattentive stage in vision, *Psychological Review* 101(1): 80–102.

Uller, Claudia, Carey, Susan, Huntley-Fenner, Gavin, and Klatt, Laura. 1999. What representations might underlie infant numerical knowledge? *Cognitive Development* 14(1): 1–36.

Watanabe, Akira. 1992. *Wh-in-Situ, Subjacency, and Chain Formation* (Cambridge, MA: MIT Occasional Papers in Linguistics 2).

West, Rebecca E. and Young, Robert J. 2002. Do domestic dogs show any evidence of being able to count? *Animal Cognition* 5: 183–6.

Whalen, John, Gallistel, C. R., and Gelman, Rochel. 1999. Nonverbal counting in humans: the psychophysics of number representation, *Psychological Science* 10(2): 130–7.

Wiese, Heike. 1997a. *Zahl und Numerale. Eine Untersuchung zur Korrelation konzeptueller und sprachlicher Strukturen* (Berlin: Akademie-Verlag).

1997b. Semantics of nouns and nominal number, *ZAS Papers in Linguistics* 8: 136–63.

2003a. Semantics as a gateway to language, in H. Härtl and H. Tappe (eds.), *Mediating between Concepts and Language* (Berlin: Mouton de Gruyter).

2003b. Sprachliche Arbitrarität als Schnittstellenphänomen. Habilitation thesis, Humboldt-Universität Berlin.

Wiese, Heike and Piñango, Maria M. 2001. 'Mass' and 'count' in language and cognition: some evidence from language comprehension, in: J. D. Moore and K. Stenning (eds.), *Proceedings of the 23rd Annual Conference of the Cognitive Science Society, Edinburgh, August 1–4, 2001* (Mahwah, NJ: Erlbaum).

Wilkening, Friedrich, Levin, Iris, and Druyan, Sara. 1987. Children's counting strategies for time quantification and integration, *Developmental Psychology* 23(6): 823–31.

Wimmer, Heinz and Goswami, Usha. 1994. The influence of orthographic consistency on reading development: word recognition in English and German children, *Cognition* 51: 91–103.

Winter, Werner. 1992. Some thoughts about Indo-European numerals, in: J. Gvozdanovic (ed.), *Indo-European Numerals* (Berlin, New York: de Gruyter), pp. 11–28.

Wittgenstein, Ludwig. 1953. *Philosophical Investigations*, trans. by G. E. M. Anscombe (Oxford: Blackwell, 1953). German original: *Philosophische Untersuchungen*. Oxford.

Wynn, Karen. 1990. Children's understanding of counting, *Cognition* 36(2): 155–93.

1992a. Addition and subtraction by human infants, *Nature* 358: 749–50.

1992b. Children's acquisition of the number words and the counting system, *Cognitive Psychology* 24: 220–51.

1993. Evidence against empiricist accounts of the origins of numerical knowledge, in: A. I. Goldman (ed.), *Readings in Philosophy and Cognitive Science* (Cambridge, MA: MIT Press), pp. 209–27.

1996. Infants' individuation and enumeration of sequential actions, *Psychological Science* 7: 164–9.

1998. Numerical competence in infants, in: C. Donlan (ed.) (1998), pp. 3–25.

Wynn, Karen, Bloom, Paul, and Chiang, Wen-Chi. 2002. Enumeration of collective entities by 5-month-old infants, *Cognition* 83: B55-B62.

Xu, Fei and Spelke, Elizabeth. 2000. Large number discrimination in 6-month-old infants, *Cognition* 74(1): B1-B11.

Yamada, Jun. 1992. Why are kana words named faster than kanji words? *Brain and Language* 43(4): 682–93.

Index